CASES IN
# MANUFACTURING
# MANAGEMENT

# McGraw-Hill Series in Management

*Keith Davis,* Consulting Editor

**Albert N. Schrieber, M.B.A.**
Professor

**Richard A. Johnson, M.B.A., D.B.A.**
Associate Professor

**Robert C. Meier, M.A., Ph.D.**
Associate Professor

**McGraw-Hill Book Company**
*New York   St. Louis   San Francisco*
*Toronto   London   Sydney*

CASES IN
# MANUFACTURING MANAGEMENT

**William T. Newell, M.B.A., Ph.D.**
Associate Professor

**Henry C. Fischer, M.B.A.**
Acting Assistant Professor

All members are in the field of production
management on the faculty of the College
of Business Administration, University of
Washington, Seattle, Washington.

CASES IN MANUFACTURING MANAGEMENT

*Library of Congress Catalog Card Number* 64-8623

ISBN 07-055608-3

5 6 7 8 9 10 11 12 – MAMB – 7 6 5 4 3 2

# PREFACE

This book is a collection of cases in manufacturing management. All the cases represent actual situations from contemporary business operations, having been collected during the past several years by one or a combination of the five authors of this book. The cases represent situations in a variety of industrial settings, company sizes, and locations. Several cases concern companies that manufacture products for national defense. We believed it was important to include a number of these for two reasons: (1) the amount of production effort directed toward national defense and related activities by large and small manufacturers represents a very significant portion of our gross national product, and (2) many new and complex production problems are being experienced in these industries.

To preserve confidences, almost all names are fictitious and geographical locations may have been changed. In most instances the facts are authentic. In other situations the facts have been disguised by changing the data so as not to alter the basic relationships.

This book has been designed for use in a number of learning situations. The cases vary in complexity, offering solution opportunities and challenges for both sophisticated students and those with limited training in production. For example, the book may be used as a second course in production management designed to integrate the techniques, philosophy, and descriptive material that the student has experienced in a beginning course. The cases have been used by the College of Business Administration at the University of Washington as a senior course in manufacturing administration, which is the terminal course in a sequence of courses designed for production majors. In this course the objective is to coordinate and integrate the production function and to acquaint the student with the environment and problems faced by production administrators at different levels of supervision. In addition, many of the cases have been used successfully in a series of advanced management seminars for executives engaged in manufacturing. The cases presented in this book, therefore, provide sufficient descriptive and quantitative materials to have potential usefulness for different levels of analysis, that is, undergraduate, graduate, and industrial training programs.

Almost all the cases have integrative aspects where the subfunctional areas of production are related to the total operation, and in many instances consideration is required involving functions of business other than production. Most of the cases are organized around some specific problem which existed in the company that was studied. Careful review may identify problems and solutions other than the one suggested in the case and may reveal other underlying problems which have caused difficulty. The focal point of the analysis should be on the facts of the case with reference to the specific issues to be decided rather than on the descriptive background of the case. In many situations the validity of the opinions stated in the case must be considered in determining a solution.

Although specific skills and techniques may be useful and necessary in solving some of the cases, the overall solution generally requires consideration of factors beyond the application of a technique. The techniques should be used to contribute to the determination of basic policy and the recommendation for action but should not necessarily be the only focus of attention.

Many of the cases will have several alternative solutions. The best analytical approach will be to compare numerous feasible courses of action and to recognize that many decisions must be made with incomplete knowledge about all the relevant factors. Often there may be a lack of unanimous agreement among the class members in determining the most workable solution. Differences of opinion are valuable because they lead to a better understanding of the problem, the general concepts that are involved, and the many interrelationships affecting the solution.

The cases have not been selected as examples of typical or recommended practices. The situations described in the cases were selected primarily to serve as a pedagogical device for developing the student's facility in analyzing a wide variety of production-oriented problems. It is not likely that many students, if any, will ever find themselves involved in the exact types of situations which are described in the cases. The experience gained from studying these cases, however, should prove valuable in understanding and analyzing other production situations which the student may face in the future. Success in solving the cases is not dependent on the memorization of formulas or "pat" solutions, but rather on one's ability to approach a new situation with an open-minded and analytical problem-solving attitude.

The following suggestions of study procedure may be helpful to students who have not had practice in case analysis. An almost universally accepted approach is to read the case several times. In the first reading the student should gain a general impression of the situation and determine the kind of information presented. A second, more careful reading should include note-taking, detailed study of all exhibits, determination of problems, analysis of the facts, weighing alternative courses of action, and proposing a program to activate the most workable decision. Subsequent readings of the case should be made to determine whether all the pertinent facts have been considered and properly integrated.

Analysis of a case may reveal that some of the data given may be superfluous to the particular problem in the case or that additional data which would be desirable to have are not provided. This is typical of complicated business situations where the real test of effective management involves the manager's ability to select the pertinent data from large quantities of data, much of which may not be relevant, and his ability to make plausible assumptions about other factors which are relevant but unavailable or unknown.

There are several questions at the end of each case. These questions are not intended to be exhaustive but are designed to initiate and stimulate the student's thinking about some of the key issues.

Many of the cases include special or unusual terms. This reflects the wide difference in terminology among industries and even among companies within an industry. Technical words and titles are merely "tags" which provide in shorthand form the identification of complex ideas. Many of these expressions originated as slang but later became accepted as a legitimate addition to our language. The student should be alert to terminology which may be uniquely used in a given case, company, or situation. He should try to identify its true meaning in the environment of the case so that it may be properly used within the context of the situation.

Occasionally it will be necessary for students to review reference material in connection with a case study. A list of readings is suggested for each case. In specific instances where unusual or condensed references may be difficult to locate, they have been included in the case or in the Appendix. This is particularly true for materials relating to the defense industry. For example, the Appendix includes information on improvement curve theory and the Armed Services Procurement Regulations. In addition, other materials have been included for the convenience of the student, for example, tables for present value analysis.

*Albert N. Schrieber*
*Richard A. Johnson*
*Robert C. Meier*
*William T. Newell*
*Henry C. Fischer*

# CONTENTS

## APPENDIX

# AERODYNE
# INCORPORATED

Aerodyne Incorporated was a large, well-financed firm which had been a major producer in the airframe industry for over twenty-five years. Its primary aircraft manufacturing facility was located in southern California. In recent years Aerodyne expanded into the missile field and acquired additional plants in Texas and Florida.

Aerodyne Incorporated had developed by 1960 a new commercial jet-powered airplane, the Aerodyne-4, which it was preparing to put into production and which seemed to enjoy the acceptance of several major commercial airlines. The company had letters of intent from two airlines to purchase forty of the new planes on the condition that the company could deliver planes meeting the promised speed and weight specifications on a firm delivery schedule. Although the price of the company's new Aerodyne-4 was somewhat higher than that announced by its chief competitor, American Aeronautics, for its forthcoming Model 625, Aerodyne won these orders because of the slightly better weight and performance characteristics of its proposed plane and a delivery promise that was six to nine months ahead of American's.

The conditions which made this delivery commitment feasible were an early start on the design of the new airplane and a rapidly declining tooling manpower requirement for current business which permitted a smooth time-phased relationship with the tooling manpower requirements of the Aerodyne-4 program. At the end of 1960 the projected tooling manpower requirements for existing business by quarters through 1965 were as shown by the chart in Exhibit 1. Tooling for existing company programs was expected to be completed by the beginning of the second quarter of 1963, at which time the 2,900 workers in tooling would be reduced to a permanent base of 500.

It was estimated that tooling for the Aerodyne-4 program would require approximately 6,050,000 man-hours, or 13,000 man-quarters distributed over a 13-quarter period as shown in Exhibit 2. The initial proposal was based on beginning tooling in the second quarter of 1961. The rapid rise in tooling personnel needed for the Aerodyne-4 program would complement the declining needs of existing business to permit approximately level tooling employment for the next two years.

In early 1961 two events occurred which forced a delay in the planned April, 1961, go-ahead date. One involved an engineering problem and the other a top-management decision. The design engineers had not been able to work out all the detailed specifications for the new airplane and release the necessary drawings. Also, although the sales department had letters of intent from two major airlines for forty airplanes, Aerodyne's top management felt that this was too few for the company to start construction of the new craft. Management believed that firm commitments for at least eighty airplanes should be in hand before undertaking this expensive venture.

Consequently, the go-ahead was moved back in February, 1961, by two quarters to October, 1961. Potentially this could result in failure to meet the delivery promise made to the first two customers. Because of the two-quarter delay, the tooling-production-testing cycle would have to be compressed if the delivery promises were to be kept. The program planning group determined that part of the compression would have to come in the tooling phase which was compressed by one quarter, as indicated in Exhibit 3, to a total time period of twelve quarters. Because of a slight decrease in the expected efficiency of manpower utilization under the compressed program, the total manpower required for the second schedule was estimated to be 6,280,000 man-hours (or 13,500 man-quarters) instead of the 6,050,000 man-hours (or 13,000 man-quarters) contained in the original projection of the first schedule, an increase of approximately 4 per cent.

Exhibit 4 shows the projected total average tooling manpower requirements by quarters. The number of tooling employees required under the initial schedule (Exhibit 2) beginning in April, 1961, would complement the declining number required for existing business (Exhibit 1). This would permit the total employment to remain approximately stable in 1961 and 1962. Exhibit 4 also shows the impact of the delay in the schedule on total tooling personnel requirements for the five-year period 1961–1965. By the start of the Aerodyne-4 tooling program in the fourth quarter of 1961, the total average number of tooling employees on existing business would be down to 1,900 and the number on the Aerodyne-4 program would be only 50, for a total of 1,950.

Through the first quarter of 1962, the decline in manpower on existing programs would continue at a faster rate than the increase for the new program, resulting in a continued drop in total average employment for that quarter to a low of 1,450. In the following quarter, however, total employment would begin to increase.

From past experience the company had determined that its maximum recruiting and training capability permitted it to no more than double existing tooling manpower in one year. This constraint is indicated in Exhibit 4 by the line showing the maximum buildup capacity starting at the low point in the first quarter of 1962. It was apparent that the company could not achieve the required level of employment without resorting to overtime work. The extra cost of this overtime plus the termination and hiring costs resulting from reducing the employment level and subsequently building it up again is shown in Exhibits 5 to 7. Total tooling manpower costs through the first quarter of 1965 were estimated at $79,520,000 for the existing business plus the first schedule for the Aerodyne-4 program, and $83,379,750 for the second schedule. Thus, the delay added an estimated $3,859,750 to the cost of tooling manpower, an increase of approximately 4.8 per cent.

These costs were computed as follows. The company's average regular hourly tooling labor cost was $5.38. The labor cost per man-quarter was $2,500 ($5.38 per hour multiplied by 465 man-hours per quarter). The average working month was 155 man-hours, comprised of 21 man-days, or 168 man-hours, minus 13 man-hours (8 per cent) allowance for absenteeism and vacations. The cost of terminating an employee from the company was estimated to be $300. To rehire an experienced employee was estimated to cost $700, and to hire an inexperienced person was estimated to cost $900.

Straight-time capacity in the company's tooling operations was about 3,000 man-quarters, or 1,395,000 man-hours per quarter. Manpower requirements over this amount could be met by overtime work up to about 15 per cent of the available straight-time man-hours. Thus, if tooling employment was up to the maximum of 3,000 the company could handle up to 3,450 man-quarters of work in its own shop. Any manpower requirement over this would have to be provided by subcontracting work out to the company's other divisions or to outside firms.

The cost of work obtained through overtime work was about double the cost of straight-time work. This was based on an estimated extra cost of one-third for each hour of work obtained through overtime because of a 25 per cent loss of efficiency after 40 hours of work per week. This extra one-third was compounded by the 50 per cent premium paid for each overtime hour to arrive at the overtime labor cost estimate. Thus, to obtain on an overtime basis the equivalent output of 6 man-hours of normal tooling work would require 8 extra overtime hours to be incurred ($6 \times 1.333$) for which 12 hours at the straight-time wage rate would have to be paid ($8 \times 1.50$).

The cost to subcontract work was estimated to be equivalent to $4,500 per man-quarter, or $9.78 per man-hour. This amount included the subcontractor's direct labor cost ($4.05 per man-hour), overhead cost ($5.00 per man-hour), and profit (8 per cent).

In the manpower cost computations in Exhibit 6 it was assumed that all the people added after the slight slump in total tooling requirements would be experienced persons. After the slump caused by the delay that resulted in the second schedule, it was assumed that about 40 per cent of the people added would be new, as indicated in Exhibit 7.

Between the initial go-ahead date of April, 1961, and the second go-ahead date of October, 1961, the commercial airlines suffered from low volume of air traffic and found it difficult to obtain additional financing to purchase new aircraft such as the Aerodyne-4. Industry observers pointed out that some of the airlines seemed to have seriously overextended themselves in financing jet purchases, and it was not clear that air traffic was expanding fast enough to warrant the immediate purchase of additional equipment. Also, rumors were circulating that some of the lines were hoping for radical performance improvements when the revised specifications of the American Aeronautics Model 625 were released. American was redesigning its airplane around a new engine which, it was hoped, would have greater power and a lower fuel consumption and weight than existing power plants. However, the hoped-for breakthrough on the new engine had not occurred and, in fact, it was the consensus of experts in the aerospace industry that the new engine would probably not be available for two more years.

Whatever the cause, by October, 1961, Aerodyne had not been successful in obtaining orders for the eighty airplanes desired before going ahead with production of the Aerodyne-4. Orders were then in hand for fifty airplanes. It appeared that the start of production on the Aerodyne-4 might have to be delayed another nine months until July, 1962, which was fifteen months later than the initial proposal.

The tooling manpower requirements under the second delay were estimated for a third schedule as indicated in Exhibits 8 and 9. The tooling program would have to be compressed another two quarters beyond the second schedule in order to maintain reasonable delivery schedules on the airplane. The total tooling manpower requirement on the revised program would be increased by 465,000 man-hours to 6,745,000 man-hours.

Exhibits 10 and 11 indicate the timing of cash flows related to tooling manpower requirements for the first and second schedules, respectively. Exhibit 12 charts the cumulative cash flow for the original schedule and for the second schedule.

# EXHIBIT 1

## Projected tooling manpower requirements for existing business, 1961-1965

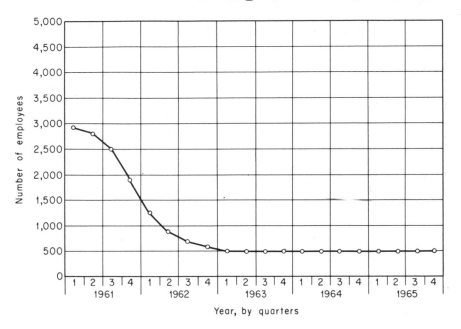

# EXHIBIT 2

## Projected tooling manpower requirements for Aerodyne-4 program, first schedule

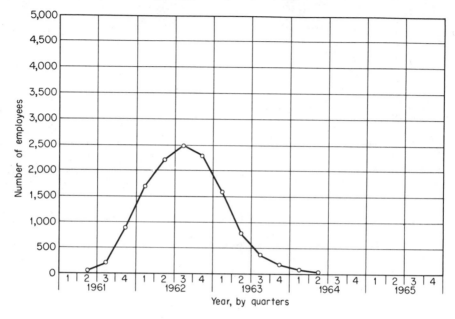

## EXHIBIT 3

### Projected tooling manpower requirements for Aerodyne-4 program, second schedule

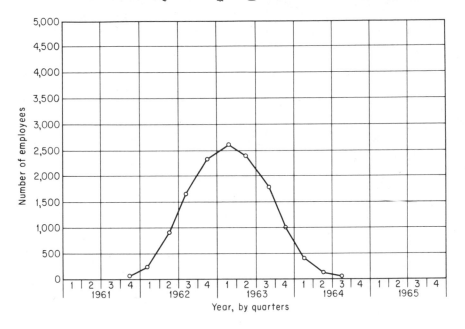

# EXHIBIT 4

## Projected total tooling manpower requirements

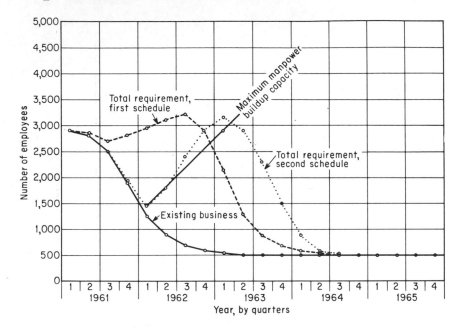

## EXHIBIT 5

# Projected tooling manpower requirements and cost for existing business, 1961–1965

| Year | Quarter | Manpower required, man-quarters | Direct labor cost* | Termination cost† | Total tooling manpower cost |
|---|---|---|---|---|---|
| 1961 | 1 | 2,900 | $ 7,250,000 | | $ 7,250,000 |
| | 2 | 2,800 | 7,000,000 | $ 30,000 | 7,030,000 |
| | 3 | 2,500 | 6,250,000 | 90,000 | 6,340,000 |
| | 4 | 1,900 | 4,750,000 | 180,000 | 4,930,000 |
| | | | 25,250,000 | 300,000 | 25,550,000 |
| 1962 | 1 | 1,250 | 3,125,000 | 195,000 | 3,320,000 |
| | 2 | 900 | 2,250,000 | 105,000 | 2,355,000 |
| | 3 | 700 | 1,750,000 | 60,000 | 1,810,000 |
| | 4 | 600 | 1,500,000 | 30,000 | 1,530,000 |
| | | | 8,625,000 | 390,000 | 9,015,000 |
| 1963 | 1 | 550 | 1,375,000 | 15,000 | 1,390,000 |
| | 2 | 500 | 1,250,000 | 15,000 | 1,265,000 |
| | 3 | 500 | 1,250,000 | | 1,250,000 |
| | 4 | 500 | 1,250,000 | | 1,250,000 |
| | | | 5,125,000 | 30,000 | 5,155,000 |
| 1964 | 1 | 500 | 1,250,000 | | 1,250,000 |
| | 2 | 500 | 1,250,000 | | 1,250,000 |
| | 3 | 500 | 1,250,000 | | 1,250,000 |
| | 4 | 500 | 1,250,000 | | 1,250,000 |
| | | | 5,000,000 | | 5,000,000 |
| 1965 | 1 | 500 | 1,250,000 | | 1,250,000 |
| Total | | 18,100 | $45,250,000 | $720,000 | $45,970,000 |

* Direct labor cost: $2,500/man-quarter.

† Termination cost: $300/man (allocated to quarter in which employment is lower than in preceding quarter).

# EXHIBIT 6  Projected tooling manpower requirements and cost for existing business and first schedule of Aerodyne-4 program

| Year | Quarter | Manpower required, man-quarters | | | Direct labor cost* | | Termination cost‡ | Hiring cost, all experienced personnel§ | Total tooling manpower cost |
|---|---|---|---|---|---|---|---|---|---|
| | | Existing business | Initial AD-4 schedule | Total | Straight-time basis | Overtime basis, excess over 3,000 man-quarters† | | | |
| 1961 | 1 | 2,900 | | 2,900 | $ 7,250,000 | | | | $ 7,250,000 |
| | 2 | 2,800 | 50 | 2,850 | 7,125,000. | | $ 15,000 | | 7,140,000 |
| | 3 | 2,500 | 200 | 2,700 | 6,750,000 | | 45,000 | | 6,795,000 |
| | 4 | 1,900 | 900 | 2,800 | 7,000,000 | | | $ 70,000 | 7,070,000 |
| | | | | | 28,125,000 | | 60,000 | 70,000 | 28,255,000 |
| 1962 | 1 | 1,250 | 1,700 | 2,950 | 7,375,000 | | | 105,000 | 7,480,000 |
| | 2 | 900 | 2,200 | 3,100 | 7,500,000 | $ 500,000 | | 35,000 | 8,035,000 |
| | 3 | 700 | 2,500 | 3,200 | 7,500,000 | 1,000,000 | | | 8,500,000 |
| | 4 | 600 | 2,300 | 2,900 | 7,250,000 | | 30,000 | | 7,280,000 |
| | | | | | 29,625,000 | 1,500,000 | 30,000 | 140,000 | 31,295,000 |
| 1963 | 1 | 550 | 1,600 | 2,150 | 5,375,000 | | 225,000 | | 5,600,000 |
| | 2 | 500 | 800 | 1,300 | 3,250,000 | | 255,000 | | 3,505,000 |
| | 3 | 500 | 400 | 900 | 2,250,000 | | 120,000 | | 2,370,000 |
| | 4 | 500 | 200 | 700 | 1,750,000 | | 60,000 | | 1,810,000 |
| | | | | | 12,625,000 | | 660,000 | | 13,285,000 |

# EXHIBIT 6  (*Continued*)

| Year | Quarter | Manpower required, man-quarters | | | Direct labor cost* | | Termination cost‡ | Hiring cost, all experienced personnel§ | Total tooling manpower cost |
|---|---|---|---|---|---|---|---|---|---|
| | | Existing business | Initial AD-4 schedule | Total | Straight-time basis | Overtime basis, excess over 3,000 man-quarters† | | | |
| 1964 | 1 | 500 | 100 | 600 | 1,500,000 | | 30,000 | | 1,530,000 |
| | 2 | 500 | 50 | 550 | 1,375,000 | | 15,000 | | 1,390,000 |
| | 3 | 500 | | 500 | 1,250,000 | | 15,000 | | 1,265,000 |
| | 4 | 500 | | 500 | 1,250,000 | | | | 1,250,000 |
| | | | | | 5,375,000 | | 60,000 | | 5,435,000 |
| 1965 | 1 | 500 | | 500 | 1,250,000 | | | | 1,250,000 |
| Total | | 18,100 | 13,000 | 31,100 | $77,000,000 | $1,500,000 | $810,000 | $210,000 | $79,520,000 |

\* Direct labor cost: $2,500/man-quarter.
† Overtime: (1⅓) (1½) ($2,500) = $5,000/man-quarter.
‡ Termination cost: $300/man (allocated to quarter lower than preceding).
§ Hiring cost: $700/man (allocated to quarter higher than preceding).

# EXHIBIT 7 Projected tooling manpower requirements and cost for existing business and second schedule of Aerodyne-4 program

| Year | Quarter | Manpower required, man-quarters | | | Over-time, man-quarters | Direct labor cost* | | Termination cost‡ | Hiring cost, 60% exper. and 40% inexp. personnel§ | Total tooling manpower cost |
| --- | --- | --- | --- | --- | --- | --- | --- | --- | --- | --- |
| | | Existing business | Second AD-4 schedule | Total | | Straight-time basis | Overtime basis† | | | |
| 1961 | 1 | 2,900 | | 2,900 | | $ 7,250,000 | | | | $ 7,250,000 |
| | 2 | 2,800 | | 2,800 | | 7,000,000 | | $ 30,000 | | 7,030,000 |
| | 3 | 2,500 | | 2,500 | | 6,250,000 | | 90,000 | | 6,340,000 |
| | 4 | 1,900 | 50 | 1,950 | | 4,875,000 | | 165,000 | | 5,040,000 |
| | | | | | | 25,375,000 | | 285,000 | | 25,660,000 |
| 1962 | 1 | 1,250 | 200 | 1,450 | | 3,625,000 | | 150,000 | $ 273,000 | 3,775,000 |
| | 2 | 900 | 900 | 1,800 | | 4,500,000 | | | 292,500 | 4,773,000 |
| | 3 | 700 | 1,700 | 2,400 | 225.0 | 5,437,500 | $1,125,000 | | 282,750 | 6,855,000 |
| | 4 | 600 | 2,300 | 2,900 | 362.5 | 6,343,750 | 1,812,500 | | 282,750 | 8,439,000 |
| | | | | | | 19,906,250 | 2,937,500 | 150,000 | 848,250 | 23,842,000 |
| 1963 | 1 | 550 | 2,600 | 3,150 | 250.0 | 7,250,000 | 1,250,000 | | 282,750 | 8,782,750 |
| | 2 | 500 | 2,400 | 2,900 | | 7,250,000 | | | | 7,250,000 |
| | 3 | 500 | 1,800 | 2,300 | | 5,750,000 | | 180,000 | | 5,930,000 |
| | 4 | 500 | 1,000 | 1,500 | | 3,750,000 | | 240,000 | | 3,990,000 |
| | | | | | | 24,000,000 | 1,250,000 | 420,000 | 282,750 | 25,952,750 |

# EXHIBIT 7 (Continued)

| Year | Quarter | Manpower required, man-quarters | | | | Direct labor cost* | | Termination cost‡ | Hiring cost, 60% exper. and 40% inexp. personnel§ | Total tooling manpower cost |
|---|---|---|---|---|---|---|---|---|---|---|
| | | Existing business | Second AD-4 schedule | Total | Over-time, man-quarters | Straight-time basis | Overtime basis† | | | |
| 1964 | 1 | 500 | 400 | 900 | | 2,250,000 | | 180,000 | | 2,430,000 |
| | 2 | 500 | 100 | 600 | | 1,500,000 | | 90,000 | | 1,590,000 |
| | 3 | 500 | 50 | 550 | | 1,375,000 | | 15,000 | | 1,390,000 |
| | 4 | 500 | | 500 | | 1,250,000 | | 15,000 | | 1,265,000 |
| | | | | | | 6,375,000 | | 300,000 | | 6,675,000 |
| 1965 | 1 | 500 | | 500 | | 1,250,000 | | | | 1,250,000 |
| Total | | 18,100 | 13,500 | 31,600 | 837.5 | $76,906,250 | $4,187,500 | $1,155,000 | $1,131,000 | $83,379,750 |
| | | | | | | | Less total cost initial schedule | | | −79,520,000 |
| | | | | | | | Cost of delay | | | $ 3,859,750 |

* Direct labor cost: $2,500/man-quarter.
† Overtime (1⅓) (1½) ($2,500) = $5,000/man-quarter.
‡ Termination cost: $300/man (allocated to quarter lower than preceding).
§ Hiring cost: 0.60 ($700) + 0.40($900) = $780/man (allocated to quarter higher than preceding).

# EXHIBIT 8

## Projected tooling manpower requirements for Aerodyne-4 program, third schedule

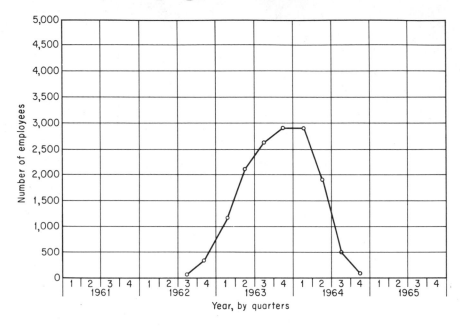

# EXHIBIT 9

## Projected tooling manpower requirements for Aerodyne-4 program, third schedule

| Year | Quarter | Manpower required, man-quarters |
|------|---------|--------------------------------|
| 1962 | 3 | 50 |
|      | 4 | 300 |
| 1963 | 1 | 1,150 |
|      | 2 | 2,100 |
|      | 3 | 2,600 |
|      | 4 | 2,900 |
| 1964 | 1 | 2,900 |
|      | 2 | 1,900 |
|      | 3 | 500 |
|      | 4 | 100 |

# EXHIBIT 10

## Projected cash flow analysis for Aerodyne-4 program, first schedule

| Year | Quarter | Original work load | Original plus first schedule | First schedule | First schedule cumulative flow |
|------|---------|------|------|------|------|
| 1961 | 1 | $ 7,250,000 | $ 7,250,000 | | |
|      | 2 | 7,030,000 | 7,140,000 | $ 110,000 | $ 110,000 |
|      | 3 | 6,340,000 | 6,795,000 | 455,000 | 565,000 |
|      | 4 | 4,930,000 | 7,070,000 | 2,140,000 | 2,705,000 |
|      |   | 25,550,000 | 28,255,000 | 2,705,000 | |
| 1962 | 1 | 3,320,000 | 7,480,000 | 4,160,000 | 6,865,000 |
|      | 2 | 2,355,000 | 8,035,000 | 5,680,000 | 12,545,000 |
|      | 3 | 1,810,000 | 8,500,000 | 6,690,000 | 19,235,000 |
|      | 4 | 1,530,000 | 7,280,000 | 5,750,000 | 24,985,000 |
|      |   | 9,015,000 | 31,295,000 | 22,280,000 | |
| 1963 | 1 | 1,390,000 | 5,600,000 | 4,210,000 | 29,195,000 |
|      | 2 | 1,265,000 | 3,505,000 | 2,240,000 | 31,435,000 |
|      | 3 | 1,250,000 | 2,370,000 | 1,120,000 | 32,550,000 |
|      | 4 | 1,250,000 | 1,810,000 | 560,000 | 33,115,000 |
|      |   | 5,155,000 | 13,285,000 | 8,130,000 | |
| 1964 | 1 | 1,250,000 | 1,530,000 | 280,000 | 33,395,000 |
|      | 2 | 1,250,000 | 1,390,000 | 140,000 | 33,535,000 |
|      | 3 | 1,250,000 | 1,265,000 | 15,000 | 33,550,000 |
|      | 4 | 1,250,000 | 1,250,000 | | |
|      |   | 5,000,000 | 5,435,000 | 435,000 | |
| 1965 | 1 | 1,250,000 | 1,250,000 | | |
|      | 2 | 1,250,000 | 1,250,000 | | |
|      | 3 | 1,250,000 | 1,250,000 | | |
|      | 4 | 1,250,000 | 1,250,000 | | |
|      |   | 5,000,000 | 5,000,000 | | |
| Total | | $49,720,000 | $83,270,000 | $33,550,000 | |

# EXHIBIT 11
## Projected cash flow analysis for Aerodyne-4 program, second schedule

| Year | Quarter | Original work load | Original plus second schedule | Second schedule | Second schedule cumulative flow |
|---|---|---|---|---|---|
| 1961 | 1 | $ 7,250,000 | $ 7,250,000 | | |
|  | 2 | 7,030,000 | 7,030,000 | | |
|  | 3 | 6,340,000 | 6,340,000 | | |
|  | 4 | 4,930,000 | 5,040,000 | $    110,000 | $    110,000 |
|  |  | 25,550,000 | 25,660,000 | 110,000 | |
| 1962 | 1 | 3,320,000 | 3,775,000 | 455,000 | 565,000 |
|  | 2 | 2,355,000 | 4,773,000 | 2,418,000 | 2,983,000 |
|  | 3 | 1,810,000 | 6,855,000 | 5,045,000 | 8,028,000 |
|  | 4 | 1,530,000 | 8,439,000 | 6,909,000 | 14,937,000 |
|  |  | 9,015,000 | 23,842,000 | 14,827,000 | |
| 1963 | 1 | 1,390,000 | 8,782,750 | 7,392,750 | 22,329,750 |
|  | 2 | 1,265,000 | 7,250,000 | 5,985,000 | 28,314,750 |
|  | 3 | 1,250,000 | 5,930,000 | 4,680,000 | 32,994,750 |
|  | 4 | 1,250,000 | 3,990,000 | 2,740,000 | 35,734,750 |
|  |  | 5,155,000 | 25,952,750 | 20,797,750 | |
| 1964 | 1 | 1,250,000 | 2,430,000 | 1,180,000 | 36,914,750 |
|  | 2 | 1,250,000 | 1,590,000 | 340,000 | 37,254,750 |
|  | 3 | 1,250,000 | 1,390,000 | 140,000 | 37,394,750 |
|  | 4 | 1,250,000 | 1,265,000 | 15,000 | 37,409,750 |
|  |  | 5,000,000 | 6,675,000 | 1,675,000 | |
| 1965 | 1 | 1,250,000 | 1,250,000 | | |
|  | 2 | 1,250,000 | 1,250,000 | | |
|  | 3 | 1,250,000 | 1,250,000 | | |
|  | 4 | 1,250,000 | 1,250,000 | | |
|  |  | 5,000,000 | 5,000,000 | | |
| Total | | $49,720,000 | $87,129,750 | $37,409,750 | |

# EXHIBIT 12

## Projected cumulative cash flow for Aerodyne-4 program

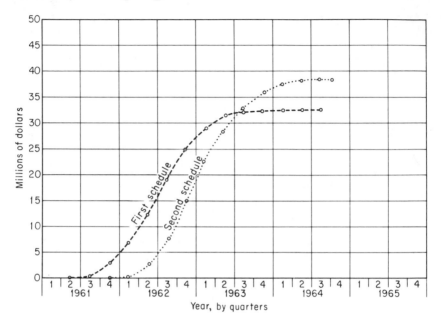

# DISCUSSION QUESTIONS

1. Evaluate the alternatives open to Aerodyne as of October, 1961. What will be the cost of the alternatives?

2. Since subcontracting tooling work is somewhat less costly than over-time work in the company's shop, why would it not be preferable to do all over-capacity work through subcontracting rather than with overtime?

3. Suppose this were a military item rather than a commercial item (e.g., a missile), and the delays were caused by funding difficulties of the government (delay in appropriating the necessary funds). How would the alternatives available to the company differ from those in the present situation?

# REFERENCES

Buffa, Elwood S.: *Modern Production Management* (New York: John Wiley & Sons, Inc., 1961), chap. 16.

than twice the standard increase normally granted by the firm. King, like Calligan, began his career as a bench inspector and was rapidly promoted to his current supervisory position. Unlike Calligan, King viewed his initial position of bench inspector primarily as a means of financing his education and not as the beginning of his lifetime career. King was thirty-one years old.

The major differences between these individuals centered about their philosophies regarding the role of inspection and quality control in a manufacturing organization. Calligan's philosophy was that:

> Quality is an essential part of every product. . . . It is the product development engineer's function to specify what constitutes quality, and the function of quality control to see that the manufacturing departments maintain these specifications. . . . Accurate and vigilant inspection is the key to controlled quality.

When asked how important process control was in the manufacturing of quality products, he stated:

> Process control is achieved primarily through the worker's attitude. If a firm pays high wages and provides good working conditions, they should be able to acquire highly capable workers. . . . A well-executed and efficient inspection program will, as it has done in my firm, impress the importance of quality on the employees and motivate high-quality production. In the few cases when quality lapses do occur, an efficient inspection program prevents defective products from leaving the plant . . . Any valid quality control program must hold quality equal in importance to quantity. . . . Quality records must be maintained for each employee and be made known to both the employee and his immediate superiors. Superior quality should be a major consideration in recommending individuals for promotion or merit pay increases.

King's philosophy paralleled that of Calligan only to the extent that, "quality was an essential part of every product." King made the following comments regarding his philosophy toward inspection and quality control:

> If quality is properly controlled, inspection becomes a minor function. The more effective a quality control system becomes, the less inspection is required. . . . The key to quality control is process control, and inspection serves only as a check to assure that the process controls are being properly administered. . . . An effective inspection scheme should locate and pinpoint the cause of defects rather than place the blame on an often innocent individual. A good rejection report will include the seed from which a solution to future rejections can be developed. . . . One sign of an unsatisfactory quality control system is a large, impressive inspection program.

Holt, Charles C., Franco Modigliani, John F. Muth, and Herbert A. Simon: *Planning Production, Inventories, and Work Force* (Englewood Cliffs, N.J.: Prentice-Hall, Inc., 1960), chaps. 1–3.

Smith, Richard A.: "How a Great Corporation Got Out of Control: The Story of General Dynamics, Part I," *Fortune*, vol. 65, no. 1 (January, 1962), pp. 64–69ff.

————: "How a Great Corporation Got Out of Control: The Story of General Dynamics, Part II," *Fortune*, vol. 65, no. 2 (February, 1962), pp. 120–122ff.

Timms, Howard L.: *The Production Function in Business* (Homewood, Ill.: Richard D. Irwin, Inc., 1962), chap. 17.

# THE AMERICAN CERAMIC AND GLASS PRODUCTS CORPORATION

John Parr, production manager for The American Ceramic and Glass Products Corporation, just completed a trip which covered eight states, seven universities, and three major industrial centers. The purpose of his trip was to recruit personnel for American's three plants. He felt that his trip had been extremely successful and that he had made several contacts which would hopefully result in his firm's acquiring some useful and needed personnel. There appeared to be a general shortage of experienced top-notch talent available, and it took more than just making a good offer to secure the services of good men. It required a sizable amount of selling, persuasion, negotiating, and apparently some luck to secure a really good man. The American Ceramic and Glass Products Corporation employed a total of approximately 13,000 people, each of its three plants employing between 4,000 and 5,000 of this total. About three-quarters of its sales volume came from standard glass containers produced on highly automatic equipment; the balance of the company's sales were of specialized ceramic and glass items produced in batches on much less automated equipment, primarily at American's Denver plant.

Parr was seeking several people to fill specific openings and positions of weakness in his firm. He was particularly anxious to secure a capable person to head up the inspection and quality control department of the American plant located in Denver, Colorado, which was the largest of American's three plants.

The position of chief of inspection and quality control had just been vacated by Downs, who had taken an indefinite leave of absence due to a serious illness. There was little possibility that Downs would be capable of resuming any normal work duties within a year, and a substantial probability that he would never be capable of working on a full-time basis. During the ten years that Downs held the position of chief of inspection and quality control he completely modernized the firm's inspection facilities and operated a continuous training program in the use of the most modern inspection equipment and techniques. The physical facilities of Downs's inspection department were a major attraction for dignitaries and industrialists visiting in the Denver area.

During his trip, Parr interviewed two men whom he felt were qualified to fill Downs's position. Although each appeared more than qualified, Parr felt that a wrong choice could easily be made. Calligan, the first of the two men, was a graduate of a reputable trade school and had eight years of experience in the inspection department of a moderately large manufacturing firm (approximately 800 employees). He began working as a production inspector and was promoted to a group leader within two years and chief inspector two years later. His work record as a production inspector, as a group leader, and as a chief inspector was extremely good. His reason for wishing to leave the firm "to seek better opportunities." He felt that within his present firm could not expect any further promotions in less than ten years. was known for its stability, low employee turnover, and slow but advancement opportunities. His superior, the head of quality was recently promoted to this position and was doing a more satisfactory job. Furthermore he was a young man, only thirty old. Calligan was thirty-two years old.

King, the second of the two men being considered recent graduate of a major southwestern university and imately five years of experience. King was currently em of inspection and quality control in a small-sized ma employing approximately 300 people. His abilities exc ments of his job and he had made arrangements w do a limited amount of consulting work for nonc major reason for wanting to secure a different posit conflict of interests between himself and his emplo to make consulting his sole source of income b position was equally unsatisfactory. He believ a large firm he would be able to fully utilize and thus resolve the conflict occurring betwee and the interests of his employer.

King's work record appeared to be good fact that he had just recently been granted

King was asked what steps he would take to develop such a program if he were to be offered and accept the job of chief of inspection and quality control in the Denver plant. He answered:

> I would design and install a completely automatic inspection and process control system throughout the plant. By automatic I do not mean a mechanical or computer-directed system, but rather a completely standardized procedure for making all decisions concerning inspection and process control. These procedures would be based on a theoretically sound statistical foundation translated into laymen's terminology. The core of the program would be a detailed inspection and quality control manual.

When asked how long this might take King continued:

> I constructed a similar manual for my present employer in a period of less than twelve months and had the whole process operating smoothly within eighteen months after beginning work on the task. Since your firm is somewhat larger, and accounting for my added experience, I would estimate it to take no longer than two years and hopefully significantly less time. . . . As previously stated, I would place major emphasis on process control and would minimize inspection by applying appropriate sampling procedures wherever possible. . . . Employee quality performance should be rated on the basis of process control charts rather than on the basis of final inspection reports. The employee should be trained and encouraged to use these charts as his chief tool toward achieving quality output.

King further stated that one of the reasons for his desire to find a new employer was that he had developed the quality control program in his present firm to the point where it was no longer offering him any challenge. He further stated that he felt this situation would recur in The American Ceramic and Glass Products Corporation, but that because of the size of the firm he could direct his attention to bigger and more interesting problems rather than be required to seek outside consulting work to satisfy his need for professional growth.

When asked what his real interests were King stated, "Application of statistical concepts to the nonroutine activities of a manufacturing organization." He cited worker training, supplier performance, and trouble shooting as areas of interest. King submitted several reports which summarized projects which he had successfully completed in these or related areas.

This was the extent of information which Parr had on each of the two individuals he felt might best fill the position vacated by Downs, the retiring chief of the inspection and quality control department.

# DISCUSSION QUESTIONS

1. What is quality, who determines it, how is it described, and how is it attained?

2. What should be the role of the chief of inspection and quality control?

3. What was Calligan's philosophy toward quality control?

4. What was King's philosophy toward quality control?

5. Under what conditions would you expect Calligan and King, respectively, to be most effective?

6. Excluding the differences in philosophies between King and Calligan, what other factors relative to each require consideration?

7. Which of the two candidates, if either, should be selected for the position of chief of the inspection and quality control department?

8. Where could each man be utilized outside of the area of inspection and quality control?

# REFERENCES

Bethel, Lawrence L., Franklin S. Atwater, George H. E. Smith, and Harvey A. Stackman, Jr.: *Industrial Organization and Management,* 4th ed. (New York: McGraw-Hill Book Company, 1962), chap. 15.

Buffa, Elwood S.: *Modern Production Management* (New York: John Wiley & Sons, Inc., 1961), chap. 18.

Feigenbaum, A. V.: *Total Quality Control* (New York: McGraw-Hill Book Company, 1961).

Mayer, Raymond R.: *Production Management* (New York: McGraw-Hill Book Company, 1962), part 7, chaps. 1–5.

Moore, Franklin G.: *Manufacturing Management* (Homewood, Ill.: Richard D. Irwin, Inc., 1961), chap. 35.

Voris, William: *The Management of Production* (New York: The Ronald Press Company, 1960), chap. 20.

# ATWOOD INDUSTRIES

The managers of Atwood Industries were at a crossroads. Should they retain the same product policy which had been practiced during the past several years, or should the company engage in an accelerated program of research and development to create proprietary items (i.e., products which differed in design from competitive products)?

## HISTORY

In 1946 four engineers from one of the largest manufacturing firms in the country decided to start their own company. George Atwood, Bob Sawyer, Oliver Running, and Tom Jackson began devoting their spare money and time to develop a new method of using feedback control technology in electronic equipment. They spent $2,000 and countless hours to develop a demonstration board. The board had five panels and five identical interchangeable controllers to operate the panels. The panels represented systems such as deicing, wing flap position indicators, and speed control, which plugged into a central control unit like a toaster. As work progressed, George Atwood left his job and devoted all of his time to the new work, while the other three men continued their regular jobs but worked for the new company in their spare time.

In 1947 the group got their first contract (an airplane windshield temperature control unit), and production work was started in the basement of George Atwood's home. In 1948 the company was incorporated and by 1950 thirty-five people were employed. In the next few years the company grew rapidly and by 1960 approximately 75,000 square feet of floor space was occupied in ten buildings located in a quarter-mile radius. By this time more than 800 people were working for the company (see Exhibit 1).

## ORGANIZATION

The basic objective of the company was to "conduct and utilize research for advances in control technology and the application thereof." This objective had not changed since the company was incorporated in 1948.

The executives of Atwood Industries were the four founders of the company. George Atwood was president and had the responsibility for determining policy and conducting long-range planning. The treasurer and general manager of the corporation was Bob Sawyer. Oliver Running was the vice-president and material director, who, along with Tom Jackson, secretary and executive engineer, was responsible for the development and design programs undertaken by the company.

The five major departments and the subareas by stated objectives were as follows:

1. Engineering:
    a. The preliminary design group specialized in flight and propulsion controls.
    b. Product design studied computing controls and servo systems.
    c. Technical services supplied information about technical materials for other departments in engineering.
    d. Administration services prepared budgets, schedules, and procedures for engineering.
    e. Research and development was responsible for research and development-planning and research development projects. This group also prepared proposals and bids for prospective customers.
2. Manufacturing:
    a. The production section was responsible for the fabrication and assembly of the product.
    b. Manufacturing engineering was concerned with production methods, planning, and scheduling.
    c. Purchasing was in charge of materials procurement, inventory control, receiving, and shipping.
    d. Quality control was responsible for inspection and quality evaluation of vendor and company products.
3. Finance:
    a. General accounting was responsible for all cash inflows, data processing, and corporate record keeping.

*b.* Factory accounting was engaged in estimating for contract negotiations, timekeeping, and production cost accounting.
4. Administration:
   *a.* Industrial relations was concerned with employees: wages, hours,
   and training.
   *b.* Facilities and plant maintenance was charged with the responsibility for forecasting facility requirements and maintaining the plant.
   *c.* Public relations was engaged in community and stockholder relations.
   *d.* General services was responsible for providing telephone service,
   company publications, and library service.
5. Sales:
   This department was responsible for directing the course of product
   development in accord with the market information collected. One
   regional office was established on the Eastern seaboard and a second
   in California. Sales representatives of the company were strategically
   located throughout the United States and Canada.

## PRODUCTS

In 1960 the company produced over 400 different items for 55
customers. The items produced could be classified under 6 categories:

|  | Per cent of sales during previous four years |
|---|---|
| 1. *Electronic controllers.* These were computers, the principal component of equipment systems in missiles and aircraft. | 44 |
| 2. *Signaling equipment.* Such equipment was used to indicate abnormal conditions, e.g., electrical system monitoring equipment. | 18 |
| 3. *Test equipment.* This was produced to facilitate installation check-out and maintenance of other products sold by the company. | 8 |
| 4. *Transducers.* This product was a flat temperature sensing device used between layers of metal, plastic, and rubber. | 8 |
| 5. *Liquid level switches.* These switches were used to indicate the level of various kinds of liquids in aircraft and missiles. | 13 |
| 6. *Other products.* These included solid state electrical converters, valves, and actuators. | 9 |
| Total | 100 |

## SALES

Exhibit 2 illustrates the sales and profits during the seven-year period between 1954 and 1960. The backlog of unfilled orders on December 31, 1960, was $4,214,000. During 1960, 89 per cent of the company's sales was to five customers. Between 1956 and 1960, approximately 90 per cent of the total production was used in military applications; however, only 4 per cent of the output was sold directly to the government. The nonmilitary sales were to companies engaged in commercial aviation.

## FACILITIES

Late in 1960 the company was planning another expansion program. It had been impossible to provide sufficient floor space for all the company's requirements even though an additional building had been leased during the year. The allocation of square footage assigned to the different departments was:

|  | Allocation, sq. ft. |
|---|---|
| Engineering and administration | 29,000 |
| Technical services | 9,700 |
| Manufacturing | 38,000 |
| Storage | 6,700 |
| Other | 10,000 |
| Total | 93,400 |

Ten buildings were used of which only two, the administration and the engineering building, were owned by the company, and the others were leased. All the buildings were in good repair; however, it was not possible to expand these facilities at their present location and very difficult to coordinate the operations of the company in so many buildings.

The expansion plans called for the construction of a large, single building in another location. The new plant would have 136,000 square feet of floor area with possibilities of expansion to 400,000 square feet. The cost of constructing and moving to this new facility would be approximately $3 million.

## MANPOWER

Eight hundred and twenty-five people were employed at Atwood Industries on July 1, 1961. A breakdown of employment by department was listed as follows:

|  | Employees |
|---|---|
| Engineering | 220 |
| Manufacturing | 468 |
| Finance | 30 |
| Administration | 62 |
| Sales | 45 |
|  | 825 |

There were seventy-eight employees in the engineering department who had science or engineering degrees. Forty-five of the seventy-eight had experience with other companies before accepting jobs with Atwood. Eight of the seventy-eight held advanced graduate degrees in their field. The other people in the department were workers assigned to support the engineering effort.

About 40 per cent of the employees were women. Women seemed better suited to working with the small, intricate assemblies and seemed less subject to fatigue in repetitious work. However, the turnover rate was nearly 40 per cent per year for the women, as compared to 3 per cent for the men.

Atwood was operated in a very friendly and relaxed manner. The employees of the company were not covered by any labor contract or bargaining agreement. The National Labor Relations Board had held two elections and in these elections the vote was against union certification by eight to one in the first instance, and twelve to one the second time. This vote against unions was explained in two ways. First, the company paid the union scale or above, and provided fringe benefits such as group health insurance, life insurance, profit sharing, retirement funds, sick leave, and paid vacation. Secondly, many of the women employees in manufacturing were not interested in a permanent position and, therefore, campaigned against accepting union representation.

## FINANCES

In 1959 Atwood Industries made a public offering of its capital stock. Three hundred thousand shares of $1 par value stock were sold for

$10.50 a share, resulting in capital surplus of about $2,850,000. In 1960 the company issued debenture bonds to raise additional money for the new building. The financial statements are shown in Exhibits 3 and 4.


## THE INDUSTRY

The electronic industry comprised one of the most rapidly growing sectors of the United States economy (Exhibit 5). During the period from 1935 to 1960, electronic output had increased about thirty-five times, compared to six times for the gross national product. No other industry manufactured such a broad and diversified group of products, or depended to such an extent upon research and development for its continued growth.

Electronic production and employment had increased more rapidly in some segments of the industry than others. Advanced systems and instrumentation—complete guided missiles and space vehicles, electronic computers, test and measuring equipment—were examples of the product lines which had shown the greatest gain in sales.

During 1957–1958 there was a change in the growth pattern; output during 1958 declined. Early in 1961 there were indications that manufacturers' shipments would be down again. Further, the capacity to produce electronic parts and equipment had been expanding more rapidly than the demand for electronic products. More than 4,000 companies were classified as electronic producers. An increasing number of military and industrial equipment producers were starting to produce parts which formerly had been purchased from the companies specializing in manufacturing components. On the other hand, component manufacturers were engaging in the production of more complex components and equipment assemblies. In addition, foreign competition was becoming more severe. Several foreign countries were building electronic industries of their own, often with government protection and financial support. Japan, as well as other countries, was providing stiff competition by exporting electronic production equipment and low-cost components.


## RESEARCH AND DEVELOPMENT POLICY

Atwood Industries began by using proprietary ideas to make original adaptations and minor improvements in thermostatic devices used in the aerospace industry. The meaning of proprietary may be clarified by classifying it into four categories:

1. *Proprietary ideas.* This refers to the skill of a supplier in modifying existing designs or products to meet the special needs of a customer. It does not involve significantly original concepts or new basic approaches to a problem.

2. *Proprietary engineering.* The customer may outline a general unsolved problem relative to a desired product. The supplier will attempt to create a solution or a design which generally is original. A new basic design or process (sometimes patentable) may result from this effort.

3. *Proprietary production.* This refers to the competitive advantage a supplier may gain from a secret process or special manufacturing capability.

4. *Proprietary items or products.* This describes the situation when the supplier identifies the need, creates and develops the design, and sells the product as a catalog or shelf item. Often such items are protected from competition by trademarks or patents.

For several years the development and manufacture of products involving proprietary ideas proved successful for Atwood Industries and profit margins were high. As the company succeeded with the first approach to a proprietary position, they moved into the second category and gradually expanded their proprietary engineering skills. Some customers had problems in designing electronic equipment and invited several suppliers (including Atwood) to apply their research and development capabilities in solving the problems. Each participating supplier would outline a solution and prepare a bid to secure the production order for the equipment. The supplier that presented the best solution to the problem usually secured the production contract for the first order but had to extend the rights to the design to the buyer. Reorders were usually subject to competitive bidding since the buyer could furnish the design details required for production.

Customers of Atwood gradually became more sophisticated in their knowledge of electronics and began not only to specify the performance characteristics desired but also to provide detailed physical designs for such electronic equipment. Competing electronic suppliers (including Atwood) were invited to bid on production contracts which involved little product research, development, or engineering on the part of the supplier. The increasing opportunities for such production contracts encouraged Atwood to expand into the third category and improve their proprietary production skills. At first the profit margins in the straight production type contracts were good, but as the electronic industry built excess production capacity, competition became more intense and profit margins decreased.

Some customers found that they could economically make some of the electronic equipment that they formerly purchased, and this trend together with competition made it increasingly difficult for the company to maintain the volume of business they desired. As a result the Atwood management felt it was necessary to expand their already acquired proprietary skills by embarking on the fourth category of developing proprietary items on their own. In connection with this program an effort was made to seek out new products, new types of markets, and new customers.

By 1960 five of the sixty engineers in the engineering department were working on projects directed toward creating proprietary items. The remaining engineers were still assigned to developing proprietary ideas, engineering, or processes.

Patents had been considered important in the early years of the company's history, and a number of patents were obtained on ideas which had been originated by technical employees, but with all rights assigned to the company. The managers of Atwood believed that patents gave the company protection from competitors that would try to copy a design and offer it at a lower price, additional sales appeal for their products, justification for higher profit margins, and a position of status in the industry.

Subsequently the value of patents began to be questioned. Idea documentation, special drawings, patent searches, patent office fees, attorney fees, and other charges involved costs for each patent totaling from $500 to many thousands of dollars, depending on the difficulties involved. Frequently these costs were in excess of any potential profit that could be made on the idea being patented. The processing and issue of a patent by the Patent Office took from two to five years. By that time the rapid technological advancement of the industry often had made the original idea obsolete.

After a patent was issued, the idea became public knowledge and copies of the patent could be obtained by anyone for a few cents. With thousands of manufacturers and tens of thousands of products it became almost impossible to discover when infringement of a patent took place. Even if an infringement were discovered, it required long and expensive legal action to prove the validity of the patent issued by the Patent Office and to prove that a specific violation of patent rights had occurred.

The alternative course of action for protection of original ideas involved the avoidance of patents. The new idea was not publicized to competitors. Further, most of Atwood's products were sold in small quantities to specific users, which sometimes made it difficult for a competitor to obtain physical possession of the product for examination. Even if a competitor obtained the product, the complexity of the design and the use of special production processes and materials made it almost impossible to discover all the essential secrets and know-how of the idea through "reverse engineering."[1] This was particularly difficult when the products were encapsulated or "potted in a black box."[2]

The lack of patents, however, introduced other complications. Most of the sales made by Atwood were under contracts which were subject to the Armed Services Procurement Regulations or other government procurement regulations. These regulations provided that design rights would pass to the government if the ideas were developed with government funds, and particularly if the type of contract was other than a fixed-price contract. Under such a situation Atwood was required to provide complete design and production drawings to the buyer who in turn could distribute them to competitors in order to solicit competitive bids. In 1961 the precise design rights of the buyer and seller were in a "legal jungle" with a great deal of controversy involved between the various branches of government and industry. Atwood executives were anxious to maintain the protection of their ideas and know-how from competitors but they were uncertain as to how to accomplish this effectively.

George Atwood was also very concerned about the reduced profit picture of the company and about the inability of the company to establish sales prices which he believed were in proper relation to costs. In July of 1961 he appointed a committee to determine the kinds of proprietary items Atwood Industries might develop and the problems the company might incur in the increased development and sale of products under its own brand name. The initial assignment for this committee was to list alternate product areas and general problems. An intensive evaluation session was scheduled to follow this initial report, and the best alternatives would be selected for detailed study and planning. Oliver Running and Tom Jackson were appointed as a two-man subcommittee to suggest product policy alternatives, and Bob Sawyer was asked to prepare a list of questions and problems arising from a program to create and develop proprietary items. Excerpts from these preliminary reports were as follows.

*Alternative Product Policies* (prepared by Running and Jackson)

1. Create and develop electronic control products under the Atwood trademark—products which could be used as complex electronic systems built by large companies in the aerospace industries

---

[1] Reverse engineering consists in obtaining a competitor's product and preparing engineering drawings that copy its design.

[2] Encapsulation involved inserting the electronic components and circuitry in a container and filling it with a liquid plastic which hardened into an opaque solid. To examine the electronic parts required that the solid mass be broken, which in turn destroyed the electronic parts and circuitry.

2. Create and develop electronic control products under the Atwood trademark for potential sale to industries other than the aerospace industry

3. Create and develop *complete* electronic systems for the aerospace industry

4. Specialize in *producing* electronic equipment and concentrate on improving production efficiency, thus minimizing or eliminating proprietary products in favor of concentrating on proprietary ideas, engineering, and processes

*Questions and Problems Relating to Proprietary Products* (prepared by Sawyer)

1. What trends in the electronic industry are significant and pertinent to the product policy decision Atwood Industries should make?

2. How would profit margins be affected by each alternative policy?

3. What about the current patent laws and government regulations?

4. Could each of the product proposals be financed under the current capital structure of Atwood Industries?

5. How could the company administer a research and development program to produce proprietary products, e.g., how should the R and D group be organized, scheduled, budgeted, stimulated, rewarded, and evaluated? How could the right talent be recruited?

# EXHIBIT 1
## Number of employees

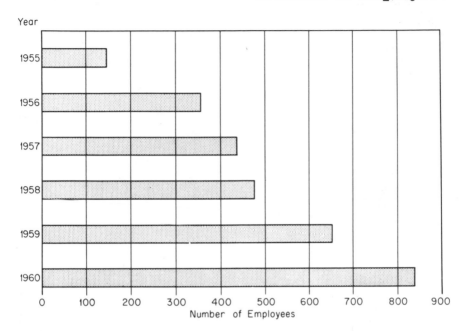

# EXHIBIT 2
## Sales and profits

| Period | Sales | Profit/(Loss) |
|---|---|---|
| 1954 | $ 1,557,000 | $150,000 |
| 1955 | 2,250,000 | 284,000 |
| 1956 | 4,942,000 | 582,000 |
| 1957 | 7,957,000 | 810,000 |
| 1958 | 6,112,000 | 440,000 |
| 1959 | 12,558,000 | 485,000 |
| 1960 | 12,251,000 | (382,000) |

# EXHIBIT 3
## Consolidated balance sheet, December 31, 1960

*Assets*

Current assets:

| | | |
|---|---|---|
| Cash | | $   250,420 |
| U.S. government securities, at cost | | 1,280,440 |
| Receivables | | 2,420,248 |
| Inventories, at lower of cost or market: | | |
| Raw materials, purchased and fabricated parts | $1,680,797 | |
| Work in process | 986,166 | |
| Finished goods | 488,248 | 3,155,211 |
| Prepaid expenses and deposits | | 70,359 |
| Total current assets | | $7,176,678 |
| Investments at cost | | 42,400 |
| Property, plant, and equipment, at cost: | | |
| Land, mainly new plant site | $   425,840 | |
| Buildings | 210,400 | |
| Equipment | 890,705 | |
| Leasehold improvements | 84,225 | |
| Construction in progress, mainly new building | 720,245 | |
| | $2,331,415 | |
| Less allowance for depreciation and amortization | 498,345 | |
| Net property, plant, and equipment | | 1,833,070 |
| Unamortized engineering and development costs | | 520,210 |
| Other deferred charges, etc. | | 324,560 |
| Total assets | | $9,896,918 |

*Liabilities*

Current liabilities:

| | | |
|---|---|---|
| Notes payable: | | |
| Bank | $   605,650 | |
| Current installments on long-term debt | 64,000 | |
| Total notes payable | $   669,650 | |
| Accounts payable, trade | 630,400 | |
| Accrued salaries and wages | 420,223 | |
| Contribution to profit-sharing retirement trust | 20,736 | |
| Other accrued taxes and expenses | 120,008 | |
| Total current liabilities | | $1,861,017 |
| Long-term debt | | 2,486,200 |
| Accrued compensation due officers | | 387,240 |
| Deferred Federal income taxes | | 286,400 |
| Total liabilities | | $5,020,857 |

*Net Worth*

Common stock:

| | | |
|---|---|---|
| $1 par value, authorized 2 million shares, outstanding 821,100 shares | $   821,100 | |
| Capital surplus | 2,840,324 | |
| Earned surplus | 1,214,637 | |
| Total net worth | | 4,876,061 |
| Total liabilities and net worth | | $9,896,918 |

# EXHIBIT 4

## Income for the year ending December 31, 1960

| | | |
|---|---:|---:|
| Sales, less returns and allowances..................... | $12,250,967 | |
| Cost of goods sold................................. | 9,240,324 | |
| Gross profit............................................. | | $3,010,643 |
| Research and development........................... | $ 1,240,820 | |
| Field servicing and rework.......................... | 84,252 | |
| Selling, general, and administrative.................. | 1,965,640 | |
| | | 3,290,712 |
| Operating (loss) after provision for depreciation and amortization........................................... | | $ (280,069) |
| Other deductions: | | |
| Interest........................................ | $ 72,490 | |
| Contributions to employees' profit-sharing retirement trust........................................ | 25,840 | |
| Miscellaneous, net............................... | 3,248 | |
| | | 101,578 |
| Net (loss)................................................ | | $ (381,647) |

# EXHIBIT 5

## Electronic output in 1947 and 1950–1962*
(In millions of dollars)

| Year | Consumer-type radio and television receivers and related products† | All other electronic equipment‡ | Electron tubes | Semiconductor devices | Electronic components other than tubes and semiconductors |
|------|------|------|------|------|------|
| 1960 | 1,850 | 4,570 | 860 | 540 | 2,000 |
| 1959 | 1,790 | 4,000 | 865 | 395 | 1,750 |
| 1958 | 1,350 | 3,250 | 790 | 210 | 1,340 |
| 1957 | 1,500 | 3,100 | 820 | 150 | 1,450 |
| 1956 | 1,470 | 2,800 | 790 | 90 | 1,360 |
| 1955 | 1,500 | 2,500 | 770 | 40 | 1,360 |
| 1954 | 1,420 | 2,470 | 690 | 25 | 1,275 |
| 1953 | 1,593 | 2,503 | 734 | 25 | 1,445 |
| 1952 | 1,340 | 2,330 | 690 | 20 | 1,110 |
| 1951 | 1,296 | 843 | 473 | § | 788 |
| 1950 | 1,687 | 473 | 443 | § | 697 |
| 1947 | 810 | 469 | 122 | § | 349 |

* Data cover manufacturers' shipments. The totals represent the factory value of production or shipments (output) of electronic products, whether incorporated in other products or used in maintenance and repair of end equipment.

† Not including sales of phonograph records and magnetic tape.

‡ Not including payments on research and development contracts or electronic services.

§ Data for years prior to 1952 are included under "Electronic components other than tubes and semiconductors."

SOURCES: Bureau of the Census; Electronic Industries Association Marketing Data Department; Electronic Division, BDSA; and other sources.

# DISCUSSION QUESTIONS

1. Evaluate the alternate product policies suggested for Atwood Industries. Can you suggest any other possibilities?

2. What is the advantage of creating proprietary products? Disadvantages?

3. What changes in the organization of the R and D group may be necessary?

4. Do you believe the practice of reverse engineering is ethical?

5. What would be the advantage of merging with or acquiring another electronic firm? Disadvantages?

6. What decision should the managers of Atwood make at this time?

7. Must a small company constantly generate new product items to compete in a dynamic industry?

# REFERENCES

Bethel, Lawrence L., Franklin S. Atwater, George H. E. Smith, and Harvey A. Stackman, Jr.: *Industrial Organization and Management*, 4th ed. (New York: McGraw-Hill Book Company, 1962), pp. 113–133.

Moore, Franklin G.: *Manufacturing Management*, 3d ed. (Homewood, Ill.: Richard D. Irwin, Inc., 1961), pp. 268–289.

# THE BETHANY STEEL CORPORATION

During the 1930s Roger L. Bethany, a veteran industrialist in the steel industry, was responsible for the merger of four small, independent steel manufacturers located in western Pennsylvania. The four firms were in serious financial difficulty due to the depressed condition of the steel market. By astute financial maneuvering and by adopting a policy of manufacturing specialty steels, Mr. Bethany was able to bring the plants into a sound operating and financial condition by the close of World War II.

Mr. Bethany's managerial skill was again tested as Bethany faced the transition from wartime to civilian production. For several years the firm operated at or slightly below its breakeven point. By the mid-1950s, however, because of its proved skill in the production of specialty steels The Bethany Steel Corporation received several new long-range contracts to supply a relatively large quantity of a special type of high-strength heat-resistant stainless steel for the United States space program. The critical physical properties of this steel required that it be heat-treated and aged under accurately controlled conditions prior to its use. Only one of Bethany's several plants had the equipment for this particular process.

Because of capacity and expansion limitations at the Latrobe plant, where Bethany was currently producing this type of steel, Bethany management decided also to equip their plant located at Blairsville to produce the steel. In addition to providing the required extra capacity, this arrangement would also serve as a dual source of supply in case one or the other of the plants ran into difficulties in meeting its production schedule. The added assurance of supply provided by dual production facilities had been an important factor in Bethany being able to obtain the large orders for the special type of high-strength heat-resistant stainless steel.

The processing facilities at the Blairsville plant were constructed as identically as possible to those of the Latrobe plant. All equipment was purchased from the same manufacturers and the same models were used whenever possible. When this was not possible, equipment as similar as possible was selected and altered. Even the operating and test procedures used at the Blairsville plant were similar to those used at the Latrobe plant. The significant difference was that only 60 to 65 per cent of the lots of material produced by the Blairsville plant was acceptable, whereas 95 per cent of the lots processed by the Latrobe plant was acceptable.

Engineers from both plants had studied the problem and recommended solutions, all of which failed. Their only comment as to the difference between the two processes was "It just can't be!"

Brad Varney, part-time technical consultant for The Bethany Steel Corporation, was contacted and asked to investigate the matter. Varney was not a heat-treat expert; he stated that he was not sure that he could solve their problem but that he would make a one-week study of the problem and report on what he felt could be done. Bethany Corporation officials agreed.

In conducting his study Varney noted that the heat-treat process was a three-stage process: (1) the material underwent a six-hour heat treatment at a temperature approximating 2700°F, (2) the material was transferred to cycling furnaces and aged for four days under temperatures varying from 1200 to 1800°F, and (3) the material was tested to assure compliance with all specifications. The only specification with which the Blairsville plant appeared to have any difficulty was the minimum tensile strength of the final product.

Varney's report was brief and stated the following:

1. He could neither offer nor guarantee an immediate solution to the problem.

2. He felt that he could possibly isolate the cause of the problem to one of the three stages of the process.

3. He proposed to design and carry out an analysis-of-variance experiment for the Latrobe and Blairsville plants.

4. To carry out the analysis-of-variance experiment, the Latrobe plant would have to work in close harmony with the Blairsville plant.

Varney's suggestion was accepted, and the following experiment was designed and conducted: Forty samples of equivalent raw material were selected. On a random basis twenty of the samples were sent to each of the two plants. At each plant the twenty samples were divided into four equal groups and identified as "W," "X," "Y," and "Z." Each plant was to completely heat-treat, age, and test the samples in group "W." Samples in group "X" were to be heat-treated and aged at the respective plants and then sent to the other plant for testing. Group "Y" samples were to be heat-treated at their respective plants, then sent to the other plant for aging, and finally returned to the original plant for testing. The remaining group "Z" samples were to be only heat-treated in their respective plants and sent to the other plant for aging and testing. Since aging did not have to follow heat-treating immediately, this arrangement was possible. The data obtained are summarized in Exhibit 1.

Using these data Varney carried out the appropriate analysis-of-variance calculations and concluded that the problem originated somewhere in Blairsville's testing process. Although this possibility had already been considered, recalibration tests were ordered; and as expected, the equipment tested out perfectly. Varney then carefully compared the test and calibration procedures of the two plants. Again no difference in the procedures was ascertainable. As a last resort, Varney suggested that samples of acceptable material from the Latrobe plant which tested near the rejection limit be obtained and tested on the Blairsville facilities. Twenty-five such samples were obtained and tested on Blairsville equipment. Eighteen of the samples were rejected. As a double check, twenty samples of material which were produced by the Blairsville plant and which tested as slightly unsatisfactory were sent to the Latrobe plant. When tested at the Latrobe plant all the samples were accepted.

This reaffirmed the results obtained from the analysis-of-variance experiment, and a complete recertification of the Blairsville testing process was ordered. In the recertification process a critical balance weight was found to be overweight. This was corrected and the process again put in operation. The Blairsville plant's process thereafter produced almost 100 per cent acceptable material. Comparisons of overall process averages indicated that the Blairsville plant produced material of slightly greater tensile strength than the Latrobe plant. All previous batches from the Blairsville plant which had not been scrapped were retested, and over 95 per cent proved to be acceptable.

To prevent the reoccurrence of such a situation the two plants decided to exchange samples of all lots of rejected material for comparative testing. This appeared to be an inexpensive precaution when compared to the costly episode which had just been experienced.

As part of his final report, Varney included Exhibit 2 as an explanation of the analysis-of-variance technique that he used. This explanation was intended to be of help to the management and engineers of the Latrobe and Blairsville plants.

# EXHIBIT 1

## Test data

(Tensile strength in 1,000 pounds per square inch)

| Lot number | Originating plant | | | | | | | | | |
|---|---|---|---|---|---|---|---|---|---|---|
| | Latrobe | | | | | Blairsville | | | | |
| "W" | 671 | 673 | 674 | 678 | 676 | 677 | 680 | 681 | 682 | 677 |
| "X" | 659 | 661 | 658 | 661 | 661 | 682 | 683 | 685 | 685 | 690 |
| "Y" | 672 | 674 | 674 | 672 | 670 | 667 | 669 | 675 | 669 | 669 |
| "Z" | 655 | 662 | 662 | 662 | 665 | 676 | 681 | 680 | 682 | 684 |

# EXHIBIT 2

## A brief comment on analysis-of-variance experiments

In comparing the performance characteristics of two or more processes, two measurable characteristics are generally of significance. The first of these is the mean or average value of the process outputs. If the benefits of a process are cumulative and one is interested primarily or exclusively in long-run advantages, the mean value of the output of each of the individual processes often provides sufficient information for a proper evaluation of alternatives. If, however, the benefits are not cumulative, or the gain from the next single or few events is of primary importance, the mean value alone generally does not provide sufficient information for making a proper decision.

The second measure required is the variability between individual or successive outputs of each of the processes in question. If the variation between successive outputs of a process is small, the character of the next and succeeding outputs can be predicted with a relatively high degree of accuracy. If the variability between successive outputs is large, predicting the next and successive outcomes is subject to substantial error and uncertainty. This is particularly true when the only basis for making a prediction is the process average and the probability of each possible value which the process may yield. Such a process is called a random process.

All other things equal, the process with the most desirable mean is the overall most desirable process. It, however, is improbable that two processes with different means are identical in all other respects. It is entirely possible for a process to have an acceptable mean and an unacceptable variability and similarly for a process having an unacceptable mean to have an acceptable variability. This is often the case in a machine shop where close tolerances are required. A machine may produce parts with a mean length of 1.000 inch, but if the parts range from 0.900 to 1.100 inches few of the parts will be acceptable if the specification is 1.000 ± 0.0015. A process that produces parts between the limits of 1.015 and 1.016 has an unsatisfactory mean but a satisfactory variability. A satisfactory process must possess both an acceptable mean and an acceptable variability.

When a process has an unsatisfactory mean but a satisfactory variability a resetting of the process may remedy the situation. When a process has an unsatisfactory variance it is often necessary to determine the basic causes of the excess variation in order to correct the process. In a complex process where many factors contribute to the overall variability of the final product, determining the extent to which each of the individual factors contributes to the overall variability of the process can be a difficult task. In many instances an analysis-of-variance experiment may be the most efficient method of performing this task.

As an example, assume that three machines are performing identical operations and that their aggregate output displays excess variability. This could be the result of several combinations of variability among the individual machines:

1. All or some of the machines have excess variability.
2. All or some of the machines are centered about an inappropriate mean dimension.
3. All or some of the machines have a combination of excess variability and are centered about an inappropriate mean dimension.

Taking the proper corrective action depends upon knowing which of these conditions exists for each of the machines. If the output of a particular machine displays excess variability, often little can be done except to reduce the basic variability of the process. Correction might require the use of a different process or a major revision or overhauling of the current process. If the output of the same machine were to display a satisfactory variability but be improperly centered, a relatively simple resetting of the machine would often correct the situation. Inappropriate action in the first case, resetting the mean when in fact the variance is excessive, will degrade the process rather than correct the situation. Inappropriate action in the second case, attempting to reduce the variability when in fact the mean is in error, would probably correct the process but likely at an unnecessarily large cost. In this case obtaining the required information about the output of each of the machines offers no more of a problem than separating the output of each machine and comparing each output with the product specifications.

Assume now that each machine is operated by a different individual and that the variability of the output of each machine is determined by the combined capabilities of the particular machine and operator. Having determined that a machine-operator pair displays unacceptable variability no longer provides sufficient information to take appropriate corrective action. The unsatisfactory variability may now be attributable to an unsatisfactory machine, an unsatisfactory operator, both an unsatisfactory machine and an unsatisfactory operator, or an unfortunate pairing of the machine and operator. To determine if a particular machine is unsatisfactory, all operators could be assigned to operate the machine in question and if all were unable to achieve an output with acceptable variability the machine could be considered unsatisfactory. A similar experiment could be designed to determine whether a particular operator was unsatisfactory. With this information the beginnings of a rational or scientific solution to the problem become apparent.

Still other information would be useful. For example, it would be useful to know what portion of the overall variability of the machine-operator pair is attributable to the machine, what portion is attributable to the operator, and what portion is attributable to factors not explicitly considered. Furthermore, it would be useful to know if the variability attributable to each of these causes would remain constant if machines and operators were interchanged, and if not to what extent particular pairings of machines and operators displayed unusually large or small variability in their combined output. With this information optimal, machine-operator assignments could be made; and if a particular machine or operator required improvement, this information would specify the amount of improvement required to achieve an output with acceptable variability.

Individuals unaware of analysis-of-variance techniques could possibly imagine ways of determining the answers to all of these questions independently; but, except in very rare cases, they would dismiss this possibility as being overly costly. Were it necessary to conduct a separate experiment to answer each of the questions this would certainly be true. However, by means of an appropriate analysis-of-variance experiment all these questions can often be answered from the results of a single experiment whose cost may be surprisingly low. The Bethany Steel Corporation case illustrates this point.

By means of an appropriate analysis-of-variance experiment the overall variability of a complex process can be partitioned into specific components which are attributable to:

1. Differences in the basic mean dimensions of the individual factors assumed to contribute to the overall variability

2. Differences in the inherent variability possessed by the individual factors assumed to contribute to the overall variability

3. Interaction between the variables assumed to contribute to the overall variability

4. The overall variability attributable to factors not explicitly considered to contribute to the overall variability

Given appropriate information, analysis-of-variance techniques allow the maximum amount of information to be derived from a given quantity of data. By predesigning the experiment, analysis-of-variance techniques allow a specified amount of information to be obtained with the smallest amount of experimental data. In each case the confidence one can have in the resultant answer is determinable. It should be noted that to determine the variability attributable to a particular factor, the process must be able to be operated in such a way that the factor under consideration can be varied.

Analysis of variance is a powerful tool if used correctly. When one uses this technique certain assumptions about the situation being analyzed are implied. If the situation does not meet these conditions the results can be invalid. Therefore, when using analysis-of-variance techniques or any similar technique, one should either familiarize himself with the assumptions and implications included in the model used or employ the services of a qualified statistician. This is particularly important where an incorrect decision may be costly.

# DISCUSSION QUESTIONS

1. In reviewing the data obtained from the analysis-of-variance experiment what would one look for first?

2. What additional information would a complete analysis of variance provide?

3. Carry out the appropriate analysis-of-variance calculations for the given data.

4. What does the analysis of variance reveal?

5. How much additional support did Mr. Varney's second sampling experiment give to the hypothesis that the two test facilities were not comparable?

6. If no imperfection in the Blairsville facility had been discovered what should have been done next?

# REFERENCES

Bowman, Edward H., and Robert B. Fetter: *Analysis for Production Management* (Homewood, Ill.: Richard D. Irwin, Inc., 1961), chap. 8.

Bryant, Edward C.: *Statistical Analysis* (New York: McGraw-Hill Book Company, 1960), chap. 8.

Buffa, Elwood S.: *Modern Production Management* (New York: John Wiley & Sons, Inc., 1961), chap. 6.

# THE BIRD COMPANY

Joe Dickson, assistant to Jim Jackson, manager of the computer division of The Bird Company, was about to summarize his findings with regard to the memorandum shown as Exhibit 1. The memo was given to him ten days earlier by Jackson, who requested him to draft a statement for the coming cost control meeting. In reviewing past events and any mental and written notes regarding the investigation he had just completed, Joe Dickson felt that the following facts and information were pertinent to his problem.

The Bird Company was a large, well-established firm in the commercial radio-television and electronics field. For over thirty-five years it was one of the major radio producers in the United States.

In 1945 top management made a gross miscalculation in predicting that large-scale commercial television was still ten to fifteen years off. On the basis of this prediction they decided to adopt a wait-and-see attitude regarding television. Although TV sales were almost non-existent in 1946 and low in 1947 when only 179,000 sets were produced, the total market jumped to 975,000 sets in 1948, to 3,000,000 sets in 1949, and 7,464,000 sets in 1950. In the late 1940s the management of The Bird Company recognized their previous forecast error and initiated a crash program to make up for lost time. They were unable, however, to acquire an appropriate share of the television market, and they finally withdrew from the market in 1959 when total TV industry sales fell sharply and production dropped to only 5,385,000 sets.

Since the radio market also declined in the 1950s and was extremely competitive, new product and market possibilities were investigated. In 1955 two new markets and product classes were selected: (1) electronic computers and (2) electronic instrumentation. These were two areas in which competition was moderate and where a doubling or tripling of the market was anticipated within the succeeding five to ten years. Also, these were both products requiring substantial design and manufacturing skills. Top management viewed these as distinct advantages in that they felt that the personnel within their company had both the specialized skills and experience required and that such talent would become increasingly scarce as the market demand for these products increased. Because these two new markets were substantially different from the radio market, the computer and instrumentation operations were administratively separated from radio sales and production. The firm was therefore organized into three separate sections: (1) the radio section, (2) the computer section, and (3) the instrument section.

The radio section possessed the major fabrication and processing facilities. The computer and instrument sections primarily performed the assembly and distribution activities related to their respective products. During the succeeding years when radio sales declined, the operations of the radio section were held relatively stable by producing related commercial products such as shortwave transmitters, receivers, intercommunication systems, etc. It appeared that the radio section would continue to play a dominant role in the firm's operations.

In 1958, three years after management's decision to enter the computer and instrumentation fields, the computer section and instrument section almost simultaneously secured several large, long-term contracts amounting to approximately 25 per cent of the firm's then existing total business. This appeared to be a turning point in the history of the firm. Thereafter, the sales volume of the computer and instrument sections grew while the sales volume of the radio section declined. Increasing competition and rising internal costs appeared to plague the radio section. By the middle of 1962 only 40 per cent of the radio section's total effort was devoted to its own products. The remaining 60 per cent was devoted to supporting the computer and instrument sections' increased processing requirements.

In order to stimulate initiative within each product section, to shorten lines of communication, and to improve the locus of decision making, it was decided to make a major organizational change. This change officially decentralized the activities of the three previously semi-dependent operating sections. In the new organization each section became an independent division and retained its basic name with the exception of the radio products section, which became the general processing division. The change became effective January 1, 1963. Due to the skill, facilities, and production know-how contained in the radio section, it was decided to keep this section intact. However, because its major activity no longer consisted of producing radios and radio parts, but rather in providing the other divisions with fabrication and processing services for which they had no comparable facilities, the radio section was renamed the general processing division. At this same time it was decided that a concerted effort to regain a major share of the market which had been lost by the radio section would be made. It was informally agreed upon that if sufficient gains in this direction could be achieved, a new radio division, comparable to the computer and instrument divisions, would be formed and the general processing division would continue solely as a service division for the product divisions.

In addition to the minor name changes, the reorganization included the installation of a new cost accounting and control system and a new set of formal authority relationships. The new relationship placed the corporate officers (vice-presidents of sales, manufacturing, engineering, and finance) in a functional relationship with their counterparts at the divisional level. Previously each had line authority, but with this new relationship each division gained a large measure of autonomy. To exercise this autonomy a general manager who reported directly to the president was placed at the head of each division (see Exhibits 2 and 3).

The final change was the installation of a new cost control system. Operationally the new cost system was an extension of the old system which charged all direct labor and direct material costs to specific orders and accumulated all other costs in a single general overhead account for the entire company. This account was cleared monthly by distributing the accumulated overhead costs to specific jobs in proportion to the direct labor expended on each job during the month. Thus all jobs had the same overhead rate.

The major procedural change instituted by the new system was to allow the old functional overhead account number to be prefixed by a division number, work center number, and/or functional account number. Each division could thereby determine its own cost centers, develop independent and different overhead rates for each cost center, and still utilize the existing data processing and accounting system. Exhibit 4 and the following paragraphs describe the new system.

Under the new cost collection system, corporate level costs (salaries, supplies, and expenses of the president, vice-president, and their staffs, etc.) were collected by function and whenever practical charged directly to an appropriate divisional counterpart account. Costs from the corporate level which could not be charged directly against any single division were prorated among the counterpart accounts of all three divisions in proportion to each division's respective gross sales dollars. A vast majority of the corporate level costs were of this nature.

At the divisional level, all direct costs were collected by manufacturing cost centers. Indirect costs were assigned either to a manufacturing cost center or to an appropriate functional cost account such as sales expenses, cost records, production control, etc. Manufacturing cost center overhead rates in dollars per direct labor hour were calculated for each manufacturing cost control center by dividing the total overhead charges levied against each cost control center by the total direct labor hours expended within each respective center.

Subfunctional overhead rates and an overall functional overhead rate were also calculated for each division. The subfunctional overhead rates were calculated by dividing the total indirect and corporate charges accumulated in each of the divisions' functional accounts by the total direct labor hours expended within the specific division. The determination of these numerous subfunctional overhead ratios was designed to permit interdivisional cost and performance comparisons. The ratio currently under study constituted one of these numerous subfunctional overhead ratios. The overall functional overhead rate was merely the sum of all of the subfunctional overhead rates for each respective division.

The total or item cost of a specific job or project was obtained by accumulating the appropriate direct labor, material, and overhead charges for the specific job. The overhead charges consisted of the divisional overhead rate multiplied by the total direct labor hours that were applied to the specific job, plus each manufacturing cost center overhead rate multiplied by the respective direct labor hours expended in each respective cost center.

The computer division and the instrument division were charged the item cost plus 10 per cent for all support work performed for them by the general processing division. It was a general company policy that no division should subcontract work outside the firm as long as internal capacity was available. This latter policy was designed to allow each division to work as near to capacity as possible and thus operate at the lowest possible average cost per direct labor hour.

The final decision to allocate overhead costs, determine item costs, and allow a 10 per cent profit on all support work as just described was determined partly on an objective basis, partly by negotiation, and partly on the basis of expediency and past practice. At the corporate level considerable controversy developed with regard to what specific costs should be charged against a particular functional account and whether certain costs should be charged to a single division or prorated among the divisions. At the divisional level major compromises were made in classifying various costs as direct or indirect and in deciding whether particular indirect costs should be charged against a manufacturing cost center or against a functional account number. For situations exclusively within a division, these decisions were left to the discrimination of the executives within each division. Although each division tended to follow similar practices, numerous differences in procedure resulted.

The validity and usefulness of the new cost control system continued to be the subject of extensive debates among the various executives. One group, which favored the new system, claimed that under the old system of a single overhead rate, jobs requiring more than an average amount of indirect and overhead services were allocated less than their proportionate share of these costs and that: (1) inappropriately high profits were credited to these products, (2) sales were unwisely encouraged, and (3) unwarranted price reductions were made. Products requiring less than average indirect and overhead services were alleged to be assigned an excessive share of overhead costs resulting in: (1) inappropriately low profit assignments, (2) unjustified discouragement of sales, and (3) unwarranted price increases. The total sequence of events was thought to be:

1. An invalid distribution of overhead costs
2. An incorrect pricing policy
3. A loss in the sale of products having a low actual overhead to direct labor ratio
4. An increase in the sale of products having a high actual overhead to direct labor ratio
5. A continuous increase in the overall overhead rate

It was further claimed by the proponents of the new system that the increasing overhead rates made it impossible for the radio section, whose products required a minimum of overhead services, to meet competitive prices. Prices were determined by adding the divisional and corporate overhead rates to direct labor and material costs and applying a nominal profit. The proponents of the new system stated that, even at a zero profit rate, the radio section could not match competitive prices and that bidding a negative profit rate (a loss) was not considered a good business practice.

The proponents of the old cost system, led by Daniel Woods, the chief cost accountant, strongly resisted the change in systems. They stated that the above argument was based largely on conjecture and hypothesizing and that markedly changed market conditions and the increasing size of the firm were the major causes for the sales shifts. This group also claimed that the old cost system could easily be modified to correct any minor inaccuracies which it might contain. They also stated that the new system did not offer sufficient evidence of improving the situation to warrant the increased complexity, cost, and risks involved in such a change in procedure. In spite of these objections the new system was adopted.

After six months of operation, the new cost system was operating routinely and most major objections had disappeared. Each division had been able to reduce its own direct costs and the redistribution of overhead and indirect costs resulting from the new cost center system had not appeared to disturb the sales of either the computer or instrument division even though the effective overhead rates charged against these products were above the previous single overhead rate and the price of most computer and instrument division products had been increased slightly. Adequate time had not elapsed to evaluate the effect on the sale of radio products. This conclusion was based on previous experience which indicated that recapturing a lost market was often more difficult and time consuming than acquiring a new market.

The new cost collection and allocation system resulted in significant differences in the calculated cost of many items. The change in the calculated cost of the J7-Crystal Detector Set was an example of a large but typical change (see Exhibit 5).

The model J7-Crystal Detector Set was completely assembled from purchased parts. Direct labor consisted of hand assembly and packaging, which was done by individuals working at a small bench using inexpensive hand tools such as a soldering iron, pliers, wire clippers, scissors, etc. Under the new cost center system the overhead rate for this work center was only 35 per cent compared to the division's average work center overhead rate of approximately 95 per cent. The 25 per cent general overhead allocation shown in Exhibit 5 was the division's overall functional overhead rate applied to all jobs on the basis of total direct labor costs. This figure included all indirect charges not directly assignable to a particular work center as well as all corporate overhead charges assessed against the division.

Once an excellent seller in the hobby radio field, the J7-Crystal Detector Set had become practically unsalable. It was believed that this was the consequence of a 20 per cent increase in the selling price resulting from increased manufacturing costs being passed on from the manufacturer to the wholesaler, from the wholesaler to the retailer, and subsequently from the retailer to the customer. The increased manufacturing cost stemmed primarily from a continuous rise in the general overhead rate applied to all direct labor during the three-year period prior to the installation of the new cost system. Under the new system the work centers used in the production of J7-Crystal Detector Sets possessed overhead rates substantially below the previous single overhead rate. Other work centers possessed overhead rates substantially higher than those used in the production of J7-Crystal Detector Sets and the previous single rate. As a result the total overhead cost applied to the J7-Crystal Detector Set was reduced by 50 per cent (see Exhibit 5). This promoted a price reduction which placed the wholesale price of the J7-Crystal Detector Set approximately 5 per cent below the average competitive price. Unfortunately, even at this price, little of the lost market had been regained to date.

In addition to having a significant effect on the calculated costs and the pricing structure, the new cost system permitted functional cost comparisons between the three divisions. Such a comparison led the controller to request an analysis of the production control costs of the three divisions. Since the divisions were of unequal size, an absolute measure did not appear appropriate and the ratio of production control cost to direct labor hours was selected as the appropriate measure of performance. The attempt to find a satisfactory explanation and subsequent remedy for the large differences in the production control to direct labor cost ratios for the three divisions was one of the first tests of the usefulness and value of the new interdivisional cost comparisons made possible by the determination of the subfunctional overhead rates for each division.

Shortly after the introduction of the new cost accounting system an initial study was made when the ratio of production control to direct labor costs was reported as shown in Exhibit 6. These results were contrary to all intuitive reasoning and a cursory investigation revealed several major errors in the cost accumulation procedures. It was decided that the study should be postponed until the new cost accounting system had time to "shake down." A similar check of the accuracy of the latest figures, included in the comparative production control overhead cost report (Exhibit 7) and in the memo designated as Exhibit 1, indicated no apparent errors in the accumulation process. It was thus felt that an analysis of these latest figures was in order.

As a basis for the required analysis Joe Dickson decided to identify and describe the major production control functions common to each division and to compare respective costs for each function. Since all divisions were using a similar production control system there appeared to be no major functions which were not common to all divisions. The items listed in Exhibit 8 constitute the major production control functions.

An investigation of the magnitudes of the costs associated with each function indicated that the combined cost of items 1, 3, 4, 10, and 11 in Exhibit 8 accounted for about 5 per cent of the total production control costs and that they were similar enough on a percentage basis to warrant exclusion from further investigation. The study was thus limited to the following six functions:

| | |
|---|---|
| Parts accountability | Scheduling |
| Dispatch | Production records |
| Parts expediting | Stores control |

A breakdown of the total production control costs for each division into the above functions and other miscellaneous cost data which Dickson was able to obtain is included in Exhibits 9 and 10.

Dickson carefully studied these figures. The course of action he selected was to investigate thoroughly each function, beginning with the function having the largest total expenditure and proceeding to the lesser valued functions. After a series of conferences, discussions with people in each division, and an examination of many reports, he collected the information shown in Exhibit 11.

Having refreshed his memory, Joe Dickson began organizing the report which his boss requested and which was to be presented at the next cost control meeting on October 20.

# EXHIBIT 1

## Memo: October 5, 1962

To:    Messrs. Jackson—Manager, Computer Division
                Karson—Manager, Instrument Division
                Jacobs—Manager, General Processing Division
From:  John Krass, Controller
Subject: Comparative Production Control Costs

In accordance with our objective to reduce divisional operating costs, ratios of overhead to direct labor costs are now being calculated for all major overhead functions. The first such monthly report was completed last week and should now be in your hands.

In order to derive the maximum benefit from these new statistics, all major differences and/or changes in overhead to direct labor cost ratios will be reviewed at our monthly cost control meetings. The agenda distributed two weeks in advance of each meeting will announce specific ratios to be discussed. The division possessing the least favorable ratio will be responsible for presenting the facts and an analysis of the situation. All other divisions are obligated to make any necessary information available. An informal discussion will follow each presentation.

The first such ratio to be discussed will be the production control to direct labor cost ratio. Last week's comparative production control cost report determined these figures to be as follows:

| Division | Production control cost per direct labor hour |
|---|---|
| Computer | $0.53 |
| Instrument | 0.12 |
| General Processing | 0.18 |
| Average for company | $0.31 |

In compliance with the above directive the computer division will be responsible for presenting an analysis of the above differences at the regular cost control meeting on the twentieth of this month.

Any significant changes in cost ratios within a division will be discussed at the respective division's subsequent cost control meeting. Such discussions cannot begin until a reasonably stable base rate has been established for each division. This is expected to require from one to three additional cost reporting periods.

                                        J. Krass
                                        Controller

# EXHIBIT 2

## Abbreviated organization chart prior to January 1, 1963

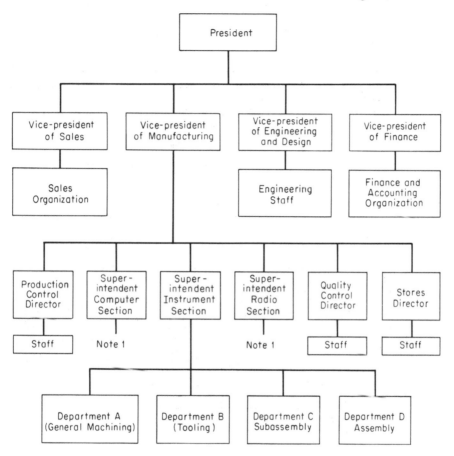

Notes: 1. Similar to Instrument Section.

# EXHIBIT 3

## Abbreviated organization chart after January 1, 1963

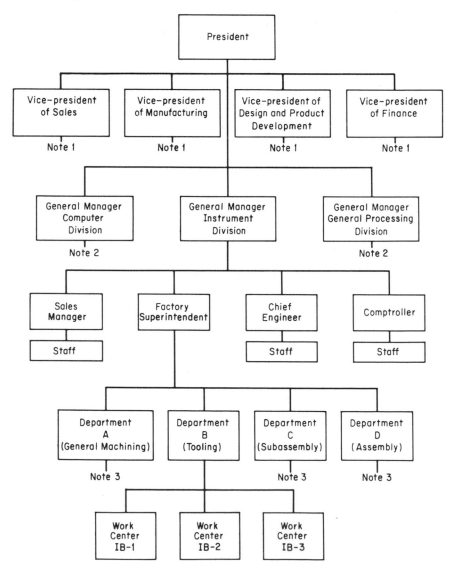

Notes:
1. Functional authority over counterparts at divisional level.
2. Similar to Instrument Division.
3. Similar to Department B.

# EXHIBIT 4

## Schematic diagram of new cost system

### (Flow of overhead charges)

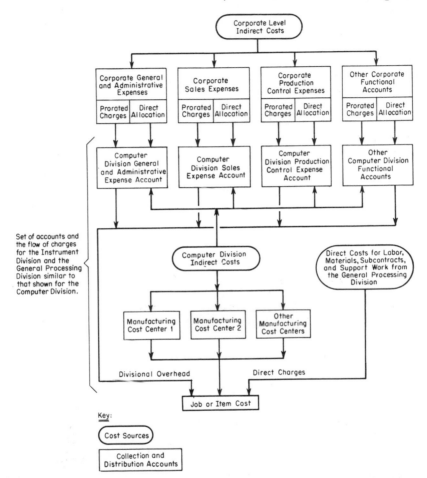

# EXHIBIT 5

## Cost comparison, model J7-Crystal Detector Set

| Item | Old system, four years ago | Old system, one year ago | Cost center system, current |
|------|---------------------------|--------------------------|----------------------------|
| Material | $0.50 | $0.60 | $0.60 |
| Direct labor | 2.00 (0.90 hr.) | 2.30 (0.90 hr.) | 2.30 (0.90 hr.) |
| General overhead | 2.00 (100% D.L.) | 2.76 (120% D.L.) | 0.58* (25% D.L.) |
| Cost center overhead | | | 0.80 (35% D.L.) |
| Total cost | $4.50 | $5.66 | $4.28 |
| Profit | 0.45 (10%) | 0.29 (5%) | 0.51 (12%) |
| Selling price | $4.95 | $5.95 | $4.79 |

\* Total functional overhead.

# EXHIBIT 6

## Comparative production control overhead cost report, May, 1963

| Item | Computer division | Instrument division | General processing division | Total |
|------|-------------------|---------------------|----------------------------|-------|
| Production control costs | $ 45,400 | $ 51,600 | $ 233,000 | $ 330,000 |
| Total overhead costs | 219,000 | 645,200 | 4,247,000 | 5,111,200 |
| Direct labor hours | 456,000 | 286,400 | 416,000 | 1,158,400 |
| Production control cost ÷ by direct labor hours | $0.10 | $0.18 | $0.56 | $0.29 |
| Total overhead cost ÷ by direct labor hours | $0.48 | $2.25 | $10.20 | $4.41 |
| Production control cost ÷ by total overhead cost | 21% | 8% | 5% | 6% |

# EXHIBIT 7

## Comparative production control overhead cost report, September, 1963

| Item | Computer division | Instrument division | General processing division | Total |
|---|---|---|---|---|
| Production control costs | $   230,900 | $   32,620 | $   72,260 | $   335,780 |
| Total overhead costs | 3,564,000 | 1,300,000 | 1,032,600 | 5,896,600 |
| Direct labor hours | 432,000 | 268,000 | 400,000 | 1,100,000 |
| Production control cost ÷ by direct labor hours | $0.53 | $0.12 | $0.18 | $0.31 |
| Total overhead cost ÷ by direct labor hours | $8.25 | $4.85 | $2.58 | $5.36 |
| Production control cost ÷ by total overhead cost | 6.5% | 2.5% | 7.0% | 5.7% |

# EXHIBIT 8

## Description of major production control functions

| Function | Definition |
|---|---|
| 1. Blueprint control | Produce and issue blueprints and maintain process description master file |
| 2. Dispatch | Report operation completions; receive parts into and release parts from a production control hold area to the work center responsible for the next operation |
| 3. Change commitment | Negotiate and implement changes in existing schedules resulting from part or process design change orders |
| 4. Change notice control | Maintain records and issue documents covering change orders |
| 5. Parts accountability | Maintain inventory and status records for material, work in process, and finished goods |
| 6. Parts expediting | Follow up and expedite parts to accelerate movement of behind-schedule items |
| 7. Production records | Prepare, code, reproduce, and release work orders; maintain a continuous record of the status of all in-process work orders |
| 8. Scheduling | Schedule the fabrication and subassembly of parts in support of end-item production schedules |
| 9. Stores control | Physically maintain stores facilities for purchased, in-process, and finished parts and subassemblies |
| 10. Tool crib | Maintain inventory control and accountability records for standard shop tools and equipment; issue and requisition standard tools |
| 11. Typing pool | Provide clerical assistance in the typing, filing, and maintenance of production control records |

# EXHIBIT 9

## Production control costs by function, September, 1963

| Function name | Computer division | Instrument division | General processing division | Total |
|---|---|---|---|---|
| 2. Dispatch | $  4,320 (2%) | $ 1,340 (4%) | $ 1,960 (3%) | $  7,620 (2%) |
| 5. Parts accountability | 23,820 (10%) | 4,280 (13%) | 8,200 (11%) | 36,300 (11%) |
| 6. Parts expediting | 8,640 (4%) | 1,320 (4%) | 2,040 (3%) | 12,000 (4%) |
| 7. Production records | 134,000 (58%) | 15,560 (48%) | 40,680 (56%) | 190,240 (56%) |
| 8. Scheduling | 22,560 (10%) | 5,900 (18%) | 4,280 (6%) | 32,740 (10%) |
| 9. Stores control | 28,060 (12%) | 2,940 (9%) | 9,960 (14%) | 40,960 (12%) |
| Subtotals | $221,400 (96%) | $31,340 (96%) | $67,120 (93%) | $319,860 (95%) |
| Other costs (items 1, 3, 4, 10, 11) | 9,500 (4%) | 1,280 (4%) | 5,140 (7%) | 15,920 (5%) |
| Total | $230,900 (100%) | $32,620 (100%) | $72,260 (100%) | $335,780 (100%) |

# EXHIBIT 10

## Miscellaneous direct and overhead cost data collected by Dickson, September, 1963

| Item | Computer division | Instrument division | General processing division | Total |
|---|---|---|---|---|
| Total production control cost | $230,900 | $32,620 | $72,260 | $335,780 |
| Direct labor hours | 432,000 hr. | 268,000 hr. | 400,000 hr. | 1,100,000 hr. |
| Direct labor dollars | $1,417,000 | $849,800 | $1,236,000 | $3,502,800 |
| Average direct labor cost | $3.28/hr. | $3.17/hr. | $3.09/hr. | $3.19/hr. |
| Total production control cost ÷ by direct labor hours | $0.534/hr. | $0.122/hr. | $0.181/hr. | $0.319/hr. |
| Total production control cost ÷ by direct labor dollars | $0.16 | $0.04 | $0.06 | $0.10 |

# EXHIBIT 11

## Dickson's findings

1. Dispatching and expediting were the only functions whose magnitudes were clearly related to the direct labor hours expended by a division.

2. All the remaining functions were performed by the division originating the work order and were independent of the location where the processing was actually performed.

3. Most functions were more closely related to the number of work orders in process and the number of operations performed on each order rather than to direct labor hours. This was deduced from the fact that a majority of the functions had to be performed periodically or at the beginning and end of an operation rather than during the entire processing cycle. Jobs also tended to be checked when idle as well as when being processed.

4. An increase in the number of urgent jobs substantially increased expediting costs. A sample of 100 new job releases for each division indicated that 30 per cent of the computer division jobs were released with a priority of urgent or greater. Similar figures for the instrument division and general processing division were 10 per cent and 13 per cent, respectively. Urgent jobs were jobs that had less than 80 per cent of their normal processing and wait time remaining before they were due for completion. A sample of completed jobs showed that 58 per cent of the computer division's job had received a priority of urgent or higher before completion. These figures for the instrument division and general processing division were 12 per cent and 8 per cent, respectively.

5. A majority of all jobs released under an urgent classification was done within the division originating the work order because of the added control which could be exercised.

6. Order sizes, operations per order, and direct labor per operation varied widely for individual orders. There was no clear relationship between any of these variables and specific products, except that computer work orders appeared to have a greater number of operations per order and had shorter processing times for each operation. No quantitative or statistical measures were made or were immediately available.

7. No quantitative measures of the number of work orders or the number of respective operations performed on particular work orders were available for this study.

8. The general processing division's work in terms of direct labor hours consisted of approximately 40 per cent radio products, 33 per cent computer division products, and 27 per cent instrument division products.

9. The computer division performed 67 per cent of its total work

requirements and the instrument division 80 per cent of its total work requirements. The remaining work for these divisions, plus all of the work for radio products, was done in the general processing division.

10. Approximately 4 per cent of the direct labor hours accumulated for the computer division and 2 per cent of the direct labor hours accumulated for the instrument division were of a type which the general processing division would have classified as indirect and overhead costs. However, none of these hours could be classified within any of the production control functions listed.

11. Approximately 6 per cent of the production control costs for the computer division and 2 per cent of the production control costs for the instrument division consisted of premiums paid for overtime work. The general processing division worked no overtime. Overtime was charged to a separate divisional overhead account and allocated to appropriate jobs as a per cent of direct labor. Only jobs for which overtime was authorized were charged for overtime. On rare occasions when the general processing division worked overtime it charged all overtime to its support work for the other divisions on the basis that it was their work that made overtime necessary. Overtime was authorized only when no additional personnel who had the necessary skill requirements were available within or outside of the firm.

12. Each division utilized the services of a single corporate digital computer for processing its production control records and data. Only direct labor charges for the computer's operation were charged directly to the respective production control cost centers and subsequently included in the determination of the production control cost ratios. All computer rental, maintenance, and supply charges were charged to a separate overhead account (cost center) which was closed into each division's general overhead account on the basis of the number of hours of computer service utilized by the respective divisions. Appropriate non-direct labor charges to the production control function were estimated to be $0.05 per shop direct labor hour for the general processing division, $0.01 per shop direct labor hour for the instrument division, and $0.015 per shop direct labor hour for the computer division.

# DISCUSSION QUESTIONS

1. Which of the two groups was correct with regard to the appropriateness of the new cost system in view of the fact that the new system did not succeed in regaining sales for the radio division and that the effective overhead rate charged against computer division and instrument division products was in general higher than the previous single overhead rate?

2. Why didn't the sale of computer division and instrument division products decline when the effective overhead rate caused prices to be increased?

3. How can the low overhead rates charged against the J7-Crystal Detector Set be justified?

4. Is it necessarily inappropriate to apply a negative profit rate when pricing a product in the manner described under the single overhead rate system? Explain.

5. Are the production control overhead to direct labor ratios included in the memo to the division managers a valid basis for measuring the relative efficiencies of the production control functions of each division?

6. What adjustments, if any, should be made to the reported figures to make them better satisfy their intended purpose? Assume that the factors described in items 3 through 7 of Exhibit 11 can be neglected.

7. Prepare a revised comparative production control overhead cost report by incorporating the adjustments that you recommend in your answer to question 6.

8. What conclusion do you draw with regard to the relative efficiencies of the production control functions in each division?

9. Do you agree with the company policy that there should be no outside subcontract work negotiated as long as internal capacity was available? Why?

# REFERENCES

Anthony, Robert N.: *Management Accounting, Text and Cases* (Homewood, Ill.: Richard D. Irwin, Inc., 1956), chaps. 10, 12, 14.

Buffa, Elwood S.: *Modern Production Management* (New York: John Wiley & Sons, Inc., 1961), chap. 21.

Carroll, Phil: *Overhead Cost Control* (New York: McGraw-Hill Book Company, 1964).

Dearden, John: *Cost and Budget Analysis* (Englewood Cliffs, N.J.: Prentice-Hall, Inc., 1962), chaps. 3–5.

Folts, Franklin E.: *Introduction to Industrial Management*, 5th ed. (New York: McGraw-Hill Book Company, 1963), chap. 22.

Matz, Adolph, Othel J. Curry, and George W. French: *Cost Accounting* (New Rochelle, N.Y.: Southwestern Publishing Co., Inc., 1962), chaps. 9–11.

Timms, Howard L.: *The Production Function in Business* (Homewood, Ill.: Richard D. Irwin, Inc., 1962), chap. 20.

# THE BOWMAN COMPANY

Lionel Mallick was an analyst in the value analysis section of the purchasing department of The Bowman Company. This organization was a major manufacturer of fabricated metal parts whose employment over the past ten years had been one of the largest in its industry.

Although the value analysis section of the purchasing department was four or five years old, it had only recently begun investigating savings opportunities resulting from inventory standardization. In fact, Mallick had made the first and only study that had been completed using this approach. This study, called the screw project, had been undertaken for the purpose of reducing the number of sizes and types of screws used by the MRO stores (the storeroom that serviced the maintenance, repair, and operational requirements, but did not handle production requirements.

The first step in his study of screws involved a review of the inventory records to determine the rate of usage of the various sizes and types of screws. From the 242 accounts, one for each size and type of screw, he found that almost half appeared to be used in relatively small quantities on a yearly basis. He reviewed this list of low-usage items with the chief storekeeper and with several of the foremen who used substantial quantities of screws. In most cases he was able to persuade the users to substitute one size for another and to agree that the lengths of screws carried in stock could be limited to ¼-inch increments so that the ⅛-inch or even ¹⁄₁₆-inch increments could be discontinued. The occasional requirements for nonstandard sizes could be satisfied by petty cash purchases and expedited service. This phase of the study resulted in the elimination of 81 items. It was estimated that each item eliminated saved the company approximately $50 a year in out-of-pocket expenses by eliminating the cost of paper work and handling involved in the purchasing, receiving, storing, and checking procedures. Exhibit 1 illustrates how some of the substitutions were made.

In his routine checking with stores clerks, buyers, and vendors, Mallick observed that all requirements for machine screws in the MRO stores were procured in standard one-gross containers. The next standard-sized container was a bulk keg weighing approximately 100 pounds. Since many of the items were used in substantial quantities, Mallick suggested the idea of purchasing such items in bulk to obtain the large discounts which were available when quantities of 25,000 or more of a single item were ordered. The proposal met with considerable opposition because it was claimed that bulk containers would increase the cost of handling, sorting, and issuing the machine screws and more than offset any savings that could be derived from quantity purchases. Most of the stock clerks were women for whom the heavy keg would be unwieldy and in some cases impossible to handle. It also meant that all issues would have to be either weighed or hand counted when disbursed to the workmen. The chief storekeeper estimated that such a change would require two extra people to accomplish these additional tasks.

Mallick was not satisfied with the explanation and decided to investigate further. He noted that a 10-32 $\times$ $\frac{1}{2}$-inch flathead machine screw had a usage of 235,500 screws during the previous year. These were listed at $1.50 per gross when packaged in gross quantities. If procured in bulk kegs the price dropped to $4.85 per thousand. The price quoted for gross quantities was the equivalent of $10.42 per thousand, and thus was more than double the bulk price. Savings of over $1,300 could have been made during the previous year if the procurement had been on a bulk basis on just this single item.

Many other specific items were checked and it was found that the potential savings averaged approximately 45 per cent if the items were purchased in bulk. Additional investigation revealed that approximately 40 per cent of all sizes had usages of more than 25,000 units per year that amounted to $22,800 in purchases during the past year. It seemed to Mallick that the possible savings justified further study to overcome the difficulties involved in the handling of bulk quantities.

Mallick contacted the local vendor who had been supplying most of the machine screws to the company and discussed the problem with him. The vendor suggested that the screws be supplied in special packages of 1,000 each which he would be willing to provide for a penalty of 5 per cent above the bulk price. The proposal was presented to the chief of the MRO stores and to the buyer who also had responsibility for the inventory records. These men then studied the effect of the proposed change in terms of record keeping, storage, and material handling. On all counts the 1,000-unit packages met with approval, and it was agreed that all items used in the quantity of 25,000 units per year or more would be purchased in 1,000-unit packages while items that were used in smaller quantities would continue to be purchased in gross packages.

During one of his conversations with the buyer, Mallick discovered that requisitions for similar types of machine screws were received from several different stores units in the company. He then discovered that a substantial number of the machine screws were also stocked in a special maintenance stores unit which purchased the items in relatively small quantities and received very minor quantity discounts from the list prices. After discussing the matter with the storekeepers of the various units involved it was decided to transfer all inventory stock accounts to the MRO stores. This eliminated sixty-four stock accounts from the special maintenance stores units that duplicated the identical items carried in the MRO stores unit.

In the course of his study Mallick observed that stove bolts were being stocked in addition to machine screws. During one of his trips to the storeroom he noticed that the stove bolts and machine screws up to 3 inches in length appeared to be identical in all but one respect—the only difference being that stove bolts came with square nuts included in the same box. These were screwed onto the stove bolts and the workmen were inevitably required to remove them before the bolts could be used as a fastener. An analysis of the $\frac{1}{8}$-32 $\times$ 1-inch stove bolts indicated that in the previous year purchases of $1,830.84 had been made that were packaged in boxes containing gross quantities. The equivalent quantity of number 5-40 $\times$ 1-inch machine screws which could be substituted for the stove bolts would have cost $420.77 and the square nuts would have cost $410.88 if purchased separately in 1,000-quantity boxes. The cost relation for other sizes was found to be similar. Eighteen sizes of stove bolts were carried in inventory and purchases of $6,229.38 of these items had been made during the previous year.

Mallick therefore suggested that the stocking of stove bolts be discontinued and that separate square nuts be stocked which could then be used with the machine screws which were already standard items in inventory. This proposal was accepted.

The screw project study had taken approximately a month to complete. As a result of this investigation Mallick then received the assignment of determining ways to reduce the cost of office pencils. From a preliminary study he learned that the company purchased pencils from four major manufacturers. Only first-grade quality pencils were procured and these were carried in inventory in five degrees of hardness. The sources of supply for these office pencils were as follows:

American Pencil Company, #3557-Velvet
Dixon Pencil Company, #1388-Ticonderoga
Eagle Pencil Company, #174-Mirado
E. Farber Pencil Company, #482-Mongol

During the previous year the company had purchased 1,000 boxes of office pencils, each box containing ½ gross of pencils consisting of 6 individual packages each containing a dozen pencils. This was the method for packaging used by all manufacturers in the pencil industry. Prices for the first-grade pencils were quite uniform at about $7.20 per box, but due to the quantities purchased The Bowman Company received volume discounts which averaged 65 per cent of the list price.

About seven years previously the company had gone to lower-grade pencils in order to obtain cost savings. These pencils, however, had resulted in a number of complaints, especially from the accounting department, and as a result it was decided to purchase only first-grade quality pencils.

During recent months the company had been solicited by a number of companies which produced second-grade pencils at a price about 30 per cent below the prices Bowman was currently paying for first-grade pencils. Second-grade pencils were available from more than a dozen sources, including the four companies from which the company was buying first-grade pencils. In starting his new assignment Mallick had tried out several second-grade pencils and from casual observation was unable to detect any significant difference between these and the first-grade pencils which he had been using.

# EXHIBIT 1

## Partial list of discontinued machine screws

| Items discontinued | Types of item | Substitute |
|---|---|---|
| 6-32 × ⅝ in. | Machine screws, round head | 6-32 × ¾ in. |
| 12-28 × ⅝ in. | Machine screws, round head | 12-28 × 1 in. |
| 12-28 × ¾ in. | Machine screws, round head | 12-28 × 1 in. |
| 5⁄16-18 × 2¾ in. | Machine screws, round head | 5⁄16-18 × 3 in. |
| ½-13 × ¾ in. | Machine screws, flat head | ½-13 × 1 in. |
| ½-13 × 5 in. | Machine screws, flat head | Close account |
| ¼-in. aluminum post screws | .................... | Transfer stock to stationery stores and close account |

# DISCUSSION QUESTIONS

1. What do you think of Mallick's study of screws? Are there any additional areas of investigation that you could suggest?

2. How much was saved as a result of the screw project? Was this a satisfactory payoff after considering the cost of making the study?

3. How would you go about making the study of office pencils? What data would you seek and what kind of problems would you expect to run into?

# REFERENCES

Aljian, George W. (ed.): *Purchasing Handbook* (New York: McGraw-Hill Book Company, 1958), chap. 11.

Ammer, Dean S.: *Materials Management* (Homewood, Ill.: Richard D. Irwin, Inc., 1962), chap. 18.

Heinritz, Stuart F.: *Purchasing Principles and Applications* (Englewood Cliffs, N.J.: Prentice-Hall, Inc., 1959), chap. 12.

National Committee on Education: *Cutting Costs by Analyzing Values* (New York: National Association of Purchasing Agents, 1952).

# BUCKNELL
# INDUSTRIES, INC.

Bucknell Industries, Inc., originated in the early 1900s as a small back-yard shop manufacturing tools and fixtures for local industrial concerns. When a major railroad car manufacturing and repair depot was located in the same town, K. R. Bucknell, the original owner and manager of what was then called the Bucknell Machine and Foundry Works, negotiated several contracts to supply the depot with pins, bushings, and other small fittings for railroad cars. Because of the nearness of Mr. Bucknell's facility and his willingness to do everything possible to satisfy the needs of the repair depot, his firm gradually acquired a large share of the depot's outside manufacturing business. With the growth of the business, the original shop and various other buildings which were leased in the immediate vicinity became too small to house the firm's manufacturing activities. Consequently, a new plant was built on the outskirts of town on a large tract of land which had been owned by the Bucknell family for several generations. The plant occupied only a small part of the tract; the balance was leased as pastureland and farmland.

In a period of some twenty years after the plant was constructed, the Bucknell Machine and Foundry Works bought out two local firms, and early in World War II it became a major subcontractor for machined parts for various military weapons and vehicles. At that time the name of the firm was changed to Bucknell Industries, Inc., and four separate divisions were formed: the railroad products division, the defense products division, the machine tools division, and the tool, die, and fixture (TDF) division. The machine tools division and TDF division continued to occupy the separate plants in which they were located before being acquired by Bucknell. The defense products division took over a portion of the original Bucknell plant, which was underutilized because of a decline in railroad business, and a new building which had been constructed adjacent to the original plant. The railroad products division continued to occupy the remainder of the original plant which had not been relinquished to the defense products division.

Over a period of years the total sales of the four divisions rose to $125 million per year and remained fairly constant at that level. At first profits rose in proportion to sales. However, when sales leveled off at $125 million, profits slowly began to decline. Part of the reason for the decline was a substantial decrease in sales of the railroad products division which pushed that division's sales far below its breakeven volume. Also the other three divisions were faced with increasingly severe competition which forced profit margins lower than they had ever been previously.

Faced with a continuing decline in profits which apparently could not be reversed by usual cost-cutting methods, the management of Bucknell Industries undertook a complete reevaluation of the operations of the four divisions.

The reevaluation began with a meeting of the regional sales managers and several field sales representatives to discuss the possible reasons why Bucknell was losing its former leadership position for many of its specialty products. All the sales executives admitted that they were aware of the situation and emphasized the highly competitive condition of the market, particularly with reference to prices. In fact, some of those present at the meeting suggested the possibility of secret price cutting on some products.

The sales manager presented a comprehensive study that he had prepared from several interviews between Bucknell's field representatives and customer purchasing agents conducted shortly after Bucknell had lost several significant orders. In no case did a purchasing agent express dissatisfaction with Bucknell's quality of service. The typical explanation as to why the order went to another supplier was that a better deal was offered. The sales representatives were unable to clearly determine how the competitor's deal differed from Bucknell's, but they all felt that price was the determining factor.

From industry reports and trade association data it appeared that several other older firms in the industry were in the same situation and that two relatively new firms were making the only significant gains evident in the entire industry. Secret price cutting had not previously been a problem in the industry. Bucknell and most of its competitors belonged to a strong trade association which advocated open price competition by the independent setting of fair catalog prices. The association violently denounced secret price cutting and cutthroat competition, and to date the major firms had been known to conscientiously uphold these principles.

A review of competitive catalog prices revealed only negligible price differences. Any existing price advantage resulting from differences in catalog prices amounted to only a few per cent and were often reversed when special shipping and handling charges were taken into account.

Bucknell had already made numerous reductions in catalog prices, but in spite of this, major losses in sales were being experienced in the big seller items. Some gains were evident in the small sellers that were priced at or below total costs because of low volume. The sales meeting concluded with a remark from one of the field salesmen: "We don't have a sales problem. Just get production costs down so I can offer the right price and I'll get you all the business you want."

The sales review was followed by an examination of internal operating policies and procedures. This study brought to light the fact that a considerable amount of fully depreciated equipment was still being used, that work loads between departments were out of balance, and that the manufacturing methods used were those that tradition and experience had proved to be sound. Several of the production executives were incensed at the position taken by the sales organization and charged that "if you salesmen knew your job you would be able to sell what we can manufacture. With our long experience we can out produce and out compete anyone in the industry."

The conclusion reached by Bucknell's top management as a result of this study was that the organizational structure consisting of four divisions, each maintaining separate staffs and facilities, was a luxury which could no longer be afforded. Accordingly, three of the four divisions—the railroad products division, the machine tools division, and the TDF division—were merged into a single industrial products division. The new industrial products division occupied the plant area formerly occupied by the railroad products division and also took over a portion of the new plant in which the defense products division was located. The defense products division continued to occupy the remainder of the new plant area. Both of the plants which had been acquired when the two local firms were purchased some years before were sold by Bucknell along with some surplus equipment which was not needed after the consolidation.

Under the new organization many similar manufacturing operations which had previously been done independently in the three separate divisions were now centralized in the industrial products division. It was found that the consolidation of these activities reduced the requirement for some machinery and equipment to less than one-half of that previously required by the three separate divisions. Also, some of the machine work being done in the defense products division which was similar to that done in the new industrial products division was transferred to the industrial products division. In effect, the industrial products division became a large metalworking job shop with some facilities for assembling machine tools.

In selecting a management team to guide the new industrial products division, it was decided to rely primarily on personnel from the three divisions which were being merged into the new industrial products division. It was felt that the management team had to know the ways of Bucknell Industries to reach an efficient operating position quickly, but they also had to know "how to get $1.10 of value out of every $1.00 spent." Guy Wilkinson, with seven years of experience as manager of the machine tools division and ten years of experience as a major executive in the automobile industry, was selected to head the industrial products division. Steve Statten, with five years of experience in the railroad products division and fifteen years of previous experience as an industrial engineer, was selected as manufacturing manager of the division. Knowing that reduced manufacturing cost was the sole reason for creating the industrial products division, Statten immediately set out to create an organization to achieve this goal. The line and staff structure which was developed is shown in Exhibit 1.

To get an immediate "fix" on operational efficiency and to prevent the development of lax work habits, one project which was given first priority was the determination of a set of production standards for all standard items to be produced in the machine shops. Although this could be a very lengthy project, it was hoped that the standards could be established fairly quickly since the standards would not have to be completely perfect. It was a basic company policy not to reveal individual production standards to individuals having responsibility below the cost center level. Hence specific production standards would not be known to the individual workers. Even first-line supervisors ordinarily would not know the standard unless they were specifically requested by job number and operation, and authorization to release the figures was secured from the section foreman.

The policy of not revealing production standards below the cost center level was based on considerable previous experience which indicated a marked reduction in quality when individual worker performance was measured against an inflexible standard. Two of the old divisions, the railroad products division and the machine tools division, had used incentive wage systems for short periods of time. Under these plans incentive payments were made to individual workers who produced above the existing standard. Both divisions had given up the systems and reverted to straight hourly pay rates when quality declined drastically and the cost of inspection, scrap, and rework rose to such levels that the benefits of increased production were erased. As a result of this experience, it was believed that training individual workers in the use of proper methods and applying appropriate nonfinancial incentives at the supervisory level would best achieve an optimum between quality and quantity.

The determination of the correct method, the training of the employee in the use of the method, and the determination of production. standards were considered to be the functions of the methods group. From that point it was the foreman's responsibility to see that the specified method was maintained and to place the appropriate emphasis on quality and quantity. The foreman also had the responsibility for all future job training once an initial employee was trained in the proper job method. An exception to this occurred in certain cases where special training programs in specific techniques and methods were conducted by the methods group. Production standards were considered to serve primarily as an efficiency benchmark for managerial information and control and as an assurance that proper methods were being followed. Any radical deviation from specified production rates was assumed to indicate a change in method which should either be corrected or accepted as the proper method if it were found to be better than the existing method.

By means of a great deal of effort and the assistance of several persons from other groups within the manufacturing staff, the methods group either located or devised standards which covered approximately 40 to 50 per cent of the jobs in the fabrication and machining departments within a period of less than one month. These standards covered approximately 80 per cent of the direct labor performed in the industrial products division. Some of the standards were projected from time studies made as long as twenty-five years previously in the plants of the old railroad products division and machine tools division. Although most of the time studies from which standards were determined were of much more recent vintage, none of the time studies had been preformed in the consolidated manufacturing shops of the new industrial products division. Some of the time data also were adjusted to reflect anticipated savings from rearrangement of equipment and purchase of new equipment which had taken place when the industrial products division was formed. In a few instances where no time study data were available, standards were established by means of predetermined time techniques using MTM data.[1]

As soon as the standards went into effect, it became apparent that some corrective action was necessary. In a few instances cost centers significantly exceeded their expected output, whereas in most instances output was 20 to 40 per cent below expectations. On an overall basis, out-

---

[1] "Method-time-measurement" predetermined standard time data.

put was more than 20 per cent below expectations. To determine whether this inconsistency was due to improper standards or poor performance, sample time studies were conducted in work centers which displayed above-standard outputs and also in work centers which were below standard. The sample studies indicated that the errors in the hastily developed standards were such that all the standards would have to be redetermined before performance could be measured accurately. Previous experience indicated that neither supervisors nor workers were particularly sympathetic toward work standards and any attempt to use inaccurate standards for managerial control would be doomed to almost certain failure.

To develop a revised set of standards for each specific job by the traditional series—(1) job analysis, (2) methods development, (3) employee training, and (4) stopwatch time study—was impractical as a short-range solution to the problem. It was decided, therefore, to determine, initially, new stopwatch standards based on existing methods. Methods improvements would be suggested only where the gains were obvious and quickly attainable. Also, standards were not to be based on studies of each and every detailed operation, but only on a sample of selected operations which could be used to determine a set of basic elemental times from which standards for all production items would be calculated.

It was hoped that the total number of different basic elements would be limited to less than 200. These elements were expected to range from less than one minute to several minutes in length. The basic requirements for an element were that the motions or operations included in a single element were repeated for a large number of parts and that they were all performed in a single work center. This did not imply that the motions or processes which comprised a single element necessarily constituted a continuous series of motions. "Process and final inspection" satisfied the conditions for a single element if all of the work was charged to a single cost center. Similarly, "rough and finish grind" could also be a single element even though an inspection intervened.

Each basic element could be assigned more than a single time value depending, possibly, on such characteristics as part length, weight, or tolerance specifications. In such cases it was necessary to make several studies of an element to determine what factors were relevant in determining the correct time. It was considered that, on the average, four studies of such elements would be sufficient: two to represent extreme cases and two to represent intermediate or normal situations.

Since a single time study would cover several basic elements, it was estimated that the total project would require at most 1,500 separate studies. If each represented two hours of effort, the total time required was equivalent to about 1½ man-years of work. Accordingly, three men were assigned to the job of making the necessary time studies with a tentative completion date six months after the beginning of the project. A sample time study made by one of the men is shown in Exhibit 2. Each reading in Exhibit 2 was made by the snapback stopwatch technique and shows the elapsed time for each element in hundredths of a minute and the speed rating of the worker as a percentage of normal. Five operating cycles were observed and recorded. The column head TOT refers to total time for the five cycles AVG refers to average time per cycle, RF refers to speed rating factor in per cent, and BASE refers to the calculated standard time for the element (AVG × RF).

The operation shown on the time study sheets of Exhibit 2 was a carburizing heat-treating operation in which parts were packed in a carburizing compound and placed in a heat-treating furnace for from one to eight hours depending on the size of the part and the carbon penetration desired. In performing this operation the worker placed a layer of carburizing compound on the bottom of a large, heavy, metal box; he filled the box with parts and additional compound; and he tamped the compound to assure full contact with all parts. He then placed a heavy cover on the box and moved it adjacent to the heat-treating furnace. He might load one or more boxes before placing them in the furnace.

Before loading the furnace the employee had to put on protective clothing consisting of a face mask and gloves. He then opened the furnace, removed the boxes which were completed, and placed the newly loaded boxes in the furnace. He placed the hot boxes on a conveyer where they were carried outdoors by gravity and allowed to cool. When sufficiently cool the boxes were dumped, the parts placed in a wash rack, the carburizing box stacked, and the carburizing compound placed in a hopper. At the wash rack the parts were cleaned of adhering particles and placed in an outgoing tote box. Although this was the normal sequence which each part followed, the employee seldom carried out this sequence without interruption. Several different parts were processed simultaneously and the operator constantly shifted his activities between various operations.

It was hoped that this study in combination with numerous similar studies would provide basic data on various elements required in the carburizing process from which standard times could be determined. These times would be used to determine production rates on such tasks as carburizing medium-sized railroad bushings ($2\frac{1}{2}$ to 5 inches in diameter), carburizing large bearing races ($4\frac{1}{2}$ to 8 inches in diameter), and carburizing small railroad pins (1 to 2 inches in diameter). These standards would in turn be used to measure and control costs for the heat-treat and carburizing work center.

**EXHIBIT 1** Organization chart for the manufacturing department, industrial products division

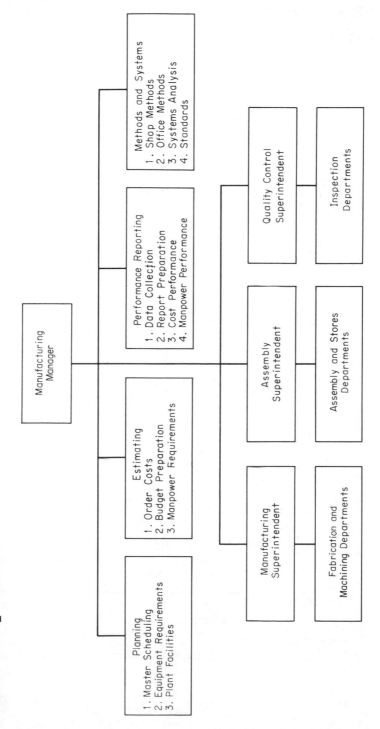

# EXHIBIT 2

# Time study sheet

**TIME STUDY SHEET**

DEPT. *Heat treating*  
PART NAME *Bushings*  
PART NO. *6420, 4631, 4286, 7138*  
OPERATION *Continuous time study of heat treat*  
*carburizer processing performed on batch basis*

OPER. NO. *62*  
STUDY NO. *486*  
SHEET NO. *1 of 2*  
DATE *2/24/64*  
OBSERVER *Ames*  
OPERATOR *Jensen*

| | ELEMENTS | 1 | 2 | 3 | 4 | 5 | 6 | 7 | 8 | 9 | 10 | TOT. | AVG. | RF | BASE |
|---|---|---|---|---|---|---|---|---|---|---|---|---|---|---|---|
| 1 | Obtain carburizing box | 41 | 30 | 29 | 35 | 35 | | | | | | 1.70 | | 90 | |
| | | 80 | 90 | 90 | 100 | 90 | | | | | | | | | |
| 2 | Add bottom compound | 32 | 25 | 30 | 10 | 30 | | | | | | 1.27 | | 100 | |
| | | 100 | — | 100 | 110 | 90 | | | | | | | | | |
| 3 | Load bushings | 38 | 122 | 160 | 112 | 32 | | | | | | 4.64 | | 91 | |
| | | 100 | 80 | 85 | 100 | 90 | | | | | | | | | |
| | (Number of bushings) | (2) | (10) | (12) | (10) | (2) | | | | | | (36) | | | |
| 4 | Fill box and tamp | 109 | 87 | 108 | 138 | 90 | | | | | | 5.32 | | 96 | |
| | | 100 | 110 | 100 | 80 | 90 | | | | | | | | | |
| 5 | Strike off and close | 21 | 25 | 19 | 22 | 28 | | | | | | 1.15 | | 92 | |
| | | 100 | 90 | 100 | 90 | 80 | | | | | | | | | |
| 6 | Move racks | | 19 | | | 21 | | | | | | .40 | | 90 | |
| | | | 100 | | | 80 | | | | | | | | | |
| | (Number of racks) | | (3) | | | (3) | | | | | | (6) | | | |
| 7 | Don protective clothing | 85 | 99 | 68 | 87 | 95 | | | | | | 4.34 | | 92 | |
| | | 100 | 90 | 100 | 90 | 80 | | | | | | | | | |
| 8 | Open furnace and unload | 160 | 100 | 33 | 310 | 291 | | | | | | 8.94 | | 100 | |
| | | 100 | 100 | 100 | 100 | 100 | | | | | | | | | |
| | (Number of boxes) | (1) | (1) | (0) | (2) | (2) | | | | | | (6) | | | |
| 9 | Load furnace | 83 | 70 | 95 | 105 | 68 | | | | | | 4.21 | | 94 | |
| | | 100 | 100 | 90 | 80 | 100 | | | | | | | | | |
| | (Number of boxes) | (1) | (1) | (1) | (1) | (1) | | | | | | (5) | | | |
| 10 | Close and set | 95 | 35 | 90 | 90 | 35 | | | | | | 3.45 | | 96 | |
| | | 100 | 90 | 90 | 100 | 100 | | | | | | | | | |
| 11 | Move to cool | 19 | 21 | | 32 | 41 | | | | | | 1.13 | | 93 | |
| | | 100 | 80 | | 100 | 90 | | | | | | | | | |
| | (Number of boxes) | (1) | (1) | (0) | (2) | (2) | | | | | | (6) | | | |
| 12 | Dump pick and rack | 452 | 416 | 292 | | 392 | | | | | | 15.52 | | 90 | |
| | | 90 | 80 | 100 | | 90 | | | | | | | | | |
| | Number of boxes and bushings | (2-20) | (2-19) | (1-10) | | (1-13) | | | | | | (6-57) | | | |
| 13 | Move to wash area | 100 | 35 | 90 | | 90 | | | | | | 3.15 | | 90 | |
| | | 90 | 90 | 90 | | 90 | | | | | | | | | |
| | Number of racks | (1) | (1) | (1) | | (1) | | | | | | (4) | | | |
| | TOTALS | | | | | | | | | | | | | | |

| FOREIGN ELEMENTS | | ALLOWANCES | % |
|---|---|---|---|
| | | STD. TIME | MIN. |
| | | HRS./C PCS. | HRS. |
| TIME FINISHED *11:01 AM* | | PIECES/HOUR | PCS. |
| TIME STARTED *9:05 AM* | | LABOR GRADE | |
| ELAPSED TIME *116 Minutes* | | | |

# EXHIBIT 2

## (*Continued*)

### TIME STUDY SHEET

DEPT. *Heat treating*

PART NAME *Bushings*

PART NO. _____

OPERATION _____

OPER. NO. *62*

STUDY NO. *486*

SHEET NO. *2 of 2*

DATE *2/24/64*

OBSERVER _____

OPERATOR _____

| | ELEMENTS | 1 | 2 | 3 | 4 | 5 | 6 | 7 | 8 | 9 | 10 | TOT. | AVG. | RF | BASE |
|---|---|---|---|---|---|---|---|---|---|---|---|---|---|---|---|
| 14 | Wash parts | 499 90 | | 603 80 | | 469 90 | | | | | | | 15.71 | | 87 | |
| | (Number of racks) | (1) | | (1) | | (1) | | | | | | | (3) | | | |
| | | | | | | | | | | | | | | | |
| | Miscellaneous productive elements | | | | | | | | | | | | | | | |
| 15 | Talk to foreman | 350 | | | 100 | | | | | | | | 4.50 | | | |
| 16 | Shovel compound | | | 560 | | | | | | | | | 5.60 | | | |
| 17 | Sweep area | | 35 | | 15 | 25 | | | | | | | .75 | | | |
| | | | | | | | | | | | | | | | |
| | Miscellaneous non-productive elements | | | | | | | | | | | | | | | |
| 18 | Talk | 150 | | 325 | | 200 | | | | | | | 6.75 | | | |
| 19 | Stand or wait | | 100 | | 135 | | | | | | | | 2.35 | | | |
| 20 | Leave area | | | 1560 | | 580 | | | | | | | 21.40 | | | |
| 21 | Others | 350 (Smoke) | | | | | | | | | | | 3.50 | | | |
| | | | | | | | | | | | | | | | |
| | | | | | | | | | | | | | | | |
| | | | | | | | | | | | | | | | |
| | | | | | | | | | | | | | | | |
| | | | | | | | | | | | | | | | |
| | | | | | | | | | | | | | | | |
| | | | | | | | | | | | | | | | |
| | TOTALS | | | | | | | | | | | | 115.78 | | | |

| FOREIGN ELEMENTS | | ALLOWANCES | % |
|---|---|---|---|
| | | STD. TIME | MIN. |
| | | HRS./C PCS. | HRS. |
| TIME FINISHED | | PIECES/HOUR | PCS. |
| TIME STARTED | | LABOR GRADE | |
| ELAPSED TIME | | | |

# DISCUSSION QUESTIONS

1. Why didn't the time standards first established for the industrial products division work satisfactorily?

2. How would standards be determined from the data shown in Exhibit 2?

3. Using the limited data provided in Exhibit 2, what is the best estimate of the normal time to perform element 7 (don protective clothing), and what accuracy can be attributed to such an estimate?

4. How accurate can the new standards be compared to the previous standards? How accurate should they be?

5. In what ways will the new basic elemental times to be established differ from predetermined time standards, such as MTM? Are they likely to be as useful?

6. What problems will be involved in making the new program of production standards successful?

7. What do you think about the company's policy normally not to reveal time standards to the workers or the first-line supervisors?

8. For what specific purposes does Bushell intend to use the standards? Are there other possible uses?

9. What are the reasons that the company changed to a more centralized form of organization? Should they also consolidate the defense products division and the industrial products division? What are the advantages and disadvantages of the centralized versus decentralized form of organization in this situation?

10. Evaluate the organization structure of the new manufacturing operations in the industrial products division.

11. The sales executives and the production executives had divergent views as to each other's responsibilities. Whose view should dominate?

12. Was Bucknell's experience with incentive pay plans typical of what should be expected?

# REFERENCES

Bailey, Gerald B., and Ralph Presgrave: *Basic Motion Timestudy* (New York: McGraw-Hill Book Company, 1958), chaps. 1–3, 11–14.

Barnes, Ralph M.: *Motion and Time Study*, 3d ed. (Homewood, Ill.: Richard D. Irwin, Inc., 1948), chaps. 1–4, 20–23.

Buffa, Elwood S.: *Modern Production Management* (New York: John Wiley & Sons, Inc., 1961), chaps. 11–13, 19–21.

Carroll, Phil, Jr.: *Timestudy for Cost Control*, 3d ed. (New York: McGraw-Hill Book Company, 1954).

Crossan, R. M., and Harold Nance: *Master Standard Data* (New York: McGraw-Hill Book Company, 1962), chaps. 1–6, 16, 17, 20–26.

Hadden, Arthur A., and Victor K. Gender: *Handbook of Standard Data for Machine Shops* (New York: The Ronald Press Company, 1954).

Krick, Edward V.: *Methods Engineering* (New York: John Wiley & Sons, Inc., 1962), chaps. 12–21.

Maynard, Harold B., G. J. Stegemerten, and John L. Schwab: *Methods-Time Measurement* (New York: McGraw-Hill Book Company, 1948), chaps. 1–3, 29.

Mundell, Marvin E.: *Motion and Time Study* (Englewood Cliffs, N.J.: Prentice-Hall, Inc., 1960), chaps. 1–3, 17–29.

Nadler, Gerald: *Work Design* (Homewood, Ill.: Richard D. Irwin, Inc., 1963), chaps. 1–3, 19–21, 23, 34.

# CANBURY
# MANUFACTURING
# COMPANY

"The policy regulating interdivisional work needs to be reviewed immediately." This was the conclusion stated by John Boyd, manufacturing manager of the consumer division, Canbury Manufacturing Company. Boyd had been in opposition to the interdivisional work policy for several months, but recently he had become very adamant about the subject. "Why should our division be assessed additional costs because another division does not reduce their costs? Perhaps the initial statement of the policy was logical, but the application has gone far beyond the original intent."

Canbury Manufacturing was an established firm in the electric and electronic industry. It served the consumer, industrial, and military markets and produced products which included electric appliances, motors, and electronic components and systems. The company had been reorganized into five major divisions (see Exhibit 1), and inasmuch as several of the divisions operated similar equipment, it was believed advantageous for each division to utilize the idle capacity of other divisions whenever possible. The various divisions were in separate buildings located contiguously to each other.

The central division included the president of Canbury, Stan Hall, and his staff of advisors. Major company policy was established by this division which had no manufacturing facilities but concentrated on coordination of overall company activities. The consumer division manufactured a wide variety of electric and electronic appliances for the consumer market. The industrial division made motors and electronic control systems for automated machinery. The military division had been organized to manufacture several different electronic components (including transistors) but gradually had expanded its capability to produce complete electronic control systems for military weapons. The special order division specialized in producing electric and electronic parts which were needed in small quantities or were of unique design. This division solicited business from the industrial market and from the other divisions of Canbury.

The product line produced by the four manufacturing divisions was so similar that the policy statement (see Exhibit 2) issued by President Hall appeared logical to the division managers when it was issued. Pursuant to the corporate policy on interdivisional work transactions a supplemental document was issued indicating the standard accounting and business arrangements which would govern these transactions (see Exhibit 3).

Standard definitions were created for all the terms used to describe interdivisional work transactions. These definitions included:

1. *Prime division.* The division that had administrative responsibility for a contract.

2. *Support division.* The division that provided a portion of the prime division's product and/or tooling.

3. *Task support.* An identifiable direct work assignment or group of such assignments which required the support division to provide for planning, procurement of raw materials, purchased equipment, etc., shop order releases, and necessary related support functions in the performance of the work assignment.

4. *Direct assist.* A direct work assignment between divisions which required the prime division to provide for planning, shop order release, direct material procurement, etc.

5. *Program document.* A listing or a grouping of records, forms, and data from which all information pertinent to an interdivisional transaction could be obtained. A separate document was required for each identifiable program.

6. *Interdivisional work authorization (IDWA).* An agreement between responsible managers of the prime and support divisions which described (directly or by reference) the requirements of a specific interdivisional work agreement. The IDWA did not apply to more than one program document. Subsequent work not covered by initial agreement required a revised IDWA.

A general procedure was outlined to provide the ground rules, responsibilities, and instructions for administering interdivisional work transactions (see Exhibit 4).

Several months prior to Boyd's statement that the interdivisional work policy should be changed, the consumer division had negotiated for the special order division to produce a transformer (Model 141) for a combination stereo-television set the company had just designed. The special order division already was producing three other types of transformers for the consumer division. The other three types had been produced for periods of time ranging from one to three years.

The IDWA was negotiated as a task support transaction. There was no firm target on price, but instead a definite number of man-hours were allocated by month to cover this program and the standard company overhead rate was to be used to make final cost determination. The man-hours budgeted for all transformers, and the actual man-hours expended, are illustrated in Exhibit 5.

The total budget of man-hours had been forecast on standards developed for each transformer. The time standard for each type of transformer was estimated relative to the size of the component and the amount of handwork required, and based on a 90 per cent improvement curve. The standards were as follows:

| Model | Man-hours |
|-------|-----------|
| 111 | 15 |
| 121 | 14 |
| 131 | 36 |
| 141 (new) | 13 |

The quantities of transformers required by model had been scheduled for monthly delivery (see Exhibit 6).

By May the scheduled delivery program was approximately on time but the overrun of man-hours from January through April totaled 27,000, and Boyd requested that the entire program be reviewed.

In response to Boyd's request, President Hall asked both John Boyd and Ben Thompson (the manufacturing manager of the special order division) to report their views in writing. Within a few days the president received their memorandums (Exhibits 7, 8).

# EXHIBIT 1
## Divisional organization

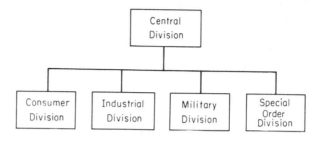

# EXHIBIT 2
## Interdivisional work transactions
## corporate policy

Normally division managers are free to determine their own sources of supply and to contract for goods and services which are not within the capability of their division. In certain cases it will be in the best interests of the company and the customer for a division to obtain goods and services from another division. These cases will ordinarily involve one or more of the following objectives: (1) to minimize cost and/or flow time, (2) to level abnormal fluctuations in manpower requirements, or (3) to take advantage of special products, facilities, and capabilities of another division.

Arrangements for interdivisional work usually will occur through mutual agreement of the respective division managers or their delegates, but in exceptional cases they may be directed by the president. When such interdivisional work has been determined appropriate, the work will be arranged on the basis of sound business practice.

Arrangements between the prime and support divisions must include documentation of at least the following items:

1. The reason or reasons for placement of the work with the support division
2. Agreement on a work statement or arrangement which clearly defines, to the extent practical, the performance responsibilities and

commitments of both parties and covers—as appropriate to the particular transaction—schedules, costs, and an expression of responsibilities accepted for performance of the product and for provision of spares and service

3. Agreement on procedural matters for administration of the transaction including documentation, change control, cost control, status reporting, and criteria for judging compliance with the agreement

4. Agreement on the price or pricing method

The pricing of interdivisional work may be done on a fixed-price or cost reimbursement basis (including time and material type arrangements) as appropriate to the circumstances and type of work being performed. A profit factor may or may not be included in the pricing, depending upon agreement between the divisions, except that agreements involving only overhead services or loaned employees shall be priced at actual cost.

Any profits made or losses incurred by one division on work performed for another are to be recorded in the participating divisions' financial records. For government contracts, however, the actual costs incurred by the support division (but not profits) are to be charged to the benefiting contract. The exception to this general rule is that if the transaction occurs on the basis of competitive procurement or on any other specific arrangement under which interdivisional profit is an allowable cost on the prime contract (such as a straight fixed-price prime contract), the full price (including any profit) will be charged to the benefiting contract but any overrun of price will be recorded as a loss by the support division.

The finance vice-president will issue and maintain a supplement to this policy documenting the standard accounting and business arrangements to be followed when one division does work for another division.

Each division manager is responsible for the appropriate use and control of interdivisional work transactions in compliance with this policy and its supplement.

The manufacturing vice-president is responsible for monitoring compliance with this policy and will initiate action to keep it up-to-date.

Stan Hall
President

# EXHIBIT 3

## Supplement to interdivisional work transactions corporate policy

I. An interdivisional work authorization (IDWA) is to be executed when one division does work for another division. The form is to be executed by the managers responsible for the work involved and to whom this authority has been delegated by the division general manager or corporate staff executive.

II. Standard accounting:

A. The detail accounting treatment of interdivisional costs and profits is to be established by the company controller and documented in divisional procedures. Such procedures will receive the concurrence of the company controller prior to release and implementation.

B. The basic accounting practices with respect to costs incurred and any profits or losses if negotiated, in connection with direct work transactions, are as follows:

1. Actual costs will be transferred to and reported on the books of the prime division.

2. Should the divisions agree on an interdivisional profit or loss arrangement, the difference between actual costs and negotiated prices will be recorded as additional (or reduced) cost by the prime division and as interdivisional profit (or loss) on the books of the division doing the work.

3. The government will not be charged for interdivisional profits except where the transaction occurs on the basis of a competitive procurement or on any other specific arrangement under which interdivisional profits are allowable costs on the prime contract (such as a straight fixed-price prime contract).

4. If the work transaction will require the support division to utilize substantially all its normal overhead services such as production control and procurement of necessary materials, the full burden rate of the support division will be included in the transfer of actual costs to the prime division. Such work transactions will be referred to as task support.

5. If the prime division performs procurement, production control, and other overhead functions associated with an interdivisional work transaction, only the applicable overhead of the support division will be included in the transfer of actual costs to the prime division. Such work transactions will be referred to as direct assist.

*C.* The basic accounting practices with respect to overhead support transactions are as follows:

1. For overhead support the costs to be transferred from the support division will include all appropriate overhead costs.

2. For loaned employees the costs to be transferred from the support division will, by definition, include only the salaries and wages involved: 25 per cent of such salaries and wages for applicable employee costs and other costs directly identifiable and associated to an employee loan, such as travel expenses.

III. The minimum reporting requirements are that:

*A.* Each support division will provide appropriate reports to each prime division.

*B.* The company controller will establish a summary report format for use by each support division in providing data required for the maintenance of a corporate summary report on all interdivisional work transactions.

W. N. Seftie
Finance Vice-president

# EXHIBIT 4

## General procedures for interdivisional work transactions

1. Lines of communication will normally be directed between corresponding organizations in each division.

2. Cost commitments or costing arrangements will be established by direct negotiation between the two finance departments. Manufacture of hardware will commence in accordance with delivery requirements following acceptance of the support division's preliminary cost commitment. The costing arrangement will be indicated on the IDWA.

3. The prime division will have the option of performing necessary rework on delivered items or returning them to the support division for rework. Appropriate documentation and notification of rework activity will be made.

4. Responsibility for specific functions, e.g., material procurement, may be excluded from a transaction by mutual agreement of the manu-

facturing managers. Finance departments will be notified of such agreements.

5. The prime division will be responsible for the plan for shipping, routing, and traffic. The traffic control organizations of both divisions will coordinate routing plans for each item.

6. The prime division finance department will assign reference numbers to all proposed IDWAs. The prime and support division finance departments will maintain a central file of all approved IDWAs.

7. IDWAs will be identified with their related support division work order numbers for purpose of charge accountability.

## EXHIBIT 5

## Man-hour allocation for model 111, 121, 131, and 141 transformers

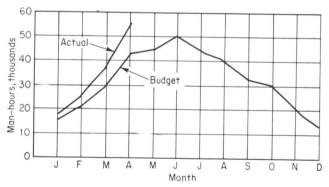

# EXHIBIT 6

## Quantities of transformers scheduled by model and month

| Period | 111 | 121 | 131 | 141 (new) |
|--------|-----|-----|-----|-----------|
| Jan. | 100 | | 50 | 900 |
| Feb. | 100 | 80 | 50 | 1,200 |
| Mar. | 200 | 150 | 150 | 1,500 |
| Apr. | 200 | 200 | 250 | 2,000 |
| May | 200 | 100 | 200 | 2,500 |
| June | 150 | 100 | 200 | 3,000 |
| July | 100 | 100 | 150 | 2,800 |
| Aug. | 100 | 100 | 100 | 2,500 |
| Sept. | 200 | 100 | 100 | 2,000 |
| Oct. | 150 | 100 | 100 | 1,800 |
| Nov. | | 50 | | 1,500 |
| Dec. | | | | 1,200 |
| Total | 1,500 | 1,080 | 1,350 | 22,900 |

# EXHIBIT 7

Stan Hall, President
Canbury Manufacturing Company

Dear Mr. Hall:

I am sure that you have heard of my dissatisfaction with inter-divisional work assignments. I am in general agreement with the basic policy but I believe some of the ground rules need review, and further, I believe that the administration of this program has not been in accord with the intent of your original policy statement.

During the past three months the costs in the consumer division have gone up because we have been charged more hours for the transformer program than the original budget specified. I recognize that we are all part of the same team, but if our division could have secured bids on this program from outside vendors I am sure that we would have received a better price and produced a greater profit for our company.

I believe that whenever interdivisional work is warranted an exact price should be negotiated and the supporting division should be required to live with the quoted price. When the supporting division can transfer actual costs there is little incentive for them to be cost conscious. Why shouldn't the supporting division bid on work for a prime division just like they bid on outside work? Perhaps they ought to charge a lower overhead rate for internal orders than they do for outside work.

It is my opinion that changes in policy and/or procedure are in order. It has been difficult to deal with the other divisions when the organizational structure and the philosophy of costing are not the same. Our division would be substantially more effective if we were more self-sufficient; therefore, I suggest that we purchase additional machines to improve the production capability of our division. If this is not practical we must make every division competitive by using only fixed prices and removing any internal pressure to direct business to our own divisions.

Sincerely,
John Boyd, Manufacturing Manager
Consumer Division

# EXHIBIT 8

Stan Hall, President
Canbury Manufacturing Company

Dear Mr. Hall:

Mr. Boyd has expressed his concern over the number of man-hours charged to the transformer project. There are several reasons for the over-budget figures and most of the reasons are the direct responsibility of the consumer division. For example, after our division received the work order for the Model 141 transformer and had based the budget on producing 16,000 units, we were informed that the order had been increased to 22,900 units for the coming year. This increased our plant load to near capacity, made necessary some overtime work, and required our shops to utilize some less efficient machines than those previously scheduled. Further, there have been two significant engineering changes, and the improvement in employee skill has not reached the level used in estimating the standard time. Moreover, Model 141 has had a significant impact on the total man-hour cost for transformers.

In the past our division has maintained great flexibility by not committing our group to exact price quotations. On numerous occasions we have reacted quickly to bail out another division in trouble when one of their suppliers failed to deliver acceptable parts on schedule. We have acted as a cushion to absorb overloads and a consultant to solve knotty production problems. Order cancellations are typical and occur whenever the other division can reschedule and produce the work they have authorized for our division.

I believe the special order division is performing a valuable service for our company which is not really appreciated.

Sincerely,
Ben Thompson, Manufacturing Manager
Special Order Division

# DISCUSSION QUESTIONS

1. Is there evidence in this case that the administration of interdivisional work has been inconsistent with the policy stated by President Hall?
2. Should there be a fixed-price contract between divisions?
3. Would such a contract destroy the flexibility feature suggested by Ben Thompson?
4. Should a support division grant a different overhead rate to a prime division from the one granted to external customers?
5. Should facilities be transferred from the special order division to the consumer division?
6. How valid are Thompson's reasons for explaining the over standard man-hour charges?
7. What action should President Hall take?

# REFERENCES

Johnson, Richard A., Fremont E. Kast, and James E. Rosenzweig: *The Theory and Management of Systems* (New York: McGraw-Hill Book Company, 1963), pp. 89–108.
Moore, Franklin G.: *Manufacturing Management* (Homewood, Ill.: Richard D. Irwin, Inc., 1961), pp. 83–86.

# COLUMBIA CO., INC.

During the late 1950s and early 1960s industrial firms in the United States began to realize that transportation and inventory costs comprised a significant portion of the total cost incurred by the manufacturer in delivering a finished product to the consumer. For decades attention had been focused on methods of increasing in-plant efficiency through both better control procedures and technological advances. At the same time, little attention had been given to the problem of reducing warehousing, freight, insurance, interest, and other costs associated with the distribution of the finished product. In the early 1960s, however, the importance of distribution costs began to be realized by an increasing number of manufacturers, and the concept of looking at the total system for moving goods from the manufacturer to the consumer gained widespread acceptance. As a result, many firms undertook detailed analyses of their distribution systems and methods with the objective of reducing total system costs. A surprising number of them found that airfreight, which at one time was thought to be of use only for small, high-value, or perishable items, was a feasible method of moving many types of goods when such costs as warehousing, insurance, deterioration, obsolescence, and interest on inventory investment were considered.

At the same time that this change in attitude toward distribution practices was taking place in industry, technological advances in the design of cargo aircraft, such as the development of more efficient jet engines and improvement in cargo handling systems, led to a continual decline in the cost per ton-mile of airfreight. By 1962 the impact of these simultaneous developments was to create a growing market for cargo aircraft for the movement of both domestic and foreign freight.

Columbia Co., Inc., had followed these developments closely since it had been in the aircraft manufacturing business for over thirty years.

Columbia Co., Inc., was the successor to Columbia Aircraft Company which was formed in 1931. Columbia Aircraft originally manufactured sport planes, racing planes, and a few military aircraft. Volume was low and total sales were never more than $3 million per year until the Second World War when the company became a major producer of training planes for the Air Force. During the war Columbia Aircraft manufactured aircraft in a large plant owned by the government in southern Wisconsin. At the end of the war Columbia purchased the plant and its adjoining airfield for a nominal sum with the intent of entering the luxury light plane and executive aircraft field. However, the market for these types of aircraft was not as large as anticipated and, aside from a brief period during the Korean War when it obtained a large subcontract for a major subassembly for a jet fighter, Columbia was never able to utilize fully the facility it owned for aircraft manufacturing.

After the Korean War, Columbia Aircraft changed its name to Columbia Co., Inc., and made a concerted effort to diversify into fields other than aircraft. Its efforts to diversify were not completely successful. By 1960, 75 per cent of the total sales volume still was derived from the sale of light and corporate executive planes and subcontract work from several missile and aircraft manufacturers. Although the company had not made a conscious effort to assemble a large engineering and research staff, the gradual evolution of the missile and aircraft subcontract work toward more sophisticated designs and the use of new materials resulted in the development within the company of an extremely competent engineering and research department. At the same time, the production facilities were capable of producing the types of parts used in the latest missile and aircraft designs.

In assessing its position in early 1960, the executive committee of Columbia took note of the fact that missile and aircraft subcontract work did not provide an opportunity for Columbia to develop a stable sales base for future growth. Also, the outlook for this type of business was not overly favorable since Columbia's aircraft subcontracts, in particular, called for a diminishing production rate in the future. The outgrowth of the executive committee's concern for sources of future business was a formal attempt to prepare plans for the next five years and the following ten years, in which estimates were made of the volume of business expected from present and possible future products.

One product which the executive committee felt would make use of Columbia's facilities and manufacturing, engineering, and research capabilities was a jet cargo plane. The executive committee felt that Columbia's long experience as an aircraft manufacturer and its experience as a subcontractor for large aircraft and missile components and structures well suited it for the production of such an aircraft. Also, its technical capabilities would be fully utilized in the development of a jet cargo plane. Columbia's market research department added further assurance that this would be a good choice for a major development effort with its report that the domestic civilian market should be able to absorb 100 planes by the mid-1960s and at least that many aircraft would also be required by the military by that time. Accordingly, Columbia embarked on a major design and development program coupled with an intensive effort to sell the proposed cargo plane to both civilian customers and the military.

Within a year after the development work began, preliminary designs were completed and the company obtained reasonably firm commitments for the sale of thirty aircraft. The design was for a medium-sized, four-engine plane with a swing tail for efficient loading. First deliveries of the aircraft were scheduled in thirty months. The market research department estimated that the company might expect to be able to sell a total of 100 aircraft for delivery during the next four years.

Because of the complicated nature of aircraft production, a number of different departments were involved in the preparations for production of the new cargo plane. The engineering department had the basic responsibility for the design of the aircraft. The manufacturing-engineering coordination department was responsible for the translation of engineering drawings into workable methods of manufacture. Usually the manufacturing-engineering coordination department attempted to suggest two methods of manufacture whenever possible so that the manufacturing department, or vendor in the case of a purchased part, would have some flexibility in choosing the least costly method of manufacture. The production engineering unit in the manufacturing department was responsible for working out the details of processing in the manufacturing department shops. The purchasing department was responsible for the purchase of materials for use in the shops and also for the purchase of finished parts. Finally, the industrial engineering department was responsible for estimating costs, preparing schedules, determining the number of jigs required, allocating shop space to various operations, and planning the flow of parts.

After the engineering drawings were released by the engineering department, initial planning was undertaken by the manufacturing-engineering coordination department and the industrial engineering department. As the engineering releases became available, the manufacturing-engineering coordination department established methods of manufacture. The industrial engineering department, in turn, worked backwards from the scheduled delivery dates to determine when parts would be needed and the approximate number of labor-hours required for tool design, tool fabrication, parts fabrication, etc. These estimates were then compared with the capacity of Columbia's facilities, taking into consideration the fact that parts for other aircraft and missile subcontract work were scheduled to be made at the same time. The result of this preliminary planning was the discovery that for some types of work Columbia did not have sufficient capacity available in its shops. Therefore, it was decided to subcontract a sufficient number of items to bring the shop work load within the limits of the existing capacity.

At one stage in this process of preliminary planning, over 100 different medium-sized aluminum items were selected for outside procurement. Although Columbia's shops had the capability for handling these parts, they did not have sufficient capacity, particularly in the milling department. The 100 parts were turned over to the purchasing department for procurement from outside sources. The purchasing department located two suppliers with sufficient capacity to do the work and with experience in producing similar aircraft-quality parts.

Both vendors were given the opportunity to bid on each of the 100 items with bids to be based on an initial order of 30 ship sets[1] of each item with possible follow-on contracts for 70 more ship sets. Since many of the parts involved complex machining operations and alternative manufacturing methods were available, engineers from the two vendors spent a considerable amount of time discussing possible methods of manufacturing with the manufacturing-engineering coordination department. The vendors then bid on each of the parts based on a certain method of manufacture. Out of the total group of slightly over 100 different parts, one vendor, Bryant Products Company, won the bidding on 60 items and the other vendor received contracts for the remaining items.

One of the largest and most difficult to manufacture parts in the group of 60 which were subcontracted to Bryant Products was a structural member located in the rear section of the fuselage. The fuselage was designed with a swing tail for ease of cargo loading. Also, to enable Columbia to compete for military orders, it was necessary to design the fuselage section immediately forward of the. swing tail section with a hinged loading ramp that became a part of the cargo section floor after loading. On commercial planes the hinged loading ramp was not usually required, and this section of the lower fuselage and floor was integrated into the rest of the fuselage. However, for simplicity of design no major changes were made in the structural design of major members regardless of whether individual planes had movable loading ramps or not. The part which Bryant Products contracted to produce was the main struc-

---

[1] A "ship set" is the number of parts required for one aircraft. If a certain part is needed ten times on an aircraft, a ship set is ten.

tural member running along either side of the loading ramp. The location of the two parts required per plane is shown schematically in Exhibit 1.

These members were designed as T sections with the top of the T on the outside of the fuselage and the leg of the T projecting into the fuselage. The cross section of the T varied along the length of the member since there were numerous points where other structural members attached to the T section. At these points additional thickness was required for strength. At the forward end of the loading ramp the T section had a compound bend and twist at a single point which further complicated the part. The engineering department had considered designing the member in two or three sections, but finally decided on a single part because of weight considerations and the fact that there was less chance of metal fatigue without the additional joints.

When the manufacturing-engineering coordination department received the engineering releases for the two T sections used on each plane, an attempt had been made to determine at least two methods of manufacture in keeping with the usual policy of offering alternatives to either Columbia's own shops or outside vendors. Because of the complexity of the part, the planning engineer assigned to work on the T section was able to specify only one method which he felt would be satisfactory. This method was to start with an oversized T-shaped aluminum extrusion, make the proper bend and twist in the extrusion, and then machine the rough extrusion down to the required cross sections. By starting with a sufficiently large cross section on the extrusion, any deformations caused by the bending and twisting could be rectified in the machining process. The other method which was considered was to machine the proper cross section into the extrusion first and then bend and twist the member. This would be cheaper, since it would permit a smaller-sized extrusion and would require milling the cross section of a straight rather than a bent extrusion. After consultation with a metallurgist in the engineering department, however, this method was rejected since the metallurgist was of the opinion that the section would crack if an attempt was made to keep the leg of the T section in line while the bend and twist were being made.

The T section had been primarily included in the group of subcontracted items because the industrial engineering department had determined that there was insufficient overall milling capacity available. In addition, milling the T section after bending and twisting operations would require some modifications in one of Columbia's milling machines to permit it to handle the bent extrusion in production volume. When the bids had come in on the T section, Bryant Products had won the contract with a low bid of $35,000 for tooling and $60,000 for the 30 ship sets. Their bid, however, had been based on machining the extrusions first and then bending and twisting them, which they claimed was a feasible method of manufacture in view of their experience. The other vendor's bid was $30,000 higher than Bryant's on this part: $10,000 more for tooling and $20,000 more for the T sections themselves. The much higher bid was due to the fact that the other vendor did not feel that the part could be made by machining first and then bending and twisting, but agreed with the method specified by the manufacturing-engineering coordination department. Bending and twisting the extrusions first and then machining them required more complicated tooling and also necessitated providing more material in the basic extrusions from which the parts were made.

Although the manufacturing-engineering coordination department was aware of the changed method of manufacture and expressed its doubts about the method, the basic responsibility for procurement and manufacture after the planning was completed was that of the purchasing department and also the production engineering unit. Accordingly, Bryant's bid and method of manufacture were accepted by the purchasing department, partly because of their reputation for technical competence and also because they had submitted a satisfactory small sample part manufactured by the machining-bending-twisting method. Because of time considerations and the cost of tooling, a finished full-sized test part was not required prior to the acceptance of Bryant's proposal. Another important consideration was the extreme cost-consciousness of Columbia's management and the continual efforts which were made to encourage innovations in designs and production methods which would cut costs. Every purchased part, in particular, was thoroughly scrutinized by a value analysis section in the purchasing department. The recommendation of the value analysis section was strongly in favor of the lower cost method of manufacture proposed by Bryant Products, particularly in view of Bryant's reputation for technical competence.

Bryant Products received the contract for the T sections in September with first deliveries scheduled in five months, during the following February. Columbia's schedule for assembly of the first two aircraft required that the T sections be ready for incorporation in a fuselage subassembly two months later in April. Following receipt of the contract, Bryant Products completed the design of the tooling for the T sections and began fabrication of the tooling in its own shops. The tooling was completed on schedule, and the first two parts were machined in December. When an attempt was made, however, to put the proper bend and twist into the sections, the parts cracked at the bend.

Bryant Products immediately reported the difficulty to Columbia's purchasing department since it would be impossible to meet the first delivery date, although they felt confident that they could produce the parts successfully by altering the way in which the bend and twist were made. Since the T sections were not actually required in the assembly operation until April and since Bryant Products had an excellent reputation for technical competence, the purchasing department saw no reason for alarm and agreed to a delay of three weeks in the delivery of the first two parts.

After the third and fourth units were machined, however, Bryant found it impossible to bend and twist the sections properly while still maintaining the specified angle between the top of the T and the leg of the T. On both parts, the angle between the leg of the T and the top of the T was off by about 4 degrees at the point where the bend and twist occurred. When Bryant Products reported this further difficulty, the purchasing department discussed the problem with the production engineering unit which was responsible for all processing in Columbia's own shops.

In view of the tight schedule which would now have to be met in procuring the parts, it was decided to bring the imperfect third and fourth units made by Bryant into Columbia's own shops for correction. Although Columbia's production engineering staff had felt confident of the shop's ability to correct the improper angle on the leg of the T, both the third and fourth parts were broken in the process by the shop.

At this point the situation would have been critical had it not been for a revision of the assembly schedule which delayed all assembly completion dates by four weeks. With the extra time available, the purchasing department and production engineering unit decided, as a temporary measure, to cut off the straight ends of the third and fourth units from the broken bend and fabricate stub knees in Columbia's machine shops with the bend and twist machined into them. (This was similar to the method of manufacture originally specified for a single extrusion by the manufacturing-engineering coordination department.) The stub knees were then joined to the original straight portions of the T sections using a specially designed connector.

The net result was that the third and fourth units, one ship set, were available on schedule for the assembly of the fuselage section of the first aircraft. Although the parts met design specifications for strength, Columbia expended an estimated $1,500 per piece on connector design and fabrication and on the machining of the stub knees. This cost did not include the unmeasurable costs of changing schedules in the shop to provide the necessary machine-hours and man-hours to do the job, nor did it include the cost of tooling at Bryant Products which would have to be altered or scrapped if this method were adopted. In addition, the resulting parts weighed 9 pounds per piece more than the original parts because of the splice. The increase in weight was a serious matter in view of the fact that the aircraft was already overweight, and penalties of $100 per pound would have to be paid for all excess weight over the the maximum guaranteed delivery weight.

While the third and fourth T sections were being reworked in Columbia's shops, Bryant Products had continued with the production of the fifth and sixth units which would be required four weeks after the earlier units. Without further instructions from Columbia regarding a change in the method of manufacture, Bryant had no alternative but to start production of these units using the same method that had been unsatisfactory for the first units. It was not until the fifth and sixth units were about two-thirds completed by Bryant that the third and fourth units were broken at Columbia and plans were made for producing the stub knees in Columbia's shops.

As soon as it was definitely determined that satisfactory parts could not be made by the method specified in the contract with Bryant Products, a meeting was called of representatives of each of the departments that had been involved in the design, planning, procurement, and manufacture of the T sections. Those concerned were the engineering department, manufacturing-engineering coordination department, industrial engineering department, purchasing department, production engineering unit, and the shop superintendent. In actuality, the first meeting was followed by three more meetings during the course of which the entire problem involving the procurement of the T sections was explored in detail. Among the questions raised in these meetings were the following:

1. What should be done about the fifth and sixth units?
2. What should be done about succeeding units?
3. Who is responsible at Columbia for the difficulties with the T sections?
4. To what extent is Bryant Products responsible for the failure of the T sections?
5. Who should be charged with the excess costs incurred because of the failure of the T sections?
6. To what extent were Columbia's internal procedures and purchasing procedures to blame for the difficulties?
7. Should Bryant Products be given further contracts in view of their failure to perform on this contract?
8. Who should pay for the tooling at Bryant Products which does not make a satisfactory part?

# EXHIBIT 1

## Location of major structural member produced by Bryant Products Company

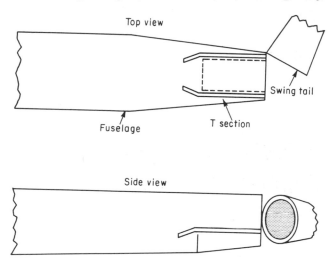

Top view

Swing tail

Fuselage    T section

Side view

# DISCUSSION QUESTIONS

1. If you were a representative of one of the departments participating in these meetings, what would your position be on these questions?

2. If you were a representative of Bryant Products, what would your position be with regard to your company's inability to perform on the contract?

# REFERENCES

England, Wilbur, B.: *Procurement: Principles and Cases*, 4th ed. (Homewood, Ill.: Richard D. Irwin, Inc., 1962), pp. 205–211.

Koontz, Harold D., and Cyril J. O'Donnell: *Principles of Management*, 2d ed. (New York: McGraw-Hill Book Company, 1959), chaps. 8, 27.

# CONSOLIDATED
# PRODUCERS

Consolidated Producers was a major producer of mechanical and sheet metal parts of a proprietary nature and also was a subcontractor manufacturing to the designs and specifications of others. James Homer had been the coordinator for the electronic data processing center of Consolidated Producers for six years. During this period several different tasks had been programmed on the computer, e.g., payroll, manufacturing scheduling, and certain applications of inventory control. Top management, however, was not yet convinced of the feasibility of expanding the electronic data processing (EDP) program. Their uncertainty was based on three issues: (1) there was a lack of understanding about electronic data processing systems among middle management, (2) Homer often was unable to satisfy middle management's requests for new information by pointing out that their requests would require reprogramming, and (3) there was no specific evidence that the machines were paying for themselves.

Homer attempted to meet the first criticism by an informal educational program for interested executives. He explained that "data processing systems ordinarily consist of a combination of units including input, storage, processing, and output devices. The devices may vary but typically the operations can be performed either by paper and pencil or by machines."

The transfer of the data processing function from manual to electrical accounting machines and electronic computers had been gradual at Consolidated Producers. During the 1930s the company used a manual system. Information was recorded and reproduced by hand or typed, transactions were posted by hand, calculations were made with adding machines and desk calculators, and information was stored as paper forms in filing cabinets.

During the 1940s the company introduced electrical accounting machines (EAM), sometimes referred to as punched card accounting. The basic element in this system was the punched card. The holes in the cards actuated the machines to perform various operations for keeping records. Some of the operations performed included reading, printing, adding, subtracting, multiplying, dividing, comparing, classifying, and summarizing. The initial step in this data processing system was to transfer information from printed or handwritten documents to punched cards. That was done with the card punch machine. Other electrical-mechanical machines verified the information, printed the information on the face of the card, sorted the cards by selected characteristics, matched or merged similar cards from different decks, calculated the arithmetic data on the cards, and returned the punched information back into the printed word in the form of invoices, reports, purchase orders, checks, etc.

"The computer," Homer stated, "distinguishes an electronic data processing system from an EAM system. The computer is able to store information in the form of an electronic code and select and use this information when it is needed. Further," Homer continued, "the computer can follow a sequence of instructions (the program) from beginning to end; and these instructions can require the computer to choose between alternatives."

Most of the same peripheral equipment was used to receive or expel information in the EDP system as in the EAM system. New and faster equipment, however, had been designed (e.g., magnetic tape input and output, high-speed printers, etc.) to keep pace with the tremendous processing speed, accuracy, and reliability of the computer.

James Homer responded to management's second criticism by stating:

> The EDP system has been damned by some for its inflexibility and praised by others for its flexibility. This paradox stems from characteristics which are common to large-scale EDP efforts, particularly those in the field of manufacturing control. Unlike payroll computations, the basic policies relating to manufacturing control are subject to considerable fluctuation. This is caused by the need to respond to changed conditions in shop load, labor market, vendor relations, customer needs, clerical manpower restrictions, and sales contingencies, to name but a few. The biggest single factor contributing to system inflexibility is caused by the time required to define a change with the precision needed by EDP and to translate the definition into machine instructions: in other words, to reprogram.

An EDP system cannot operate effectively without careful planning. The equipment is uncompromising and intolerant of value judgments which somehow exist in the less sophisticated manual system. This aspect of EDP does not apply to changes in quantities or revision of parameters. It applies particularly to changes involving processes of logic and decision.

Management has an inherent horror of becoming subservient to the EDP system or, more precisely, of being forced by circumstances to be dependent on the EDP programmer's estimate of how long it will take to reprogram what to the manager is a simple, straightforward, and very necessary change in ground rules. All too frequently the reprogramming estimate is so long that the manager will override the request to reprogram and supplement the current EDP output by manual means. When this happens, the suspicion may remain in the manager's mind that the reprogramming time was not estimated honestly, and further, the manager may be frustrated because he cannot prove his suspicions.

There have been times, however, when the EDP system has been able to extract data which have proved significant. The data were prepared in hours in contrast to the typically long flow time requirement or to being unavailable by manual methods.

The final criticism, that of proving savings from EDP installations, often was very difficult to resolve. Manual and EDP systems were different and usually not directly comparable. That is, the EDP systems not only replaced the manual systems but produced more and different kinds of information faster. Homer pointed out, therefore, that the machines were doing a larger and more effective job than the manual systems they replaced. The methods of cost analysis, however, usually failed to give full credit to the larger quantity and higher quality of work performed by the machines, and often the actual cost savings could not be proved.

There had been at least one application in Consolidated Producers, however, where the actual results were measured. It had involved the transfer of an existing program from EAM to EDP based on an International Business Machines Corporation (IBM) 1401 data processing system.

The 1401 system was completely transistorized and could perform the basic functions of reading, printing, comparing, adding, subtracting, editing, storage, etc., and variations of these functions. There were five interrelated units in the 1401 card system:

1. The IBM 1401 processing unit which contained 1,400 positions of alphameric core storage, each storing six characters of information

(expandable to 2,000, 4,000, 8,000, 12,000, or 16,000 positions), and the circuitry that performed the machine logic.

2. The IBM 1402 card read-punch unit containing the read-feed section which could read 800 cards per minute and the punch section which could punch 250 cards per minute, each card containing up to 80 characters of information.

3. The IBM 1403 printer unit which was capable of printing as many as 600 lines per minute, with a print span of 100 to 132 print positions of alphabetic and numerical data per line.

4. The IBM 729 magnetic-tape units which handled ½-inch-wide plastic tape coated with metallic oxide that could be magnetized in tiny spots to store 200 or 556 characters per inch and could be processed at speeds up to 112.5 inches per second to read or write up to 62,500 characters per second. A 10½-inch-diameter tape containing 2,400 feet could store up to 14,000,000 characters.

5. IBM 1405 magnetic-disk storage units which contained thin metal disks 24 inches in diameter, coated on both sides with a metallic oxide on which information could be recorded by means of magnetic spots located in concentric tracks. Access arms containing reading heads could move to any position on the disk which were revolving at 1,200 rpm. Thus, the information stored could be written or read on a random access basis rather than on a sequential basis as was the case with the tapes. The 50 disks in the unit had a storage capacity of 20 million alphameric characters, and data could be read or recorded at the rate of 22,500 characters per second.

The savings forecast in transferring the application to the 1401 card system were summarized as follows:

EAM systems cost:
| | |
|---|---:|
| Total basic lease cost/month | $ 4,378.00 |
| Average extra shift lease cost/month | 1,607.86 |
| Total manpower costs (including support group)/month | 9,372.00 |
| | $15,357.86 |

Anticipated EDP systems costs with 1401:
| | |
|---|---:|
| Total basic lease cost/month | $ 5,474.50 |
| Average extra shift lease cost/month | 289.92 |
| Total manpower costs (including support group)/month | 4,998.40 |
| | $10,762.82 |

| | |
|---|---:|
| Total savings/month | $ 4,595.04 |
| Total savings/year | $55,140.48 |
| Reprogramming costs | $28,450.00 |

The management of Consolidated Producers had approved this conversion to the 1401 computer. The actual costs of the program were summarized two years later as follows:

| | |
|---|---:|
| Systems cost with 1401: | |
| Total basic lease cost/month | $ 6,487.00 |
| Total manpower costs (including support group)/month | 3,456.50 |
| | $ 9,943.50 |
| | |
| Total savings/month | $ 5,414.36 |
| Total savings/year | $64,972.32 |
| Reprogramming costs | $56,343.60 |

One additional piece of equipment had been ordered to support the 1401. The rental cost of this piece of supporting equipment had not appeared in the original estimate of costs. The 1401 equipment had been scheduled to arrive on March 1 and the program scheduled to be in operation by April 1. Actually, the equipment arrived April 1, and it was August 1 before the program was functioning as planned. Once the program was in operation, however, it proved to be more effective than the estimate, and several workers were transferred to other assignments.

Later in the same year, Homer proposed an integrated data processing system to maintain perpetual inventory records, initiate reorders, and perform many other administrative and control functions. His estimate of costs and savings was based on the following data.

Twenty-four systems and programming personnel would be required for 21 months, twelve manufacturing conversion personnel for 2 months, ten material conversion personnel for 6 months, and five engineering conversion personnel for 2 months. The pay scale for these people averaged $550 a month. Machine time for testing and parallel operations would cost $69,200; the conversion key punching, $34,000; and the operation of peripheral machines during the implementation, $120,000.

The rental on the new equipment would cost $48,200 a month, and the manpower cost to operate the equipment (including support machines) would be $54,000 a month. This operation would eliminate the rental cost of machines which were renting for $24,000 a month and reduce the manpower requirement for different clerical operations by 210 people, whose average pay was $475 a month.

This new system involved the control of parts and materials (COPAM) and was designed to assist in the attainment of such objectives as: reduced flow time, increased inventory turnover, uniformity of systems, reduced paper work by personnel in the line organizations, closer integration among departments, and simplification of operating procedures. Consequently, there were many benefits to be gained which could not be measured in dollars and cents.

Management had reviewed the presentation of this proposed new system with skepticism: First, would the system work? And second, would the savings be sufficient to justify the high conversion cost? One area of concern was the electronic data processing system which was being used to record shop time for timekeeping and cost control. This system had been in operation for over a year and was still troublesome. The greatest problem was related to the need to have the workers insert the correct information input at the work stations. The men in the shop and their foremen seemed to have little concern for using care in inserting the correct data in the system. In spite of this difficulty, however, the accountants pointed out that the EDP system allowed them to account for more than 85 per cent of the costs incurred in the shop. Prior to the introduction of the system, the reverse had been true, i.e., only 15 per cent of the costs were accountable directly, while the remainder had to be prorated by formula. If the costs were not charged to the correct order, however, the additional information was of limited value.

Many of the supervisors of the company were opposed to the new system. Homer felt this opposition was caused by (1) their unwillingness to learn and use a new system, (2) their dislike of reducing the size of their work group, and (3) their reluctance to delegate any of their decision-making authority to the machine.

No employee of the company had ever lost his job because of EDP. Every employee who had been replaced by machines was transferred to another group or assigned to perform other services in the same group. The total work force of the company was approximately the same as it had been during the past five years. The output was slightly higher.

John Olson, the manager of the purchasing department, wondered if he could depend on the new system to give him an accurate account of inventories. Years ago the company had used a system of perpetual parts inventory. Clerks were stationed in every store area to account for the receipt and issue of parts. A separate ledger page was maintained for each part and when parts arrived the ledger was credited with the quantity received. The ledger was debited with the quantity of every issue of the part. When the minimum inventory levels were reached, the clerk initiated a recorder for parts.

This system had not worked effectively. There were countless situations when the balance shown on the ledger record did not agree with the bin count. Consequently, it became necessary to check the quantities in the bins frequently to make sure the inventory recorded on the ledgers actually existed. Finally, the company decided to drop the ledger record and depend on the storekeepers to maintain inventory levels. The new system was based on bundling a quantity of parts as a safety stock. Whenever a storekeeper had to break open the safety stock to fill a parts requisition, he issued a request to purchase a new supply of parts. This system had worked well and was still in use.

Homer believed that COPAM would be a successful system providing that the basic policies and conditions upon which the system was designed would remain constant. Moreover, he stated that Consolidated Producers could not hope to retain its position as a major concern in the industry if it did not adopt and use new tools and techniques to improve its operating efficiency.

# DISCUSSION QUESTIONS

1. How long would it take Consolidated Producers to recover the costs of developing the COPAM program? Is this a reasonable period of time?
2. Would this be a good return on the investment? Make whatever assumptions you feel are necessary.
3. How much confidence can be placed in the accuracy of the cost estimate? What might cause errors and how serious might these errors be? How can the estimate be improved?
4. What is the significant difference between setting up an EDP program for payroll computation and for manufacturing control?
5. What is meant by changes in parameters in contrast to changes in logic?
6. Is there any way to measure the value of reduced flow time, increased inventory turnover, and other intangible benefits attributed to the proposed system?
7. What advantages of the manual system might be lost in the changeover to EDP?
8. It is possible to design an effective control system when the decentralized units are not responsible for correct input?
9. Can a company achieve the cost advantage of machine efficiency when the total work force is not reduced?
10. What are the advantages of EDP? The disadvantages?

# REFERENCES

Buffa, Elwood S.: *Modern Production Management* (New York: John Wiley & Sons, Inc., 1961), pp. 247–286.
Johnson, Richard A., Fremont E. Kast, and James E. Rosenzweig: *The Theory and Management of Systems* (New York: McGraw-Hill Book Company, 1963).

# CYCLOPS AIRCRAFT INDUSTRIES, INC., PART A

Henry Jackson, chief of the production control unit of the missile division of Cyclops, faced the problem of convincing the cost accounting department and other production control groups that they should accept his proposal for changes in their well-established system for controlling quantities of parts placed in manufacture and for collecting manufacturing costs. The present system required rigid adherence to manufacturing by lots, each lot in sequence having a predetermined quantity specified for it. Jackson felt that greater flexibility in the quantities specified for each lot would reduce excessive scrap losses and rework costs and aid in scheduling work in the shop. His proposal, however, would require the other production control groups to change their present system or require the cost accounting department to maintain two systems for collecting costs. The cost accounting department contended that maintaining two systems would result in added expense and confusion that would more than offset the gains to the missile manufacturing operations.

Cyclops Aircraft Industries, Inc., was a well-established firm in the airframe industry. For many years the company's principal product had been medium-sized commercial and military planes. Because of the changing character of the aircraft industry, however, the company had been forced to withdraw from the marketing a line of its own planes. To meet the new conditions the company redirected its efforts toward acting as a major subcontractor to the larger companies who were the prime manufacturers of planes and missiles in the United States. The company was particularly interested in expanding into the missile field as a manufacturer of major and minor missile sections and parts involving both large and small production quantities. Cyclops was organized on a product division basis for purposes of planning, selling, and administration, but due to the similarities in manufacturing aircraft and missile hardware much of the fabrication of part and small subassemblies was performed by common manufacturing shops serving all product divisions. The balance of the manufacturing and assembly was performed by shops located in the respective product divisions.

Over a period of years the firm had developed a parts control system which was a modified economic lot-size plan to control quantities of parts placed in manufacture. The plan also served as a basis for collecting costs of manufactured parts to be used in computing the total cost of the end product. The plan did not involve the complications of computing an economic lot size for each part based on individual usage rate, setup charges, and carrying charges. Instead the plan involved the classification of parts into four broad classes and the use of a simple table to determine the proper lot sizes for parts being placed in production.

The criteria for classifying any part into a certain class were based on the size of the part and its complexity. The parts assigned to a given class had approximately the same manufacturing, setup, tooling, and storage costs. Exhibit 1 shows the descriptions of the four classes. These very brief descriptions were supplemented by a detailed description of the types of parts and subassemblies fitting into each of the classes. The detailed descriptions had been distributed in loose-leaf form to persons working directly with the system. As the variety of the company's products increased it was necessary to modify the original detailed descriptions of the classes by including in the descriptions additional criteria relating to setup costs and manufacturing costs.

The production planners were one of the groups of persons who had received copies of the detailed descriptions of the physical characteristics and costs of parts falling into each of the classes. When a part was to be made, the production planners consulted the descriptions to determine the proper class for the part and then consulted a table (Exhibit 2) to determine the number of parts which should be ordered. Exhibit 2 shows the size of each succeeding lot for a part in any of the four classes. The table was tabulated in terms of end-item sets. Determining the order quantity for any particular part and lot number required that the number in the table be multiplied by the number of times the part was used in each end-item. For instance, for a Class A part the order quantity in the first lot produced would be for the number of parts required for 15 of the end-items (missiles, aircraft, etc.) in which this part was used. Thus, for an airplane requiring 10 units of a specific part per plane, the first lot size of the part would be 150 (or 10 × 15). The next lot would be for 30 sets and so on up to a maximum production run of the number required for 1,100 end-items at lot number 9. At lot number 10 the long-run production lot size was reached for all part classes. All succeeding lots were manufactured to these lot sizes. The purpose of gradually building up to the long-run production lot size was to approximate the pattern of the company's increasing parts usage rate over time and, on the early production runs, to avoid excessive scrap and waste when design changes and changes in the method of manufacture were made.

Although it was necessary to arbitrarily categorize parts into classes and use average costs in order to develop a workable lot-size plan as shown in Exhibit 2, the table was based on the fundamental economic lot-size equation:

$$Q = \sqrt{\frac{2RS}{I}}$$

where $Q$ = lot size
$R$ = annual usage rate
$S$ = setup cost for each lot
$I$ = inventory carrying cost per end-item set for one year

As an illustration of the derivation of the table, the average inventory carrying cost per end-item set per year $I$ of Class A parts was found to be about $3. This included space charges, interest on cost of the inventory, obsolescence and deterioration allowance, etc. Average setup cost per lot $S$ was $6.75. Initial usage rates $R$ averaged about 50 end-item units on a yearly basis, thus giving a $Q$ of about 15 for the first lot of Class A parts. As Exhibit 2 shows, the lot size increased for subsequent lots because of the typical rise in production rate or usage rate $R$.

Subsequently, because of the company's financial position, it became necessary to place a limit on the amount of in-process and in-inventory parts. In order to accomplish this an overriding restriction was placed on the size of the production lot in any part classification. The maximum quantity that could be ordered out for each classification was the number of manufacturing days' usage shown in Exhibit 3. The following is an example of how this restriction operated. The lot size shown in Exhibit 2 for lot number 10 of a Class A part was 1,100 end-product sets. If this were enough for a 480-day supply at current usage rates, the lot would be cut in half to comply with the days' usage restriction. A 240-day usage was permitted for Class A parts because they represented only about 10 per cent of the total dollar value of inventory.

In practice the system had worked well for the production of parts used in end products such as aircraft, which were of relatively stable design and which were required in reasonably large quantities and at fairly constant rates. The system offered several advantages. One of the most important was that the system had been tailored to aid in shop loading of the total manufacturing facility. Traditionally, Cyclops had experienced demand for its products that was low in the early production runs but which increased fairly rapidly to a point that often was close to production capacity. Consequently, it was necessary to anticipate this high production level, which the control plan attempted to do by gradually building up to the maximum production lot size.

Another advantage was that it made it possible to identify particular lots of parts produced at various times against particular end-item units. This permitted cost accounting to accumulate man-hours by production lots of end-items and to apply improvement curve theory for estimating man-hours of successive production runs. This identification was accomplished by assigning a production planning number to each production lot which identified the part number, the end-item, the lot number, and the part classification, as well as the type of production (parts manufacture, assembly, rework, etc.) and the source of production authority (stock, customer's order, military contract number, etc.). The data thus collected were particularly useful in the administration of certain types of military contracts, such as fixed price with redetermination contracts and some forms of incentive contracts.

While the system usually required rigid adherence to producing parts in the lot sizes indicated in Exhibit 2 (with the maximum restriction of Exhibit 3), it was possible occasionally to produce different quantities. If a smaller lot quantity than specified in the table was produced, the sublot was identified by a letter subscript, such as 1a. This would indicate the "a" run of this part for lot number 1. Succeeding quantities were divided into sublots 1b, 1c, etc., to accumulate the total quantity specified for lot number 1 from Exhibit 2. Similarly, if a quantity of parts greater than that called for in a particular lot was required immediately, the order was broken down into lots of the sizes specified in Exhibit 2 and the lots were released together. Thus, a production run of an item might on occasion contain more or less than the specified lot quantity, but this required that extra care be taken to properly identify the particular lot in question so that it could definitely be related to the lots in Exhibit 2. This practice was discouraged by the manufacturing manager.

In a rather short period of time Cyclops experienced a radical change in some of its product line. Instead of fairly long production runs on aircraft of stable design, some of the product line was replaced with missiles made in small quantities and with numerous changes in design. The effect of this change was to require parts whose usage rate was sometimes erratic and whose design might change several times during early production runs.

As the shift in the product line took place, the men in Henry Jackson's production control unit in the missile division began to experience increasing difficulty in adhering to the established part classes and lot sizes. They felt that the net result of the attempt to apply this particular system to their product line was that it was cumbersome and added to the confusion in preparing and following their production orders. They wished to be permitted to vary the quantities placed in production based upon their judgment of the situation—subject, of course, to the in-process inventory restrictions indicated in Exhibit 3. For instance, because of the unsettled missile design situation, it often happened that after the first lot for a part was produced, the part design was found to be unsatisfactory and a new part was designed. This required scrapping of parts already produced. The missile production control people wished to try to avoid this situation by producing initial lot quantities of just one part when they felt that there was a great possibility that the design might be changed.

To accomplish this would require changing the parts classification system to allow the exercising of judgment in the selection of production quantities in place of using the rigid system of Exhibit 2. Such a change in the system would necessitate altering the production planning number used by the cost accounting department. Under the proposed change the lot number and part classification would be dropped from the production planning number, and a number would be substituted which would represent both the quantity in the particular production lot and the cumulative quantity of the part produced in that lot.

The production planners for the company's other product lines, principally aircraft, felt that the existing system was necessary and workable as it stood. An objection to the proposed change was that if the missile production planners were permitted to vary the size of the lots, it would be difficult to equalize the load on the shop. It was thought by some that the cost of an excessive number of setups in the shop, due to very small initial runs, and of the subsequent likelihood of running into manufacturing capacity limitations as demand for the parts increased would far exceed the cost resulting from having to scrap some parts already made because of design changes. Consequently, the production control people for the company's other product divisions did not favor making any change in the system.

If the missile division production control group were allowed to change their system without changing the system used by other production control groups, cost accounting would have to operate two systems. While cost accounting had determined that it would be possible to make the proposed change in the existing system and still yield the required man-hour data, they were quite reluctant to operate two systems simultaneously. At the request of Henry Jackson the accounting group had estimated the cost of operating two systems to involve an initial outlay of $5,000 to develop new procedures and $20,000 per year of extra cost to operate the two systems. In addition the machine time available on the data processing equipment was rather limited, and accounting felt that any attempt to operate two systems simultaneously would put a severe strain on this equipment.

Henry Jackson felt that savings to the missile division in terms of eliminating confusion, scrap losses, and rework costs would far outweigh the expense of operating two systems or any difficulties which might arise in shop loading if the system were altered. He also felt that a definite decision would have to be reached at once.

# EXHIBIT 1

## Classification of parts

---

Class A:   Small sheet metal parts up to 6 by 8 by $\frac{1}{8}$ inches; simple subassemblies consisting of not more than three components

Class B:   Sheet metal parts larger than Class A parts; small machined parts; more complex subassemblies consisting of not more than ten components

Class C:   Machined parts larger than Class B parts; more complex assemblies

Class D:   Hammer-formed or die-cast parts

---

# EXHIBIT 2

## Production lot quantities

(Number of end-item sets)

| Lot number | Part class | | | |
|---|---|---|---|---|
| | A | B | C | D |
| 1 | 15 | 5 | 2 | 2 |
| 2 | 30 | 10 | 3 | 2 |
| 3 | 30 | 15 | 5 | 2 |
| 4 | 50 | 15 | 5 | 3 |
| 5 | 75 | 15 | 10 | 3 |
| 6 | 100 | 15 | 10 | 3 |
| 7 | 350 | 25 | 15 | 5 |
| 8 | 700 | 50 | 15 | 5 |
| 9 | 1,100 | 50 | 25 | 5 |
| 10 | 1,100 | 100 | 25 | 10 |

# EXHIBIT 3

## Maximum permissible production quantities

| Classification | Manufacturing days' usage |
|---|---|
| A | 240 |
| B | 80 |
| C | 40 |
| D | 40 |

# DISCUSSION QUESTIONS

1. Is the present lot-size system adequate for the changing needs of the missile division?

2. To what extent should the needs of the accounting department and other departments determine the lot-size system used by the missile division?

3. What is the justification for using a modified lot-size system such as that shown in Exhibit 2 rather than a theoretically optimum lot size which could be calculated by using the fundamental formula?

4. What effect does the budgetary limitation have on the lot-size system? Is there any theoretical justification for the budgetary limitation, or is it an ill-advised modification to the system?

# REFERENCES

Buffa, Elwood S.: *Modern Production Management* (New York: John Wiley & Sons, Inc., 1961), chap. 16.

Magee, John F.: *Production Planning and Inventory Control* (New York: McGraw-Hill Book Company, 1958), chaps. 1–5.

# CYCLOPS AIRCRAFT INDUSTRIES, INC., PART B

The general manager of Cyclops Aircraft Industries, Inc., had just concluded a discussion with his administrative assistant, George Staugher, regarding a meeting to be held in his office in several minutes. The general manager, B. Z. Manne, was scheduled to attend meetings on the same afternoon concerning equipment purchases involving several millions of dollars and a crucial change in design and method of manufacture of a major airframe component. However, he had agreed to take time out from his busy schedule to hear a presentation by one of his department heads on a suggested solution to a problem involving several of the company's departments.

George Staugher had arranged the meeting to include several members of each of the departments concerned with the problem and had met with the department head making the presentation to familiarize himself with the history of the problem. Insofar as George Staugher had been able to determine, the problem had arisen about six months ago when separate missile manufacturing and aircraft manufacturing divisions were formed out of the previous single manufacturing division under a plan to decentralize certain operations. The separation had been necessitated by the growing differences between aircraft and missile design and production problems. Although two new divisions had been formed by the reorganization, the aircraft division was in fact really the successor to the old manufacturing division, while the missile division was largely a new organization. The two new divisions were in-

119

dependent organizationally, but some of the manufacturing activities had been left intact in a manufacturing shops department which operated essentially as a service department for the two new divisions (see Exhibit 1 for reorganization chart).

The problem for discussion at the meeting concerned the use of the company's parts control plan. This plan was a modified economic lot-size plan for determining lot sizes for production orders in the manufacturing activities. The plan had been used successfully for some years when the single manufacturing division controlled the manufacturing operations which now served both of the new divisions. Shortly after the separate aircraft and missile manufacturing divisions had been formed, the aircraft manufacturing division called a meeting with the missile manufacturing division to review the economic lot-size plan. This meeting actually was merely the first in a series of meetings culminating in the presentation to be made to the general manager this afternoon. From the information George Staugher had been able to obtain by personal contacts, the series of meetings had taken place approximately as described in the following statements. (Unfortunately no written minutes of the meetings were available, so that it was impossible to determine exactly the course that the discussions had taken at each meeting.)

## FIRST MEETING: JANUARY 8

The meeting was called by Ole D. Immer, head of the production control unit of the aircraft manufacturing division, to review the parts control plan with the missile group. In attendance were Immer and several members of his staff; and Henry Jackson, who was head of the production control unit of the missile manufacturing division, and several members of his staff. One of Immer's staff members gave the actual presentation, using flip charts, of the modified economic lot-size plan which had been successfully used in the past. In the discussion following the presentation, Henry Jackson and his staff members questioned the appropriateness of the plan for their operations because of the different conditions, particularly the number of design changes, found in missile manufacturing. One of the arguments put forth, however, for the existing plan was that government contracts required its use. Further discussion of this point led to the clarification that *some* plan was necessary for controlling lot sizes but not necessarily the plan currently in use. As an alternative to the economic lot plan presented by the aircraft manufacturing division, the missile manufacturing division suggested that they be allowed to use a different system[1] which would give them considerable freedom, particularly to decrease lot sizes on early production lots where they thought that smaller quantities were warranted by impending design changes. The meeting ended without any resolution of the different points of view, although the existing economic lot-size plan remained in effect as official policy.

## SECOND MEETING: JANUARY 15

A second, and less formal, meeting was held one week later involving largely the same persons who had attended the first meeting. The existing economic lot-size plan was discussed in greater detail, as was the proposal by the missile manufacturing division for a plan more suitable to what they considered to be the particular needs of their department. Because the aircraft people (Immer's group) did not seem inclined to consider any changes in the existing classification plan for their operations, the discussion was enlarged to a consideration of the effects on other departments of running two different systems simultaneously, one for aircraft and one for missiles. The principal problems in using two systems appeared to be in the possibility of confusion in planning shop loads for the manufacturing shops department, which still did work for both aircraft and missiles, and in the effect on the cost accounting department. Discussion of these points indicated that further exploration of the matter was necessary, particularly of the effects on the cost accounting system.

## THIRD MEETING: JANUARY 20

Henry Jackson, the head of the production control unit of the missile manufacturing division, organized a meeting with representatives of the cost accounting department to explore the possibilities of either changing the existing classification plan or using two different systems and to determine what effect this would have on cost accounting methods. Henry Jackson and his assistant explained their proposed revision to the cost accounting representatives. The major change for cost accounting as far as missile manufacturing people could see was that a different serial numbering system would be used on production lots. This would mean that cost accounting would have to modify its system of cost collection and allocation to accommodate the use of two

[1] For details of the plan see Cyclops Aircraft Industries, Inc., Part A.

methods of lot numbering and the identification of the quantities of items in the lot. The cost accounting representatives were skeptical but said that they would discuss the matter further within their own department.

## FOURTH MEETING: FEBRUARY 4

After due investigation by various section heads in the cost accounting department, a meeting was held within the department to determine what attitude the department should take in the matter. The consensus was that the proposed system was possible and that a dual system would be feasible although not desirable. The overall cost accounting system could accommodate the operation of two systems, and it would also be possible to change some of the computer programs to make them compatible with the operation of two lot-size systems. However, this would naturally lead to increased expense and confusion.

## FIFTH MEETING: FEBRUARY 10

The meeting was attended by representatives of the cost accounting department, missile manufacturing division production control unit, aircraft manufacturing division production control unit, and shop load unit for the manufacturing shops department, which produced items for both the missile manufacturing division and the aircraft manufacturing division. Because of the aircraft group's continuing opposition to changes in their system, the discussion centered generally on the possibility of using two lot-size systems and how this would affect the shop load unit and its relationships with the cost accounting system. The representatives of the shop load unit stated that since the several different organizations now placing orders with them had different ordering practices, presumably the same but in reality inconsistent, it didn't make much difference to them whether aircraft and missile parts were ordered under different lot-size systems. The shop load unit felt that under actual working conditions the lot-size system which had been used had not been of much help to them in planning and scheduling work loads. (Subsequent to the meeting, however, the shop load unit changed its position on this last point and said that the existing lot-size system was useful to them in predicting loads and leveling their operations). The meeting was adjourned without reaching an agreement.

## SIXTH MEETING: FEBRUARY 19

At the sixth meeting an attempt was made to agree on a letter which would authorize the missile manufacturing division production control unit to deviate from the existing economic lot-size system and in effect operate a separate system. The meeting was attended by Jackson and Immer, by their assistants, and by representatives from the cost accounting department. In the discussions of how to resolve the situation the cost accounting department took a stronger stand than previously, stating that, while it had the capability to operate with two labor cost collecting and lot-size systems, as a matter of policy it would not support both systems. The matter then seemed to become one of choosing between the two systems. Before any decision could be reached as to what to do, Immer had to leave the meeting. The meeting finally broke up without any decisions being reached.

## SEVENTH MEETING: FEBRUARY 24

The last meeting involved the same participants as in the sixth meeting. Between the sixth and seventh meetings the cost accounting department had made an estimate of the cost of operating the two systems concurrently. This was done at the specific request of the missile group. Cost accounting stated that it would cost $5,000 to change over to the dual system and about $20,000 extra a year to operate both systems. In response to this, Jackson stated that the dual system would be well worth the money since his department would save five to ten times that much per year by being allowed to use its own system. The cost accounting department was still adamant about not operating two separate systems because of the many other disadvantages which it envisioned, among them a shortage of data processing machine time. No decision was reached at the meeting except that Jackson concluded that it would be necessary to take the matter to Manne, the general manager.

Following the seventh meeting, Jackson contacted George Staugher, Manne's assistant, to make an appointment for a meeting with him. Jackson directed one of his assistants to prepare a flip-chart presentation comparing the two systems. George Staugher had just recounted to Manne this series of events leading up to the impending meeting, and they discussed some possible solutions to the problem. However, as Manne sat in his office for a few minutes before the meeting, his mind was occupied not so much with possible solutions to the problem as it was with the hope that the problem could be dispatched quickly and to the satisfaction of all concerned so that he could attend to the other important decisions to be made that afternoon.

# EXHIBIT 1

## Organization chart

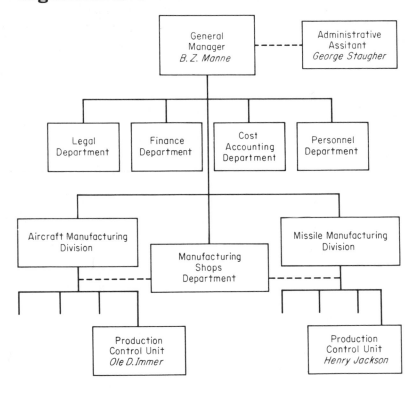

# DISCUSSION QUESTIONS

1. Should there be a single lot-size plan, or should each department be allowed to develop its own plan?

2. Who should have the authority to determine which system (or systems) should be used?

3. What should be the role of the general manager and his assistant in resolving conflicts of this nature?

4. Why did seven meetings take place without a decision or agreement by the participants?

5. To what extent will the increasing size and complexity of corporations affect the likelihood of conflicts of this nature? To what extent will the development of control systems and the use of data processing equipment affect the likelihood of conflicts of this nature?

# REFERENCES

Koontz, Harold D., and Cyril J. O'Donnell: *Principles of Management*, 2d ed. (New York: McGraw-Hill Book Company, 1959), chaps. 6, 12, 14, 27.

Newman, William H., and Charles E. Summer, Jr.: *The Process of Management: Concepts, Behavior, and Practice* (Englewood Cliffs, N.J.: Prentice-Hall, Inc., 1961), chaps. 5, 20, 28.

# DELAWARE BAY SHIP & FABRICATION COMPANY

Preparation of the annual budget was always a difficult task for James Peters, production manager of the Delaware Bay Ship & Fabrication Company. Peters was responsible for all parts fabrication, the indoor assembly shop, all outdoor yard work, and the overhead departments which supported these activities. When Delaware Bay's business consisted largely of small boat and barge contruction, it was relatively simple to estimate manpower and dollar requirements based on the construction program forecast for the year. The company, however, had expanded into the manufacture of heavy machinery and equipment some ten years previously, and it had become increasingly difficult to prepare budgets for the activities necessary to support the many different manufacturing programs under Peters's control.

In 1964, in particular, the budget for overhead activities was a source of more than usual concern. During the past several years the overhead rate had gradually risen to the point where Delaware Bay's prices were out of line with competitors in the heavy machinery and equipment business. In small boat and barge construction, where most work was obtained through competitive bidding, Delaware Bay's high overhead rate had been a major factor in the loss of several contracts during the past six months—contracts which Delaware Bay needed badly to keep its facilities busy. As a result, the president of the company had directed Peters to reduce the portion of the company overhead under Peters's direct control by 15 per cent for the coming year. Since the contribution to the company overhead rate per direct man-hour by the activities reporting to Mr. Peters had been $1.81 in the previous year, this meant a reduction of these overhead charges by $0.27 per direct man-hour in the coming year.

The organizations included in the overhead charges of the production department were Peters's office and staff, the production control unit, the industrial engineering unit, the production engineering and services unit, and the general superintendent's office. The overall organization of the production department is shown in Exhibit 1. The internal organization and description of duties for each of the units and offices are illustrated in Exhibits 2 to 6. The actual overhead charges for the past year, 1963, together with the actual direct man-hours expended in the shops and yard are shown in Exhibit 7. Actual overhead expenditures in 1963 were 6.5 per cent over the amount budgeted for 1963, while the direct man-hours worked in 1963 were only 92.4 per cent of the anticipated number of hours.

Peters was faced with the task of reconciling the 1964 budget requests from his organization with the president's order that he reduce the overhead rate per direct man-hour by 15 per cent. As shown in Exhibit 8, the forecast of direct labor man-hours for 1964 showed a further decline of more than 9 per cent from the total for 1963. However, the budget requests for the various overhead activities (including Peters's estimate of the cost of operating his own office) totaled $5,593,000 (Exhibit 9). If these budget requests were submitted to management without change, the forecasted overhead rate would rise to $1.84 per hour rather than be reduced to $1.54 per hour as directed by management.

Before making his decision as to where and by what amount the overhead budget requests should be cut, Peters decided to hold individual conferences with the heads of each of the overhead groups under his jurisdiction, at which time the basis for the budget requests could be discussed.

The first conference was held with the general superintendent, Karl Schulz. Schulz began the discussion of his budget request by noting that in the previous year the number of first-line supervisors had been reduced to the point where the ratio of supervisors to workers was one supervisor for every sixteen employees. This reduction in the relative amount of supervision was made even though the fabrication, assembly, and yard operations were spread out geographically, and in spite of the fact that the nature of work was becoming more specialized and required more supervision. As a result of the reduction in first-line supervisors, it was not uncommon for workers to be unsupervised when the supervisor was ill or was attending meetings. Also, the lower work load had not reduced the number of shifts worked so that, in many areas, the work load might be down, but it was still necessary to assign supervisors to all three shifts.

Schulz explained that the reduction of over $200,000 in his 1964 budget request from the 1963 actual was accomplished by removing several more first-line supervisors and completely eliminating a level of supervision between the fabrication shop, assembly shop, and yard superintendents and the first-line supervisors in these areas. The effect of the removal of the level of supervision directly under the superintendents was to make it necessary for all the first-line supervisors to report directly to the superintendent of the area. This meant that between thirty and thirty-five first-line supervisors would report to each suprintendent in the future. Schulz stated that it would be impossible to reduce the amount of supervision further without seriously reducing shop efficiency. He also said that if there were reductions in the budgets of production control, industrial engineering, and production engineering and services, it would be necessary for the shop and yard supervisors to perform some of the functions now performed by these organizations.

Peters met next with Richard Wall, the industrial engineering unit chief. The industrial engineering unit's budget request was $65,000 lower than the actual amount spent in 1963, which Wall explained to be the result of a general reevaluation of the number of personnel required to support the various industrial engineering programs. The nonlabor portion of the budget had been reduced very little from the previous year's actual expenditure since a large part of the $97,000 was for data processing and computer services necessary to operate the performance reporting system. Because of the nature of the system, it was not possible to reduce the cost of the performance reporting system without giving it up entirely. Wall did not think that a manual system would be any less expensive than the computerized system since an extensive study made several years previously of the cost of a manual system compared to a computerized system had indicated that the computerized system would be more effective and 25 per cent less costly.

Wall stated that he believed the budget request represented a fair estimate of the cost of maintaining the industrial engineering programs at a minimum level. It would, of course, be possible to reduce the budget still further, but this would mean giving up some of the programs. The industrial engineering department already had severely curtailed some of its programs such as forecasting shop loads and attempting to level them. This had caused some difficulties with overloads in certain areas and had resulted in some unanticipated overtime. Wall suggested that further reduction in the industrial enginering programs would have damaging effects immediately and perhaps some long-run harmful effects as well.

The third conference was held with Edgar Reeves, production control unit chief. Reeves had reduced his budget request by almost $100,000 from the actual amount expended in 1963. This reduction, according to Reeves, was accomplished largely by reducing the number of expediters and the number of people conducting physical inventories of parts in storage. Both of these functions could be reduced without affecting the basic production control functions, although there was likely to be an increase in the number of parts shortages caused by lack of expediting and inaccurate parts records. Reeves said that it was impossible to tell what the cost of these additional parts shortages might be because the effects were not felt immediately or directly. As far as the possibility of reducing the amount of manpower in records, scheduling, and dispatching was concerned, Reeves said that the increasing complexity and variety of products were such that the work load of these units was actually increasing, although the total shop and yard work load was decreasing. He felt that maintaining staffs at their present levels in these areas was equivalent to a reduction in force, considering the work loads. The $163,000 budgeted for nonlabor charges for the production control unit was only slightly reduced from the actual charges during 1963. Almost $150,000 of this amount was for computer and data processing services used in maintaining parts and tool records and for scheduling, and there did not seem to be any way to reduce these costs without eliminating the scheduling system or ceasing to maintain the parts and tool records.

Dow, unit chief of production engineering and services, was the last to confer with Peters on the 1964 budget. The budget for Dow's unit was quite large, principally because all the perishable tools (items assumed to last for less than one year), shop and yard supplies, contracted services, and bottled gases (acetylene, oxygen, etc.) used in the shops and yard were charged to his budget. Dow said that he was not able in most cases to reduce the level of these nonlabor charges. The use of drill bits, cutters, degreasing compounds, acids, welding rods, acetylene, oxygen, and other supplies was essentially determined by the products being fabricated and the processes being used. While Dow and the shop and yard supervision made every effort to impress upon the workers the need for conservative use of these items, it was impossible to cut the usage arbitrarily and still produce the product. Dow said that he had incorporated in his budget substantial cuts in the level of contracted services such as towels and overalls, but he did not feel that there was any more room for reduction in the nonlabor budget request.

Dow further indicated that he had made some personnel reductions in production engineering, tool and supply distribution, and packaging and preservation which accounted for most of the reduction in the budget for 1964 below the actual 1963 expenditures. He then explained the situation in each of the areas. Production engineering was cut somewhat although the variety and complexity of items being manufactured had actually increased the work load. Further cuts seemed out of the question if the work was to be done. The number of personnel in tool and supply distribution had been cut to the point where some toolrooms and supply points were only open for a portion of each day. Workers needing tools or supplies either had to walk to a more distant point or wait until the attendant arrived. Packaging and preservation, normally a small operation, had been cut by two men, one-third of the work force.

The other area under Dow's supervision was the planning group which prepared estimates and documentation for bids for new business. This group also assisted Peters in long-range planning for the department. Dow had made no cuts in this group since the declining work load in Delaware Bay's shops made it imperative that more effort be expended on bids for new business and long-range planning for the department.

Following the series of conferences, Peters looked once more through the budget requests and began the difficult task of cutting almost $900,000 from them.

# EXHIBIT 1

## Production department, organization chart

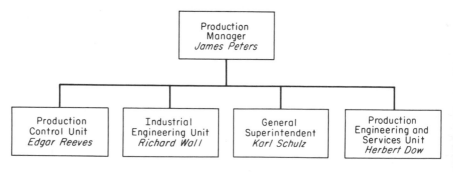

# EXHIBIT 2

## Production department office, organization chart

Establishes policies and plans for the
production of all ships, barges, machinery,
and equipment. Establishes policies and plans
for carrying out all supporting activities.
Coordinates fabrication and assembly operations with company policies and other departments.

| Assistant Production Manager | Office Supervisor |
|---|---|
| Assists manager in establishing policies and plans for departmental operations. Acts for manager in absence of manager. | Establishes and maintains such records and reports as may be required by manager. Supervises office staff. |

# EXHIBIT 3

## Production control unit, organization chart

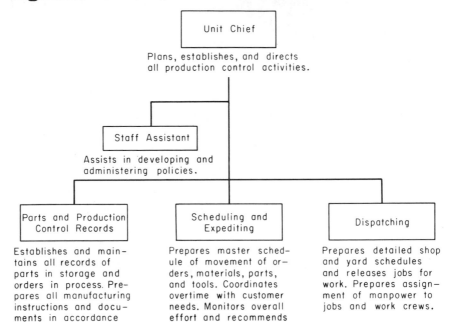

| | Unit Chief | |
|---|---|---|

Plans, establishes, and directs all production control activities.

| | Staff Assistant | |
|---|---|---|

Assists in developing and administering policies.

| Parts and Production Control Records | Scheduling and Expediting | Dispatching |
|---|---|---|
| Establishes and maintains all records of parts in storage and orders in process. Prepares all manufacturing instructions and documents in accordance with master schedule. | Prepares master schedule of movement of orders, materials, parts, and tools. Coordinates overtime with customer needs. Monitors overall effort and recommends courses of action to management. | Prepares detailed shop and yard schedules and releases jobs for work. Prepares assignment of manpower to jobs and work crews. |

# EXHIBIT 4

## Industrial engineering unit, organization chart

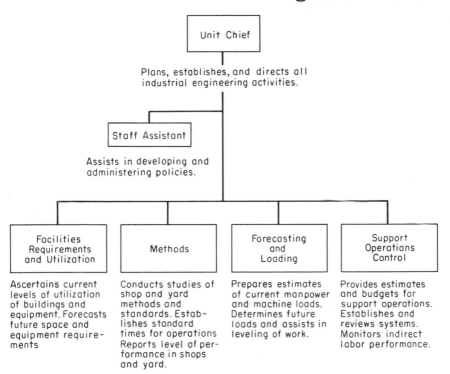

Unit Chief

Plans, establishes, and directs all industrial engineering activities.

Staff Assistant

Assists in developing and administering policies.

| Facilities Requirements and Utilization | Methods | Forecasting and Loading | Support Operations Control |
|---|---|---|---|
| Ascertains current levels of utilization of buildings and equipment. Forecasts future space and equipment requirements | Conducts studies of shop and yard methods and standards. Establishes standard times for operations Reports level of performance in shops and yard. | Prepares estimates of current manpower and machine loads. Determines future loads and assists in leveling of work. | Provides estimates and budgets for support operations. Establishes and reviews systems. Monitors indirect labor performance. |

# EXHIBIT 5

## Production engineering and services unit, organization chart

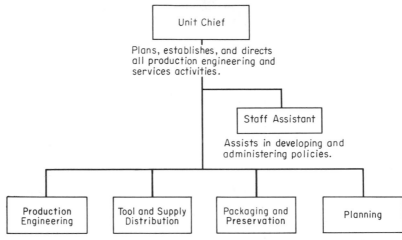

| Production Engineering | Tool and Supply Distribution | Packaging and Preservation | Planning |
|---|---|---|---|
| Engineers necessary tools, jigs, and fixtures for manufacturing and assembly operations. Determines method of manufacture and assures producibility of parts, assemblies, and completed units. | Maintains toolrooms, distributes tools, and maintains records of location of all tools. Maintains stocks of all shop supplies, issues all supplies, and records usage. Issues blueprints and other documents. | Determines methods of packaging and preserving all items to assure delivery without damage or deterioration. Issues instructions for packaging and preservation. Provides material and supervises packaging and preservation. | Prepares necessary estimates and documentation for new business. Assists fabrication and assembly department manager in formulating long-range plans for department. |

# EXHIBIT 6

## General superintendent's office, organization chart

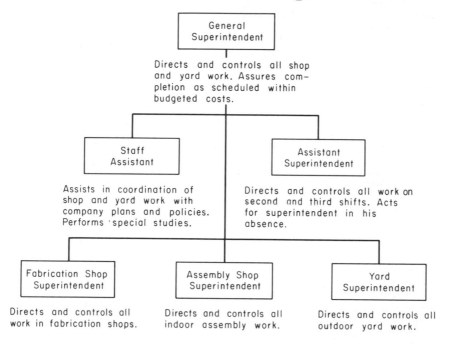

# EXHIBIT 7

## Production department overhead charges—actual, 1963

| | Month | | | | | | |
| --- | --- | --- | --- | --- | --- | --- | --- |
| | Jan. | Feb. | Mar. | Apr. | May | June | July |
| Production manager's office | $ 5,273 | $ 4,781 | $ 5,937 | $ 4,781 | $ 4,425 | $ 5,674 | $ 4,781 |
| Production control unit | 79,189 | 71,554 | 88,777 | 71,555 | 68,109 | 86,616 | 71,554 |
| Industrial engineering unit | 49,390 | 44,708 | 55,673 | 44,708 | 42,930 | 53,622 | 44,710 |
| Production engineering and services unit | 326,781 | 295,006 | 360,953 | 269,498 | 349,115 | 344,642 | 216,780 |
| General superintendent's office | 109,215 | 99,732 | 124,690 | 99,733 | 94,804 | 122,982 | 99,732 |
| Total | $569,848 | $515,781 | $636,030 | $490,275 | $559,383 | $613,536 | $437,557 |
| Direct man-hours—Actual, 1963 | 307,880 | 320,085 | 313,369 | 305,887 | 269,443 | 263,509 | 270,229 |

| | Month | | | | | Total |
| --- | --- | --- | --- | --- | --- | --- |
| | Aug. | Sept. | Oct. | Nov. | Dec. | |
| Production manager's office | $ 4,793 | $ 6,046 | $ 5,830 | $ 6,398 | $ 8,560 | $ 67,279 |
| Production control unit | 71,557 | 77,300 | 59,430 | 59,162 | 69,511 | 874,314 |
| Industrial engineering unit | 44,709 | 50,367 | 39,754 | 37,905 | 47,346 | 555,822 |
| Production engineering and services unit | 222,907 | 270,010 | 250,009 | 230,661 | 206,066 | 3,342,428 |
| General superintendent's office | 99,732 | 120,058 | 82,713 | 90,111 | 104,005 | 1,247,507 |
| Total | $443,698 | $523,781 | $437,736 | $424,237 | $435,488 | $6,087,350 |
| Direct man-hours—Actual, 1963 | 264,752 | 259,836 | 253,908 | 269,018 | 259,003 | 3,356,919 |

# EXHIBIT 8

## Production department forecasted direct labor man-hours, 1964

|  | Man-hours |
|---|---|
| January | 258,000 |
| February | 264,000 |
| March | 265,000 |
| April | 263,000 |
| May | 255,000 |
| June | 254,000 |
| July | 252,000 |
| August | 252,000 |
| September | 250,000 |
| October | 244,000 |
| November | 243,000 |
| December | 242,000 |
| Total | 3,042,000 |

# EXHIBIT 9

## Production department budget requests for overhead activities, 1964

|  | Labor | Nonlabor* | Total |
|---|---|---|---|
| Production manager's office | $    61,000 | $    4,000 | $    65,000 |
| Production control unit | 616,000 | 163,000 | 779,000 |
| Industrial engineering unit | 394,000 | 97,000 | 491,000 |
| Production engineering and services unit | 879,000 | 2,340,000† | 3,219,000 |
| General superintendent's office | 1,022,000 | 17,000 | 1,039,000 |
| Total | $2,972,000 | $2,621,000 | $5,593,000 |

* Travel, miscellaneous supplies, and services including data processing and computer charges.

† Perishable tools, shop and yard supplies, contracted services, and bottled gases.

# DISCUSSION QUESTIONS

1. Do you agree with the president's instructions to Peters directing him to reduce the overhead rate by 15 per cent?
2. On what basis should Peters make the reduction—a straight percentage cut in all areas or on some other basis?
3. Assuming that Peters has to submit a budget which would result in an overhead rate of no more than $1.54 per direct man-hour, what should that budget be?
4. Should overhead budgets be related to direct labor man-hours, or should some other basis be used?

# REFERENCES

Buffa, Elwood S.: *Modern Production Management* (New York: John Wiley & Sons, Inc., 1961), chap. 21.
Hodges, Henry G., and Raymond J. Ziegler: *Managing the Industrial Concern* (Boston: Houghton Mifflin Company, 1963), chap. 12.

# THE DYNAMONICS
# CORPORATION

Jack Lawton, production supervisor of the instrument division of The Dynamonics Corporation, had just received his month-end shipping report (see Exhibit 1). Shipments of the model 2J-67B binary control unit, a major component in a series of specialized ground based computers which were designed to control the firing and guidance system used in the first stage of the Neptune Satellite Booster, had again fallen behind schedule. Lawton felt he had to find a way to get the division on schedule and keep it on schedule.

The binary control unit consisted of several hundred modular subassemblies assembled in a large metal chest. Each subassembly was constructed so that it could be removed and replaced without disturbing other subassemblies in the unit. Eighty per cent of the modular subassemblies comprising the binary control unit consisted of hand-assembled electromechanical devices. Each device consisted of from twenty to forty components assembled and sealed into a plastic cartridge. All the components used in these modular subassemblies, including the cartridge type containers, were purchased from outside sources.

Although the instrument division produced and assembled other items and products of similar nature, the reliability requirements and number of binary control unit subassemblies required made it most practical to separate (physically) the production of these items from the other activities of the division. This pertained primarily to the process of assembly and subassembly, and did not include such service functions as purchasing, stores, etc. In fact, one central pur-

139

chasing organization serviced the whole firm and one central store serviced the entire instrument division.

A review of the situation by Lawton revealed that the inability to meet shipping schedules for the binary control unit resulted from a shortage of modular subassemblies of the type just described. An investigation as to why particular subassemblies were not available revealed an alarming parts shortage. When asked by Lawton what might be done immediately to relieve the situation one employee commented, "Close the plant down." The departmental foreman admitted that the situation was approaching this degree of seriousness and saw no method of improving the situation within the next few months. This serious problem was amplified by the fact that a doubling of current output levels over the next twelve to eighteen months was specified by the master production schedule.

Further discussion by Lawton with the foreman indicated no obvious reason for the parts shortage problem. Total in-process inventory for binary control unit production was in excess of $4½ million. This was a relatively large dollar value in relation to the overall value and delivery requirements of the contract. The overall complexity of the end product was less than that of many items produced by other divisions of the company. Reliability and quality standards were considerably greater than required by any previous product. This, however, did not appear to be an insurmountable problem with regard to meeting production requirements. The departmental foreman and his group leaders unanimously agreed that with adequate parts, production schedules could be met. Design changes were frequent but not significantly greater in number or scope than those experienced on other products. Other problems existed, but none alone appeared to be sufficient to cause such a critical parts situation.

A review by Lawton of the parts ordering procedure indicated that all standard ordering procedures were being followed. If anything, less than the normal number of human errors were occurring within the system. The parts ordering procedure was instituted several years ago and indicated no weakness in the years that it had been used. Parts shortages and other problems did arise, but they could always be assigned a cause and corrected within the system. In fact, this ordering system was instituted because of its successful history in other divisions of the firm (Exhibit 2 briefly describes the system in use). It was evident that a more detailed analysis of the problem was necessary to detect the cause of the parts shortage and effect a solution.

The first step was to determine exactly which parts were in short supply and how quickly they could be obtained. Lawton had such a report prepared and it immediately became evident to him that all critical parts shortages were within a single class of parts. These were purchased parts which required special processing by the vendor and in many instances were parts never previously manufactured. The minimum lead time for such parts was 4 months and could extend to 7 months if no similar part had ever been produced. In addition many of the parts required a 45-day curing and test period after delivery to The Dynamonics Corporation and before being assembled. Because of the special nature of the parts and the lack of manufacturing experience, rejection rates were abnormally high. Practically all rejections occurred either at receiving inspection or during the 45-day curing and test cycle. For most of the parts which were rejected during the curing and test cycle, the first indications of unsatisfactory performance appeared during the latter half of the test cycle. In such situations it was not uncommon for an entire lot ultimately to prove unsatisfactory and be rejected. If an immediate reorder were instituted a minimum delay of 4 months plus 45 days was required before the rejected lot could be replaced and made available for assembly. In practice a 10-day to 3-week additional delay was incurred in carrying out the reordering procedure.

Although a 4- to 9-month lead time was not uncommon for parts used on other products, the number of such parts in a typical binary control unit subassembly was unusually large. Often as many as 10 to 15 different parts of this nature were used in a single subassembly. This was the first real indication that the problem might be arising from a group of extreme circumstances rather than a set of entirely new circumstances.

A detailed report of these items, approximately 300 of the 8,000 part numbers used in the binary control unit, was made. A small portion of this report which related current inventories to production requirements is shown in Exhibit 3. Each period in the table is identified by a week number and represents five working days (one workweek). The period marked with an asterick designates the current period. Figures in the body of the table represent the number of parts required in each period to fulfill planned production schedules. Figures for periods prior to the reporting period represent overdue subassembly requirements for which parts have not been drawn from central stores.

A summary of the entire report indicated that 23 per cent of the parts required for current and overdue production schedules were completely out of stock and that 10 per cent of the parts in stock were not required within the period covered by the report. In terms of total pieces of stock, current inventory was equal to approximately a 3½-week supply. This estimate was somewhat high as it was calculated on the basis of a constant output rate over the period covered by the report. In actuality, the production rate was increasing and current output was above the mean for the period. The correct figure was probably close to 2½ to 3 weeks. Total current usage was approximately 16,000 pieces per week for the approximately 300 part numbers included in this report.

More detailed investigation revealed other possibly useful information. The binary control unit required various quantities of approximately 200 different modular subassemblies. Each configuration consisted of 25 to 40 individual parts hand-assembled and hermetically sealed in a plastic container. This in itself did not constitute an overly complex end-item as each subassembly could be produced as an independent entity. One unusual factor, however, was that each module and its components had to be as free from dirt, dust, and moisture as humanly possible. This required that all parts used in a given module be completely decontaminated, assembled in a dust-free and humidity-controlled atmosphere, and immediately hermetically sealed in its container. The entire process had to be completed within an eight-hour period. No work could commence on a module or its components until all parts were in stock and ready for use. Partial assembly, parts substitution, and other irregular production measures to compensate for parts shortages were not permitted.

In addition, a given part was often used in several different subassemblies. In the past, and on other products produced in the instrument division, most assemblies and subassemblies consisted of a set of relatively unique parts. With the exception of fasteners, no specific part was included in more than a few different assemblies or subassemblies. Most often a given part was unique to a specific assembly. In the binary control unit, however, some parts were used in as many as 80 per cent of the modular subassemblies. In fact a majority of the parts were used in more than one modular configuration. Although a few of the parts were used on other products produced by the instrument division, a majority of the parts were used only on the binary control unit.

Binary control unit subassembly production schedules were projected 10 weeks in advance to determine potential parts shortages and needs. At times all parts required to produce an item scheduled for production in 3 to 4 weeks would be available only to have one or more of the parts requisitioned by another department by the time actual assembly time had arrived. The cost and fragility of both the electrical and mechanical components made it impractical to withdraw parts from stores more than 3 to 5 days before actual assembly. Wholesale practice of a scheme of advance withdrawals by all departments could cause complete havoc within the already faltering system. An exhaustive check, however, indicated that the correction of this problem would have only a marginal effect toward solving the general parts shortage problem.

Due to the urgency of the Mars satellite program which used the Neptune booster, the master schedule for production of the binary control unit contained a minimum of wait and idle time. This provided little or no flexibility in scheduling work and resulted in an irregular work load within the shop. Because of the skill and training requirements of the job, varying the capacity of the binary control unit subassembly shop (that is, hiring and firing personnel as requirements changed) was impractical. Likewise, allowing idle time was not only costly but interfered with product quality and the development and maintenance of good work habits. The solution to this problem was load leveling. Since little idle time was scheduled, leveling consisted of attemping to produce ahead of the master schedule during slack periods and when parts shortages prevented the assembly of scheduled items. Delaying an item in order to level the load during overload periods meant almost certain failure to meet the final delivery requirements.

The specific procedure for assigning work ahead of schedule to level the shop load included: (1) maintaining a current listing of all outstanding binary control unit subassembly requirements in the order of their due dates on the master schedule; (2) constructing biweekly a complete parts availability listing from inventory stores records; (3) from these listings and from the individual subassembly parts lists determining a final list of subassemblies for which there was currently 100 per cent parts availability. Although no actual notations were made on the inventory records, this final list was constructed so that parts required on more than one subassembly were preempted by subassemblies having the earliest master schedule completion date. The listing was then used as a basis for making actual subassembly assignments for the subsequent two-week period, after which the entire process was repeated. Subassemblies for which parts were missing were not considered until all shortages were eliminated.

These were the facts Lawton was able to obtain with regard to his division's failure to meet binary control unit deliveries. He was sure that somewhere in this maze of information was a logical explanation to the parts shortage problem. He also felt that once the cause was discovered a solution would become evident. With this in mind he instructed his secretary to divert all but absolutely necessary interruptions and he withdrew to his private office to find an explanation and solution to the parts shortage problem.

## EXHIBIT 1

## The Dynamonics Corporation instrument division

| Summary shipping report for month of March | | | |
|---|---|---|---|
| Classification | Number of items | Total dollar value | Average weeks late |
| Shipped on time | 135 | $2,365,000 | 0 |
| Shipped late | 7 | 365,000 | 5 |
| Due but not shipped | 5 | 1,268,000 | 19 |
| Total | 147 | $3,998,000 | |

| Listing of overdue items as of end of month of March | | | | |
|---|---|---|---|---|
| Item name | Order number | Quantity overdue, units | Weeks late, maximum | Dollar value |
| Binary control unit | 2J-67B | 10 | 15 | $ 892,000 |
| Altitude stability regulator | 773-K | 4 | 2 | 176,000 |
| Sway level gauge | SK7-2B | 25 | 3 | 114,000 |
| Manefred pressure translator | 46-46-4 | 7 | 4 | 53,000 |
| Rufuss gauge | 11A2B | 300 | | 33,000 |
| Total | | 346 | | $1,268,000 |

## EXHIBIT 2

## Description of parts ordering and release system, instrument division

All part requirements originated in the form of a parts release. This document was prepared immediately after the final design and drawings were accepted by the customer. A separate part release was written for each part on every customer order. Thus, several releases for a specific part could be in existence simultaneously. When an unusually long lead time was anticipated, a special advance release could be written. This advance release allowed a specified quantity of a given part to be ordered prior to the final drawing release. These releases were usually for small quantities due to the increased probability that a design change might occur which would make the part obsolete.

Regular releases were issued for the entire quantity required to satisfy a particular customer order.

Parts releases were forwarded to the order determination department daily as they were written rather than by complete orders or contracts. The order determination department designated whether the part was to be purchased or made within the plant and forwarded the release to the purchasing or production control department as the situation required. (Since this exhibit is concerned with purchased parts, only this segment of the system will be traced.)

The purchasing department was organized on a commodity basis by the type of item purchased, i.e., one group of buyers purchased electrical components, another group lubricants, etc. Within each group further specialization occurred. It was the purchasing department's responsibility to determine lot order sizes and schedule the arrival of parts to satisfy the master schedule requirements. Order quantity, scrap allowances, and other factors governing the purchase of each particular part were determined by a standardized routine tailored to the particular type of item purchased.

The master schedule was constructed by an entirely different group of individuals. Start times for all manufacturing operations were determined by applying standard lead and wait times for all operations and counting backward from a final delivery commitment. The procedure provided that a check be made to assure that adequate lead time was available for securing purchased parts. The master schedule specified manufacturing lot sizes and thus placed a lower limit on the purchase lot size unless there was an overage remaining from another production lot. Purchase orders, however, could combine the needs of more than a single production lot when economical to do so. The purchase quantity could even combine the requirements of several part releases.

The time span from final drawing release to placement of the first order for an item was often five to six weeks. The transfer of responsibility for a purchase order occurred when the parts arrived at the proper storeroom. The firm was serviced by several storerooms, with each division having at least one storeroom. The entire instrument division was serviced by a single storeroom. The storeroom disbursed parts to the shops on receipt of a requisition signed by a departmental foreman or person of higher rank. No department was allowed to draw more parts than were covered by outstanding part releases. However, parts could be drawn ahead or behind master schedule requirement dates. This freedom was allowed to provide some flexibility in scheduling and in coping with minor irregularities which persist in any manufacturing operation, no matter how well planned. Controlling the flow of parts in compliance with the master schedule would require a substantial increase in record keeping. Other divisions functioned without this control and incurred no apparent overburdening consequences. To institute this type of control in the instrument division would require complete justification to higher levels of management.

# EXHIBIT 3

## Binary control unit, inventory status report

(Purchased items with lead time exceeding 15 weeks)

| Part number | On hand | Requirements by week number | | | | | | | | | | | | | | | Total |
|---|---|---|---|---|---|---|---|---|---|---|---|---|---|---|---|---|---|
| | | 35 | 36 | 37 | 38 | 39 | 40 | 41 | 42 | 43 | 44 | 45* | 46 | 47 | 48 | |
| 315-26A | 319 | 161 | | 3,710 | | | | 3,710 | 644 | | 805 | 805 | 8,225 | 805 | 805 | 19,670 |
| 368-21K | | 1 | | 540 | | | | 540 | 4 | | 5 | 5 | 1,085 | 5 | 5 | 2,190 |
| 372-89F | 9,037 | 190 | | 3,330 | | | | 3,330 | 760 | | 950 | 950 | 7,610 | 950 | 950 | 19,020 |
| 399-01P | 14,200 | | | | | | | | | | | | | | | 0 |
| 428-97L | 9,555 | 5 | | 3,020 | | | | 3,020 | 20 | | 25 | 25 | 6,065 | 25 | 25 | 12,230 |
| 662-82M | 8,496 | | | 5,710 | | | | 5,710 | | | | | 11,420 | | | 22,840 |
| 663-88M | | | 120 | | | | 120 | | | | | | 120 | | | 360 |
| 999-99Z | 142 | | | | | | | | | | | | | | | 0 |
| 1087-235 | 1,903 | | | 180 | | | | 180 | | | | | 360 | | | 720 |
| 2075-687 | 867 | | | 30 | | | | 30 | | | | | 60 | | | 120 |
| 2757-444 | | 3 | | 200 | | | | 200 | 12 | | 15 | 15 | 415 | 15 | 15 | 890 |
| 2872-392 | 120 | | 90 | 50 | | | 90 | 50 | | | | | 190 | | | 470 |
| 3629-220 | 207 | | 60 | 20 | | | 60 | 20 | | | | | 100 | | | 260 |
| 3630-987 | | 7 | | | | | | | 28 | | 35 | 35 | 35 | 35 | 35 | 210 |
| 3876-421 | 1,465 | | 30 | 640 | | | 30 | 640 | | | | | 1,310 | | | 2,650 |
| 3899-481 | 3,380 | 16 | 30 | 930 | | | 30 | 930 | 64 | | 80 | 80 | 1,970 | 80 | 80 | 4,290 |
| 4000-300 | 484 | 15 | | 30 | | | | 30 | 25 | | 25 | 25 | 85 | 25 | 25 | 285 |

* Current week.

# DISCUSSION QUESTIONS

1. List the factors which were either primary or secondary causes of the parts shortage problem. (Primary causes are causes which originate a problem, whereas secondary causes amplify or aggravate a problem once in existence.)

2. Which of the stated causes were correctable only in the long run?

3. What causes were subject to short-run or immediate improvement or correction?

4. What useful and what possibly detrimental functions did the "work ahead of schedule" procedure serve?

5. Was the purchasing department optimally organized for the type of operations required for the division and the binary control unit program?

6. What immediate action would you have instituted to cope with the problem at hand?

# REFERENCES

Bierman, Harold, Jr., Lawrence E. Fouraker, and Robert K. Jaedicke: *Quantitative Analysis for Business Decisions* (Homewood, Ill.: Richard D. Irwin, Inc., 1961), chap. 5.

Bowman, Edward H., and Robert B. Fetter: *Analysis for Production Management* (Homewood, Ill.: Richard D. Irwin, Inc., 1961), chap. 11.

Broom, H. N.: *Production Management* (Homewood, Ill.: Richard D. Irwin, Inc., 1962), chaps. 11, 12.

Magee, John F.: *Production Planning and Inventory Control* (New York: McGraw-Hill Book Company, 1958).

Timms, Howard L.: *The Production Function in Business* (Homewood, Ill.: Richard D. Irwin, Inc., 1962), chap. 18.

# FARRINGTON COMPANY[1]

Ralph Pierson, an industrial engineer for the Farrington Company, metal fabricators, was preparing to estimate a follow-on contract for structural hatch closures. Farrington was completing their first contract for 60 units. From an analysis of the cost data, Ralph Pierson knew that the first contract had improved on about a 75 per cent improvement curve. The latest accounting data indicated that the forty-fifth unit completed had required 152¼ man-hours. The follow-on contract was for 100 units.

1. What man-hours could be expected for the last unit of the first contract if the improvement ratio remained at 75 per cent?
2. Estimate the total man-hours for the first contract.
3. Estimate the average man-hours for the 60 units on the first contract.
4. Estimate the total man-hours for the follow-on contract of 100 units.
5. Estimate the average man-hours for the 100 units and the man-hours for the last unit on the second contract.
6. Plot the unit values line on a sheet of log-log paper and identify the points for the first, forty-fifth, sixtieth, and one-hundred-sixtieth units.
7. At what unit on the first contract will the man-hours drop to the average for the first contract? Use the unit values line drawn for question 6 and check the answer using the tables.

[1] Farrington Company is a practice problem to be used with Appendix B, Supplemental Notes Regarding Improvement Curves.

8. Repeat question 7 for the second contract.

9. If additional units were to be built beyond the second contract, at what unit would you expect the man-hours to drop to 50?

10. Calculate the percentage of the slope of your curve by comparing units 1 and 2, 10 and 20, 100 and 200 from the chart and the tables.

11. The actual man-hours turned out to be 12,794 for the first contract and 11,461 for the second contract. What man-hours would you estimate for a third follow-on contract for 340 units.

# THE FASTER
# FASTENER COMPANY

The Faster Fastener Company was a large producer of standard and special fasteners. The size of items produced varied from rivets $\frac{1}{32}$ inch in diameter and $\frac{1}{16}$ inch in length to special lock-clamp fasteners weighing over 75 pounds. The value of the fasteners produced and sold by The Faster Fastener Company varied from $0.001 to over $100 per piece. Less than 5 per cent of the items handled, however, sold for over $5 per piece. Items selling for more than $5 per piece were referred to as expensive items and were primarily special fasteners made to customer order, i.e., not shipped from stock. Besides its extremely wide product line coverage, the Faster Fastener Company was noted for the quality of its products and its dependable delivery performance.

The Faster Fastener Company advertised 72-hour delivery of its standard products anywhere in the continental United States provided the customer was willing to pay all special shipping and handling charges. For small orders these charges often exceeded the value of the items shipped. However, when this kind of service was needed by the customer it was well appreciated, even at high cost.

Since most customers knew of their needs well in advance of 3 days only a small percentage of orders fell in this category. Most orders for standard parts provided for a 7- to 12-day interval between the receipt of an order and its due date at the customer's plant. Depending on the distance between the customer and the Faster Fastener plant, a 7-day lead time allowed for 1 to 2 days to process the customer's purchase order, 1 to 2 days to assemble and package the order, and 3 to 5 days for shipment. If orders were received more than 7 days in advance of the due date at the customer's plant, The Faster Fastener Company paid shipping charges; if not, the order was priced f.o.b. the Faster Fastener plant. Consequently the order processing and shipping system was geared to this pace. To assure the timely arrival of parts at the customer's plant all items on an order had to be in stock or in production in a state of near completion.

When an order could not be filled from inventory due to a parts shortage or stockout, special measures were taken. If an order for the particular part was in the shop, it was rushed to completion. If there was no order in the shop, a quick check was made to see whether any existing order or finished part could be modified or reworked to meet the crisis. If there was no other way, a new order was originated and expedited through its entire processing cycle. To minimize the necessary processing time the special order included only a sufficient quantity to meet the immediate need. At the same time a normal reorder was instituted and routed through regular channels.

Time lost in acquiring the out-of-stock parts was regained by shipping the order airfreight at the company's expense. Although almost any stockout or parts shortage could be compensated for in this way without failing to meet delivery promises, the costs of such action were prohibited except for isolated, infrequent occasions.

The average net profit, before Federal income taxes, on standard items was estimated at 4 per cent of the selling price. Depending upon the order size, added costs resulting from a parts shortage could equal two to ten times the selling price of the item. The added cost of airfreight alone often equaled or exceeded the order value. In addition other costs such as overtime, breaking into an existing setup, holding a machine idle awaiting the rush order, and similar interruptions of the normal processing cycle were generally incurred. It was a stated policy of The Faster Fastener Company that contributing to an inventory runout or parts shortage was the greatest "sin" that could be committed within the company. Management was in full agreement that tight and accurate inventory control was a requisite to low costs.

The primary responsibility for the management and control of the finished goods inventory was vested in B. I. Crimp, controller of finished inventory stores. For eight of the thirteen years that Crimp held this position he fought a constant battle against inventory runouts and parts shortages. During this period a complete paper inventory control scheme was in effect. A complete record of all transactions was recorded on individual stock cards. All receipts and disbursements from finished goods stores were recorded and a current balance on hand figure maintained. Postings to all stock cards were maintained current to within three hours of the actual transaction. Approximately fifty clerks were employed to maintain the records for the approximately 150,000 standard parts stocked. Every measure conceivable to Crimp was taken to prevent and eliminate errors from occurring within the system. It was Crimp's opinion that random sampling was his most effective tool in maintaining the system in a state of control.

To check on inaccurate balances, postings, and other procedural errors, Crimp had all parts receivers (a document reporting the completion or arrival of a part) routed through his office. Weekly he would grab a fistful of parts receivers and have his assistant check the bin count with the stock record balance for the group of receivers selected. If Spaulding, assistant to Crimp, found a disagreement between the bin count and stock card balance, he would attempt to discover the cause of the difference and locate the person responsible for the error. Spaulding would then discuss the situation with the responsible party. This discussion often involved clearing up a misunderstanding about the correct procedure, teaching correct procedure, or reprimanding an individual for lax work habits.

Upon completing his sample check Spaulding summarized his findings in a report to Crimp. The report specified the number of errors found, a description of the error, and the magnitude of the error. If the number of errors or their magnitude became disturbing to Crimp, he ordered a 5 per cent sample of the entire inventory to be taken. If the sample revealed that the inventory records were less than 5 per cent in error, only the errors found were corrected and no further action was taken. If the sample indicated an error in excess of 5 per cent a physical check between the stock card count and actual bin count was made for all subsequent parts received until such time that Crimp felt that all records were in order. Crimp considered the situation to be corrected when a subsequent 5 per cent sample indicated that the records were in error by substantially less than 5 per cent. Since the average reorder cycle for parts ranged from 3 to 6 months, approximately 5 per cent of the items were physically checked each week. No additional help was provided and no one was relieved of any of his normal duties during the time the inventory records were being corrected.

The major causes for incorrect balances and errors on the stock cards were:

1. Failure to post a receipt or disbursement of parts.
2. Failure to reorder at the appropriate time. (Reorder points and reorder quantities were stated on all stock cards.)
3. Arithmetic errors in calculating a new balance after a disbursement or receipt of parts.
4. Unexplainable differences between stock card balance and bin counts. (Bin counts were generally below stock card balances.)

Each of the above causes appeared to be of approximately equal importance in terms of the number of actual inventory runouts incurred. Under this system runouts amounted to approximately 4 per cent per month and inventory losses or shrinkage from $\frac{1}{4}$ to $\frac{1}{2}$ per cent per month. Looking back on this eight-year losing battle Crimp wondered if life was worth living.

Five years ago Crimp, taking the attitude that "if you can't lick 'em, join 'em," recommended that the then existing inventory system be converted to a two-bin automatic reorder system. This system was essentially a standard two-bin inventory control scheme. In converting to the new system Crimp recommended that all current reorder points and reorder quantities be reviewed. He was particularly concerned about the reorder point and suggested that, wherever serious doubt with regard to the correct reorder point existed, the largest practical reorder point should be adopted to provide the longest lead time. Also, because of his experienced difficulty in controlling manual posting and arithmetical errors, Crimp recommended that the new system eliminate all manual posting and transcribing other than the dating and signing of prewritten documents. He stated that this could be achieved through the use of prepunched mechanical tabulator cards or mechanically prepared documents.

Each storekeeper was to maintain a master card file in which each item stocked was represented by two master cards. In addition there was a reorder card included in each safety stock package. The safety stock package was to consist of a securely packaged or segregated batch of parts equal in number to the reorder point for the specific part. The safety stock package was to be stored in the same location as the main stock but was not to be disturbed until the remaining stock was completely depleted. At this time the safety stock package would be broken and used to satisfy part requirements until a new batch of parts could be ordered and manufactured. When the stock chaser opened the safety stock package he was to place the enclosed reorder card in a conveniently located reorder box.

Two or three times daily the reorder boxes were to be emptied by the inventory records group and the reorder process completed. This consisted of removing one of the two master cards associated with the part from the master file and noting the expected arrival date for the new batch on the second card which remained in the master file at all times. The card removed from the master file was to be placed in a weekly tickler file in accordance with the expected arrival date of the new order. The reorder card removed from the safety stock package was to be forwarded to the manufacturing control group. Manufacturing control was to complete the reordering process by preparing all necessary shop and purchase orders. The manufacturing control group was responsible for all items until they passed inspection and arrived at the proper storeroom.

Upon receipt of an order at the appropriate storeroom area a new reorder card was to be placed with the order. The new reorder card was to be prepared by the manufacturing control group from the previous reorder card and forwarded to the stock receiving group during the manufacturing or procurement cycle. A new safety stock package was then to be assembled and the order placed into stock. Simultaneously the receiver (a copy of the inspection report which was sent to the storeroom receiving station with the order) was to be forwarded to the inventory records group who would remove the master card currently in the tickler file, return the card to the master file, and note the receipt date on the card which remained in the master file.

The tickler file would serve primarily as a double check against late arrivals. On critical parts an early arrival date could be specified and would serve notice to initiate expediting activity if the part failed to arrive on or before the specified due date.

A management committee thoroughly reviewed Crimp's proposal for a two-bin automatic reorder system and authorized provisional approval to test the proposed new system. The provisional approval provided that Crimp operate his proposed system in parallel with the existing system and show positive evidence of improvement within six months. Management, however, did not provide him with any additional funds or other assistance.

Crimp assigned his staff assistant to this task on a full-time basis. Because of limited resources Crimp decided to test his proposal on a single class of parts. He selected miniature rivets because this class of parts was traditionally the most difficult type of inventory to control. Also he knew that a reduction in parts shortages would be almost immediately recognizable.

Within two months the two-bin system was in limited operation and, on the merits of the new system or by the constant vigilance of Crimp and his staff assistant, not a single parts shortage occurred during the succeeding four-month period. Prior to this time miniature rivet parts shortages were considerably above the 4 per cent per month average for all parts.

Crimp reapproached management with this new evidence and received approval to convert the entire inventory system to a two-bin system. He also received permission to discontinue any unnecessary aspects of the old system. By discontinuing the detailed recording of all disbursements of parts required by the old system, Crimp was able to complete the entire conversion process in six months. Parts shortages showed a steady decline and leveled off at an all-time low of 1 per cent per month. In the succeeding years additional improvements were made and parts shortages were reduced to a range of ½ to ¾ per cent. The major causes for these shortages were: (1) unanticipated high usage over a short interval, (2) unusually long delays in processing fabricated parts, (3) failure of a vendor to meet delivery promises, and (4) rejections by inspection. In addition to the reduction in parts shortages, thirty-five of the fifty clerks required to maintain the records required by the old system were transferred to tasks outside the inventory control function.

On several occasions the question of how inventory shrinkages and losses under the new system compared with similar losses under the full control system was posed. On each occasion Crimp avoided a direct answer by reiterating the large reduction in direct labor costs and parts shortages resulting from the new two-bin system. He also stated that he could conceive of no practical and economical control on such losses under a two-bin inventory system.

On one occasion the cost accounting department was asked to supply comparative data on inventory losses between the two systems. They said that under the current system there was no direct way of measuring such losses and hence such information was unavailable. The chief cost analyst stated that he felt that there would automatically be an increase due to the lack of control but that any quantitative measure would require considerable subjective judgment and thus be subject to error. In addition he pointed out that a preconceived opinion regarding such losses existed and that any estimate would very likely be subject to bias. He further stated that in view of the fact that previous losses were as small as ¼ to ½ per cent per month, current losses could easily be twice as large and very likely go undetected. The chief cost analyst was in full agreement that no simple and inexpensive control against losses was apparent under the two-bin system.

After approximately five years of reasonably successful operation of the two-bin inventory system, top management of The Faster Fastener Company made a decision which placed considerable pressure on Crimp to return to a full control system. On the basis of a comprehensive nine-month study by the system development section, top management decided to automate the operations of manufacturing control. All material and part requirements forecasts, purchase and manufacturing orders, production schedules, and similar reports were to be prepared by means of an integrated electronic data processing system. On the basis of the systems development section's final report, negotiations were initiated to acquire a basic electronic data processing system. Based on the advice of several computer manufacturers and the experience of other firms, a system with considerably larger capacity than was currently warranted was selected.

Because of the expected excess capacity of the proposed system and the fact that the inventory control function was closely related to the manufacturing control function, the committee suggested that the inventory control function also be included in the system. It was pointed out that much of the information required by each of the two functions was common and/or similar. Thus, the operation of two independent systems would incur considerable duplication of effort. Also, the operation of incompatible systems in the data processing sense, i.e., manual versus electronic, would require much unnecessary data transformation. It was further suggested that the new inventory control system be a full control system rather than a two-bin system. The automated system, it was claimed, would not be subject to arithmetical or clerical errors or fail to reorder when the reorder quantity was reached. Under the automated full control system all posting and clerical tasks would be performed by a computer which was purported to literally possess flawless accuracy. In addition, the proposed full control scheme would eliminate the need for the packaging of safety stock bundles and further reduce the amount of direct labor required to operate the system.

Crimp, not being fully familiar with computers and modern computer techniques, was somewhat apprehensive of the computer group's proposal, particularly in view of the difficulties he encountered under the old manual full control system. He was particularly interested in determining what problems the computer would eliminate and what new problems might arise.

In reviewing the problem from both a personal and a company viewpoint, Crimp came to the following conclusions. First, if parts shortages and runouts under the computer system were to rise to 2 per cent per month or higher (one-half the level under the old manual full control scheme), the current two-bin system should be maintained even though the cost might be greater. Second, if there was any rise in parts shortages and runouts, the relative cost savings of the proposed system should be carefully weighed against the potential added costs of additional runouts. Third, if he were to successfully oppose the recommendation to abandon the current two-bin system, Crimp would subject himself to the risk of being thought of as a nonconformist and possibly as lacking initiative. Finally, if he unsuccessfully opposed the proposal and it in fact proved successful, he would be in the worst possible position.

In view of these facts Crimp decided that he ought to acquire additional information before making a decision. Due to his regular activity schedule he saw little opportunity for outside reading or any other time-consuming research. His best approach appeared to be to schedule a luncheon meeting of his staff and discuss the issue in as much detail as possible. He invited several people from outside his supervisory jurisdiction whom he felt could add useful information to the discussion.

Crimp planned to conduct the meeting in such a manner as to encourage free discussion of the problem and thus acquire the greatest amount of possible information.

Crimp realized that he would have to base his decision on what he currently knew, what he could learn in the succeeding few days, and what would transpire at the planned luncheon meeting. Due to his work load the luncheon meeting appeared to be his only real hope of gaining any additional knowledge. At the meeting Crimp felt that two specific areas should be considered at some depth: (1) the effects of substituting computer effort for human effort on the performance of a full control inventory system, and (2) the possibility of automating the clerical portions of the current two-bin inventory control system to make it compatible with the proposed manufacturing control system.

# DISCUSSION QUESTIONS

1. What problems experienced with the original full control inventory system would be eliminated by use of an electronic computer?
2. What problems experienced with the original full control system would continue and possibly be aggravated by the newly proposed system?
3. What advantages does the proposed system offer above and beyond those offered by the original full control system and the current system?
4. How can the current two-bin system be modified to eliminate the major disadvantages claimed by the proponents of the new control system?
5. What would your decision be if you were Crimp?
6. What quick sources of information, if any, did Crimp overlook?

# REFERENCES

Chorafas, Dimitris N.: *Statistical Processes and Reliability Engineering* (Princeton, N.J.: D. Van Nostrand Company, Inc., 1960).

Dummer, G. W. A., and N. E. Griffin: *Electronic Equipment Reliability* (New York: John Wiley & Sons, Inc., 1960).

Feigenbaum, A. V.: *Total Quality Control* (New York: McGraw-Hill Book Company, 1961), chap. 14.

Henney, Keith: *Reliability Factors for Ground Electronic Equipment* (New York: McGraw-Hill Book Company, 1956).

# THE FIBERTEX
# PLASTIC CORPORATION

The management of The Fibertex Plastic Corporation of Bellevue, Washington, a suburb of Seattle, faced the problem of planning for the proper location of the company. The existing lease on the building used as their factory was due to expire within the coming year. The management was considering five possible courses of action:

1. Remain in their present location
2. Move to a new location within the Seattle metropolitan area
3. Move to a new location within the Pacific Northwest
4. Move into the Middle West
5. Move to California

The Fibertex Corporation manufactured translucent building panels made from polyester resins reinforced with fiber glass mat. The paneling was made as flat or corrugated sheets varying in width from 24 to 42 inches and in length from 8 to 14 feet. There were 6 different corrugations such as sine-wave form, shiplap form, hat section form, etc. Up to 14 different colors could be used for each corrugation although most items were limited to 4 or 6 colors. The intensity of the color could be varied from complete opaque to as much as 80 per cent light transmission. Surface finish could also be varied to produce either a smooth finish or a crinkle finish. The panels were manufactured in light weight of 6 ounces per square foot or in heavy weight of 8 ounces per square foot.

The corporation had pioneered the development of a new method of manufacture. At the Bellevue plant the paneling was made in a continuous process in which the raw materials were inserted at one end of a 150-foot-long machine and emerged from the other end completely processed. The method of manufacturing involved the impregnating of the fiber glass mat with the polyester resin between sheets of cellophane and passing the material through an oven containing platens which guided the material into the proper configuration. The heat in the oven caused the resin to cure into a hard, permanent material. Upon emerging from the oven the panel was trimmed on the sides and cut to proper length ready for inspection and shipment. The continuous process machine had been designed and patented by the owners of the company.

Other companies generally manufactured paneling by the batch method, in which the mat was impregnated by hand and molded on caul plates which were piled one on top of another and rolled on a rack into an oven for curing. The continuous process machine at Bellevue produced a superior panel at lower cost than could be made by the batch method. The batch method, however, had the advantage of greater flexibility for small runs in that it permitted easier changeover between colors and configurations than the continuous process machine.

Translucent plastic paneling was introduced to the market shortly after the end of World War II. Since that time it had received enthusiastic acceptance by the public. The paneling had the characteristics of light weight, great strength, corrosion resistance, transmission of light, and ease of handling. The material could be sawed, nailed, and handled in a rather rough manner without any damage. In contrast to glass, it was highly resilient to impact.

The major home market for translucent plastic paneling was in patio roofs and enclosures, over breezeways, for skylights, for awnings, for greenhouses, and for carports. In addition, it was used for interior partitions and other decorative effects. In industry the material was used in roofs, windows, and partitions. There also appeared to be a potential market in such applications as truck bodies and fabricated parts, but this market had not yet been fully explored.

Although the price of the plastic paneling had been greatly reduced during the past several years, it was still considered a relatively expensive building material item. Lightweight paneling sold in the retail market at about 45 cents per square foot and the heavyweight material sold at about 60 cents per square foot.

The Fibertex Corporation distributed their translucent plastic paneling through the Panelette Distributing Company of Santa Monica, California. Panelette had succeeded in building up a national market for paneling under their trade name.

The management of Panelette had urged Fibertex to move their manufacturing plant to some location in the Middle West or in California

They felt the potential market in California or in the Middle West was so much larger than in the Pacific Northwest that it would be more economical to locate manufacturing facilities in the large market areas and ship to the small market areas. The management of The Fibertex Plastic Corporation felt that the growing market in the Pacific Northwest justified a machine in this area although they recognized the desirability of production facilities close to the large market areas. The senior executives of Fibertex had lived in the Pacific Northwest for many years and they and their families had a strong preference for remaining in the area.

The Bellevue plant was operated by a crew of ten men that consisted of an engineer, a manager of production operations, six men who worked on the continuous machine, an inspector, and a shipping and receiving clerk. These men were paid the average going rate in the community. Mat was received by rail at an average cost of 49 cents per pound. Approximately $1\frac{3}{4}$ ounces of mat was used per square foot for the light paneling and $2\frac{1}{2}$ ounces of mat was used per square foot for the heavy paneling. Practically all of the balance of the paneling was resin which was trucked from the Seattle warehouse of a national chemical manufacturer. Mat was purchased f.o.b. Huntington, Pennsylvania, while the resin was sold nationally by the chemical companies at a uniform delivered price of 26 cents per pound. Freight charges on mat shipped to the West Coast were $2.88 per hundredweight in carload quantities.

The resin was normally shipped in 475-pound barrels. Near the manufacturing plants of the resin companies it was possible to obtain bulk shipments of the resin at a savings of approximately 2 cents per pound. Fibertex bought resin from manufacturing plants located in Azusa, California, and in Cleveland, Ohio. Other materials used in the manufacturing process averaged 3 cents per square foot. The value of the machine at Bellevue was upwards of $100,000 and was depreciated on a 5-year basis on the assumption that it would be obsolete by that time. It had a capacity ranging from 2 to 15 lineal feet per minute, averaging about 6 feet per minute on most types of paneling.

Dealers received a 25 per cent markup on the paneling that they handled. Regional distributors had a 15 per cent markup for their operation and Panelette as the general distributor had a markup of 20 per cent. Approximately six major companies were attempting to sell the paneling on a national basis and had forced prices down to where the margins were considered very thin. In addition, there were a large number of regional or local manufacturers operating on very small volume using the hand-batch methods in very simplified form. In the Seattle metropolitan area there were two such small local manufacturers.

Some manufacturers had made very lightweight panels down to

5 ounces and even 4 ounces per square foot in order to offer a very low-priced product. These panels were sold for as little as 25 cents per square foot. Fibertex had refused to produce such panels because they felt the sacrifice in quality made very lightweight panels a poor buy for the customer even at very low prices.

Transportation charges for shipping the finished paneling between the Pacific Northwest and southern California were $3.84 per hundredweight for small quantities by truck down to $1.84 per hundredweight for carload quantities by rail. Transportation charges from the West Coast to east of the Mississippi River were approximately double the rates between the Pacific Northwest and southern California.

The Fibertex Plastic Corporation had most of its funds tied up in equipment and working capital requirements for raw inventory, accounts receivable, and current cash needs. As a result they found it necessary to rent their building. An offer had been made by a local investor to provide them with a building of their choosing anywhere within the Seattle metropolitan area which would be rented to the corporation on the basis of 1 per cent per month of the cost of the building. The company anticipated that it needed for manufacturing operations 12,000 square feet at an average building cost of about $10 per square foot. At the present time the company was renting a building in Bellevue, 50 feet wide by approximately 160 feet long. Rail facilities were considered to be important although not absolutely necessary. One of the problems the company faced in building in the city of Seattle was the restrictions contained in the zoning code, the building code, and the regulations of the fire department. The company operated on a nonunion basis although the management had expressed their willingness to work with any union that the employees desired to have as their representative. Four unions had already attempted to organize the workers but the employees of the corporation had felt that the enlightened personnel policies of the company did not make the cost and obligation of union affiliation desirable.

While all the marketing problems at the present time were taken care of by the Panelette Distributing Company, the management of the Fibertex Corporation anticipated that they might have to handle their own marketing problems at some future date. This would require a capital investment in finished inventory as well as 8,000 square feet of additional space for warehousing. At the present time all finished paneling was shipped as rapidly as manufactured in lots of 10,000 to 15,000 pounds. Most shipments left the Bellevue plant by rail although a small number were shipped by truck. Over 80 per cent of the production of the Bellevue plant was sent to the southern California market. The balance was largely consumed in the Pacific Northwest with a small volume of drop shipments being made to the Middle West.

The expiration of the lease on the Bellevue property was still a year away, and the management of The Fibertex Plastic Corporation felt they had plenty of time to work out a satisfactory solution to their problem. Hence, it was reviewed in a casual way from time to time.

# DISCUSSION QUESTIONS

1. Assume you have been hired as a consultant to study the company's problem of plant location. Prepare a plan of how to organize and proceed with this study.
2. What are the possible advantages and disadvantages of Fibertex remaining in their suburban location as compared to relocating in the metropolitan area?
3. Compare Seattle, Los Angeles, and Chicago as locations for Fibertex by selecting appropriate business statistics from census data and other sources.
4. Select your home city or town, or another city, and evaluate it as a potential location for Fibertex.
5. How do you evaluate the approach of Fibertex's management to their problem?

# REFERENCES

Buffa, Elwood S.: *Modern Production Management* (New York: John Wiley & Sons, Inc., 1961), chap. 14.
Isard, Walter: *Methods of Regional Analysis: An Introduction to Regional Science* (New York: John Wiley & Sons, Inc., 1960).
Maynard, H. B. (ed.): *Industrial Engineering Handbook* (New York: McGraw-Hill Book Company, 1956), sec. 7, chap. 1.
Moore, Franklin G.: *Manufacturing Management* (Homewood, Ill.: Richard D. Irwin, Inc., 1961), chap. 11.
"Survey of Buying Power," *Sales Management Magazine*, June 10, 1964 (or latest issue).
U.S. Bureau of the Census, *U.S. Census of Business: 1958*, 1961 (or latest issue).
U.S. Bureau of the Census, *U.S. Census of Manufacturers: 1958*, 1961 (or latest issue).
U.S. Bureau of the Census, *U.S. Census of Population: 1960*, 1964 (or latest issue).
Yaseen, Leonard C.: *Plant Location* (New York: American Research Council, 1960).

# THE HITONIC MACHINERY CORPORATION

The Hitonic Machinery Corporation ranked among the upper ten firms in the production and sales of machine tools and equipment in the United States. Over the past several years there had been a major shift in production and sales from conventional machinery to numerically controlled machinery. Although there was still good reason to expect a further shift toward numerically controlled equipment, definite indications were appearing that a balance between the sales of conventional and numerically controlled equipment was approaching. This was evidenced by the fact that sales of conventional machinery were holding their own while sales of numerically controlled machinery were increasing, but at a decidedly lower rate.

Insofar as the manufacturing activities of The Hitonic Machinery Corporation were concerned, the amount of manufacturing activity generated by a sales dollar of conventional equipment was considerably greater than that generated by a sales dollar of numerically controlled equipment. This was partly due to the fact that the numerical control portions of the numerically controlled machinery were purchased from outside the firm, and partly due to the fact that engineering and development costs for numerically controlled machinery represented a greater proportion of the total cost than for conventional machinery. Furthermore, all numerically controlled machinery was built on a semicustom basis, whereas the greatest portion of conventional machinery was built to standard specifications.

However, if one looked only at the basic machine, there was surprisingly little difference in the parts comprising the two types of machinery. Given a part at random it was difficult to know whether the part in question would eventually become part of a conventional or a numerically controlled machine. Conventional machines had been produced over a much longer time period and were much more uniform in design than numerically controlled machines. As yet no two completely identical numerically controlled machines had been built except to satisfy a single order. Conventional machinery was in a relatively stable technological state; numerically controlled equipment was continually undergoing major technological change.

In reviewing the performance of his firm over the past decade, M. O. Ree, president of The Hitonic Machinery Corporation, had much to be satisfied about. During this transition period Hitonic had grown from a secondary position to that of a leading producer in the machine tool industry. Ree attributed a major portion of his firm's success to aggressiveness in the design, development, and production of numerically controlled machinery. In successfully carrying out this transition, a major portion of the technical and managerial resources of Hitonic had been devoted to this single end. Ree realized that this had caused a certain lack of attention to less immediately important organizational and operational problems of the firm.

One specific area that Ree felt had received inadequate attention over this period was that of facilities planning and modernization. This oversight was intentional and was less critical than might be expected. Hitonic had completed a major modernization program just prior to the introduction of its numerically controlled line of equipment. At that time considerable new equipment had been added. The quality of Hitonic's current manufacturing facilities was still above average for the machine tool industry. To remain a leader, however, in the machine tool field on both a product and price basis, Ree felt this area required renewed attention.

One anomalous fact particularly troubled Ree. Although Hitonic was a major producer and seller of numerically controlled machinery, they utilized a very small proportion of such equipment in their own manufacturing processes. Several numerically controlled machines were included in Hitonic's manufacturing facilities, but it could not be stated that they comprised a really significant portion of their total manufacturing capability. In addition, a substantial amount of the capacity of this equipment was used for experimental and sales purposes. Less than 10 per cent of the parts made by the firm had any processing done on a numerically controlled machine. With this in mind it appeared to Ree that a study to determine the economic advantages of adding additional numerically controlled equipment to the existing facilities was in order. Because of the high initial cost of numerically controlled equipment and the tight production schedules required by the demand for such equipment, Ree felt that it would be advisable to attempt to determine both the company's immediate needs and the medium- to long-range needs for such equipment.

J. L. Crow, controller for The Hitonic Machinery Corporation, strongly supported Ree's feelings with regard to the need for determining the firm's long-run facility needs. He stated that the firm was financially strong but that rapid expansion and high design and development costs were making long-range planning of any major expenditures increasingly necessary.

M. A. Gnett, director of numerically controlled equipment sales, saw two additional uses for the long-run forecast of the firm's need for numerically controlled equipment. First, although it was theoretically possible to perform almost any machining operation on a numerically controlled machine, there appeared to be a limit to the proportion of such operations which could be performed economically in any given situation. Knowledge of where this point might be would give Hitonic's sales organization some feeling as to the true saturation point for numerically controlled equipment, would assist in making long-range sales forecasts, and would provide useful information relative to the proper approach in selling numerically controlled equipment. Also it would provide a means of determining whether or not additional products and designs should be added to the existing line. Gnett agreed that a quantitative figure might be difficult to obtain and undoubtedly would be subject to error. However, it appeared to him that estimates with a reasonable foundation would be superior to pure, unfounded conjecture.

The second use which Gnett foresaw was in the development of a sound methodology for establishing the saturation point for individual firms. Repeatedly Gnett had received requests from customers to assist in making long-range predictions of their needs for numerically controlled equipment for purposes of financial planning. On each occasion Gnett had to admit that he had no answer except to quote the relative proportions of numerically controlled equipment possessed by specific firms and also to state that they were all increasing this proportion. This, of course, did not assist those firms which already possessed the highest proportions of numerically controlled equipment in their field. Most important from a sales point of view was the fact that these specific firms were the ones usually desiring to determine their long-run needs.

With all these reasons in mind Ree organized an operations research team from among his staff and assigned them to the project of developing a systematic routine for determining Hitonic's immediate and long-run needs for numerically controlled equipment. S. M. Ample, head of facilities and equipment planning, was appointed director of this operations research team. In attacking the problem the group proposed to devise a scheme specifically suited to their own firm and, on the basis of the results obtained, to decide whether or not to attempt to generalize the scheme to make it adaptable to the needs of a wider range of firms. Two months after having been assigned the task, Ample's group submitted their first official report outlining their approach to the problem. Exhibit 1 summarizes the basic elements of their proposed methodology and approach to the problem.

# EXHIBIT 1

(The following is a brief summary of the first report submitted by the operations research group of The Hitonic Machinery Corporation outlining their proposed method for the determination of an economic saturation point for numerically controlled equipment.)

The initial task of the operations research group was to determine if any previous attempts had been made to arrive at such a figure or its equivalent. A review of current literature and other available sources of information was made with little success. To simplify the problem, and thus get more immediate useful results, it was decided that a specific solution would be attempted prior to seeking a general solution to the problem. It was felt that early practical results would encourage more studies of this type, whereas a prolonged delay in arriving at useful results could easily cause the project to lose momentum and be displaced by projects of a more immediate but less important nature. It was also felt that the experience gained in determining a specific solution would serve as a useful guide in developing a general solution procedure.

In addition, the operations research group decided to design the procedure so that a minimum amount of original data would have to be collected; i.e., the study would minimize the need for new data which were not available within the firm's current data reporting system or in its historical records. It was realized, however, that some original data would have to be collected, particularly cost estimates for operations currently being performed on conventional machinery but suitable for processing on numerically controlled equipment.

The specific problem selected was to determine Hitonic's own short- and long-run saturation ratio for numerically controlled equipment. The saturation ratio was to be defined as the maximum proportion of the total work load (expressed in conventional machine hours) that could economically be performed on numerically controlled machines. Because of the similarity in manufacturing methods used to produce the various mechanical parts required for the numerous classes of machines (milling, boring, grinding, etc.) and types of machines (conventional and numerically controlled), it was suggested that the facilities mix required by kind of operation was *constant*, even though the product mix *varied*. If the hypothesis of a constant facilities mix was valid, the task of determining the saturation ratio would be greatly simplified.

The essence of this hypothesis was that the proportion of the total work load for each work center had remained constant in the past and would continue to remain constant in the future. For purposes of testing the hypothesis the total work load and the work load of each work center was to be adjusted to include both the actual work performed within the company and any machining work that had been subcontracted. Work centers were the established administrative units composed of groups of machines capable of performing similar operations. The logic of the hypothesis was based on the assumption that a far greater change in Hitonic's product mix, in terms of both *classes* and *types* of machinery produced, had occurred in the past ten years than was expected to occur during the next fifteen to twenty years.

If the constant-facilities-mix hypothesis was acceptable, it appeared possible to determine the overall saturation ratio by analyzing a simple sample of parts. If, however, facility requirements had significantly changed over time because of changes in the product mix or other factors, it appeared that the overall saturation ratio would also change over time. Under these conditions, the satisfactory prediction of future overall saturation ratios might require that many samples of parts be taken in order to determine individual work-center load factors for each product class and to determine saturation ratios for each work center. The work-center load factor represented the average proportion of the work load associated with a given product which was performed by a given work center. It was even conceivable that separate saturation ratios for each work-center-and-product combination might be necessary. Since the acceptance of a constant-facilities-mix hypothesis would substantially reduce the cost and time required for the study, it was recommended that the potential validity of this hypothesis be tested statistically.

Two approaches for determining the past validity of the constant-facilities-mix hypothesis were to be considered: (1) a series of chi-square tests and (2) a linear-regression analysis. The basic data available were histories of eight years of monthly work loads (expressed in actual machine hours) for each work center.

The initial step for the chi-square tests was to determine for the *overall* eight-year period the proportion of the total work load performed within each work center. These ratios were to be called "eight-year ratios." For the first set of chi-square tests the eight-year period was to be divided into four successive two-year periods. For each two-year period the "expected" work load for each work center was to be calculated by multiplying the total work load for the period by the appropriate eight-year ratio for each work center. A simple chi-square test was to be performed to determine if the *expected* work loads of the work centers for each period were sufficiently similar to the *actual* work loads to support the constant-facilities-mix hypothesis. If this test failed to support the hypothesis, a similar chi-square test was to be performed in which the eight-year period would be divided into two successive four-year periods. This test would be less conclusive than the first test, but was recommended in order to reduce the possibility of rejecting the constant-facilities-mix hypothesis because of some unusual short-term condition which might have existed during specific two-year periods but which would be unlikely to persist over the longer four-year periods.

In the event that *either* of the chi-square tests failed to support the constant-facilities-mix hypothesis, a linear-regression analysis would be performed. This analysis would consist of determining whether the variation in the proportion of the total work load performed in each cost center possessed any recognizable trend with respect to time. A linear-regression equation, with time as the independent variable, would be calculated for the proportion of the total work load performed within each work center. The time coefficients for these equations were to be statistically tested to determine if they were significantly different from zero.[1] If so, they would be reviewed to determine what practical consequences, if any, might result from still accepting the constant-facilities-mix hypothesis.

If on the basis of the chi-square tests and the linear-regression analysis the constant-facilities-mix hypothesis was rejected, a recommendation would be made to reconsider the cost of the project, since a more expensive approach would probably be necessary. After allowing for this possibility, however, the remainder of the report was based on the tentative assumption that the constant-facilities-mix hypothesis would prove acceptable.

It was impractical to determine the percentage of work currently

---

[1] This can be done by performing the test shown on page 126 of Bryant (see references at end of case) by setting $B_0 = 0$.

economical to process on numerically controlled machinery on the basis of a 100 per cent analysis. A sampling scheme appeared necessary, and it was suggested that approximately 200 parts be selected for the sample. This amounted to approximately 2 per cent of the number of active parts fabricated by Hitonic. The sample was to be selected by randomly determining a part number and selecting every fiftieth part number thereafter until the full sample size was attained. Only parts which had been produced during the immediate 12-month period were to be included in the sample. Part numbers which were selected by the basic sampling procedure but did not meet this criterion were to be replaced by suitable part numbers.

Every operation of each part selected was to be analyzed to determine the relative economy of producing the part on a numerically controlled machine as compared to processing the part on a conventional machine. For most of the parts the tooling, setup, and average production costs for processing on conventional equipment were available. For a few jobs the tooling, programming, setup, and average production costs were also available for processing on numerically controlled equipment. Whatever information required for such comparisons that was lacking was to be estimated by the process engineering department.

From these estimates the total processing requirements represented by the sample were to be separated into three classes:

1. High savings through numerical control processing
2. Moderate savings through numerical control processing
3. Marginal and negative savings through numerical control processing

Because of the magnitude of the programming costs and the volume requirements of particular parts, it appeared that the relative economy of producing the part on a numerically controlled machine might well depend on whether or not conventional tooling was already available. With this in mind it was recommended that all parts be analyzed under two conditions: first, under the condition of the actual current situation regarding tooling; and second, under the assumption that no tooling existed for either type of processing. The saturation point determined under the first condition would represent the short-run saturation point, and the saturation percentage determined under the second condition would represent the long-run saturation point.

Since it appeared that it would take several months to accumulate and carry out the calculations suggested in the previous discussion, no further planning had been completed. Detailed plans regarding additional aspects of this study and future studies were to be delayed until the results of the current phase of the project were obtained and evaluated.

The report also noted that the preliminary estimate of the overall cost of the proposed study was $10,000.

# DISCUSSION QUESTIONS

1. Is the proposed study worth undertaking at the estimated cost? If so, is the design of the study satisfactory?

2. What advantages will Hitonic achieve by having a knowledge of the saturation point for numerically controlled equipment for its own operations?

3. Will the solution technique proposed have wide applicability or be primarily restricted to Hitonic's own operation?

4. If the proposed tests support the constant-facilities-mix hypothesis, does it follow that the percentage of the total work load which can be done economically on numerically controlled equipment will also remain stable?

5. What different environmental and technological conditions prevail with regard to numerically controlled equipment as contrasted to conventional equipment?

6. Assuming an acceptable result is obtained by completing the proposed study, what problems with regard to achieving an optimum amount of numerically controlled equipment remain unsolved?

7. Realizing that there is a substantial amount of judgment involved in making the necessary cost estimates and other decisions required by the proposed study, what kind of bias if any might be anticipated?

8. Are the recommended tests of the constant-facilities-mix hypothesis adequate, or can they be improved?

9. If the constant-facilities-mix hypothesis was not acceptable, why would the cost of developing an overall saturation ratio be so greatly increased?

# REFERENCES

Broom, H. N.: *Production Management* (Homewood, Ill.: Richard D. Irwin, Inc., 1962), pp. 676–735.

Bryant, Edward C.: *Statistical Analysis* (New York: McGraw-Hill Book Company, 1960), pp. 286–306.

Buffa, Elwood S.: *Modern Production Management* (New York: John Wiley & Sons, Inc., 1961), pp. 114–170.

Freund, John G., and Frank J. Williams: *Modern Business Statistics* (Englewood Cliffs, N.J.: Prentice-Hall, Inc., 1958), pp. 100–135, 245–269.

Kurnow, Ernest, Gerald J. Glasser, and Frederick R. Otman: *Statistics for Business Decisions* (Homewood, Ill.: Richard D. Irwin, Inc., 1959), pp. 401–445.

# HORIZON
# INDUSTRIES, INC.

Prior to the Second World War Horizon Mining Enterprises engaged primarily in the mining and smelting of nonferrous metals which it sold in pig form. Its activities were centered in the western United States with some smaller mining operations in Central America and the East Indies. During the war the company expanded its mining and smelting operations to three times their prewar size and, at the same time, became involved in the fabrication of the metals into basic items used in the manufacture of military equipment. Fabrication operations were carried on in five government-owned plants, three of them in the South and two on the West Coast. Shortly after the war Horizon purchased the five fabricating plants from the government, as a part of a program of diversification. Within ten years thereafter Horizon, renamed Horizon Industries, Inc., in keeping with its diversified nature, had increased its annual sales volume to about $400 million, of which less than 50 per cent was derived from its original mining and smelting facilities.

During the time that the diversification program was being placed into effect, the corporate management encouraged the development of relatively autonomous divisions for each major product line. This arrangement worked well during the boom years immediately following the Second World War and also during the prosperous years in the early 1950s. However, by the late 1950s increasing competition and falling profits caused the company's top executives to increase their control over the activities of the various divisions. This control was exercised through newly established central corporate marketing, finance, accounting, personnel, manufacturing, and research staffs. While these staffs did not exercise direct-line authority over the division activities, their investigatory and advisory activities resulted, in effect, in the return of a substantial degree of control to the corporate headquarters located in Denver.

The corporate manufacturing staff was quite active in encouraging the manufacturing departments of the various divisions to develop cost control and industrial engineering programs. Major attention was given to activities other than the mining and smelting activities since it was believed that the fabricating plants could derive more benefit from this kind of assistance than the mining and smelting operations. Also, in view of the fact that many of the men in top-management positions had come up through the mining and smelting segment of the business, it was not considered good company politics to look too closely at practices which they may have had a hand in developing. However, by late 1963 the mining and smelting division had become so unprofitable that the central corporate functional staffs were directed to undertake a thorough review of the mining and smelting activities. As part of this review program Ralph Norton, from the corporate manufacturing staff in Denver, was assigned to spend approximately six months in investigating production operations in the mining and smelting division.

Toward the end of his six-month assignment Norton undertook an analysis of the lumber department, which was organizationally responsible to the production department of the mining and smelting division. The inclusion of the lumber department as a part of the mining and smelting division's production department was the result of the development of certain mining properties in the western part of the United States more than fifty years previously. At the time the mines were being opened the economical availability of mine timbers, lagging, and framing materials by purchasing was not certain. To assure itself of an adequate and economical supply of timbers, the production department acquired timberland and constructed a sawmill to cut the necessary timbers. Although the lumber department was originally intended only to supply the timber requirements for Horizon mines, the amount of timberland acquired over the years was considerably in excess of the limited needs for the company operations. As a result the lumber department gradually shifted to producing commercial lumber, in both rough and finished condition, for the open market. In spite of the fact that commercial products had eventually increased to over 90 per cent of its total output, the lumber department had remained under the direct control of the production department of the mining and smelting division.

Since Norton, like many of the executives in Horizon's headquarters offices, was completely unfamiliar with the lumber department, he decided to visit its offices in Ashworth, Oregon. Wayne Logan, the manager of the lumber department, met Ralph Norton at the Ashworth airport and, while driving to the offices, gave him a brief description of the lumber operations. The lumber department landholdings comprised about 300,000 acres of timberland in several counties. This land was adjoined by various private landholdings and also by land owned by the United States Forest Service. When originally acquired, the land was forested with virgin timber of which a considerable amount remained uncut. The lumber department owned and operated a lumber mill at Ashworth which had started operation in 1907. In addition to timbers for the mining operations and commercial lumber, the lumber department also produced a full line of moldings and had recently begun to produce trusses, laminated beams, and prefabricated building components on a small scale.

At the lumber department offices in Ashworth, Norton met Nat Grinstead, Wayne Logan's assistant. Grinstead was an accountant who had been sent to the lumber department several years previously from the mining and smelting division's accounting department. Grinstead originally was brought in as Logan's assistant to aid in the establishment of proper accounting procedures. After the accounting system was revamped, however, Logan believed that Grinstead was able to accept some additional assignments. Consequently, Logan and Grinstead had divided the managerial responsibilities in the following way: Logan retained the responsibility for mill operations, forest operations, and sales; while Grinstead was placed in charge of accounting, purchasing, office management, inventory control, and traffic. In addition, Grinstead handled such miscellaneous matters as personnel, legal problems, and log sales. In talking with Grinstead, Norton concluded that Grinstead was probably a capable individual, although Norton observed that Grinstead tended to view most problems from an accountant's point of view.

Norton's first tour through the lumber mill on the day following his arrival in Ashworth was a revealing one. The mill superintendent showed Norton around the mill, in which he personally took a considerable amount of pride. The mill superintendent, who reported directly to Logan, was a veteran employee of the company, having started work in the mill in 1928 as a cutoff saw operator. He had worked at virtually every job in the mill and was obviously familiar with the duties of each of the ninety-six men working in the mill. According to Logan, the mill superintendent took a strong hand in supervising the workers and stepped in frequently to solve production problems as they arose. Logan considered the mill superintendent to be one of his most capable supervisors since he ran the mill practically single-handedly and rarely bothered Logan with any mill problems.

The mill itself was not a modern facility, although the buildings were well kept from outward appearances. The original mill building, built in 1907, had been expanded in 1923 and again in 1948. It now housed two headrigs, a gang saw, edgers, trimmers, and other equipment for sawing rough green lumber from logs.[1] From the sawmill the rough lumber was conveyed into a long shed on the green chain[2] from which men pulled the various grades and dimensions of boards and placed them in temporary stacking pockets. After stacking, most of the green lumber was moved to an adjoining shed to await drying in the kilns. A small percentage was moved out into open storage in the yard either for sale as rough green lumber or to be air dried. The majority of the lumber was kiln dried, cooled in cooling sheds, and then placed on the dry chain (similar to the green chain) from which men pulled and sorted the various grades and dimensions of boards and placed them in pockets. Although general sorting was done on the green chain it was necessary to resort after drying due to change in grade of some boards during the drying cycle. Some of the dry lumber moved directly to a separate building called the planing mill which housed the trimmers, matchers, blankers, ripsaws, and other equipment necessary to produce surfaced lumber and moldings. However, the majority of the kiln-dried rough lumber was consolidated into loads which were placed in open storage in the yard to await processing in the planing mill when orders were received for specific sizes.

As Norton walked through these facilities, the mill superintendent explained that the sawmill, kilns, and planing mill had never really been designed as an integrated unit but were the result of continual additions and modifications through the years as the product mix of the mill changed and as new equipment was obtained. When asked about the age and condition of the equipment, the mill superintendent said that it varied from some pieces which were as old as the original mill to some which had been acquired as recently as last year. However, he believed that the exact age of the various pieces of equipment was mainly of

[1] Each headrig used a single, large circular saw to saw logs into smaller pieces or into boards. The gang saw consisted of several saws arranged side by side and used for simultaneously cutting smaller logs or pieces of logs into several boards. Edgers and trimmers were smaller saws used to cut the edges and ends of the boards to their final rough dimensions.

[2] The green chain was a long conveyor carrying the lumber away from the edgers and trimmers. Men were stationed at intervals along each side of the green chain. As the lumber moved past the men, they pulled the boards from the chain and stacked them in pockets, each pocket containing a single size and grade of lumber. "Green" refers to lumber freshly cut from logs and containing a high moisture content. "Dry" refers to lumber which has been air dried by exposure to air for an extended period of time or has been kiln dried in a short period of time. Dry lumber has a low moisture content and is dimensionally more stable than green lumber and less subject to warping or cracking.

interest to the accounting department which kept records of book value and depreciation for tax and financial statement purposes. From his standpoint, the mill superintendent stated that it was sufficient for him to know that the regular mill maintenance force of six men, with some assistance from the operators themselves, was able to keep the equipment operating without too many breakdowns. Occasionally, when a piece of equipment seemed to be getting too old and unreliable, he would request that Logan buy a new piece of equipment. There was, however, usually a long delay in getting anything new since authorization for release of funds for capital expenditures had to be made through the production department of the mining and smelting division. In numerous instances in the past, authorizations had been held up for a year or more because the mining and smelting division had stopped all capital expenditures due to poor sales in the primary metals market.

The mill superintendent felt that, in general, the mill was reasonably efficient. However, there were no cost centers and no detailed cost accounting as such was done. The mill superintendent had visited other mills in the local area and was convinced that the mill would compare favorably in the industry. He also noted that mill production had increased through the years while the labor force had stayed relatively stable. He attributed the reduction in labor force relative to output mainly to his own close attention to worker supervision and the fact that over the years several pieces of automatic equipment, including conveyors, had been installed. The mill superintendent was not familiar with any of the industrial engineering programs that the corporate manufacturing staff had been encouraging at Horizon Industries' other plants, nor was he particularly sympathetic to the idea since the lumber industry in the local area had not, to his knowledge, ever made use of industrial engineers.

Adjacent to the main sawmill and planing mill was a smaller building in which trusses, laminated beams, and prefabricated building components were produced. This building was only five years old and was the most modern of those located at Ashworth. The mill superintendent introduced Norton to the foreman of the manufacturing and fabrication operations who reported to the mill superintendent. In showing Norton around the building, the foreman explained that the lumber department had begun manufacturing trusses on a very small scale about ten years previously and had expanded the operation five years ago when the new building was constructed. The trusses, beams, and prefabricated components were all made on special orders which came from two sources. One source of orders was the local construction and architectural firms that contacted Logan when they needed special components for industrial and commercial construction projects. The other source of orders was from those building materials supply yards which the lumber department operated in Ashworth and two neighboring towns. These supply yards generally ordered components for residential construction for which they were supplying materials to local contractors. Although the total dollar volume of production was currently only about $150,000 per year, the foreman felt that sales could be much larger. The foreman also noted that quite often it was possible to take poor-grade lumber, which would sell for about $50 per thousand board feet, and use it in manufacturing products which sold for three or four times that amount.

Following his tour through the plant facilities, Norton had a lengthy conference with Logan and Grinstead at which time they discussed in detail various aspects of the lumber department's operations. Logan began the discussion by explaining the lumber department's profit picture and place in the lumber market. Total sales of the lumber department in the previous year, 1963, has been $4,064,000 and profits before taxes were $344,000, or 8.5 per cent of sales. The breakdown of sales is shown in Exhibit 1. This represented a return of 5.0 per cent on a book value of $6,889,000 for the company's investment in timberland, plant, and equipment. The company's lumber sales constituted less than 0.1 per cent of total softwood lumber sales in the United States.

When asked about the low profit rate on lumber sales, Logan explained that the lumber market conditions in general were poor in 1963. During the year the industry average price, according to a trade publication, had been for pine, spruce, and fir and larch (the principal species marketed by the lumber department) respectively only $97, $70, and $74.50 per thousand board feet. All these were considerably below the highs attained in 1959 when the wholesale price index for softwood lumber had reached a ten-year high. Under these circumstances, Logan, who personally dealt with the wholesale brokers through whom most of the lumber department's output was marketed, had been forced to accept lower prices than in the previous year. In the course of their discussion of the condition of the lumber market, Logan gave Norton copies of several analyses which had been prepared of lumber sales in 1963. These are shown in Exhibits 2 to 4.

In addition to lumber sales, Logan also took personal responsibility for the sales of trusses, beams, and prefabricated components. Since the total sales volume of these items was small, they did not take much of Logan's time. Logan said that sales were generally handled on an informal basis. Local contractors and architects knew that the lumber department had a small facility for producing such items and either contacted Logan directly (in the case of unusual items or when relatively large quantities were involved) or ordered them from one of the lumber department's three building materials supply yards. On fairly standard items Logan had set prices based on the estimated cost of materials plus a rough estimate of the labor involved in producing them. For special items Logan made an estimate of the cost of materials and labor and checked these with the shop foreman before making a firm quotation. Logan indicated that the shop foreman, because of his familiarity with the operations and because of the small volume involved, was able to take care of most of the details of handling orders and supervising the shop. In fact the foreman usually accepted purchase orders directly from the lumber department's building materials supply yards without consulting Logan, and he occasionally dealt directly with other customers.

The three building materials supply yards were run by managers who reported to Logan. The three managers had all worked in the yards for many years and were promoted to their positions largely on the basis of their practical experience with yard operations and seniority. Logan did not feel that it was necessary to take a strong hand in the operations of the yards since they had consistently shown a profit. A summary of yard operations prepared for Logan is shown in Exhibit 5. Although Logan did not have an exact breakdown of the figures immediately available, he estimated that the sawmill supplied about 85 per cent of the lumber sold in the yards and about 50 per cent of the shingles, lath, and millwork. Trusses, beams, and prefabricated components were included in the millwork category.

Logan explained that the other major area for which he personally took responsibility was forest operations. The lumber department's landholdings consisted of 300,000 acres of timberlands lying mostly to the south and west of Ashworth, and it was from these forest lands that virtually all the logs for mill operations were obtained. Unlike many lumber producers, the lumber department bought logs from other sources only on very rare occasions. Some logs were sold to other local producers when the sawmill did not need them or when the location of the timber was such that it would be more economical to sell the logs than to haul them to the sawmill in Ashworth. For some years the landholdings of the lumber department had been fairly static with only minor changes when lands were sold or exchanged to consolidate the holdings. Because of the difficulty of building roads to gain access to timber when ownership in an area was mixed, efforts had been made whenever possible to work out exchanges of lands of equal value so that the lumber department gained ownership of continuous, large blocks of forest land. The accounting records showed a total of 1,055,600,000 board feet of timber on lands owned by the lumber department. This figure was based on the original timber cruises made when the land was acquired with adjustments for estimated harvesting and growth since that time.

Logan described present forest operations as an attempt to cut mature and overripe timber stands and to salvage infested, blown down, and burned timber. The current annual harvest was much less than could be cut on a sustained yield basis, although it was not certain exactly how much could be cut because of a lack of adequate information. In the past year the lumber department had embarked on a program of obtaining a complete, up-to-date timber inventory, but this was far from complete. Preliminary data obtained this program indicated that the company lands might average about 6,800 board feet per acre. Unfortunately, much of the timber was inaccessible because of the lack of roads into many areas. Logan estimated that it would take about twice as many roads as now existed to gain access to most of the timber which could be logged at reasonable cost.

Having described the operations for which he took responsibility, Logan suggested that Norton and Grinstead spend the rest of the afternoon going over the areas for which Grinstead assumed primary responsibility. Grinstead's major interest, of course, was in the accounting system which he had developed when he first arrived at Ashworth. Grinstead described the system in considerable detail, and it was apparent that the system provided adequate information regarding the lumber department's financial condition. In place of the chaos which existed prior to Grinstead's arrival, particularly in the control of billings, accounts receivable, and inventories, the systems provided very up-to-date and accurate information through the use of systematic accounting practices and punched card accounting equipment.

Besides his responsibility for the accounting system, Grinstead had assumed responsibility for purchasing, traffic, inventory control, and managing the lumber department office at Ashworth. Grinstead indicated that these functions were relatively minor in importance with the exception of inventory control. In the last year, control of inventories had become increasingly difficult, partly because of the depressed character of the lumber market. Because of lack of demand for lumber, yard inventories of rough kiln-dried lumber had increased to over a seven-month supply at current sales rates.

Grinstead also discussed problems which he had experienced with the processing of customer orders. Because of his responsibilities for accounting, traffic, inventory control, and office management, Grinstead, in effect, managed the order processing system, although this was not considered as a separate function in the organization. Grinstead described the system as operating in the following way. Wayne Logan received most of the orders for lumber from the wholesale brokers. These he passed on to an order clerk who worked in the office under Grinstead's control. Usually Logan made delivery promises to the brokers based on his personal knowledge of the planing mill's work load, and the order clerk attempted to schedule the orders to meet these deadlines. Some of the local brokers gave their orders directly to the order clerk, and all the lumber department's building materials supply yards orders were placed directly with the order clerk. The order clerk, in turn, wrote up planer tickets for each of the separate items on the order. These tickets served as directions to pick up rough lumber and deliver it to the planing mill and also as directions to the planer operators to produce the items.

Each day the order clerk released the planer tickets for the shipments scheduled during the day so that all the items for an order could be run and loaded in trucks or rail cars in the same day. The planer tickets were released to the forklift operator in batches corresponding to one customer's order. Except on large orders involving several carloads of the same item, one planer operator worked on one customer's order and was supplied with all of the rough lumber by a single forklift driver. Delays occurred when the forklift drivers were not prompt in getting the raw material to the planers and also when the planers were shut down to change the cutting knives or to reset the planers for another item. Depending upon the nature of the changeover, a new setup might take from ½ minute to 10 or 15 minutes. Lost production as a result of resetting the planers might range from virtually nothing up to 2,000 or 3,000 board feet.

Aside from small overruns which inevitably occurred, no stocks of surfaced lumber or molding were carried since there was insufficient space for a surfaced lumber and molding inventory. Also, the wide variety of items produced, particularly moldings, made it impossible to carry all the different items in inventory.

As Grinstead described it, the difficulties which had recently appeared were in getting the orders out on time and in keeping the planer production volume up to a reasonable level. In spite of efforts by the foremen to exercise closer supervision over the planing mill workers, efficiency seemed to be decreasing gradually in the planing mill. As part of his efforts to pinpoint the nature of the difficulty, Grinstead had made several special analyses of one month's shipments. The results are shown in Exhibits 6 and 7.

After some further discussion with Grinstead of the office operations, Ralph Norton noticed that it was getting quite late in the afternoon. Since Grinstead still had several matters requiring his attention that day, Ralph Norton excused himself and returned to his hotel room where he reread the notes he had made during the day.

# EXHIBIT 1

## Lumber department sales, 1963

| Product | Sales | Profit | Profit/Sales, per cent |
|---|---|---|---|
| Lumber | $2,330,000 | $ 42,000 | 1.8 |
| Chips | 241,000 | 79,000 | 32.8 |
| Land (including timber thereon) | 360,000 | 192,000 | 53.3 |
| Trusses, beams, and prefabricated components | 147,000 | (18,000) | (12.2) |
| Logs | 16,000 | 2,000 | 12.5 |
| Building materials supply yards | 970,000 | 47,000 | 4.8 |
| Total | $4,064,000 | $344,000 | 8.5 |

# EXHIBIT 2

## Lumber department sales by species, 1963

| Species | M bd. ft. | Sales |
|---|---|---|
| Pine | 12,680 | $1,124,000 |
| Spruce | 640 | 46,000 |
| Fir and larch | 14,100 | 1,012,000 |
| Production department, mining and smelting division (breakdown by species not available) | 2,420 | 148,000 |
| Total | 29,840 | $2,330,000 |

## EXHIBIT 3

# Lumber department sales by region, 1963

| Region | Sales | Per cent |
|---|---|---|
| Oregon | $    841,130 | 36.1 |
| Ten other Western states | 552,210 | 23.8 |
| Rest of United States | 906,370 | 38.8 |
| Export | 30,290 | 1.3 |
| Total | $2,330,000 | 100.0 |

## EXHIBIT 4

# Lumber department sales by product, 1963

| Product* | M bd. ft. | Sales |
|---|---|---|
| Surfaced dry | 25,810 | $1,784,300 |
| Surfaced green | 1,190 | 64,900 |
| Rough dry | 70 | 1,800 |
| Rough green | 20 | 500 |
| Moldings | 2,750 | 478,500 |
| Total | 29,840 | $2,330,000 |

* Rough lumber has been sawed but not planed. Surfaced lumber has been planed to obtain smooth surfaces.

# EXHIBIT 5

## Lumber department building materials supply yard operations, 1963

| Product | Total sales | Gross profit | Gross profit, per cent | Net profit, per cent |
|---|---|---|---|---|
| Lumber | $231,900 | $ 52,200 | 22.6 | 2.1 |
| Shingles, lath, and millwork | 199,200 | 50,900 | 25.6 | 5.1 |
| Builders' supplies | 517,000 | 137,200 | 26.6 | 6.1 |
| Miscellaneous | 21,900 | 5,100 | 23.2 | 2.7 |
| Total | $970,000 | $245,400 | 25.3 | 4.8 |

# EXHIBIT 6

## Analysis of shipments: surfaced dry lumber, October, 1963*

| October shipments, M bd. ft. | Number of items |
|---|---|
| 0– 5.0 | 856 |
| 5.1–10.0 | 61 |
| 10.1–15.0 | 16 |
| 15.1–20.0 | 13 |
| 20.1–25.0 | 4 |
| 25.1–30.0 | 1 |
| 30.1–35.0 | 3 |
| 35.1–40.0 | 1 |

* Exhibit 6 is an analysis of the first product in Exhibit 4. The October shipments for an item represent the total quantity shipped during the month for a single dimension, grade, and species.

# EXHIBIT 7

## Average customer order size: lumber and moldings, October, 1963*

| Average customer order size, M bd. ft. | Number of items |
|---|---|
| 0–1.0 | 1,036 |
| 1.1–2.0 | 215 |
| 2.1–3.0 | 82 |
| 3.1–4.0 | 31 |
| 4.1–5.0 | 15 |
| 5.1–6.0 | 18 |
| 6.1–7.0 | 9 |
| 7.1–8.0 | 7 |
| 8.1–9.0 | 5 |
| 9.1–10.0 | 2 |
| 10.1–11.0 | 4 |
| 11.1–12.0 | 1 |
| 12.1–13.0 | 0 |
| 13.1–14.0 | 0 |
| 14.1–15.0 | 1 |
| 15.1–16.0 | 2 |
| 16.1–17.0 | 0 |
| 17.1–18.0 | 0 |
| 18.1–19.0 | 1 |
| 19.1–20.0 | 4 |
| 20.1–21.0 | 2 |
| . . . . . . . . . | . . . . . |
| 33.1–34.0 | 1 |

* Exhibit 7 is an analysis of all the products in Exhibit 4. The average customer order size for an item represents the total quantity shipped during the month for a single dimension, grade, and species divided by the number of shipments.

# DISCUSSION QUESTIONS

1. Based on the information that Ralph Norton had obtained so far at the lumber department, what would be your analysis of the strong and weak points of the lumber department operations? What tentative recommendations would you consider at this point?

2. How should Ralph Norton proceed with his investigation? What areas warrant further investigation? What information should be obtained? Where can Ralph Norton get the information?

# REFERENCES

Bethel, Lawrence L., Franklin S. Atwater, George H. E. Smith, and Harvey A. Stackman, Jr.: *Industrial Organization and Management,* 4th ed. (New York: McGraw-Hill Book Company, 1962).

Moore, Franklin G.: *Manufacturing Management* (Homewood, Ill.: Richard D. Irwin, Inc., 1961).

Villers, Raymond: *Dynamic Management in Industry* (Englewood Cliffs, N.J.: Prentice-Hall, Inc., 1960).

# MIDCENTRAL FOODS, INC.

Midcentral Foods, Inc., produced and marketed a broad line of grocery products including cake mixes, dried soups, coffee, refrigerated bakery goods, and some specialty canned goods. Midcentral, which maintained its home offices in Cleveland, operated thirteen plants, most of them east of the Mississippi, and distributed its products from twenty-two warehouses scattered across the country. For many years, Midcentral had exported a limited quantity of its products to the larger markets in eastern Canada. With the growth of these markets and increasing pressure from the Canadian government to limit the growth of imports from the United States, Midcentral built a plant and warehouse in London, Ontario, to serve the Canadian market. The Canadian operation was established as a separate corporation, Midcentral Foods of Canada, Ltd., in which Midcentral held a controlling interest and the balance of which was owned by Canadian investors. Because of this controlling interest, the London plant was treated similarly to the United States plants rather than as a separate company. Considerable control over the plant's operations was exerted by the line and staff departments at Midcentral's head offices, although these departments had no formal organizational responsibility for the Canadian plant.

The company's plan at the time the London plant was constructed was to build a facility which would be used initially for manufacturing one product with a gradual expansion into the full line of Midcentral products. The building also contained space for warehousing other Midcentral products imported from the United States. The first product selected for manufacture in the London plant was cake mix.

In the United States Midcentral produced a full line of cake mixes of various types in several package sizes. Since cake mixes were rather new to the Canadian market and because of the limited size of the market, the London plant produced only five basic flavors: dark chocolate, chocolate malt, white, yellow, and spice. White and yellow mixes were also available with a package of marbling mix for making white marble and yellow marble cakes. The mixes were produced on a mixing and packaging line similar to the ones in Midcentral's United States plants; in fact, some of the equipment was surplus and outdated equipment from the United States plants.

In the three years that the cake mix line had been operating, most of the initial difficulties with equipment breakdowns had been eliminated. Although the condition of the equipment prevented the line from reaching the 1,000 cases per shift production rate of similar lines in the United States, the maximum production rate of 500 to 600 cases per shift was more than sufficient to produce enough cake mix to fill the requirements of the Canadian market. Because of the continuous nature of some of the processing, the line was operated on a three-shift basis five days a week unless it was shut down for changeover or because of mechanical difficulties. On this basis the average production rate of the line, even allowing for shutdowns, was almost double the average sales rate. When the line was shut down for changeovers, for repairs, or because there was no requirement for additional production, workers who were not needed on the line were used for cleanup and maintenance work and in the warehouse. While this kept them busy, the underutilization of labor resulted in labor costs averaging about 30 per cent higher in the London plant than in Midcentral's United States plants (after adjustment for the difference in wage scale). As a result, some of the anticipated lower costs of producing cake mixes in Canada rather than importing them from the United States had failed to materialize.

When the London facility was built, two of the men who had previously managed the distribution of Midcentral's products in Canada were chosen to manage the new plant. The former sales manager, an American who had lived in Canada for nine years, was designated as general manager of Midcentral Foods of Canada, Ltd. In spite of his new title, however, in effect he continued to spend most of his time performing the duties of sales manager since the title of general manager did not convey with it a great deal of authority over the Canadian operations. The line and staff departments at Midcentral's main offices controlled much of the London operation through frequent visits of the United States executives to the London plant and offices and by insisting on a close adherence by the Canadian operation to the policies and procedures followed in the United States. The assistant general manager in Canada was the former accountant and office manager of the old distribution organization in Canada. He also continued to perform largely the same duties as previously. One other man who had an important role in the operation of the London plant was the production manager, Norman Goodfield, an American who had been transferred from a United States plant when the London plant was built. The production manager controlled all the operations in the plant and warehouse, although this in actuality involved much less responsibility than he had formerly had in the United States because of the small size of the plant.

One problem which had been rather serious since the start of production in the London plant was that of controlling the amount of inventories of both the cake mixes which were produced at London and the other Midcentral products which were imported from the United States for distribution in Canada. Prior to the construction of the London plant and warehouse, inventories had been maintained in public warehouses and controlled from the main office in Cleveland. However, after the London facility was completed, the use of public warehouses was discontinued and these inventories became the personal responsibility of the assistant general manager. The difficulties stemmed from both improper ordering of products from the United States and improper scheduling of production on the London cake mix line. After a year of confusion, during which time it became obvious that the assistant general manager did not have the time or the necessary training to develop an adequate control system, a man was hired as production and inventory control clerk to work under the assistant general manager.

The production and inventory control clerk, Stan Penkovich, was a displaced person from eastern Europe who had emigrated to Canada five years before being hired by Midcentral. He was trained informally by having him visit several United States plants and the head office in Cleveland where he observed the operation of the production and inventory control systems. After several weeks of indoctrination, Stan took over complete responsibility for ordering products from the United States plants and issuing production schedules for the cake mix line. Some serious errors were made in the first few months after Stan took charge, but the situation gradually improved, particularly with regard to the inventories of products made in the United States. Although the ratios of inventories to sales of these products were higher than the comparable ratios in the United States, and although shortages occurred more frequently than they were experienced in the United States, they seemed to be controlled as well as might be expected in view of the small and erratic character of Canadian sales. However, the scheduling of the cake mix line was not generally regarded as satisfactory and became an increasing point of contention between the production and inventory control clerk and the production manager. In particular, Norman Goodfield blamed the incompetence of the production and inventory clerk in scheduling the cake mix line for the fact that labor costs were always higher than the standard cost per case in the United States plants (after adjustment for wage scale).

The ordering of products from the United States plants presented a much less difficult problem than that of scheduling the cake mix line. While the products from the United States plants were ordered individually from warehouse stocks, the scheduling of the cake mix line presented problems in the determination of the proper sequence for producing the different flavors, length of a total production cycle through all flavors, length of run for each flavor, and amount of safety stock of each flavor.

In the United States plants, the scheduling of lines similar to the cake mix line at London was accomplished through the use of a complex system developed by Midcentral's operations research group. This system involved the use of exponential smoothing with adjustments for trend and seasonal factors to determine the expected usage during the production cycle, determination of the optimum length of a complete cycle through all flavors, and determination of optimum run lengths for individual flavors. During his visit to the United States plants, Stan Penkovich was introduced to the basic ideas underlying this system, and the suggestion was made that he try to use some of the concepts in simplified form. However, Stan did not gain enough understanding from the brief introduction to the system to enable him to implement any of it, and the operations research group did not feel that the size of the London plant justified a full study of the problem in view of their commitments to potentially more profitable studies in the United States. As a result, Stan developed his own system in which he issued a schedule each Thursday for the following week.

The flavors to be run the following week were scheduled on the basis of the warehouse stocks on hand each Thursday and the sales rate. When a flavor was run, Stan tried to schedule about a four-week supply. This was the maximum amount that could be made in a single run because of very strict limits set by quality control on the maximum number of days that the product could remain in the warehouse before being shipped. In scheduling the maximum amount whenever possible, Stan felt that he was helping to reduce the number of costly changeovers in the plant. Also, the minimum amount of any flavor which was scheduled under any circumstances was 1,000 cases, since Stan understood that this was the smallest amount of any flavor that could be economically run on the continuous processing equipment on the cake mix line.

Whenever possible, dark flavors were scheduled to follow light flavors. A full cleanout was not necessary when going from light to dark, whereas it was necessary to clean the line thoroughly when going from dark to light. In practice, however, it was often not possible to schedule a four-week supply of a flavor or follow the light-to-dark sequence. Warehouse stocks of more than one flavor might run low at the same time or they might run low in such a fashion as to force changeovers from dark to light.

Although the method of scheduling seemed to be reasonable to the production and inventory control clerk, there was substantial dissatisfaction with the cake mix inventory levels. The production manager was generally critical of schedules which caused too frequent changeovers and changeovers from dark to light flavors, and the general manager had on several occasions planned seasonal cake mix deals and promotions requiring special packaging which could not be carried out because production of the specially packaged mixes would have resulted in overstock of the standard packages. Over a period of two years, poor scheduling was increasingly blamed for high labor costs, excess stocks of cake mix, inability to carry out promotions of cake mixes, difficulties in controlling stocks of raw materials and packaging, and the discarding of substantial quantities of mix which became overaged.

The situation finally reached crisis proportions when a planned promotion of cake mixes for the Christmas holiday season resulted in the advertising appearing several weeks before the special cake mix packages were available on the grocers' shelves. The plant also found it necessary to repackage about half of the specially packaged mix back to a standard package when it was found that the mixes would not be sold before the holiday season was over.

Following the cake mix promotion failure, the corporate sales manager, manufacturing manager, and production and inventory control manager from Midcentral's main office in Cleveland all made separate trips to London, as they had frequently done in the past, to ascertain what had happened and to offer their advice on what should be done to remedy the situation. The amount of money which was lost on the promotion was inconsequential when compared with the scale of similar promotions in the United States and did not warrant the attention of the highest executives in the company on that basis. However, the London plant was supposed to have potential for tremendous growth and was intended to serve as a pilot operation for future expansion in other foreign countries. Failure of the London plant to develop into a profitable, volume operation was causing serious misgivings about building plants in other countries further removed from the United States and with markets less similar to that of the United States than the Canadian market. The London plant operated at a loss in its first two years of operations, and preliminary figures indicated that the third year would show only a small profit amounting to about 2 per cent on Midcentral's investment. In contrast to this, Midcentral earned 15 per cent (before Federal corporate income taxes) on its United States operations.

Although the personnel at the London plant were accustomed to frequent visits by various executives from the head office, the visits of the three executives from Cleveland, all in a period of less than a month, had such a disturbing effect that the general manager of the plant requested Midcentral's vice-president for foreign operations to do something about the situation. (Midcentral's vice-president for foreign operations held the nominal title of president of Midcentral of Canada and was the only formal direct organizational link between the United States and Canadian companies.) The result of this request was a meeting between the vice-president for foreign operations and the three executives who had just visited London, at which meeting it became apparent that there was no general agreement as to how to remedy the situation. When the discussion had gone on for some time without any decisions being reached, the production and inventory control manager suggested that perhaps the operations research group should be requested to study the situation since the operations research group had developed the production control system used in the United States plants on the cake mix lines. This suggestion was agreeable to all, and a memo was written to the corporate operations research group requesting that a man be assigned to study the problem at the earliest possible date.

The man assigned to the study, John Brooks, had been involved previously in the installation of the production control system for the cake mix lines in the United States, so he was quite familiar with the problems of scheduling the lines. After discussing the situation individually with the three executives and the vice-president for foreign operations, John scheduled a trip to London to talk personally to the plant personnel and gather data which would be used in analyzing the problem. John Brooks' first reaction to the assignment was that it would be a simple matter to install a system similar to the ones used in the United States plants.

In his initial discussion of the problem with the general manager of the London plant, John received a long lecture about the difficulties of selling in the Canadian market generally and the particular difficulties of selling cake mix when the plant seemed to be unable to deliver the merchandise in spite of the fact that they had too much capacity. The general manager supplied the sales figures shown in Exhibits 1 and 2. Only aggregate figures for all cake mix sales were relevant for 1960, 1961, and part of 1962 because of the frequent changes that had been made in flavors during that period in an effort to determine Canadian preferences for various flavors. Before the plant began making cake mixes in March, 1960, a wider variety of mixes were imported from the United States. However, because of the small volume in the Canadian market, it was not economical to produce all the flavors in the London plant and a decision was made to restrict the number of flavors which would be sold. A period of adjustment ensued when the elimination of some flavors resulted in some unanticipated changes in sales of other flavors.

The general manager also supplied the most recent figures, shown in Exhibit 3, for the cost of manufacturing the various flavors of cake mix. He explained that the differences in cost between the flavors were due to ingredient cost differences except in the case of the marble mixes where some additional labor costs were incurred in making and inserting the marbling mix packets. In giving the figures to John Brooks, the general manager commented that it was difficult for him to see how the costs could be very accurate in view of the fact that there was so much moving of the men from the cake mix line and to other work in the warehouse. It was not easy, in his opinion, to determine the labor that should be charged to cake mixes and the labor that should be charged to the other products in the warehouse. Warehousing costs were allocated to each product line on the basis of the number of cases handled.

Following his interview with the general manager, John Brooks talked at some length with Stan Penkovich. Stan was obviously pleased to talk to John since the continuing friction between Stan and Norman Goodfield regarding the production schedules had led to a virtual ostracism of Stan by the plant personnel. Stan described the simple scheduling system which he used and emphasized that he was trying to do as well as he could within the limitations as he understood them. In particular, Stan felt that the lower limit of 1,000 cases in a run of a flavor and the upper limit of a four-week supply severely restricted the flexibility in scheduling. Also, erratic sales and the fact that promotions were planned long before he was ever informed of them added to his problems in scheduling.

Another chronic problem that he faced but was unable to do anything about was the enthusiasm of the general manager regarding future sales. On frequent occasions plans were made for sales far exceeding anything that ever materialized, and Stan was pressured into scheduling quantities of special packages that he knew were far in excess of requirements. It was clear that Stan felt that everyone in the plant expected him to do things that he either couldn't do or that were against his better judgment and that he would have quit long before had it not been for the encouragement which the production and inventory control manager from the main office had given on his visits to the London plant.

The last person to whom John Brooks talked was Norman

Goodfield. Norman made it very explicit that he did not feel that any fancy system of scheduling was required. In his judgment, the crux of the scheduling problem was "that ignorant foreigner in the front office who does the scheduling." Norman said that he had long ago given up trying to teach Stan anything about the problems of running a cake mix line, as his early efforts to help him had not improved the scheduling at all.

After his initial caustic comments about the production and inventory control clerk, Norman Goodfield explained some of the characteristics of the cake mix line at London. The experience of the London plant was that their line operated best at a rate of about 500 to 600 cases per shift before allowance for changeover time. This was slower than in the United States plants but necessary because the equipment on the line could not operate at higher speeds. Also it was not economical to operate at a much slower rate because of difficulties in blending and mixing which arose when the processing was done too slowly.

The major problem was, of course, short runs and costly changeovers. It was the plant's experience that about an hour's production was lost in shutting down the cake mix line and another hour was lost in starting it up. This was done routinely each weekend, but each unnecessary shutdown in midweek added to the labor cost on the line. The entire mixing and packaging line normally was run by nine men except when marble mixes were being packaged, in which case an additional man was used to put the marble mix in the packages. When the line was shut down for a changeover to a new flavor, five men were used for cleanout and the extra men were used in the warehouse, used on general cleanup work, or used to mix and package the packets of marble mix. The men were used interchangeably at the various stations on the line. The average cost per man hour was estimated at $2.16 including all fringe benefits. When changeovers occurred, the best sequence was from light to dark as this avoided the costly complete cleanout necessary to avoid contaminating the light color. In general, the cost of a changeover was the labor cost alone; the amount of cake mix lost was negligible. The production manager estimated the amount of time necessary to make the changeovers using a five-men crew as shown in Exhibit 4. This time was in additon to shutdown and start-up time.

When asked about the cost of storing the cake mix in the warehouse, Norman Goodfield showed John Brooks a cost study prepared several months previously which indicated a cost of $0.13 per case per month, almost twice the cost of public warehousing used before the plant was built. The high cost was explained by Norman as being due to the underutilization of the men from the cake mix line in the warehouse when the cake mix line was not operating and also to the fact that the warehouse was filled to less than one-half of its capacity even when inventories were at their highest level in the late fall.

At the conclusion of his interview with Norman Goodfield, John Brooks returned to the main office in Cleveland where he reviewed his notes and the data collected during his visit to London.

# EXHIBIT 1

## Total cake mix sales

( Thousands of cases )

|           | 1960 | 1961 | 1962 | 1963 |
|-----------|------|------|------|------|
| January   |      | 19.6 | 18.0 | 21.9 |
| February  |      | 15.8 | 17.6 |      |
| March     | 14.2 | 13.1 | 16.7 |      |
| April     | 12.5 | 12.6 | 15.3 |      |
| May       | 8.9  | 10.3 | 10.9 |      |
| June      | 9.1  | 7.9  | 10.6 |      |
| July      | 8.8  | 6.5  | 8.5  |      |
| August    | 7.4  | 4.5  | 6.8  |      |
| September | 9.7  | 10.5 | 12.1 |      |
| October   | 17.1 | 15.7 | 14.5 |      |
| November  | 21.0 | 20.9 | 18.9 |      |
| December  | 19.4 | 23.0 | 23.5 |      |

# EXHIBIT 2

## Cake mix sales by flavor

(Thousands of cases)

|  | Dark choco-late | Choco-late malt | White | Yellow | Spice | White marble | Yellow marble | Total |
|---|---|---|---|---|---|---|---|---|
| 1962: April | 4.1 | .9 | 3.8 | 3.2 | 1.2 | 1.2 | .9 | 15.3 |
| May | 2.8 | .7 | 2.7 | 2.3 | .9 | .8 | .7 | 10.9 |
| June | 2.3 | .3 | 3.4 | 2.8 | .8 | .6 | .4 | 10.6 |
| July | 2.0 | .4 | 2.5 | 2.2 | .5 | .4 | .5 | 8.5 |
| August | 1.6 | .3 | 2.2 | 1.6 | .5 | .5 | .1 | 6.8 |
| September | 3.5 | .7 | 3.0 | 2.5 | .9 | .8 | .7 | 12.1 |
| October | 4.8 | .7 | 3.2 | 2.8 | 1.2 | 1.0 | .8 | 14.5 |
| November | 5.7 | 1.2 | 4.4 | 3.7 | 1.5 | 1.3 | 1.1 | 18.9 |
| December | 6.8 | 1.7 | 5.4 | 4.4 | 2.0 | 1.6 | 1.6 | 23.5 |
| 1963: January | 6.9 | 1.5 | 5.0 | 4.1 | 1.7 | 1.4 | 1.3 | 21.9 |
| Total | 40.5 | 8.4 | 35.6 | 29.6 | 11.2 | 9.6 | 8.1 | 143.0 |

# EXHIBIT 3

## Total cost per case for manufacturing and warehousing cake mix, January, 1963

|  | Cost per case |
|---|---|
| Dark chocolate | $2.33 |
| Chocolate malt | 2.27 |
| White | 1.81 |
| Yellow | 1.95 |
| Spice | 1.99 |
| White marble | 1.96 |
| Yellow marble | 2.10 |

## EXHIBIT 4

### Estimated cleanout times on cake mix line

(5-man crew; all times in elapsed hours)

Change to

| Change from | White | White marble | Yellow | Yellow marble | Spice | Chocolate malt | Dark chocolate |
|---|---|---|---|---|---|---|---|
| White | | * | 2 | 2 | 2 | 2 | 2 |
| White marble | * | | 2 | 2 | 2 | 2 | 2 |
| Yellow | 3 | 3 | | * | 2 | 2 | 2 |
| Yellow marble | 3 | 3 | * | | 2 | 2 | 2 |
| Spice | 6 | 6 | 6 | 6 | | 2 | 2 |
| Chocolate malt | 6 | 6 | 6 | 6 | 6 | | 2 |
| Dark chocolate | 6 | 6 | 6 | 6 | 6 | 3 | |

* Cleanout time negligible since mix does not change. Changeover requires only loading of different packages into packaging line.

## DISCUSSION QUESTIONS

1. If you were John Brooks, what would be your recommendations regarding the use of exponential smoothing to forecast sales?

2. If you were John Brooks, what would be your recommendation regarding the use of optimum cycle length, flavor sequence, and flavor run lengths for scheduling cake mix production?

3. What would be your immediate, short-term recommendation for resolving the apparent crisis in scheduling cake mix?

4. What are the real problems at the London plant and how can they be solved?

## REFERENCES

Brown, Robert G.: *Statistical Forecasting for Inventory Control* (New York: McGraw-Hill Book Company, 1959), chaps. 1, 2, 3, 5.

Eilon, Samuel: *Elements of Production Planning and Control* (New York: The Macmillan Company, 1962), chaps. 10–14.

Magee, John F.: *Production Planning and Inventory Control* (New York: McGraw-Hill Book Company, 1958), chaps. 4, 6, 9.

# MORRISON MANUFACTURING, INC.

During World War II, Morrison Manufacturing, Inc., an automotive parts producer, operated a medium-sized ordnance plant for the government. The plant turned out small parts and assemblies for tanks, trucks, and self-propelled guns. Following the war, Morrison purchased the plant and equipment from the government with the intention of expanding its capacity for producing automotive, truck, and tractor parts. However, the planned expansion of the parts business did not meet the expectations of Morrison's management, and the plant was underutilized until the outbreak of the Korean War. At that time Morrison obtained contracts for the production of ordnance parts and assemblies which enabled it to operate the plant at close to its full capacity and to replace most of the obsolete equipment in the plant. In addition, Morrison started the development of a lightweight, heavy-duty compressor which was thought to be superior to any other compressor on the market in size, weight, and performance characteristics. After the production of several experimental models, a production contract was obtained from the Navy for 250 units for use in both land and ship installations.

In 1952 the compressor division was formed to continue the development and production of compressors. The division made several important technological advances in the design and manufacture of the product and soon became recognized as a leader in the manufacture of high-performance compressors. Lloyd Larson, the division manager, stated that the objective of his organization was to make compressors of a kind which would challenge the engineering and production capabilities of this division of Morrison Manufacturing. He did not believe his group should compete in the manufacture of inexpensive or standardized compressors.

Morrison Manufacturing was divided into four divisions, of which the compressor division was the newest. The oldest of the divisions was the automotive parts division which was the direct descendant of the original manufacturing operations which existed prior to World War II. In 1947 an appliance division had been formed to produce private brand appliances for mail order houses and chain stores, and an electronics division was formed in 1950 to produce various electronics components for military equipment and systems.

Each of the four divisions had its own facilities and each was run by a general manager who reported directly to the president of the company. The general manager was responsible for the success or failure of his unit and, within the general policy and financial limit imposed upon him from the central staff, he was free to operate his division as he wished. A current organization chart is shown in Exhibit 1.

The central office of Morrison Manufacturing was located adjacent to the plant of the automotive parts division. The compressor division occupied the ordnance plant which had been purchased from the government, located 40 miles from the plant of the automotive parts division; the appliance division and electronics division plants were 75 and 125 miles, respectively, from the automotive parts division plant. Both the appliance division and the electronics division operated almost as autonomous divisions from the standpoint of manufacturing. However, because of its excellent casting and machining capabilities the compressor division performed some support work for the automotive division. In addition, the compressor division did a very limited amount of commercial precision casting and machine shop work for firms in the immediate vicinity.

The compressor division had a foundry in which some of the best patternmakers in the industry were employed and which was capable to producing all types of aluminum castings. There were tentative plans to produce magnesium castings in the near future. The division's primary capability, however, was in machining. It operated many types of metal cutting machines, all in excellent condition. Some of the work accomplished in the compressor division required machining to tolerances as close as 0.0001. The division had the only gear grinding, broaching, hobbing, and chemical laboratory facilities in the company. Some numerical control equipment had been introduced to replace the more obsolete machines. The major equipment available in the division consisted of the following:

A brazing furnace
Heat-treat ovens
Arc and seam welding
500-ton press
Knee mills
Vertical mills
Two 36-inch vertical stroke
broaches
Turret lathes

Engine lathes
Gear hobbing equipment
Gear grinding equipment
Drill presses
Complete aluminum foundry
15-inch rolls
Jig-mill, 96 × 16 × 36-inch DeVlieg
Borematic

In addition, there were seven numerically controlled machines:

2 number 3 Milwaukee-matics
1 Brown and Sharpe drill with Warner and Swasey controls
1 Cincimatic drill press
1 vertical spindle Hydrotel
1 Jones and Lamson turret lathe
1 horizontal mill

The division was capable of producing more than $30 million worth of compressors a year with the plant and equipment currently available.

There were firm contracts for the delivery of 3,600 compressors during the next 12-month period (approximately $6 million in sales). The sales department had worked diligently to enlarge both the civilian and military markets, but additional sales did not appear to be likely. The volume of compressor sales was not nearly enough to utilize the capabilities of the division, so that approximately 40 per cent of the output was directed toward supplying close tolerance machine assemblies and castings, principally for the automotive parts division. Even with this work it was evident that either the volume of compressor business had to be increased or the product base broadened in order to operate the division successfully.

The division had been profitable in the 1950s and early 1960s but had shown a substantial financial loss for the past several years. This operating loss had been due primarily to developmental expenditures on new compressors, although Larson believed the losses could be recovered on future production (see Exhibit 2). The competition in the compressor field was becoming more keen each year and it appeared that the lead which Morrison enjoyed at one time was being reduced. There were, however, certain product advantages which the company still held over its competitors.

The three-year sales forecast is summarized in Exhibit 3. The estimates of sales were based on (1) contracts on hand, (2) business not signed but where negotiations indicated there was a good possibility of receiving the order, and (3) speculative business for which negotiations were just beginning. In the past, business in the third classification had usually materialized.

Through the spring of the current year sales for the division had averaged $1.4 million a month. However, the business on hand and in the final negotiation stages for the remainder of the year was less than $1 million per month. A disturbing fact for the compressor division management was the statement by the sales manager that speculative business was not developing into firm orders as rapidly as usual.

The manpower breakdown on April 1 of the current year is summarized in Exhibit 4. During the early part of the current year the manpower had been reduced from nearly 1,400 workers to the figure shown in Exhibit 4. Any additional reductions would result in the loss of highly skilled workers which the company could not replace easily. Larson believed that the long-run forecast indicated an expanding compressor business that would solve the problem, but in the meantime something had to be done to fill the gap which was developing between sales and capacity. Larson called a meeting of the top managers of the division to see if they could generate ideas solving the problem. The following memorandum is a summary transcript of that meeting.

This memorandum outlines the objectives, ground rules, and assignments for the successful undertaking of "Operation Upswing."

*Objective*

To obtain additional business for CD (compressor division), generally for the last half of the current year.

*Ground Rules*

Work acquired shall not restrict our ability to react quickly to the C-10 compressor production requirements and meet our existing schedule commitments.

Generally, work acquired shall be on the basis of material being supplied or being readily available locally.

We shall not take work which will require substantial farming out of operations or subcontracting of parts.

We shall attempt to acquire assembly or bench type work as well as machining work and foundry work.

A special committee will be formed to review all new work opportunities and to respond promptly to all proposals. A careful cost and profitability record will be kept for all such work taken on by the division.

Before contracting for a specified job we must assure ourselves that we *can* do what we say we shall do.

We must determine more precisely the types of work we need and want.

We must carefully determine our available machine capacity before proceeding.

### Plan and Assignments

*Spares.* The sales manager is to pursue aggressively any known spares provisioning which is pending in the customer's pipeline.

*Support equipment and tools.* The service department is to be contacted to determine if any support equipment or tools can be released for fabrications.

*Castings.* Other Morrison divisions are to be contacted for possible casting work.

*Overhaul.* We intend to explore with service and sales departments the possibility of performing at CD the overhaul of customers' equipment.

*Outside production review.* The purchasing department will review our outside production programs with the aim of determining what items would be practical to return to CD.

*"Make or buy" recoding.* Production engineering is to review new releases normally coded "buy" for the possibility and feasibility of recoding to "make."

*R and D compressors.* We shall request engineering to release for manufacture those pending R and D items which can safely be put into work on the C-12-B compressors.

*Ahead-of-schedule release.* We shall review and release all advance shop orders for which raw material is available.

*Military support of manufacturing research.* Additional emphasis will be placed on obtaining contracts for manufacturing research.

*Subcontract work for other divisions.* Purchasing agents in other divisions will be contacted with the aim of acquiring subcontract work.

*Bidders' list.* Bob Conklin (company representative in Washington, D.C.) will be made aware of the exact types of work CD is interested in doing and will watch "invitations to bid" from every government agency.

Appropriate managers of manufacturing of other divisions are to be contacted for the possibility of acquiring work.

Department managers will visit other division locations for the purpose of acquiring work.

The company also was making every attempt to reduce costs. Several suggestions were being considered by Larson. The following three examples are typical of the ideas he was considering and some of the arguments for and against them:

1. *To go back to a manual system of production control.* A few years before, the division had installed an elaborate system of electronic data processing to project setup and run time by operation and to schedule and provide shop load projections. The system also was used to provide inventory controls for both raw material and finished goods and for "exploding" bills of material. The manufacturing department was charged $115,000 a year by the finance department as its share of the computer rental and operating cost. The character and low volume of business in the plant no longer seemed to warrant the elaborate electronic data processing system. The production and inventory control department believed it could operate the system manually with the same number of personnel as were being used with the mechanized system.

2. *To reduce manpower below the number listed in Exhibit 4 by laying off some of the engineers working on research and development and some of the indirect operations workers.* Morale of the workers had been affected by the recent layoffs. The lack of work had become common knowledge throughout the plant and, even though everyone appeared to be busy, productivity was low. It cost more than a thousand dollars to recruit and indoctrinate an engineer, and good engineers were hard to find. The engineers and maintenance workers who had been laid off previously had found other jobs in the local area.

3. *To use the extra manpower to start a general plant overhaul.* Sections of the plant needed painting and repair. Larson believed a clean plant would improve quality, reduce accidents, and keep the workers busy.

# EXHIBIT 1

## Organization chart

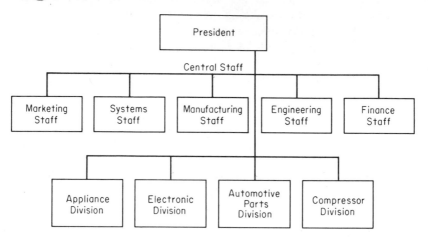

# EXHIBIT 2

## Compressor division income statement, previous year

(Thousands of dollars)

| | | |
|---|---:|---:|
| Sales............................................... | | $16,200 |
| Cost of sales: | | |
|   Material................................. | | $ 4,133 |
|   Labor: | | |
|     General administrative............. $1,850 | | |
|     Engineering (direct)............... 1,625 | | |
|     Engineering (indirect)............. 521 | | |
|     Manufacturing (direct)............. 4,940 | | |
|     Manufacturing (indirect).......... 1,812 | | |
|       Total labor........................... | 10,748 | |
|   Other expenses........................... | 2,424 | |
| Total cost of sales.................................... | | 17,305 |
| Net gain or (loss) before taxes........................ | | $ (1,105) |

# EXHIBIT 3

## Sales forecast

(In millions of dollars)

|  | Current year | Next year | Second year ahead |
|---|---|---|---|
| C-10-A compressor (commercial) | | | |
|   Orders on hand | 2.1 | 2.0 | 1.4 |
|   Expected orders | 1.9 | 1.4 | 1.0 |
|   Speculative orders | 1.0 | 1.6 | 2.7 |
| C-10-B compressor (military) | | | |
|   Orders on hand | 3.9 | 2.1 | 2.0 |
|   Expected orders | 2.0 | 1.6 | 1.3 |
|   Speculative orders | 2.0 | 5.2 | 10.0 |
| C-12-B compressor (military) | | | |
|   Orders on hand | 0.0 | 1.0 | .6 |
|   Expected orders | 0.0 | 1.0 | 2.5 |
|   Speculative orders | 0.0 | 1.0 | 1.9 |
| Other business (support work and commercial) | | | |
|   Orders on hand | 0.9 | 0.3 | 0.0 |
|   Expected orders | 4.0 | 2.5 | 1.2 |
|   Speculative orders | 1.4 | 4.2 | 4.8 |
|     Total | 19.2 | 23.9 | 29.4 |

# EXHIBIT 4

## Manpower, compressor division, April 1, current year

|  | *Manpower* |
|---|---|
| Finance, industrial relations, marketing, and general administration | 160 |
| Engineering (direct) | 128 |
| Engineering (indirect) | 40 |
| Operations (direct) | 496 |
| Operations (indirect) | 242 |
|  | 1,066 |

# DISCUSSION QUESTIONS

1. Evaluate the proposals to increase sales.
2. Which of the cost-reducing ideas would you recommend? Why?
3. Are the objectives of the compressor division sound?
4. Evaluate the sales forecast.
5. How should a company with excellent manufacturing facilities such as the compressor division react to the kind of crisis facing the division?

# REFERENCES

Timms, Howard L.: *The Production Function in Business* (Homewood, Ill.: Richard D. Irwin, Inc., 1962), chaps. 10, 11.

Villers, Raymond: *Dynamic Management in Industry* (Englewood Cliffs, N.J.: Prentice-Hall, Inc., 1960), chaps. 13, 15.

# NEUTRONICS PROPULSION
# LABORATORIES, INC.

Clare Jones, project manager of the electronics division of Neutronics Propulsion Laboratories, Inc., had been asked to make a decision concerning an improved method for recording the identity of individual parts used in the assembly of electronic circuit cards. The part identity requirement was linked to a new military standard of reliability: a standard which had caused many new problems for the manufacturing department. (Jones had been exposed to the background information on reliability contained in Exhibits 3 and 4.) As a result of the difficulty in meeting these specifications, parts had been rejected at a higher rate than expected, costs exceeded the most pessimistic estimates, and schedules were upset. In addition, Air Force representatives were hinting about the possibility of penalizing substandard performance by invoking the performance incentive clause contained in the contract.

Neutronics Propulsion Laboratories, Inc., had a contract to manufacture electronic ground equipment for a major missile program. The manufacture of this equipment involved a degree of complexity and demanded a standard of reliability well beyond anything the company had done in the past. The electronic ground equipment portion of the missile was manufactured and assembled in four stages:

1. The components (mainly purchased items such as transistors, resistors, diodes, etc.) were 100 per cent inspected and rigidly tested.
2. The components were hand-assembled on a circuit card of a standard size.
3. The circuit cards were assembled into a standard-sized drawer.

4. The drawer became one unit of the total assembly or console which contained approximately ten drawers. The console was the end product for Neutronics, who supplied it to the prime contractor for the missile system.

When the ground equipment of the missile failed in a test check, the malfunction was traced to the faulty drawer, which was removed, and a new drawer was inserted into the console by the field crew. It took only a minute or two to make this change. After being removed the faulty drawer was sent to a service center for repair. At the service center new circuit cards were inserted to replace any defective cards and the drawer became operative again. This was as far as the replacement cycle was carried. It was not practical to remove and replace a defective component from the circuit card even though every component but the defective one operated perfectly. There was too great a risk that other components would be damaged in the removal and replacement process.

Each circuit card and drawer had a standard plug-in connector. The cards varied only in terms of the components and circuitry contained in each card. The drawers varied in terms of the combination of cards and their connecting circuitry. This type of modular construction permitted the interchangeability of parts and allowed production of large quantities of certain standard items.

## ACCOUNTABILITY OF PARTS

The Air Force contract required identification of parts down to the level of the circuit card, including a system for tracing the location of any circuit card at any given time. If, for example, a specific circuit card failed, the Air Force might ask the company to locate all circuit cards which had been produced in the same lot, inasmuch as the remaining cards of the lot also might be below desirable standards. The circuit cards probably would be located at many different missile sites, repair depots, and spare parts storage areas. There were no requirements for the identification and tracing of the individual components on each circuit card.

The management of Neutronics Propulsion Laboratories, Inc., however, planned to go further than the minimum Air Force requirements. One group of executives felt that significant additional benefits could be achieved by identifying each individual component with its manufacturing lot number. In this manner when a failure occurred and was traced to a specific component, the defective component could be associated with a specific manufactured lot. Manufacturing, inspection, and test records, which were maintained by part number and lot number, could be checked for irregularities or other possible causes for the part failure. Comparisons could be made against the manufacturing and test history for different lots of the same part which revealed no defectives to date. If the difficulty was found to result from manufacturing or test procedures, corrective action could be taken on future lots.

A second group proposed that the records be capable of tracing all parts manufactured in a specific lot to the specific circuit boards on which they were mounted. Their argument was based on the premise that if the difficulty was determined to permeate the entire lot of a specific component and the lot was used on more than one specific circuit card or more than one production run of a particular circuit card, the system could not be purged of defective parts if only the circuit cards themselves were identifiable by assembly lot. Each part would have to be identifiable "backwards" to its specific manufactured lot, and all parts in the lot would have to be identifiable "forwards" to the specific completed circuit cards upon which they were assembled.

A third group went further and suggested a complete serialization of each circuit card and each component in order that complete inspection and test histories for all cards and components could be reconstructed. Test and inspection results for parts failing in service could be compared with corresponding data for similar parts having an equivalent or longer successful life and assist in designing better acceptance and test procedures to reduce operational failures.

The company decided to adopt the last of the approaches described above, i.e., serialize every part and card. Every part would thus be traceable to a specific manufacturing lot, and each item in a lot would be traceable to the card on which it was assembled. In addition, a record would be maintained of the serial numbers of the parts on each card and the physical location of each card, whether in a drawer, a console, or a spare parts bin in some repair depot.

Circuit board production currently used approximately 100,000 individual components a month and the forecast indicated that production schedules would double within the next 6 to 12 months. Due to the miniature size of the subassembly components and the endurance requirements of any identification marks placed on these parts, serialization costs varied from $0.40 to $5 per part and averaged approximately $2 per part.

## THE IN-SHOP IDENTITY SYSTEM

One of the problems in the assembly shop was to correctly record the identity of the individual components which were assembled on a particular circuit card, i.e., record the correct serial numbers of the components for a given serialized circuit card. The following procedure was in current use and several proposals were being considered for changing the procedure.

## THE CURRENT SYSTEM

In assembling a lot of circuit cards the required parts were placed in front of the worker on carrier boards. The carrier boards, as seen in Exhibit 1, were perforated plastic boards on which unassembled components were stored. The components on each carrier board were identical except for serial number. The assembler had one board for each kind of component required to perform his specified group of operations on a given circuit board. The components were located on the carrier boards in serial number sequence and the assembler received a correspondingly sequenced and numbered group of prepunched tabulator cards with each carrier board. Each tabulator card contained the serial number, part number, and manufacturing lot number for one of the items on the carrier board. Space remained on the tabulation card to add the circuit board serial number, the circuit board part number, and the assembly lot number. The completed tabulator cards served as input data to the data processing system which accumulated and cross-indexed this information with test, inspection, and other information previously collected. As the completed circuit cards proceeded to their final state as either a part of the complete console assembly, an individual spare part, or a component in a spare drawer subassembly, additional information was inputted to the data processing system and appropriately accumulated and cross-indexed. The final piece of information inputted was the terminal location of the console.

When the assembler selected a component from a carrier board, he did so in sequential order. At the same time, he selected the corresponding tabulator card associated with the specific component and placed it in a small box. When he completed his series of tasks, he passed the circuit card and box of tabulator cards to the next work station. Passing the job to the next station consisted of sliding the circuit cardholder (including the circuit card) and the box of tabulator cards to an adjacent work station along a continuous work surface (see Exhibit 2). The tasks were assigned so that each assembler attached a particular type of component to the circuit card, e.g., one worker attached resistors, another diodes, etc.

When the circuit card was completed, it was routed to the assembly inspector and a count and print-out of the punched tabulator cards was made by an electric accounting machine (tabulator). The inspector checked the card count and serial numbers on the print-out against the part numbers on the actual assembly.

## PROPOSAL A

It was proposed that the tabulator card-picking technique of the current system be replaced by a hand-recording system. The worker would record the serial number of each part installed on a sheet of paper which would accompany the circuit card through the assembly line. When the assembly was complete, the number of items recorded should agree with the number of components assembled. An inspector would check the count and the accuracy of the record. The recorded and checked data then would serve as the source document for the data processing system.

Jones felt that the new proposal would eliminate the need to check the number of tabulator cards or to print out the component numbers. However, he realized that it might be difficult to accurately transfer the written material into permanent machine language.

## PROPOSAL B

A second proposal suggested that the assembler be completely dis-associated from the serialization and that the serial numbers of parts be recorded by the inspector or performed as an independent operation after assembly was complete. It was stated that either the numbers could be recorded directly from the finished assembly and transferred to punched tabulator cards, or prepunched tabulator cards could be selected from a master file.

## PROPOSAL C

A final proposal was similar to proposal B except that it suggested that the serial numbers be recorded directly from the assembly, the data transferred to punched tabulator cards, and the punched tabulator cards used to select the appropriate prepunched tabulator cards from a master file. The prepunched tabulator cards would have previously been prepared at the time each lot of components was manufactured and serialized. The selection of prepunched tabulator cards would be done mechanically and serve as a check on the data transferring operation.

# EXHIBIT 1

## Assembling electronic components onto a circuit card

(Carrier boards containing storage of components are shown on the racks to the left and right of the worker)

# EXHIBIT 2

## Assembly line for circuit cards

(Note cleanliness features)

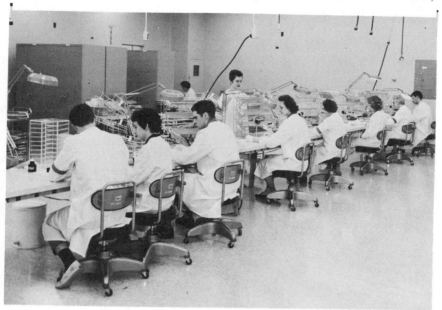

# EXHIBIT 3

## An introduction to the concept of reliability

(This is an edited transcription of a formal presentation introducing the concept of reliability as it applied to Neutronics Propulsion Laboratories, Inc., and the nation's defense program. The presentation was made by the chief reliability coordinator for Neutronics Propulsion Laboratories, Inc., to a combined group of production supervisors and reliability coordinators at a regular one-hour discussion meeting. These meetings were designed to allow and encourage the discussion of current manufacturing problems and concepts.)

Reliability is the key to our firm's growth and success as a partner in the gigantic task of maintaining and increasing our nation's military strength. Reliability represents a means of meeting our pledge to provide the greatest amount of military potential within the limits of the funds entrusted to the firm. Recent surveys investigating the cost of maintaining our nation's military capacity in a given state of readiness or reliability indicated that the annual maintenance cost for electronic equipment averaged two times the original cost of the equipment. For some of the most advanced weapons systems these annual costs were as high as ten times the original cost of the equipment. Assuming a weapon life of three to five years, it is conceivable that the total cost of a weapons system could be thirty to fifty times its original cost. A portion of these costs would prevail even if these systems were functionally perfect and free from parts or system failures over their entire useful life. The facts are, however, that a major portion of these costs are the result of parts and system failures. This portion is sufficiently large that eliminating even a small fraction of current failures would result in savings many times the original cost of the weapon. A factor of five to ten is within reason.

Chart 1 shows the typical relationship between the total cost of securing and maintaining the readiness of a typical weapons system as a function of the reliability of the individual components comprising the system. It should be noted that the cost is not minimized by utilizing either perfectly reliable or highly unreliable components. This can be best understood by dividing the total cost of maintaining the system in a state of readiness into two parts: (1) the original cost of the system, and (2) the cost of maintaining the system in a given state of readiness over its useful life.

Building a perfectly reliable weapon, i.e., a weapon guaranteed not to fail or malfunction, is impossible. After having achieved a certain degree of perfection, additional reliability is secured only at high additional cost. The right-hand portion of curve B of Chart 1 reflects this situation. As the reliability of the weapons used in the system increases, maintenance costs decrease. For perfectly reliable weapons only a small readiness crew would have to attend the system. There would be no need for spare parts or repair facilities. As the weapon becomes less reliable these costs increase rapidly. A point occurs where the weapon may be so unreliable that the only way of assuring some chance of success is to increase the number of weapons in the system. This will increase both the original and maintenance cost of the system. These relationships are schematically described by curve A and the left-hand portion of curve B on Chart 1.

The sum of the original cost and the maintenance cost is the total cost of the system and is indicated by curve C of Chart 1. Note that point X represents an optimum degree of reliability. To build a more reliable weapon would cause the total cost of the system to increase because of additional initial costs; on the other hand, a less reliable weapon would cause the costs to increase because of additional original cost or maintenance.

Realizing that it is possible to produce a product either too perfect or not perfect enough, it is important to ask ourselves where on the above reliability scale do our products fall. The answer to this question depends partly on the particular product about which we are thinking. Each product has its own set of curves and an optimum point depending on the particular system in which it is to be used. The more complex the system the greater the advantage and necessity of added reliability. If we think of commercial products such as toasters, washing machines, automobiles, etc., these systems are simple enough and the technology sufficiently advanced that industry may be operating at the optimum point already. In terms of commercial computers, aircraft, and somewhat similar systems, we hopefully are reaching the optimum technological point. By this I mean that materials, facilities, and techniques are available to achieve the optimum degree of reliability; but we have not reached this point on a day-to-day operational basis. This is not a reflection on industry's performance, as technology must lead current practice for progress to occur. For the most complex systems of today and for the even more complex systems projected for the future, we are currently technologically incapable of reaching the optimum point. This is the basis for our firm's strong emphasis on research and improved technology.

For those of us interested in production, the significant point is that a substantial part of *our* firm's products are in this latter category. This points out that we have a tremendous potential for improvement and also that large rewards are possible. We should note, however, that the rewards are long-run gains and can only be achieved by incurring the expense of higher original costs. We must be able to demonstrate the existence of these savings in order to persuade our customers to underwrite the higher original expense. Performance incentive contracts that relate total payment with the long-run performance of a product are one way of emphasizing these savings. Other ways are in the process of being developed. Reliability viewed in this light is dynamic, challenging, and profitable.

Many of you may wonder how it is possible for reliability to be a problem when we are using almost perfect components and apply seemingly flawless assembly techniques. The answer lies in the complexity of the system and the cost of a failure. We cannot afford failures in our defense system and we have already investigated the cost of avoiding failures through maintenance procedures. Let us investigate the rule for the reliability of complex systems. Assume, for example, that a certain type of switch functions properly with a certainty or probability of .999. This means that only 1 time in 1,000 will it fail to work. Assume now that we have a circuit consisting of 1,000 of these switches and that the failure of any one causes the system to perform improperly. The chances of this circuit performing properly on any trial are only slightly over 36 per cent. In addition, these switches must be connected, perhaps by soldering, which incurs additional points of potential failure. In its final form even this simple circuit could have a reliability of less than 10 per cent.

A series system is any system in which each part must function properly for the entire system to perform its function. In a series system the reliability of the whole system is the product of the reliabilities of each component. Mathematically this can be represented as:

$$R_T = r_1 \times r_2 \times r_3 \times \cdots \times r_n$$

where $R_T$ = reliability of the total system

$r_1$ = reliability of the first component

$r_2$ = reliability of the second component

$r_n$ = reliability of the last or $n$th component

This relationship applies only to a system in which every part is required to function properly and in which the failure of any one part causes a system failure or malfunction. A system which does not require every part to function properly for success will have a somewhat greater reliability. Every complex system consists of a large number of subsystems and is thus subject to this principle. Chart 2 gives the system reliability for a system containing $n$ equally reliable components or subsystems, each of which must function properly for the total system to function properly.

So far we have talked about reliability without specific reference as to how we as manufacturing and production managers fit into the picture. Since I have only a few minutes remaining before opening this meeting to informal discussion, and because this is a topic which will be discussed in a subsequent meeting, I will only touch on this matter.

One definition of the manufacturing task is to maintain, or at least reduce as little as possible, the reliability which has been designed into the product. This consists first in making laboratory methods operational on a production scale; second, in making these same methods economical; and third, in maintaining these operations in as nearly perfect control as possible. This is not an easy task and requires both technical and operational competence, a rare combination in today's human resource supply. For this reason the job has been partitioned between the production supervisor and a reliability specialist. The specialist's function is as an aid and technical assistant to the manufacturing supervisor. The supervisor remains responsible and accountable for the overall operation and therefore maintains final authority. It is impossible, however, for the supervisor to carry out his function without the proper use of the reliability specialist.

Reliability should not be confused with quality control. Quality control is one facet of reliability, just as stopwatch time study or work sampling is only one facet of a methods improvement and work standards program. Quality control is often divided into two functions: (1) acceptance sampling and (2) process control. Acceptance sampling gives the user of a product assurance that the product meets certain quality standards. Reliability calculations determine the quality required of each part in a complex system. Process control assures the operator or interested party that a process is operating within specific control limits or that a machine is operating at or near its maximum capability. Reliability studies determine the capability limits of the processing facility necessary to produce parts to meet end-item operating requirements. Reliability is a systems approach which integrates the functions of design, manufacturing, and quality control.

It is now time to open this meeting to direct questions and discussion. Before doing so I want to remind you of the next meeting of this group a week from today. In this meeting we will discuss the relationship between the manufacturing manager and his reliability specialist. It is probably a relationship with which many of you are unfamiliar or about which you may have specific questions. Between the end of this meeting and our next meeting I encourage you to talk and think about reliability and how it relates to you. I also suggest that you keep an eye open for this topic when reading trade journals and other publications.[1]

The meeting is now open for discussion and questions.

[1] Exhibit 4 of this case is a reprint of an article found by several of the production supervisors present at the above meeting. It was brought to the attention of the speaker and was reprinted and distributed at the following meeting.

# EXHIBIT 3, CHART 1

## Reliability versus total system cost

(No scale, qualitative only)

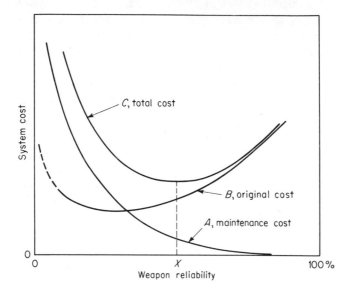

## EXHIBIT 3, CHART 2

**System reliability versus component reliability**
($n$ = number of equally reliable components)

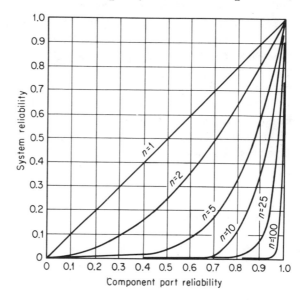

## EXHIBIT 4

**Time to change planned death policies
on commercial products[1]**

By Norman Bruns[2]

Reliability in an industrial society is broadly divided into two camps: the military and the commercial.

[1] Reprinted with permission from the *Southern California Industrial News,* Monday, November 27, 1961.

[2] Norman Bruns, a corporate staff reliability engineer with a major aerospace firm, is a member of the Los Angeles Section, American Society for Quality Control.

The differences are characterized basically by a demand for high reliability by the military; and a demand for that reliability which insures the shortest life the buyer will tolerate by the commercial.

High inherent reliability supported by an effective quality control and maintenance program geared to prevent as well as to correct failures comprises the accepted military approach.

Commercial requirements are not the same, chiefly because of their difference in goal and purpose. Though others may exist, the primary goal of a commercial enterprise is to perpetuate profit-making through maximum sales value.

Maximum sales value demands the cheapest construction for the briefest interval the buying public will tolerate. Therefore, the factor of reliability in terms of how long a product will last or require replacement has far reaching economic significance.


## DEATH DATING

It is obvious that long life products will tend to saturate consumption more than products of tolerable short life. In order to offset saturation of the market and maximize business capture, industry's policy of "dynamic or planned obsolescence" has been effected. Though planned obsolescence involves other considerations, it most directly relates to reliability. Reliability then becomes concerned with product life expectancy or death-dating. . . .


## WHOSE FUNCTION?

This brings up a key question—Who within a commercial organization should establish product life requirements. This function rightly belongs to top management.

Top management must establish the goals, directions, and life requirements and in addition the general product quality and maintenance characteristics.

The reliability organization should provide management necessary inputs concerning reliability, length of life, quality, maintenance, cost and other pertinent information for upper management decision making and planning. If decisions determining product life were solely entrusted to the judgment of reliability functions within the organization, economic disaster could result.

Reliability people are currently trained, motivated, and capable of providing long-life products, and are generally inhibited against providing short-life products.

Reliability engineers, for example, are currently solving complex missile system problems with required MTBF (Mean Time Between Failures) of 27,000 hours. If some of their attitudes and methods were applied to commercial products, increased life of 2 to 3 fold would not seem at all unrealistic.

This example may be expanded and placed in a definite setting for further clarification. We are conditioned to accept the American automobile as reliable; but is this really true?

## AUTO ANALOG

If an automobile were driven 40 mph for 1,000 hours, 40,000 miles of operation would be effected or $\frac{1}{27}$ of the MTBF of a missile system. Continuing the reasoning of this often quoted analogy, it would not be unreasonable to expect that the following items would fail or require replacement: 2 sets of tires, 2 sets of brake linings, 2 sets of hydraulic brake cylinders, 4 sets of ignition kits, 2 batteries, 1 muffler set, 1 fan belt, 2 carburetor kits, 1 generator, 1 voltage regulator, 1 set of shock absorbers, 1 set of radiator hoses, 1 thermostat, and 1 fuel pump.

Ruling out other failures and counting 1 set of tires as 1 failure and counting 1 set of sparkplugs as 1 failure, etc., then the MTBF would be $1000 \div 22$ or 45 hours. If 1 set of tires were counted as 4, 1 set of sparkplugs as 8, etc., then the MTBF would be $1000 \div 73$ or 13 hours.

This example is of course not in any way precise; however, it does illustrate that commercial products could be and can be more reliable.

A leading European automobile manufacturer representative claimed that it is not infrequent that their automobiles operate over a million miles.

Upon closer questioning, it was stated that his company provided taxicabs (used in Europe) averaging 700,000 miles, with minimal maintenance. These automobiles are currently operating economically and effectively.

Pressure points within the business environment, viz., public enlightenment and demand for longer life products, availability of reliable foreign products, etc., create a need for reappraisal of artificial demand policies.

## RECOMMENDATIONS

The key elements in the solution of this type of problem are long-range planning, product diversification and an effective and well coordinated reliability function.

Long-range planning by top management should include a ratchet-type or block-step program of gradual reliability and product life improvement. It is obvious that large reliability and life improvements (frequently obtainable without increase in cost) could contribute to market saturation and economic disaster if accomplished in haste.

An integral and most important part of this planning should be a realistic program of diversification. As attenuation of demand begins (contributed by higher reliability and longer product life), the established company or corporate plan of diversification should be put into action.

In order to keep our American way of life and our enterprise free, and prevent external authoritarian control, enterprise must provide the initiative and responsibility of disciplining itself.

# DISCUSSION QUESTIONS

1. What is reliability and how does it differ from inspection and quality control?

2. Define ideal quality or reliability, and comment on the possible difference in the case of military and commercial products.

3. What part does manufacturing play in determining the reliability of a product or system?

4. Has the management of the Neutronics Propulsion Laboratories made a practical decision with regard to part traceability?

5. Is electronic data processing the correct choice for the expanded traceability system?

6. What are the advantages and disadvantages of the current and each of the proposed data collection and input procedures?

7. Which of the proposed data collection and input procedures would be most economical?

8. How are performance incentive contracts related to the concept of reliability?

# REFERENCES

Bazovsky, Igor: *Reliability Theory and Practice* (Englewood Cliffs, N.J.: Prentice-Hall, Inc., 1961).

Boehm, George A. W.: "Reliability Engineering," *Fortune*, vol. 67, April, 1963, pp. 124–127ff.

Chorafas, Dimitris N.: *Statistical Processes and Reliability Engineering* (Princeton, N.J.: D. Van Nostrand Company, Inc., 1960).

Feigenbaum, A. V.: *Total Quality Control* (New York: McGraw-Hill Book Company, 1961).

Lloyd, David K., and Myron Lipton: *Reliability Management, Method and Mathematics* (Englewood Cliffs, N.J.: Prentice-Hall, Inc., 1962).

*Reliability Program Requirements for Aerospace Systems, Subsystems and Equipment,* Military Specification MIL-R-27542 (USAF).

# OHIO EQUIPMENT COMPANY

The Ohio Equipment Company of Sandusky, Ohio, had been in business for over three-quarters of a century. Founded in 1885 by a German immigrant, the company had established a reputation for manufacturing extremely durable, although not inexpensive, farm equipment and implements. Over the years, the company had grown from a small shop employing only a few men plus the owner to a medium-sized manufacturing company with several thousand employees and producing a full line of reapers, harvesters, combines, balers, cultivators, and other farm equipment. Although Ohio Equipment was only a fraction of the size of such industry leaders as the International Harvester Company and Deere and Company, the company's reputation for well-designed high-quality equipment was the envy of the industry. For many years, the general opinion among its competitors was that Ohio Equipment's major failing was a lack of aggressive promotion and selling which resulted in its relatively small share of the total market.

For those persons familiar with the internal organization of the Ohio Equipment Company the reason for the conservative approach to sales was apparent. Following the death of Ernst Mayer, the founder of the company, his three sons had taken over control of the company. Prior to Mayer's death, each of the sons had been in charge of the manufacture of one or more of the company's many products. In many ways the manufacturing operations were carried on as three separate projects housed in a single plant with limited central control. After Mayer's death, the three sons still continued to be interested principally in their own area of specialization. Although the eldest brother, who became president, took some steps to centralize control of the manufacturing operations, the three brothers never abandoned their long established habits of personally supervising the design and production of their own products. Each brother believed that if quality products were produced, sales would take care of themselves. In spite of this rather unconventional philosophy, the company grew at a modest, but steady rate, and the three brothers continued to operate the business without serious problems for more than twenty-five years.

However, within a period of six years each of the brothers retired from active management of the business and each sold a substantial portion of his stock in the company upon retirement. Control of the company passed to a new group of stockholders, unrelated to the Mayer family, who brought in a new president, Delbert Little. One of Little's first actions was to pull the very loosely knit organization together into a more conventional organization structure. Where previously the company consisted of three separate empires run by each of the brothers, Little created the functional structure shown in Exhibit 1.

Along with the change in organization structure, a complete physical reorganization of the manufacturing and assembly facilities was undertaken. Instead of the three separate and relatively independent manufacturing and assembly operations, the machinery and equipment were relocated and regrouped so that all similar operations were performed in the same area. A general plan of the factory after the reorganization is shown in Exhibit 2.

With the relocation of machinery it was determined that a considerable amount of surplus equipment was available. In many cases duplicate equipment had been obtained for the separate activities run by each of the brothers and the equipment was never utilized effectively. Centralization of the equipment permitted, in a number of instances, reduction of equipment requirements from three machines to a single machine. In other instances the need for six or seven similar machines was cut to three or four. When the reductions were made, the oldest and least efficient machines were declared surplus and sold. The equipment remaining was relatively modern and in good condition. The attention of the three brothers through the years to technical details and high quality had resulted in the development of a high degree of technical competence and the adoption of modern manufacturing methods. As a consequence, after the reorganization Ohio Equipment possessed manufacturing facilities as modern and technically advanced as any in the industry.

Delbert Little advocated a more aggressive policy toward sales. The sales function was lodged in two departments, the equipment sales department and a new contract sales department (see Exhibit 1). The equipment sales department concentrated on the sale of farm equipment through farm implement dealers. The contract sales department was established to solicit contracts for the production of machined parts, subassemblies, and assemblies for other manufacturers. In particular, the contract sales department solicited subcontracts from prime contractors in the defense industries. It was Little's feeling that Ohio Equipment's relatively small size and modern production facilities made it ideally suited for producing the small quantities of high-precision parts and assemblies often required for defense contracts. Because of the size of the military budget and the likelihood that it would continue to be quite large in the future, Little thought that Ohio Equipment should make every effort to obtain a portion of this potentially profitable business.

With the centralization of the manufacturing and assembly facilities and the procurement of some defense subcontracting, Ohio Equipment's plant began to operate much differently than it had in the past. Instead of specialization of workers and equipment for the production of a limited part of the farm equipment line, the production control department assigned work to shop areas based on a master schedule and the relative loads in the various areas. As a consequence, neither the workers nor the foremen were personally responsible for the production of any particular piece of equipment as they had been in the past.

As shown in Exhibit 2 the factory was physically divided into the foundry, plating, and painting departments, and the machine and assembly shops. The assembly shop was divided into subassembly and final assembly areas, and the machine shop was divided into six areas with machines of similar function grouped in each area. The foundry, plating, and painting departments were each run by a foreman while the machine and assembly shops were the responsibility of the machining and assembly superintendents. The six foremen responsible for each of the six machine areas reported to the machine shop superintendent, while the subassembly and final assembly foremen reported to the assembly superintendent. Although the foundry, plating, and painting foremen nominally reported to the assembly superintendent, they operated their departments fairly independently.

Quality control, after the reorganization, was developed as a separate function headed by a chief inspector. The workers and foremen were expected to perform a great deal of the inspection work themselves during processing and assembly, as they always had in the past. In addition, quality control inspectors performed certain inspections at key points in the factory. Generally the quality control department's inspectors checked parts before they left the foundry, plating, and painting departments. In the machine shop the quality control department inspectors usually performed an end inspection after the completion of all machining operations on a part. To satisfy requirements on some defense contracts the quality control department used MIL STD 105D[1] in some of its inspection procedures. On the average, in the foundry, plating, and painting departments and in the machine shop, there was one inspector on the floor for every forty-five direct shop people. In addition, there was one quality control inspector for the subassembly area and one for the final assembly area.

Orders for parts, assemblies, or finished pieces of equipment were transmitted by either the equipment sales department or the contract sales department to the production control department. There the orders were inserted in the master schedule and shop orders and material requisitions were prepared. In the case of orders for items which had been manufactured previously, manufacturing engineering quickly reviewed the process planning and tooling after the shop orders and material requisitions were prepared. Only rarely were any changes required on orders or requisitions already prepared. Orders for new items were sent to manufacturing engineering for process planning and development of tooling after tentative master scheduling by production control, and the orders were then returned to production control for preparation of the shop orders and material requisitions.

Material requisitions prepared by production control were sent to the purchasing department. Shop orders for fabrication were released to the area in the factory performing the first operation four weeks in advance of the date that the processing was due to start. Along with the release of the shop order, the production control department released instructions to the stores department to issue the raw material to the shop. Shop orders were also released for the subassembly and final assembly areas four weeks in advance of the time that assembly was to begin. However, fabricated or purchased parts to be used in the assembly areas were placed directly into the storage area in the assembly area immediately after receipt from the vendor for fabrication in the shops. Therefore, no instructions for release of such materials were necessary for shop orders for assembly.

The shop orders prepared and released by the production control department did not themselves contain any processing or assembly instructions. A shop order was a punched tabulator card showing the part number or assembly number, quantity required, date of start of first operation, location of first operation, completion date for the order, and reference number of the standing process or assembly orders. To signify completion of the order, there was a space on the card for the initials of the shop or assembly worker involved in the last operation or assembly, and there was a space for the inspector's initials to signify

[1] MIL STD 105D is titled "Sampling Procedures and Tables for Inspection by Attributes." This document has been approved by the Department of Defense for use by the Army, Navy, Air Force, and Defense Supply Agency.

acceptance of the order. The inspector also wrote on the card the number of items accepted and their serial numbers, if any, which were subsequently key-punched into the card. The shop order card was then used as the source document for picking up the items in the finished goods inventory records.

The reference number to a standing process or assembly order on the shop order was used to select the proper processing or assembly instructions from files maintained in the shops and assembly areas. The processing and assembly instructions were prepared by manufacturing engineering for all new items as orders were received for them, and reproducible copies were placed in the shop files. When changes or corrections were made by manufacturing engineering the shop file copies were changed so that in theory the shop files always contained the latest processing and assembly instructions for any item which Ohio Equipment had manufactured since the installation of the system.

When a shop order for the fabrication of a part was received by the foreman in the area in which the first operation was performed, the foreman obtained a copy of the standing process order from the shop files and determined the day and machine on which the order would be placed in process. Usually it was not necessary for the foreman to request issue of the raw material by the stores department since the stores department physically moved the material to the area in which the first operation was performed as soon as it received instructions to issue the material from the production control department. When the operator was ready to begin working on the job, usually several weeks later, the material was then available in the immediate area. After completion of the first operation the shop order and a copy of the standing process order were sent along with the lot through subsequent operations.

When an assembly order was received in the assembly shop, the shop superintendent assigned it to the subassembly area or final assembly area depending on the relative loads in the two areas and on the size of the items being assembled. The final assembly area was equipped to handle the final assembly of farm equipment but could, if necessary, handle smaller assemblies and subassemblies. After an assembly order was assigned to one or the other of the assembly foremen, it was the foreman's responsibility to see that the order was completed on schedule along with the other work in the shop.

The parts required for an assembly order were supposed to be in the parts storage area or delivered to it soon after the production control department released the assembly order to the assembly shops. However, since the parts were not always in the parts storage area at the proper time, the foreman who received an assembly order usually checked the parts storage area to see whether all the necessary parts were on hand before determining exactly when the assembly work would be done. If some of the necessary parts were missing, the foreman would ask the production control department to trace the missing parts and let the foreman know when they would be available. In many cases, when parts were missing and schedules were tight, part of the assembly work was done and the partially assembled lot was held until it could be completed when the missing parts arrived. By close attention to the follow-up on missing parts and by shifting manpower among the various jobs that were in process at any one time, the assembly foremen usually were able to meet schedule dates.

Because of the relatively small number of items on any assembly order, assembly work was generally done in lots. On occasion simple assembly lines were set up for orders involving larger quantities. Where small parts were involved, the usual procedure was for the worker needing parts to take the necessary parts from the shelves in the parts storage area and carry them to the assembly bench. Larger parts which could not be moved by hand were moved by a forklift truck from the parts storage area to the assembly area, with the worker requiring the parts making the arrangements for the movement.

The assembly workers either were sufficiently familiar with an assembly so that they needed no instructions, or they worked from the written assembly instructions prepared by manufacturing engineering and the exploded views prepared by the engineering department. If the assembly worker felt that he needed the assembly instructions and exploded views, he obtained copies from the files after he was assigned to work on an assembly order. When assembly instructions and exploded views were not available because of changes or delays in their preparation, some of the more experienced workers worked directly from the engineering drawings.

In the final assembly area several workers might work together on the assembly of a single piece of farm equipment. In the subassembly area it was more typical for a single worker to work on a number of assemblies at once. Because of the necessity of shifting manpower to keep all the jobs on schedule and the practice of partially completing an assembly when parts were missing, several workers might work on a single order at different times.

When the work required by an assembly order was completed, the last worker to work on the order initialed the assembly order and the quality control inspector was then asked to inspect the work. The inspection procedures which were specified by engineering varied considerably but usually consisted of a visual examination of the completed items and a check that the assemblies functioned properly. For instance, rotating gears or shafts were checked for any end play or stiffness by moving them by hand. Completed pieces of farm equipment were operated by the inspector to see that all controls functioned properly.

After completion of inspection, the quality control inspector initialed the assembly order. Serial numbers were required on all complete pieces of farm equipment, all large assemblies such as gear boxes and transmissions, and all assemblies destined for the government. After completing his inspection of these items, the inspector wrote the serial numbers on the assembly order.

Shortly after the reorganization of the production facilities, both the equipment sales department and the contract sales department began receiving complaints from farm equipment distributors and other customers regarding various problems with quality. The problems involved parts with surface defects and dimensions out of tolerance, parts manufactured to old specifications rather than incorporating the latest engineering changes, parts manufactured from incorrect materials, and —in a few cases—assemblies that had missing or incorrect parts. At first the complaints were discussed with the manufacturing department and the quality control department as they occurred. However, when the frequency of complaints had risen to the point where Ohio Equipment's reputation as a high-quality manufacturer appeared to be threatened, a meeting was called of the equipment sales vice-president, the contract sales vice-president, the manufacturing vice-president, the quality control chief inspector, and the factory manager. As a result of this meeting, the factory manager held several meetings with the shop superintendents and foremen at which quality problems were discussed. At these meetings the necessity of closer control over quality was impressed upon those attending.

At the conclusion of the meetings with the shop superintendents and foremen the factory manager submitted a report to the vice-president of manufacturing outlining the conferences which had been held and the continuing efforts that were being made by the shop supervisor to reinstill quality consciousness in the workers.

The quality control chief inspector also met with his inspectors and discussed the various complaints regarding poor quality. In an attempt to analyze the possible sources of trouble, all the rejection tags for the past year were analyzed by the chief inspector's office. These rejection tags, besides showing the identification of the items rejected and the reason for rejection, had a section in which it was mandatory for the inspector to check whether engineering, tooling, planning, purchasing, or a shop was responsible for the rejection and to indicate the specific action taken to solve the problem. In almost all cases the tags indicated that a shop was responsible and contained the notation, "Operator has been warned." The findings of the summary of rejection tags were transmitted by the chief inspector to the manufacturing vice-president who, in turn, read the riot act to the factory manager regarding quality consciousness at the operating level. Shortly afterwards the chief inspector wrote a memorandum to the vice-president in charge of manufacturing in which the chief inspector reported that his inspectors had noticed a significant increase in quality in recent weeks.

Four months later the farm equipment sales department received the following telegram from one of Ohio Equipment's largest dealers.

PLEASE BE ADVISED THAT MAIN DRIVE ASSEMBLY, SERIAL NUMBER 88-3694, ON NEW COMBINE, MODEL C-64A, FROZE AFTER THREE HOURS OF OPERATION RESULTING IN BREAKAGE OF MAIN DRIVE SHAFT. WORKER OPERATING COMBINE WAS SERIOUSLY INJURED BY BROKEN SHAFT. DISASSEMBLY OF MAIN DRIVE ASSEMBLY REVEALED THAT MISSING IDLER BEARING CAUSED OVERHEATING AND FAILURE. WE EXPECT OHIO EQUIPMENT TO ACKNOWL-EDGE LIABILITY FOR REPAIR OF COMBINE AND ANY CLAIMS FOR COMPEN-SATION BY INJURED WORKER.

FORSYTH EQUIPT. CO.
KANSAS CITY, KANSAS

A quick check of the records of serialized assemblies revealed that the particular assembly that had failed was completed one month after the quality problem was thought to have been solved. The design of the combine included a long shaft that was attached to gears at its ends. The middle of the shaft was supported by an idler bearing assembly. It was this shaft that apparently failed. Before further investigation could take place the following telegram was received.

PLEASE BE ADVISED THAT WORKER INJURED DUE TO FAILURE OF DRIVE ASSEMBLY DIED THIS MORNING BECAUSE OF INJURIES. URGENT THAT YOUR COMPANY ATTORNEY CONTACT US IMMEDIATELY TO DISCUSS LIABILITY.

FORSYTH EQUIPT. CO.
KANSAS CITY, KANSAS

**EXHIBIT 1 Functional organization chart**

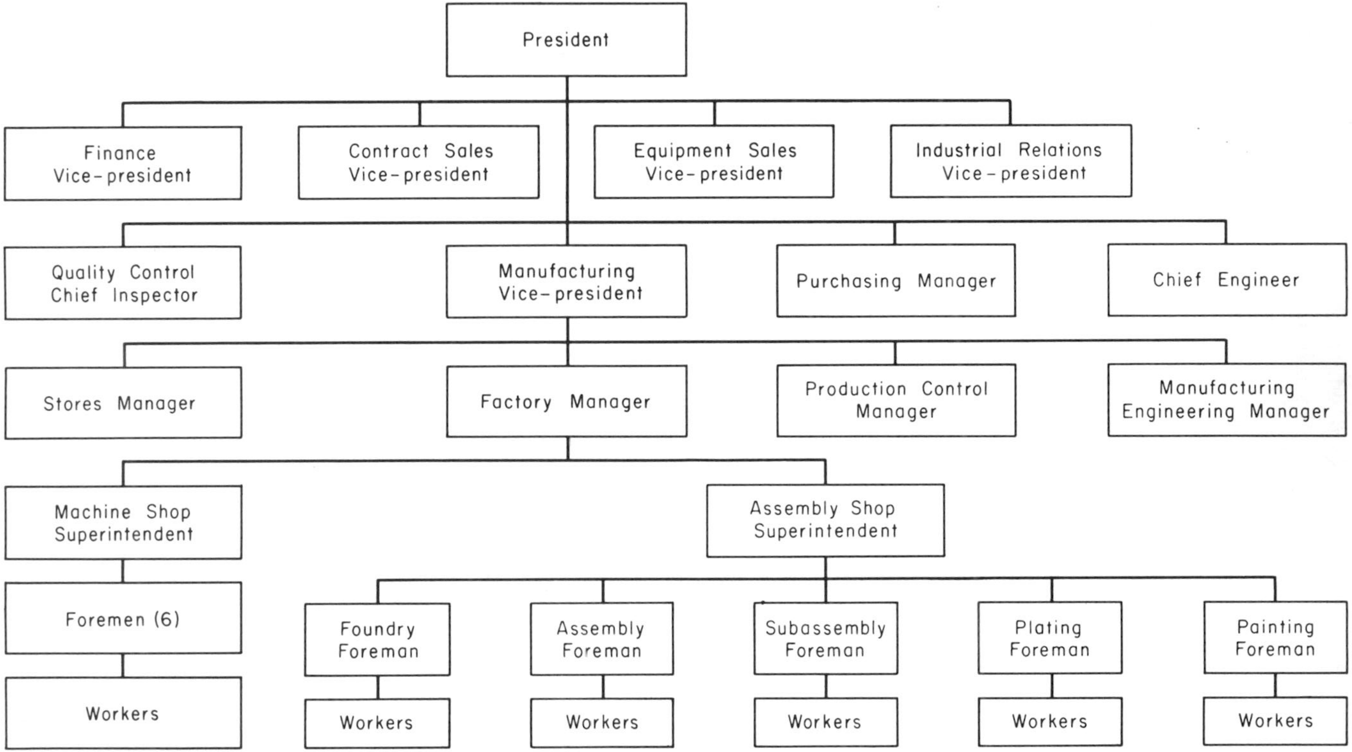

## EXHIBIT 2
### General plant layout

| Shipping and Receiving | Machine Shop | Administrative Offices |
| Stores | | Assembly Parts Storage |
| | Foundry Department | Plating Department | Painting Department | Sub-assembly Area | Final Assembly Area |

# DISCUSSION QUESTIONS

1. Who was responsible for the decline in quality after the manufacturing facilities were reorganized?

2. Were the steps taken to solve the quality problem adequate? If not, what defects still existed in the quality control system?

3. What changes, if any, would you recommend in Ohio Equipment's procedures which would reduce the likelihood of such incidents as the breaking of the combine drive shaft?

4. How much liability does a manufacturer, such as Ohio Equipment Company, have when its product fails in use and causes damage and injury?

# REFERENCES

Feigenbaum, A. V.: *Total Quality Control* (New York: McGraw-Hill Book Company, 1961).

Moore, Franklin G.: *Manufacturing Management,* 3d ed. (Homewood, Ill.: Richard D. Irwin, Inc., 1961), chaps. 35, 36.

# O-NUT, INCORPORATED

Jim Powers, Art Gross, and Fred Hatch respectively had just been appointed president, operations manager, and financial secretary of O-Nut, Incorporated, which had just taken over the entire assets of the OK Orchard Development Company. The assets consisted of 1,000 acres of planted land containing approximately 65,000 eight-year-old "O" nut trees; 2,000 acres of cleared unplanted land suitable for the growing of "O" nut trees; sufficient buildings and equipment to support the existing operation; and a substantial supply of office, maintenance, and operating supplies. Approximately 10 days prior to the transfer of ownership to O-Nut, Incorporated, the OK Orchard Development Company had completed the harvest of its second annual crop of "O" nuts. They obtained a yield of approximately 2½ million pounds of unshelled nuts and had contracted for the sale of the entire amount for $325,000.

OK Orchard Development Company was organized and operated by a group of three enterprising and aggressive businessmen for the purpose of growing, processing, and distributing "O" nuts for a heretofore undeveloped world market. The company was established on a modest capital base but had been unable to raise sufficient additional capital on satisfactory terms. As a result it was not in a position to carry out its original plans to develop its own processing and distribution facilities. Projected profits, based on the sale to existing processors of the two crops of "O" nuts previously obtained, indicated a long-run return on their investment that was substantially less than originally appeared possible under a fully integrated growing, processing, and distribution operation. In addition, the rapidly expanding yield potential of the 65,000 trees could quickly overburden existing processing facilities and possibly upset the stable market price for raw "O" nuts.

Rather than subject themselves to this risk or surrender their independence by merging with a larger company or by floating a large common stock issue, the owner-managers of the OK Orchard Development Company decided to sell their interests to the United Nut Growers (parent company of O-Nut, Incorporated). The price obtained repaid their total investment and provided a modest return for their efforts. The terms of the sale were for payment of one-third on the day of transfer of ownership and the remaining two-thirds in five equal annual installments.

The sales agreement stated that the three owners of the OK Orchard Development Company would remain in their current positions in an operating but non-policy-making capacity for three months after the official transfer agreement was signed. This was designed to provide an efficient and smooth transfer of operations to the new management. Although not included in writing, negotiators for O-Nut, Incorporated, stated that their firm would retain as many operational employees in their current positions as possible after the transfer had been effected. The negotiators, however, were careful to qualify this statement by stating that this promise was not to imply the mandatory continuance of any current company objectives or policies regarding operating practices, working conditions, or wages. This information was communicated to the employees of the OK Orchard Development Company by the original owner-managers.

"O" nuts varied in size from a filbert to a medium-sized walnut and had a texture and taste distinctly different from any currently commercially available nut. Some people likened its taste to that of an almond or chestnut, whereas others claimed it tasted similar to a filbert or brazil nut. "O" nuts could be used for party, dinner, and cocktail treats; as an ingredient or topping for cakes, pies, cookies, ice cream, and numerous other desserts; as a garnish for meats, fish, and fowl; and as an addition to various salads. A paperback book of "O" nut recipes, endorsed by a world-famed chef in a major hotel in Jamaica, was available upon request for chefs, dietitians, housewives, and others who were interested in using "O" nuts.

The discovery of the "O" nut as an edible fruit was made by Dr. Jim Adams in the late 1800s. Until 1922, however, when the first sizable commercial plantings were made, the "O" nut tree was valued primarily for its ornamental qualities and the majority of the plantings were sold for such purposes. A small portion of the plantings was used for growing "O" nuts. These generally resulted from an overoptimistic estimate of nursery requirements for ornamental plants.

For many years the primary market for "O" nuts was local natives and inhabitants of nearby islands who ate the nuts in their natural uncooked state. It was not until a group of agricultural economists took an active interest in the commercial use of "O" nuts that their potential value as a delicacy became apparent. In 1942, when the OK Orchard Development Company was formed, there were only 1,200 acres of "O" nut trees under cultivation. A majority of these trees were approaching a state of maturity, and the production of raw unshelled nuts approximated 150,000 pounds. Many of these trees were originally planted to be sold as seedlings and not for the production of nuts. The yield of most trees at this time was as low as one-fifth to one-tenth of the expected yield of the varieties developed and subsequently planted by the OK Orchard Development Company.

Few new plantings were made between 1942 and 1948 because of World War II and the numerous and more fruitful opportunities available to investors during that period. In addition, the existing, rapidly maturing trees provided a supply of "O" nuts which was neither easily harvested nor disposed of profitably in view of existing labor, equipment, and transportation problems. In the mid-1950s the OK Orchard Development Company sensed a change in existing conditions and, on the basis of an expected major increase in the demand for "O" nuts, purchased 3,000 acres of timberland suitable for growing "O" nut trees. Within a few years 1,000 acres of this land had been cleared and planted with approximately 70,000 newly grafted "O" nut trees. This planting represented a potential increase of tenfold or more in the future supply of "O" nuts and temporarily discouraged newcomers from entering the field.

At the time the OK Orchard Development Company sold out to O-Nut, Incorporated, there were approximately 2,500 acres of "O" nut trees under cultivation. Excluding O-Nut, Incorporated, the largest of the growers owned 400 acres of 3- to 5-year-old trees in the non-bearing stage. These trees were of a variety similar to those being grown by O-Nut, Incorporated. The remaining 1,100 acres under cultivation were owned by 13 independent firms and consisted of 500 acres of 7- to 9-year-old currently bearing trees and 600 acres of mature and over-mature low-yield trees. In addition to O-Nut's 2,000 acres of cleared land, other producers had available an additional 1,000 acres of land suitable for growing "O" nut trees. The 600 acres of low-yield trees could be converted to the latest varieties of high-yield trees by re-grafting. Such trees would be of bearing age within 4 to 5 years after regrafting, which would be at least 3 years prior to any yields available from new plantings made at the same time.

A major foreign nut producer was known to have been investigating the profit potential of "O" nuts. If this firm decided to enter the field it was conjectured that it would do so by purchasing numerous mature and overmature orchards, including connecting lands, and thus be able to substantially increase yields within 5 years from the entry date into the field. The financial capabilities of this foreign firm equaled or exceeded those of O-Nut, Incorporated, and its parent company, United Nut Growers.

Original plantings of "O" nut trees were made by grafting cuttings from prize growing stock to select 2-year-old nursery grown rootstock. These trees yielded their first fruits in 7 to 8 years after their grafting date. Planting could also be accomplished by regrafting to mature rootstock resulting in initial yields within 4 to 5 years after the regrafting was made. No appreciable difference in the overall yield pattern appeared to exist between new grafts and regrafts except for the approximately 3-year difference in time between grafting and initial yields. Due to the need for more careful grafting and extensive root pruning and culturing required by regrafts, the original cost of regrafting was approximately double that of purchasing and planting newly grafted trees which currently averaged $10 per tree. Part of this difference was recovered by the reduced maintenance resulting from the shorter non-bearing period of regrafted trees. Once a regraft was attempted, whether successful or not, further regrafting was inadvisable. The survival rate for new grafts was approximately 90 to 95 per cent, as compared to 70 or 80 per cent for first regrafts. For second, third, or additional regrafts the survival rate approached zero. Under ideal conditions a maximum success rate of less than 25 per cent had been achieved on second regrafts. Tree removal costs were estimated to average $5 per tree when regrafting or replanting previously planted areas.

"O" nut trees reached a maximum height of 45 feet and were planted approximately 25 feet apart. Somewhere between the eleventh and thirteenth year (the eighth and eleventh year for regrafts) the trees had to be thinned by 50 per cent to provide 35 feet of space between trees. If adequate spacing of trees was not provided, excess shading resulted and the nuts did not ripen properly. Experience indicated that as much as an 80 per cent loss in a crop could occur from overshading. Exhibit 1 gives the expected average-yield pattern for "O" nut trees of the variety existing on O-Nut, Incorporated, properties. Research with new varieties of "O" nut trees had developed trees with yields up to 25 per cent greater than those currently existing in O-Nut orchards. Indications were that further research might develop even more bountiful varieties. No other significant differences in the overall yield pattern or maturity rate had appeared.

Harvesting of "O" nuts was seasonal in nature and occurred during the months of September, October, November, and December. The mature nuts fell to the ground before being harvested. Since the nuts could not safely be allowed to remain on the ground more than sixty days without significant deterioration, they were harvested twice during the season.

Harvesting was done by handpicking nuts that had fallen to the ground. The majority of pickers were women between the ages of thirty and forty-five years. Harvesters were generally employed on a four-month basis and recruited through ads in the daily newspapers. Since worker qualifications included only a willingness to work and a strong back, applicants were given a minimal screening before being hired. The major elements in the screening process were a check of previous employment records with the firm, a check with the local police, and a physical examination to detect any back, leg, or neck injuries which might hinder the worker. Upon employment each harvester was given a pair of shoes, a pair of gloves, and a harvesting bag. This equipment was either new or used, depending on what sizes were available in used equipment. Employees were expected to return this equipment at the end of the season. Any equipment that was lost was paid for by the picker at a price equal to the company's cost of the equipment. The average cost of hiring, equipping, and terminating was approximately $30 per employee. The cost was relatively independent of whether the employee worked the full four months or some shorter time. Full-term employees generally wore their equipment quite ragged, whereas short-term employees often absconded with their equipment.

Harvesters were paid on an hourly basis and received a wage of approximately $1.38 per hour with no fringe benefits. The expected output was 1,100 pounds of nuts per picker per day. The labor market had been extremely favorable for the employer but was becoming increasingly tight as the overall production of "O" nuts increased and demand for harvesters increased. The future labor market was expected to become less favorable to the employer unless mechanical harvesting, which was still in an experimental stage, was quickly introduced and accepted.

Two of the larger and older orchards, partially owned by an orchard equipment producer, were experimenting with a newly designed mechanical harvester. Several of the existing "O" nut producers were considering a changeover in harvesting techniques pending conclusive evidence regarding the economics of mechanical harvesting. To date only preliminary results and engineering specifications were available. A fully documented report on the results of the experiments conducted was expected to be completed and released within three months. Some preliminary cost figures provided by the equipment manufacturer were included among the records of the OK Orchard Development Company.

The figures indicated that to facilitate the use of a mechanical harvester the ground surrounding each tree had to be leveled, graded, and surfaced with a 4-inch layer of pea gravel or volcanic ash. This required several tons of gravel per tree and was estimated to cost $300 per acre complete, including grading, leveling, gravel, and surfacing. This special preparation was required because of the rocky nature of the soil (3- to 6-inch-diameter rocks). The mechanical harvester accomplished its task by scooping up a ¼- to ½-inch layer of gravel including any fallen nuts, separating the nuts from the gravel by a screening process, and redepositing the gravel. Once applied the gravel surfacing was estimated to last a minimum of 20 years. When the surface became too thin, a 1- to 2-inch layer of gravel could be added to the top of the existing surface. The need for a 4-inch initial layer arose from the need to cover the numerous rocks in the orchards.

The price of a mechanical harvester which the equipment manufacturer had proposed to OK Orchard was $40,000. It was designed to harvest 20 to 25 acres per day depending on the planting configuration. The proposed mechanical harvester had a specified capacity of over 2½ times that of the two experimental harvesters in existence and was recommended on the basis of future needs. The differences in the initial cost and operating cost were substantially less than 2½ times that of the lower capacity machines. The price quoted was 1½ times that of the smaller machine and operating and maintenance costs were estimated to be only 80 per cent greater. A machine of intermediate capacity was not considered practical as it would require the same number of operating personnel and would provide a negligible original cost saving.

The harvester required three full-time operators and when moving from one area to another had a maximum speed of 5 miles per hour. Considering the difficulty of retraining competent skilled help on a part-time basis it was recommended that these employees be hired on a full-time basis and be used elsewhere during the non-harvesting season. This was consistent with the experience of most employers who found it advantageous to maintain truck drivers and similarly skilled personnel on a full-time basis even though this skill could be utilized for as little as 25 per cent of the employee's total activities. This, however, presupposed that the employee could be used to perform some useful secondary task when not occupied in performing his primary function. It was estimated that employees capable of being trained to operate and service the proposed mechanical harvester could be found and retained at a wage rate of approximately $2.50 per hour. In view of the difficulty in retraining skilled help on anything but a day shift basis and the added risk to the equipment and the operators resulting from nighttime operation, single-shift operation of the harvester was recommended. The equipment required daily maintenance and cleaning of approximately 4 man-hours. This could be performed by one to four individuals in substantially the same number of total man-hours of effort. It was felt that several of the currently employed individuals could perform this task. Gasoline, oil, and other operating and maintenance expenses were estimated at $5,000 per year per 8-hour shift. This cost would increase proportionately for any usage beyond the estimated 40 hours per week. Current delivery time for the proposed piece of equipment was 8 months from the order date.

Total single shift capacity of "O" nut processing plants was approximately 3,000,000 pounds of raw nuts per year. Approximately 80 per cent of the existing processing facilities was owned or controlled by a single distributor. "O" nut growers were responsible for delivering their harvest to a local pickup point where they were graded, weighed, and transferred to railroad cars which delivered them to the processing plant.

"O" nuts arrived at the processing plant in a paperlike husk. The husks were removed by tumbling the nuts in a high-velocity wind chamber. After this the nuts were placed in large dehydrators where they remained for at least two weeks. Once dehydrated the nuts could be kept for ten to fourteen months, which allowed the remaining processing to be conducted throughout the year rather than being required immediately following the harvesting period. Between the husking and dehydrating operations all nuts were inspected visually and any defective nuts removed.

After dehydration the nuts were graded for size and weighed into 300-pound batches to enter the final processing. The nuts proceeded to one of seven cracking machines, each machine being set up to process a specific size range. Good nuts were separated from spoiled nuts, shells, and other foreign matter by a flotation process. The good nuts sank to the bottom of the tank, whereas shells and other foreign matter remained on top. Immediately after flotation the good nuts were partially dried in a large centrifuge and, after another visual inspection, each batch passed through a flash dehydrator where any remaining traces of water or excess moisture were removed. After this second dehydration each batch was laboratory tested for moisture content, taste, and other properties. The nuts were then ready for roasting, final inspection, salting, and packaging. After roasting, the nuts were no longer separated by size and were processed in a continuous rather than a batch type process. Final packaging consisted of vacuum packing the processed nuts in unlabeled glass jars. Labels were applied just prior to shipping the processed nuts to local and regional distribution points. The approximate retail selling price of processed "O" nuts was $2.50 per pound.

Information obtained from the more successful of the two small independent processors indicated that the smallest economic unit of processing capacity was 400,000 pounds of raw nuts per shift per year. Larger plants essentially consisted of multiples of this basic unit of capacity. The current cost per basic unit of capacity (400,000 pounds of raw nuts per year) was $375,000, excluding building and installation costs. Processing costs, excluding the cost of raw nuts, averaged $0.05 per pound of raw nuts. This was equivalent to approximately $0.25 per pound of packaged nuts, since the weight loss due to shelling, de-hydration, roasting, and inferior-quality nuts averaged 80 per cent of the initial gross weight of the raw nuts. Due to the difficulty of obtaining sufficient quantities of skilled help, most processing plants also operated on a single-shift basis. The independent processor, however, from whom the majority of the cost information was obtained, was operating on a two-shift basis. Due to maintenance and other problems the second shift was from 20 to 25 per cent less productive than the first shift.

The only quantitative information immediately available for making a reasonable long-range estimate of potential "O" nut sales was current and past sales of other varieties of nuts and condiments. After examining a substantial amount of data the following conclusions were drawn:

1. From a purely objective standpoint, i.e., nutritional value, taste, stability, etc., "O" nuts were comparable to other common nuts such as walnuts, filberts, pecans, and almonds.

2. From a marketing, promotional, and processing standpoint the "O" nut industry was 15 to 25 years junior to any of the major nut industries.

3. With efficient promotion techniques and good fortune the "O" nut industry could achieve the current status of the major nut industries within 10 to 15 years.

4. A reasonably attainable 3- to 5-year goal for "O" nut sales would be a sales rate equivalent to that of filbert sales (16,000,000 pounds of raw nuts per year).

5. An optimistic yet potentially attainable 10- to 15-year goal for "O" nut sales would be a sales rate equivalent to that of walnut sales (160,000,000 pounds of raw nuts per year).

6. To achieve either of these goals "O" nuts would have to be made available in a variety of forms and prices comparable to that of the currently major nuts on either a weight or volume basis.

Exhibit 2 is an abbreviated balance sheet for O-Nut, Incorporated, immediately after acquisition of the assets of the OK Orchard Develop-ment Company. At the time of transfer, the OK Orchard Development Company employed 35 full-time employees who received an average pay of $2 per hour. These employees were nonunionized although a majority were believed to favor a union shop. During the non-harvesting season these employees performed such tasks as pruning, fertilizing, spraying, and maintaining the grounds and equipment. It appeared that they could continue to carry out this function as long as the number of trees under cultivation did not exceed 65,000. During the harvesting season these employees assisted in the harvest by acting as field supervisors and recorders, by operating local collecting stations, and by operating a shuttle service between the pickers and the local collecting stations and between the local collecting stations and the processor's pickup point.

It appeared that unless mechanical harvesting was adopted these tasks could not be performed by the 35 full-time employees after an annual yield of 5,000,000 pounds or more was achieved. The mechanical harvester would eliminate the need for field supervisors and recorders. Local collecting stations, nevertheless, would have to be retained unless a road system capable of supporting large trucks was installed throughout the orchard. However, the shuttling of nuts from the single mechanical picker to the collecting station would be considerably more efficient than from the many handpickers. An opinion had been expressed that if mechanical picking was adopted the current full-time non-harvest work crew could support the full potential harvest of the 65,000 trees currently under cultivation.

The only other major expense of operating the orchard was for materials required to maintain the trees and grounds. This amounted to approximately $2 per tree per year and was expected to slowly increase until the trees reached full maturity, at which time it would probably level off at approximately $2.40 per tree per year.

United Nut Growers and Processors of Jamaica, Incorporated, as full owners of O-Nut Incorporated, directed Jim Powers and his management team to carry out the following objectives:

1. Become the world's leading integrated producer, processor, and distributor of "O" nuts and "O" nut products
2. Attain and secure an industry leadership position by becoming and remaining the world's most efficient and low-cost producer, processor, and distributor of "O" nuts and "O" nut products
3. Promote the growth and profit potential of the "O" nut industry to the greatest extent economically feasible
4. Design an initial five-year program which would operate within the bounds of sound financial policy and limit the issuance of additional common voting stock to 80 per cent of that currently outstanding

# EXHIBIT 1

## Expected yield pattern for O-Nut, Incorporated, trees

(Yield in pounds per tree)

| Age | Yield |
|-----|-------|
| 1–6 | 0 |
| 7 | 20 |
| 8 | 40 |
| 9 | 80 |
| 10 | 100 |
| 11 | 120 |
| 12 | 160 |
| 13 | 160 |
| 14 | 140 |
| 15 | 140 |
| 16 | 120* |

* Fifteen per cent annual decrease for all subsequent years.

# EXHIBIT 2

## Balance sheet, January 1

| Current Assets | | | Current Liabilities | | |
|---|---|---|---|---|---|
| Cash | $ | 125,000 | Payables | $ | 45,000 |
| Securities | | 2,000,000 | Other | | 5,000 |
| Receivables | | 4,000 | Total | $ | 50,000 |
| Inventories | | 40,000 | | | |
| Goodwill | | 1,000 | *Fixed Liabilities* | | |
| Total | | $2,170,000 | OK Orchard Development Company | | 3,000,000 |
| *Fixed Assets* | | | *Net Worth* | | |
| Trees | | $2,950,000 | 100,000 shares common stocks | | |
| Equipment | | 150,000 | (100 per cent owned by | | |
| Buildings | | 125,000 | United Nut Growers and | | |
| Land | | 1,275,000 | Processors) | | 3,620,000 |
| Total | | $4,500,000 | | | |
| Total assets | | $6,670,000 | Total liabilities and net worth | | $6,670,000 |

# DISCUSSION QUESTIONS

1. Prepare annual estimates for 10 years for the following: physical characteristics (trees, yields, seasonal employees, etc.); profit and loss statement; and balance sheet. The estimates are to be based on the following assumptions:

   a. No additional trees are planted.

   b. No existing trees are regrafted.

   c. All yields are as shown in Exhibit 1.

   d. Trees must be thinned to 35-foot spacing after the harvest at age twelve.

   e. Harvesting is done manually at existing wages and production rates.

   f. All raw nuts produced can be sold at $0.13 per pound.

   g. Costs for purchasing, grafting, planting, and maintenance of "O" nut trees are capitalized until the initial year of yield of the trees (year 7 for new grafts and year 4 for regrafts).

   h. Capitalized costs on trees are depreciated at a rate of 10 per cent per year until fully depreciated, starting with the year the trees begin to produce a yield. If a tree is cut before it is completely depreciated, the remaining book value is immediately charged to current expenses.

   i. Tree maintenance costs are charged to current expenses after the trees begin to produce a yield.

   j. The marginal tax rate is 48 per cent of taxable profits.

   k. Executive salaries and expenses remain at $45,000 per year.

   l. O-Nut's indebtedness is interest-free if retired on schedule.

   m. Depreciation to be on a straight line basis at the rate of 10 per cent per year for buildings and 15 per cent per year for equipment.

   n. All other factors remain constant.

2. Based on their current operating situation, prepare an estimated monthly cash flow statement for the first year of operations for O-Nut, Incorporated. Assume harvest receipts are received at the end of October and December and estimated taxes are paid on a quarterly basis.

3. Prepare a projection of the potential production of raw "O" nuts for the total industry for the next ten years, assuming no new plantings.

4. What factors must be given consideration in developing an overall plan of operation?

5. What investment opportunities are available to O-Nut, Incorporated? What are the approximate funds available? How would you proceed to evaluate each investment opportunity?

6. Assume that current manual harvesting methods and costs remain constant. What rate of return is indicated by converting to mechanical harvesting? Do you recommend a change to mechanical harvesting? Why?

7. Assume that new trees would be planted at 25- or 35-foot intervals and that items (c) through (n) of question 1 apply. What would be the maximum long-run rate of return available from new plantings for:

*a.* Replanting cycle using new trees only

*b.* Replanting cycle using regrafts

Specify the cutting years for each alternative used to obtain your answers.

8. What are the factors you should consider and how would you go about determining an overall optimal plan on a long-term basis? Clearly identify what "optimal" means in this situation.

9. Evaluate the policies of operating the processing plants on a single-shift or multiple-shift basis.

10. What problems does O-Nut face and what strategy should they follow to "become the world's leading integrated producer, processor, and distributor of O nuts and O nut products"?

# REFERENCES

Folts, Franklin E.: *Introduction to Industrial Management,* 5th ed. (New York: McGraw-Hill Book Company, 1963), pp. 136–222, 477–499.

Grant, Eugene L., and Grant W. Ireson: *Principles of Engineering Economy* (New York: The Ronald Press Company, 1960), pp. 76–95.

Magee, John F.: *Production Planning and Inventory Control* (New York: McGraw-Hill Book Company, 1958), pp. 133–161.

Mayer, Raymond R.: *Production Management* (New York: McGraw-Hill Book Company, 1962), pp. 227–257, 606–626.

Moore, Franklin G.: *Manufacturing Management* (Homewood, Ill.: Richard D. Irwin, Inc., 1961), pp. 89–157.

# OSBURN MANUFACTURING COMPANY

The Osburn Manufacturing Company had an excellent record of making deliveries on schedule. At times, however, the cost of maintaining this on-schedule delivery had been high. The delivery record had been maintained by intensive expediting, adding shop personnel, overtime work, and a complex system of priorities which, when used, had required the rescheduling of most of the work a second time and often a third time.

The Osburn Manufacturing Company manufactured electric generators, mostly for the commercial market, but the company also was engaged in certain military work. The total work load was divided among three projects:

*Project A* was a commercial contract of large volume. The schedule policy associated with this project was to meet all scheduled delivery dates. Fabrication time schedule allowances were standard; however, they could be compressed by 50 per cent whenever necessary to maintain delivery schedules.

*Project B* was a commercial program which had been in production for three years. The schedule allowances were standard and reorder for the fabrication or purchase of parts was based on minimum bundle breakage (i.e., when existing quantities of available parts awaiting subassembly or assembly were reduced to predetermined levels a reorder was initiated for fabrication or purchase as required). Schedule allowances could be compressed 50 per cent in certain instances.

*Project C* was a new military contract of great importance. This project had top military priority as well as top priority within the Osburn

Manufacturing Company. Engineering design had not been finalized and many changes were being made in the design of the product.

John Jostad, the manufacturing manager of the Osburn Manufacturing Company, was in charge of the entire manufacturing operation (see Exhibit 1). Reporting to Jostad were the director of industrial engineering, the director of manufacturing shops, and the directors of projects A, B, and C. The industrial engineering group was responsible for scheduling, shop loading, and work order releases. The manufacturing shops fabricated the detailed parts, and the subassembly and final assembly were accomplished in shops under the direction of one of the three project directors.

The production schedule was prepared by the industrial engineering group. The procedure was to work back from a specified delivery date to determine when each operation should start. A simplified flow schedule is shown in Exhibit 2 to illustrate this procedure. The delivery date is shown as work day 150, the final assembly requires 15 days and is scheduled to begin on day 135, subassemblies are scheduled for completion on day 130 to allow time to deliver them to the final assembly area, etc.

Certain of the flow times were accepted as standard. For example, five days were allowed as an average flow time to transport materials, parts, or subassemblies between departments. The time allowed to fabricate parts or complete assemblies was estimated in man-hours and based on the average time required to complete identical or similar jobs in the past.

The industrial engineering group knew the capacity of each shop in terms of man-hours of output and would schedule the work into each shop accordingly. The work orders were numbered and sent to the shop in blocks. When an engineering change occurred, a new work order was issued to replace the one canceled by the change. The shops were instructed to work on the orders according to their number sequence; however, it was understood that the shop foreman could change the sequence to improve the effectiveness of work assignments in his shop.

Orders were regarded as behind schedule when the shops indicated they could not complete an order and deliver it to the next assembly area according to the stated schedule. The flow time could be compressed, however, by working overtime on the order, by providing special delivery service to the in-process part, or by performing assembly work between the regular work stations.

The scheduling policies used by the Osburn Manufacturing Company were as follows:

1. Component schedules were to support delivery of the end-item with adequate flow time allowance for each step involved in the transfer, inspection, paper flow, assembly, testing, and delivery of the end product.

2. The sales group had to consider standard manufacturing flow time requirements when negotiating contracts; however, sales should have sufficient latitude to be competitive on delivery schedules.

3. Other considerations in scheduling included the volume to be produced, the fabrication shop loads, the fabrication shop capacity, and the availability of outside sources of supply.

4. All work was to be scheduled on the basis of standard flow times for the part concerned. All orders were to be worked in sequence, according to the manufacturing work order number.

5. The fabrication shops had to periodically report work orders as "ahead," "current," or "behind" schedule.

6. Whenever behind-schedule fabrication orders exceeded manufacturing capacity for the month ahead, an initial priority was issued for the more urgent work orders.

7. When orders with priority exceeded the manufacturing capacity for the month ahead, a second, higher priority was issued and assigned to the most urgent work orders. At this point the higher priority took precedence over the previous priority. If the backlog of work orders continued to grow, then additional higher levels of priorities would be issued in turn, each subsequent priority class being effective until the capacity was saturated with its work orders. At that point another higher level of priorities was necessary. For example, if the manufacturing capacity of a shop was 100 units a month, and there were more than 100 units scheduled for the shop, a priority was established. If the work orders with the priority exceeded 100 units, they were reclassified into two levels of priorities, e.g., A and AA.

Although the amount of work involved in each order varied, the shops had processed between 280 and 320 orders per month during the previous year. Project C was integrated into the production schedule of the Osburn Manufacturing Company about July 1. The work order releases during the following twelve months are summarized in Exhibit 3. Shortly after the start of project C the number of work orders behind schedule increased. This is summarized in Exhibit 4.

John Jostad attributed the increase in the work orders behind schedule to (1) the additional work load imposed on the fabrication shops, (2) the large number of releases which did not include a sufficient flow time, (3) the large number of changes in design (whenever the design was changed a new work order was released), and (4) the added shop work required when the orders were grouped by priorities and not according to the most efficient manner of production.

In November, priority A was assigned to those orders behind schedule, and a higher priority, AA, to the orders in project C which were behind schedule. Both of these priorities authorized overtime work in the shops. Shortly after priority AA was established, the directors of the other two projects complained that their projects were suffering because the manufacture of the detailed parts for their projects was delayed due to the preference given parts being manufactured for project C. They asked Jostad for a special priority for selected orders relating to their projects.

Jostad decided to review the entire system of priorities and its impact on the present situation. He found that 84 per cent of all orders processed during May had been assigned a priority and that most of the orders for detailed parts had been produced in quantities of less than one-half the original specified lot size. Reducing quantities had been necessary to satisfy the immediate demands of the assembly lines for the three projects. The use of direct and indirect man-hours associated with the production planning, control, and operation of the fabrication shops is summarized in Exhibit 5.

S. G. Patten, the director of project A, was very upset about the entire system of priorities. He believed that the entire future of the company depended on whether or not Jostad took some action to correct the situation. To make this point and vent his feelings he sent a letter to Jostad (Exhibit 6).

# EXHIBIT 1
## Organization chart

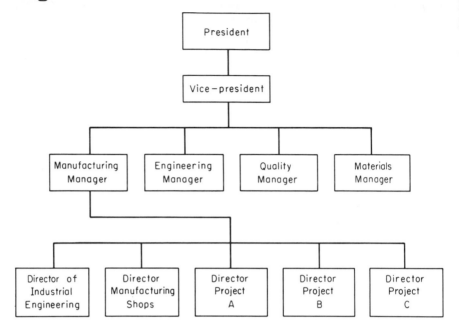

# EXHIBIT 2
## Sample schedule flow chart

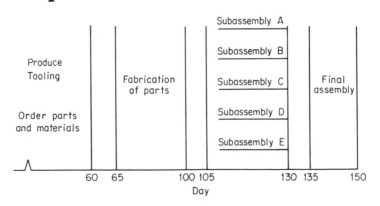

# EXHIBIT 3

## Work order releases

| Month | Project A | Project B | Project C | Total |
|---|---|---|---|---|
| July | 120 | 60 | 120 | 300 |
| August | 80 | 80 | 140 | 300 |
| September | 70 | 90 | 160 | 320 |
| October | 40 | 170 | 200 | 410 |
| November | 70 | 60 | 300 | 430 |
| December | 30 | 80 | 280 | 390 |
| January | 40 | 90 | 200 | 330 |
| February | 60 | 80 | 180 | 320 |
| March | 80 | 110 | 160 | 350 |
| April | 60 | 60 | 240 | 360 |
| May | 40 | 80 | 260 | 380 |
| June | 60 | 70 | 210 | 340 |
| Total | | | | 4,230 |

# EXHIBIT 4

## Work orders behind schedule

| Month | Project A | Project B | Project C | Total |
|---|---|---|---|---|
| July | 4 | 2 | 0 | 6 |
| August | 4 | 3 | 0 | 7 |
| September | 6 | 2 | 12 | 20 |
| October | 7 | 4 | 140 | 151 |
| November | 14 | 40 | 260 | 314 |
| December | 70 | 60 | 220 | 350 |
| January | 71 | 80 | 260 | 411 |
| February | 80 | 90 | 250 | 420 |
| March | 90 | 110 | 260 | 460 |
| April | 100 | 120 | 290 | 510 |
| May | 100 | 130 | 340 | 570 |
| June | 110 | 130 | 370 | 610 |

# EXHIBIT 5

## Direct and indirect man-hours, fabrication shops

|  | Man-hours, thousands | |
| --- | --- | --- |
| Month | Direct | Indirect |
| July | 81 | 60 |
| August | 80 | 62 |
| September | 82 | 64 |
| October | 83 | 64 |
| November | 106 | 64 |
| December | 110 | 72 |
| January | 105 | 84 |
| February | 112 | 96 |
| March | 114 | 98 |
| April | 108 | 98 |
| May | 120 | 102 |
| June | 130 | 106 |

# EXHIBIT 6

To:        John Jostad
From:      S. G. Patten
Subject:   Scheduling

Lest you feel that the parable I am going to write and the comparison I am going to make is facetious, let me assure you that it is with only a sincere desire to see a ghastly condition corrected that I illustrate it in this manner.

One time there were two cities—Johnstown and Smithtown—located fifty miles apart. There were four intermittent towns between these cities and in a direct line with each other, spaced ten miles apart.

A railroad was organized and single rails with periodic sidings were laid to join the two cities and pass through each of the interspaced towns. Trains were made up and scheduled to run regularly from one city to the other. Things went smoothly at first and the trains maintained their schedules.

Certain commitments were made by the railroad to deliver merchandise from one end of the line to the other end of the line. Soon, however, it was discovered that sometimes the promised time of arrival for some merchandise had arrived or had passed and the merchandise had not even been loaded in a car. This necessitated forced concentration on loading a car with the late merchandise and dispatching an engine under a special flag and with cleared track to rush the car through to the consignee.

This resulted in the other cars and trains along the railroad line going into sidings at each of the towns to let the Special through. This affected their schedule and made them late, causing in some cases an angry consignee to remind the railroad that his delivery date was not being met. The railroad, to meet this new urgent obligation, would dispatch this particular car or cars with special engine and flag to rush it through.

Daily more trains would start behind schedule and some of these would leave the yards with a "highball" special flag to clear the tracks. Those cars and trains that did start on scheduled time soon were forced on sidings so many times that they too fell behind schedule and were "specialed" to rush them through.

The train crews became more and more confused, trying to get all Specials through together on a single track.

Finally the railroad management concluded that the single flag would indicate just the Special, but two flags, one above the other, on the engine would give preference over just ordinary Specials.

With a sigh of relief, they sat back and congratulated each other on this simple solution.

Soon, however, they discovered most of the engines were pulling a Super-Special car with two flags.

Ah, now here was a problem! A conference was hastily called and it was decided that to get the trains through that were really important, they would fly a flag from the engine bearing a picture of the railroad president.

Now the really "hot" trains would surely get through; Specials and Super-Specials could and would go on sidings.

Soon it became impossible to assure any consignee that his car would arrive on time even though he might have it on a Special or a Super-Special train. If he couldn't promote a "picture of the president" flag on the engine he would just have to wait.

In the early days of the railroad, Sunday was designated as a day to check, maintain, and repair equipment to keep it in proper running order. But the press of Specials, Super-Specials, and Picture Flag Specials became so great that, although the same number of trains were running, they had to highball each car out of the yard as soon as it was loaded and the door shut. Seven days of each week were now required to get the trains through and there was little or no time for maintenance.

It became positively hazardous to try to cross the track because of Specials, Super-Specials, and Picture Flag Specials whizzing by at all hours.

The consignees finally became so disgusted with the service that they transferred their business to competing truck lines servicing the cities. The railroad promptly became bankrupt and went into receivership.

A new company was formed and a complete investigation was made to determine how conditions could be corrected to restore the confidence of the shippers in schedule commitments made by the railroad.

They discovered that if cars were loaded promptly and dispatched from the yards on the promised starting date, they nearly always arrived on time. The need for Specials was rare, but when required they did receive prompt attention because the train crews now felt that a Special must really be important.

Are we, too, following the example of the first railroad organization? Will we meet the same fate? To illustrate just how serious this condition is, please observe our current situation closely.

# DISCUSSION QUESTIONS

1. How serious is the situation at the Osburn Manufacturing Company?
2. Evaluate the organizational arrangement of the management.
3. How can John Jostad revise the priority system?
4. Should the Osburn Manufacturing Company slide the delivery schedule? Why?
5. How can work from different sections of the company be integrated and scheduled fairly?

# REFERENCES

Bethel, Lawrence L., Franklin S. Atwater, George H. E. Smith, and Harvey A. Stackman, Jr.: *Industrial Organization and Management*, 4th ed. (New York: McGraw-Hill Book Company, 1962), pp. 216–262.

Buffa, Elwood S.: *Modern Production Management* (New York: John Wiley & Sons, Inc., 1961), pp. 441–474.

Timms, Howard L.: *The Production Function in Business* (Homewood, Ill.: Richard D. Irwin, Inc., 1962), pp. 436–471.

# OTHELLO PRODUCTS, INCORPORATED

Othello Products, Incorporated, consisted of a plant and office area of 60,000 square feet and employed 150 hourly and 32 salaried employees. Othello had been primarily a job shop operation producing various sized lots of medium- to high-quality precision parts for a large number of local consumer goods manufacturers. For many years the volume of work in the shop had fluctuated widely from period to period. Consequently, Othello employees were either operating under "make work" or "get it out at any cost" conditions. This constant alternation between feast and famine caused numerous supervisory and managerial problems.

Labor turnover and efficiency were among the most important of these problems. Historically, Othello had little difficulty in acquiring a fair share of the local subcontracting business. Recently, however, an increasing proportion of contract invitations upon which Othello submitted bids were lost to local competitors on the basis of excessive prices. Although this was never directly stated, there appeared to be no other reason since all of Othello's customers repeatedly commented on Othello's almost impeccable quality and delivery performance.

To combat rising costs and excessive employee turnover, the management of Othello initiated two new major programs. The first of these was a work standards program, and the second a program directed toward finding kinds of work which would provide some long-term stability to Othello's volume of business.

The work standards program was designed to provide eventually a method for economically placing valid production rates on every operation of every work order issued to Othello's manufacturing organization. Considerable thought had been given to this problem. Among the alternatives considered and rejected were historical standards, MTM, BMT, stopwatch time study, and others.[1]

Historical standards previously accumulated within the company on an informal basis appeared to be of little value as it was common knowledge that low-cost production had not been one of Othello's points of strength, and to perpetuate past performance was the last thing desired. Since Othello had not officially used production standards in the past, their introduction would probably meet with considerable resistance. An arbitrary overall across-the-board increase of past performance to establish new standards did not appear appropriate. It was felt that unless the standards which would be set could be individually defended and represented reasonable and attainable levels of output, the entire venture would probably fail. MTM, BMT, and stopwatch time study offered acceptable methods from an accuracy standpoint but were considered to be uneconomical because of the large number of constantly changing items produced by Othello.

The use of predetermined standards that had elements considerably larger than those utilized in MTM and BMT studies, and somewhat comparable to those used in the determination of standard times by means of stopwatch time study, appeared to be the most reasonable solution. A review was made of available packaged plans of this nature offered by several management consultant firms. Three manufacturers were interviewed who had tried such plans, and on the basis of their advice the idea was rejected. Two complaints to such an approach were stated repeatedly: one was that the employees would not approve an arbitrary setting of standards based upon the selection and application of a fully preconceived scheme, and the second was that in each case where predetermined standards were adopted a major training and adaptation period was required. During this period the proper use of the data was learned and corrections in the data made to meet the particular situation of the using firm. In almost all cases employee relations were severely stressed. One of the firms contacted by Othello representatives ventured the opinion that if it had developed its own set of predetermined time standards, natural learning would have occurred and an overall smoother transition would have been achieved. The major advantage of the prepackaged scheme, however, was that it could be placed into effect more quickly and offered a method to achieve immediate improvement, although possibly at the cost of an overall lesser long-run improvement. No specific facts or figures had been obtained to verify or negate these

---

[1] MTM refers to "method time measurement" and BMT refers to "basic motion time study," which are systems of predetermined standard times for selected elemental motions.

statements. On this basis Othello's management decided to develop its own set of standards.

As an initial step in this direction stopwatch time studies of over 800 basic operations performed on Othello's facilities were made. After the task of collecting the time studies was completed, the individual operational elements from these studies were to be sorted, classified, and cross-referenced. The final step would be to develop a set of predetermined standard times particularly applicable to Othello's operation. It was hoped that this information would provide a means for making economical and accurate cost estimates, for setting valid shop production standards, and for controlling overall manufacturing costs. It was anticipated that this basic set of standard data would be ready for use within three weeks.

The second program consisted of an all-out effort to find one or more long-term products or contracts. An ideal product was believed to be one which was compact, easy to store, labor intensive, and yet relatively simple to manufacture. It was felt that if the product could be manufactured for inventory during slack periods, it could provide one means of leveling the overall production rate and labor force required by the firm. Also, if the product was simple to manufacture, the firm's basic labor force could be gainfully employed on this item when business was slack, and new and short-term employees could be assigned to this product during peak productive periods. After a search of approximately one year, one such product was identified. A sketch of a commercial version of this product is shown in Exhibit 1.

The product was a compact, variable-speed gear reducer used by a large conveyor manufacturer for whom Othello had previously made numerous experimental parts. The reducer appeared ideal in that the components required a considerable amount of medium-precision machining using equipment which Othello currently had available. Over 85 per cent of the reducer's finished cost (excluding overhead and profit) consisted of direct labor. The conveyor manufacturer planned to subcontract the job and had issued an invitation for bids for the first production lot to a group of selected suppliers who were known to be competent in this kind of work. All that the executives of Othello felt was required to obtain the contract was to submit a tight and accurate bid.

Since Othello had made most of the parts for the experimental model, they had relatively complete information regarding the raw material cost and machining requirements of the component parts. Actual stopwatch time studies on many of the machine operations required had been made. It was believed that it would be easy to obtain accurate estimates of the remaining machining operations by applying the standard time data which were scheduled to be available well ahead of the final date for submitting the bid. The major unsolved problem was to determine the assembly costs and allowances for cost reductions expected from high-volume continuous production.

In order to obtain accurate assembly costs, several workers and a process engineer were assigned the task of devising an appropriate assembly procedure. The data in Exhibit 2 are the result of these efforts. To obtain these data each worker was allowed, uninstructed but under the surveillance of the process engineer, five times to assemble and disassemble a reducer which had been obtained from the prospective customer. The experience gained was pooled and from the best method used by the various workers thirty-four basic assembly operations were defined. Each of these operations was then time studied using stopwatch techniques and also analyzed in terms of MTM. In most cases the two methods were within a range of $\pm 10$ per cent of each other, i.e., the stopwatch time $\pm 10$ per cent would include the MTM time. In such instances the times shown in Exhibit 2 represent the average of the standard unit times determined by each of these methods. In those instances where the MTM standard time per cycle was more than 10 per cent above the stopwatch time study standard, the stopwatch standard was selected. In cases where the MTM standard time per cycle was below the stopwatch standard by more than 10 per cent, the standard selected was the stopwatch standard less 10 per cent. This was done to provide a reasonable assurance that the workmen would be able to achieve the estimated production rate.

Both the time study and MTM standards were based on 100 per cent performance: this being the output which was expected from an average experienced worker having reasonable skill in the type of operation performed and working at a natural rate of speed. Since the time studies were made on employees who were considered to be relatively inexperienced in assembly work, an 85 per cent skill rating was assigned to all operations. Because of the highly cooperative spirit of the employees, however, practically all operations were rated for effort at or above 115 per cent. Thus, in almost all cases the stopwatch standards determined were met or exceeded in the actual assembly trials.

The only remaining task with regard to estimating the assembly cost was to lay out the assembly process in terms of specific work stations and determine the equipment and labor costs. It was a company policy to maintain good working conditions, and thus it was felt that the design of work stations should provide each employee with a minimum of 5 linear feet of work space along the assembly line. This was considered possible since an area 85 feet in length and 25 feet in width was available for the placement of the line and for in-process parts storage areas. It was felt that the entire line should be conveyorized as this would substantially reduce the problem of maintaining efficient performance. Estimates of conveyor costs indicated that the belt conveyor required for activities "a" through "d" of Exhibit 2 would cost about $2,800, plus $150 per lineal foot of conveyor. This was essentially a belt conveyor from which parts could be removed for processing and replaced for transporting to the next work station.

A chain conveyor was suggested for activities "e" through "ai" of Exhibit 2 and was estimated to cost approximately $4,300 plus $275 per lineal foot. This was a conveyor upon which the housing would be clamped and thus not removable at the work stations. This type of a conveyor would pace the line and allow completely automatic testing of the assembly as the unit would be accurately and positively located at each work station.

"Banking" facilities capable of holding up to 10 parts at any given work station were available for the belt conveyor at an additional cost of $100 per station. No such facility was available for the chain conveyor. One of the conveyor firms which had been contracted quoted a price of $1,500 plus $75 per lineal foot for small feeder conveyors which could serve as feeders to the main conveyor line for parts or subassemblies.

The contract upon which Othello was bidding was for 1,800 reducers a week for a period of six months. The invitation to bid provided that if the winning bidder wished to absorb all equipment and tooling costs, he would be free to build and sell the reducer in the open market under his own trade name. The conveyor manufacturer, however, reserved the right to procure (or to produce) any number of reducers required for use on its own products from any available source after the expiration of the original contract. The purchaser also retained the right to include any improvements incorporated during the current and all consecutive contracts with the winning supplier. In discussing the matter, representatives of the conveyor manufacturing firm stated that at present their firm had no intention of selling gear reducers other than as a component of their current products and as a replacement part. It was stated, however, that no written commitment with regard to this question would be made and that this statement was not intended to be binding if conditions changed.

To Othello management this appeared to be an excellent opportunity for Othello to develop a product line of its own, and it was decided that if the contract was received an initial single-shift five-day-week capacity would be installed that was 10 per cent in excess of the contract demand. Since Othello was currently operating on a one-shift five-day-week basis, this plan would comply with current operations and allow for up to a 200 per cent increase in production by going to two shifts of ten hours each on a six-day-week basis.

# EXHIBIT 1

## Sketch of proposed reducer

(Overall dimensions 18 × 18 × 16 inches high)

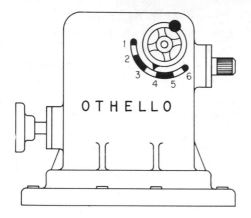

# EXHIBIT 2

## Assembly requirements, XFK-7 gear reducer

| Activity code | Activity | Quantity[1] | Unit time[2] | Handling time[3] | Cannot precede | Tooling cost[4] |
|---|---|---|---|---|---|---|
| a[5] | Start | . . . | .00 | .00 | . . . . . . | $    0 |
| b | Press main bearings | 2 | .59 | .21 | a | 3,500 |
| c | Press grease seals | 2 | .32 | .15 | a | 1,500[6] |
| d | Insert welsh plugs | 4 | .13 | .08 | a | 375 |
| e | Mount on chain conveyor | 1 | .17 | . . . . . | b,c,d | . . . . . . |
| f | Assemble main drive gear | 1 | 1.19 | .17 | e | 1,250 |
| g | Insert main drive gear assembly | 1 | .63 | .07 | e,f | . . . . . . |
| h | Position main drive gear bearing block | 1 | .30 | .07 | g | 75 |
| i | Insert and engage bolts | 4 | .04 | .02[7] | h | . . . . . . |
| j | Torque bolts | 4 | .06 | .04[8] | i | 225 |
| k | Assemble reduction gear | 1 | .63 | .14 | e | (f)[9] |
| l | Insert reduction gear | 1 | .33 | .09 | e,k | . . . . . . |
| m | Position reduction gear bearing block | 1 | .16 | .07 | l | 25 |
| n | Insert and engage bolts | 4 | .04 | .02[7] | m | . . . . . . |
| o | Shim for end play | 1 | .18 | .06 | m | 85 |
| p | Torque bolts | 4 | .06 | .04[8] | n,o | (j)[9] |
| q | Assemble idler shaft | 1 | .23 | .10 | e | (f)[9] |
| r | Insert idler shaft | 1 | .49 | . . . . . | q | . . . . . . |
| s | Position idler shaft bearing block | 1 | .20 | .05 | r | 95 |
| t | Insert and engage bolts | 4 | .04 | .02[7] | s | . . . . . . |
| u | Torque bolts | 4 | .06 | .04[8] | t | (j)[9] |
| v | Place gasket | 1 | .08 | .02 | e | . . . . . . |
| w | Place base plate | 1 | .29 | . . . . . | j,p,u,v | . . . . . . |
| x | Insert and engage bolts | 12 | .04 | .04[7] | w | . . . . . . |
| y | Torque bolts | 12 | .05 | .04 | x | (j)[9] |
| z | Insert pressure and lubricant fittings | 4 | .15 | .04 | e | 35 |
| aa | Fill lubricant | 1 | .51[10] | . . . . . | y,z | 3,800 |
| ab | Plug lubricant holes | 2 | .10 | .05 | aa | (d)[9] |
| ac | Pressure test | 1 | 3.80[11] | . . . . . | ab | 1,800 |
| ad | Remove pressure fittings and plug holes | 2 | .29 | .04 | ac | 60 |
| ae | Dynamometer test | 1 | 1.87[12] | . . . . . | aa | 4,800 |
| af | Attach name and instruction plate | 1 | .30 | .08 | e | 900 |
| ag | Wipe clean | 1 | .26 | .03 | ad,ae | . . . . . . |
| ah | Attach test results | 1 | .08 | . . . . . | af,ag | . . . . . . |
| ai | Release from conveyor | 1 | .08 | . . . . . | ah | . . . . . . |

[1] Number of cycles or repetitions of basic operation to complete the specified activity for each unit.

[2] Time to complete a single cycle of operation included in the specified activity.

[3] Time to pick up, position, lay aside tools, etc., if more than one activity is assigned to a specific work station. For example, if activities "b" and "c" are assigned to independent work stations the performance time is .59 and .32 minute,

*(Continued)*

respectively.   If they are assigned to a single work station the performance time is 1.27 minutes (.59 + .32 + .21 + .15 = 1.27).

[4] Cost of company supplied tools and special equipment to perform specified activity. Must be included for every work station at which all or any part of the specified activity is performed.

[5] Dummy operation. Requires no time or manpower

[6] Can substitute tool for operation "b." Can use common tool if this operation is performed at the same work station as operation "b."

[7] Activities "i," "n," "t," and "x" can be combined without incurring handling time since they contain identical elements and require common tools.

[8] Activities "j," "p," and "u" can be combined without incurring handling time since they contain identical elements and require common tools.

[9] Requires identical tooling as activity shown in parentheses. Can use common set of tooling if operations are performed at the same work station.

[10] Activity completely automatic, no operator required.

[11] Activity completely automatic except for operator who must visually check for leaks. One operator can oversee the testing of up to four units simultaneously. Operator cannot perform any other function regardless of how many units he oversees.

[12] Activity completely automatic except for operator who connects hydraulic dynamometer coupling, records test results, and shuts down test equipment in case of an emergency.   One operator can process up to two units simultaneously. Operator cannot perform any other function regardless of the number of units he oversees.

# DISCUSSION QUESTIONS

1. Do you agree with the thinking of Othello management that a work standards program and longer-term contracts would reduce their employee turnover and efficiency problems?

2. Was Othello's approach toward the development of a standards program sound and practical?

3. Does the reduction of production fluctuations through inventory accumulation represent sound thinking on the part of Othello's management?

4. Sketch an approximate assembly line designating specific work stations and the operations and activities performed at each work station. At what speed should the conveyor be designed to operate?

5. What are the approximate capital and labor costs per unit associated with the line you sketched? Assume direct labor costs average $3.00 per hour.

6. What information or considerations, if any, not included in the case are necessary to make a fully informed decision? Of what potential value would each be?

# REFERENCES

Bailey, Gerald B., and Ralph Presgrave: *Basic Motion Timestudy* (New York: McGraw-Hill Book Company, 1958), chaps. 1–3, 11–14.

Barnes, Ralph M.: *Motion and Time Study*, 3d ed. (Homewood, Ill.: Richard D. Irwin, Inc., 1948), chaps. 1–3, 20–23, 26, 27.

Buffa, Elwood S.: *Modern Production Management* (New York: John Wiley & Sons, Inc., 1961), chaps. 11–13.

Hadden, Arthur A., and Victor K. Gender: *Handbook of Standard Data for Machine Shops* (New York: The Ronald Press Company, 1954).

Karger, Delmar W., and Franklin H. Bayha: *Engineered Work Measurement* (New York: The Industrial Press, 1957), chaps. 1–5, 25–28.

Krick, Edward V.: *Methods Engineering* (New York: John Wiley & Sons, Inc., 1962), chaps. 12–23.

Maynard, Harold B., G. J. Stegemerten, and John L. Schwab: *Methods-Time Measurement* (New York: McGraw-Hill Book Company, 1948), chaps. 1–3, 15, 20, 28.

Nadler, Gerald B.: *Work Design* (Homewood, Ill.: Richard D. Irwin, Inc., 1963), chaps. 1–3, 19–21, 23, 24.

Nordhoff, W. A.: *Machine-shop Estimating* (New York: McGraw-Hill Book Company, 1947), chaps. 1–4.

Tonge, Fred M.: *A Heuristic Program for Assembly Line Balancing* (Englewood Cliffs, N.J.: Prentice-Hall, Inc., 1961).

# PETERSEN
# GENERAL CONTRACTORS

Petersen General Contractors was an established construction company doing work in several states in New England. Petersen generally handled small- to medium-sized commercial and industrial construction projects. Some recent projects which the company had completed were a 20,000-square-foot factory building, a four-story office building, and a water filtration plant.

The company was now in the process of preparing a bid for a television station for the erection of a 225-foot-high television antenna tower and the construction of a building adjacent to the tower which would be used to house transmission and electrical equipment. Petersen was bidding only on the tower and its electrical equipment, the building, the connecting cable between tower and building, and site preparation. Transmission equipment and other equipment to be housed in the building were not to be included in the bid and would be obtained separately by the television station. The site for the tower was at the top of a hill to minimize the required height of the tower, with the building to be constructed at a slightly lower elevation than the base of the tower and near a main road. Between the tower and building was to be a crushed gravel service road and an underground cable. Adjacent to the building a fuel tank was to be installed above ground on a concrete slab. A sketch of the tower and building site is shown in Exhibit 1.

Prior to preparing the detailed cost estimates, Petersen's estimator met with the company's general foreman to go over the plans and blueprints for the job. In addition to preparing a cost estimate, the estimator was also preparing an estimate of the time it would take to complete the job. The television station management was very concerned about the time factor and it had requested that bids be prepared on the basis of the normal time and cost for completing the job, and also for the fastest time for completing the job and the additional cost that this would entail. The result of the conference between the estimator and general foreman was to determine that the activities shown in Exhibit 2 would be necessary to complete the job. It was agreed that the estimator would prepare time and cost estimates for these activities.

In addition to determining the list of activities, the estimator and foreman discussed in some detail how these activities could be sequenced since the list of activities in Exhibit 2 did not necessarily indicate the order in which the work could be performed. In the course of the discussion, the estimator made the following notes.

Survey work and procurement of the structural steel and electrical equipment for the tower can start as soon as contract is signed.

Grading of tower and building sites can begin when survey is completed.

After tower site is graded, footings and anchors can be poured.

After building site is graded and basement excavated, building footings can be poured.

Septic tank can be installed when grading and excavating of building site is done.

Construction of connecting road can start as soon as survey is completed.

Exterior and interior basement walls can be poured as soon as footings are in.

Basement floor and fuel tank slab should go in after basement walls.

Floor beams can go in after the basement walls and basement floor.

Main floor slab and concrete block walls go in after floor beams.

Roof slab can go on after block walls are up.

Interior can be completed as soon as roof slab is on.

Put in fuel tank any time after slab is in.

Drain tile and storm drain for building go in after septic tank.

As soon as tower footings and anchors are in and tower steel and equipment are available, tower can be erected.

Connecting cable in tower site, drain tile, and storm drain can be put in as soon as tower is up.

Main cable between building and tower goes in after connecting cable at tower site is in and basement walls are up.

Tower site can be backfilled and graded as soon as storm drain, connecting cable, and main cable are in.

Clean up tower site after backfilling and grading is done.

Backfill around building and grade after main cable is in and after storm drain is in.

Clean up building site after backfilling and grading is done.

Following his meeting with the general foreman, the estimator prepared cost estimates and time estimates for completing the various portions of the job (shown in Exhibit 2). Estimates for both the normal time in which the work could be completed and the fastest possible time along with the corresponding costs were made as shown in Exhibit 3. The cost figures in Exhibit 3 are for the direct labor and equipment use costs only. Estimated costs of direct materials used in construction and purchased equipment to be installed in the tower are shown in Exhibit 4. Company experience had shown that for this kind of job indirect labor and other overhead costs could be expected to amount to 65 per cent of the direct labor and equipment use cost. The company also customarily allowed 15 per cent of the total estimated cost for contingencies. Using this information, the estimator prepared analyses for the job: one for the cost of doing the work at normal rate and one for the cost of doing the job in the shortest possible period of time.

# EXHIBIT 1
## TV tower and building site plan
(Not to scale)

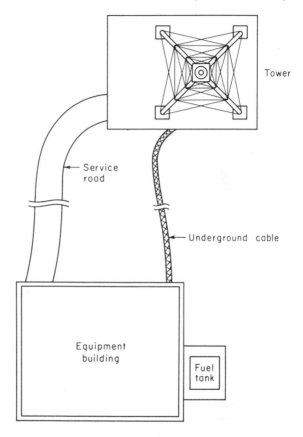

# EXHIBIT 2

## List of activities for construction of television tower and building

a   Sign contract and complete subcontractor negotiations
b   Survey site
c   Grade building site and excavate for basement
d   Grade tower site
e   Procure structural steel and guys for tower
f   Procure electrical equipment for tower and connecting underground cable
g   Pour concrete for tower footings and anchors
h   Erect tower and install electrical equipment
i   Install connecting cable in tower site
j   Install drain tile and storm drain in tower site
k   Backfill and grade tower site
l   Pour building footings
m   Pour basement slab and fuel tank slab
n   Pour outside basement walls
o   Pour walls for basement rooms
p   Pour concrete floor beams
q   Pour main floor slab and lay concrete block walls
r   Pour roof slab
s   Complete interior framing and utilities
t   Lay roofing
u   Paint building interior, install fixtures, and clean up
v   Install main cable between tower site and building
w   Install fuel tank
x   Install building septic tank
y   Install drain tile and storm drain in building site
z   Backfill around building, grade, and surface with crushed rock
aa   Lay base for connecting road between tower and building
bb   Complete grading and surface connecting road
cc   Clean up tower site
dd   Clean up building site
ee   Obtain job acceptance

# EXHIBIT 3

## Television tower and building construction time and cost estimate

| Activity code | Activity | Normal time | | Fastest time | |
|---|---|---|---|---|---|
| | | Days* | Cost† | Days* | Cost† |
| a | Sign contract and complete subcontractor negotiations | 5 | | 5 | |
| b | Survey site | 6 | $ 1,240 | 4 | $ 1,560 |
| c | Grade building site and excavate for basement | 8 | 1,300 | 6 | 1,830 |
| d | Grade tower site | 30 | 6,350 | 21 | 8,990 |
| e | Procure structural steel and guys for tower | 85 | ‡ | 85 | ‡ |
| f | Procure electrical equipment for tower and connecting underground cable | 120 | ‡ | 120 | ‡ |
| g | Pour concrete for tower footings and anchors | 42 | 8,310 | 25 | 11,670 |
| h | Erect tower and install electrical equipment | 38 | 11,350 | 25 | 15,620 |
| i | Install connecting cable in tower site | 8 | 1,740 | 4 | 1,950 |
| j | Install drain tile and storm drain in tower site | 35 | 3,600 | 18 | 5,100 |
| k | Backfill and grade tower site | 8 | 930 | 4 | 1,450 |
| l | Pour building footings | 29 | 3,030 | 21 | 4,100 |
| m | Pour basement slab and fuel tank slab | 14 | 1,050 | 11 | 1,540 |
| n | Pour outside basement walls | 34 | 2,550 | 30 | 2,810 |
| o | Pour walls for basement rooms | 9 | 800 | 7 | 960 |
| p | Pour concrete floor beams | 11 | 980 | 10 | 1,110 |
| q | Pour main floor slab and lay concrete block walls | 12 | 1,860 | 10 | 2,240 |
| r | Pour roof slab | 15 | 1,740 | 13 | 1,960 |
| s | Complete interior framing and utilities | 42 | 9,750 | 30 | 11,800 |
| t | Lay roofing | 3 | 270 | 2 | 340 |
| u | Paint building interior, install fixtures, and clean up | 19 | 920 | 13 | 1,350 |
| v | Install main cable between tower site and building | 35 | 4,360 | 25 | 4,540 |
| w | Install fuel tank | 3 | 180 | 2 | 220 |
| x | Install building septic tank | 12 | 630 | 8 | 750 |
| y | Install drain tile and storm drain in building site | 15 | 530 | 10 | 830 |
| z | Backfill around building, grade, and surface with crushed rock | 9 | 680 | 7 | 850 |
| aa | Lay base for connecting road between tower and building | 15 | 2,560 | 13 | 2,970 |
| bb | Complete grading and surface connecting road | 8 | 1,600 | 5 | 2,340 |
| cc | Clean up tower site | 5 | 240 | 3 | 500 |
| dd | Clean up building site | 3 | 210 | 2 | 400 |
| ee | Obtain job acceptance | 5 | | 5 | |

\* Days shown are working days only.
† Costs are for direct labor and rental of equipment only.
‡ Cost included in Exhibit 4.

## EXHIBIT 4

## Estimated cost of materials and equipment

| Item | Cost |
| --- | --- |
| Structural steel and guys for tower | $23,600 |
| Tower electrical equipment and connecting cable | 7,260 |
| Sand, gravel, crushed rock, and cement | 5,110 |
| Lumber and millwork | 6,400 |
| Drain tile and sewer pipe | 3,600 |
| Septic tank, plumbing fixtures, fuel tank, and other hardware | 3,300 |
| Other miscellaneous materials | 3,320 |

# DISCUSSION QUESTIONS

1. Working at a normal rate, in how many days can the job be completed? What should the bid be on this basis if Petersen attempted to obtain a profit of 10 per cent before Federal income taxes?

2. What is the shortest possible time in which the job can be completed? What should the bid be on this basis if Petersen attempted to obtain a profit of 10 per cent before Federal income taxes?

3. If the job is obtained and the work is to be completed working at a normal rate, what portions of the work should be supervised most carefully to ensure that the job is completed on time? What portions of the work should be supervised most carefully if the contract is let on the basis of completing the job in the shortest possible time?

4. If you were the television station management and felt that the estimated time for completing the job in the shortest possible period of time was still too long, what would you do?

5. What effect would the amount of other work for which Petersen had received contracts have on the bid price for this contract?

# REFERENCES

Fulkerson, D. R.: "A Network Flow Computation for Project Cost Curves," *Management Science,* vol. 7, no. 2 (January, 1961), pp. 167–178.

Kelly, J. E., Jr.: "Critical-path Planning and Scheduling: Mathematical Basis," *Operations Research,* vol. 9 (1961), pp. 296–320.

Kemeny, John G., et al.: *Finite Mathematics with Business Applications* (Englewood Cliffs, N.J.: Prentice-Hall, Inc., 1962), chap. 2, sec. 6.

Prager, William: "A Structural Method of Computing Project Cost Polygons," *Management Science,* vol. 9, no. 3 (April, 1963), pp. 394–404.

# PLASTICS AND METALS
# CORPORATION OF AMERICA

Plastics and Metals Corporation of America, known as PAMCOA throughout the plastics and metalworking industry, was a large manufacturer
and fabricator of plastic and metal products. PAMCOA produced a very
diversified line of products ranging from metal and plastic builders' hardware and supplies to complex machinery and military products. PAMCOA
produced a very
diversified line of products ranging from metal and plastic builders' hardware and supplies to complex machinery and military products.

In recent years the company faced increasing competition that made
the company's goal of a larger share of the potential market more difficult
to achieve. This environmental condition required that greater emphasis
be placed on meeting customer needs through improvements in design,
engineering, testing, manufacturing, and cost. The extensive variety of
products produced and customers served required considerable specialization in the areas of sales, engineering, and manufacturing. All this resulted
in an organizational structure consisting of four product divisions and
a manufacturing division as follows:

> Product divisions:
> Building division
> Structures division
> Machinery division
> Military division
> Service unit:
> Manufacturing division

Building products included both standard and special-order items
generally classified as builders' hardware and supplies. These items were

usually sold to local and regional wholesalers and distributors, and on occasion, directly to general contractors engaged in large residential and commercial building projects. The structures classification consisted largely of plastic and metal structural members, panels, and curtain walls. Prospective customers for this product line were typically architects and contractors.

The machinery products and the military products differed substantially from the building and structures products in that they tended to be more complex in design and manufacture. Machinery and military products often appeared visually similar, but differences between them in terms of performance, quality control, and contractual requirements were sufficient to make separate divisions advisable. It was management's opinion that the ability to provide each customer with the particular type of specialized service he required was one of the significant factors contributing to PAMCOA's past and future success.

The major source of interaction between the product divisions was through the manufacturing division. This division operated as a manufacturing service unit for the product divisions and possessed all of PAMCOA's basic processing facilities. The manufacturing division did no design work and made no contact with customers; thus it operated as a "captive" job shop to the other divisions. The product divisions, however, did have a sufficient amount of manufacturing facilities to handle emergency repair work, to make simple modifications on completed items, and to do special assembly operations. The management strongly felt that the centralization of the processing facilities in a single manufacturing division resulted in better utilization of equipment and lower manufacturing costs. It was felt that such an arrangement made the firm's entire manufacturing skill and capacity available to each division instead of having the skills and capacity partitioned and diluted among the divisions. In addition, the relatively large fluctuations in processing requirements experienced by the individual product divisions could be balanced within the manufacturing division. This eliminated interdivisional parts and cost transfers and many other associated problems that would otherwise be required, and permitted a single cost accounting and production control system, instead of multiple systems, to be used. It was also assumed that manufacturing costs would be more difficult to control under a divided set of facilities and extensive transfers of work between divisions. This manufacturing policy appeared sound, for PAMCOA's management felt it had developed a reputation for better than average cost and delivery performance.

During the past year, however, the meeting of scheduled delivery dates had become a serious problem, and the previous declining cost trends leveled off. Within a period of three months the number of late part completions more than doubled and a significant increase in late deliveries to customers occurred in spite of increased expediting action. In order to understand why this situation had developed it was decided that the production planning procedure used by each division be reviewed. Up to this time each product division was only required to specify the latest acceptable completion date for work to be performed by the manufacturing division. The manufacturing division, in the best way possible, attempted to match the requirements of the individual product divisions with their available capacity. In an attempt to correct the late delivery situation it was decided that a more formal scheduling procedure should be followed by all divisions.

The new system required that a more comprehensive scheduling procedure be performed by each product division. When an order arrived the planner assigned to the order would first establish a normal starting date by determining standard or estimated lead times for the major operations required such as engineering, tooling, material ordering, parts manufacturing, assembly, and test. The normal starting date was determined by deducting the standard lead times for each operation and all moves between operations from the requested delivery date. If the normal starting date came after the current date, then completion dates for each operation were established as determined by the application of normal lead times to the requested delivery date. If, however, the normal starting date preceded the current date, an acceleration factor was determined. This factor consisted of the total calculated standard time to complete the job divided by the available time to satisfy the customer's requirements. If this factor was less than 1.50 the job could be accepted and a set of completion dates determined on the basis of accelerated standard lead times (standard lead time divided by acceleration factor). In cases where the order was particularly desirable a further reduction in time could be made for any operation performed wholly within any given product division. This appeared reasonable in that the division instituting such action would suffer any unfavorable consequences in terms of increased operating costs.

This revision in the production scheduling procedure appeared to provide temporary relief for all divisions. However, within six months John Franks, manager of the machinery products division, felt compelled to confront management with his renewed customer delivery problems. Franks prefaced his specific complaints by stating that all of his division's business was of a very competitive nature and failure to meet delivery promises often involved substantial cash penalties in addition to impairing his division's image as a reliable producer. He stated that meeting delivery commitments was a major factor in receiving repeat business and described his feelings toward allowing schedule lapses as follows:

Falling behind schedule is the road to certain death. . . . The costs of preventing schedule failure are minor compared to those of curing a major lapse. Once behind schedule, drastic measures are necessary to meet current deliveries. These measures include large-scale use of special priorities causing inefficiencies which in turn reduce overall output capacity and cause additional lags in already tight and lagging schedules. To remedy this situation a complete replanning of activities is required and this invariably costs many times more than preventing the original lapse.

When asked about his specific complaints Franks stated that he felt the newly devised production planning scheme was inadequate and was causing his division to receive unfavorable prejudicial treatment from the manufacturing division. He augmented his argument by providing conclusive evidence that his division received a higher percentage of late completions from the manufacturing division than any of the other product divisions, and that on the average his jobs were twice as late as the average for all jobs finished behind schedule.

Archer, manager of the manufacturing division, was requested to respond to Franks's complaint. Archer stated that he was in full agreement with Franks about remaining on schedule but that this was currently impossible and, once behind schedule, it was necessary to select the best alternative from a group of possible alternatives, none of which was really satisfactory. He pointed out that he lacked both the information and resources to develop a fully rational solution to the problem and that he was doing the best possible job in view of the innumerable special requests made of him. He was constantly plagued by product managers, coordinators, and expediters, each stating a "life or death" situation. The daily volume of such requests exceeded his capacity to hear, understand, investigate, or grant them. From what information he had obtained, Archer could conceive of only one rational guide. This was (all other things equal) to give those orders with a high acceleration ratio preference over orders having lower acceleration ratios. He based this decision on the fact that orders with high acceleration ratios possessed little if any safety factors and any delay in these orders would almost certainly cause late delivery.

Since the military division was working on an almost completely crash schedule, a very high percentage of their orders had high acceleration ratios and received first preference. On the other hand, machinery product orders were almost always based on standard lead times, and thus from Archer's viewpoint, some degree of lateness for such orders appeared tolerable.

As an example, Archer constructed the chart shown in Exhibit 1. The chart indicated relative start and completion dates for a specific job having a given delivery date (day 30) but different acceleration ratios.

Archer pointed out that on the basis of normal lead times (acceleration ratio of 1.0) the scheduled completion date for machining was day 13, but for a crash program (acceleration ratio of 1.6) the scheduled completion date for machining would be day 19. He further emphasized that actual processing and fabrication times were usually much longer than those used in the example and that in general a much greater number of operations were involved. Hence, the machining completion date for the same part to be used on an identical assembly or order could differ by as much as 10 to 20 days depending on the acceleration ratio that was used.

Archer concluded his argument by stating that once a behind-schedule situation was incurred, scheduled due dates became meaningless; therefore to treat jobs with high acceleration ratios in the same manner as jobs with normal acceleration ratios when in a behind-schedule condition was completely unsound; and as a result he was duty bound to assign arbitrary priorities such that the least overall inconvenience to the firm would result. He admitted that this was no real solution to the basic problem and that the problem would not be solved until all divisions were required to use a common scheduling procedure. Archer felt that under these conditions alone could all due dates be given equal consideration under "ahead-of," "on," and "behind" schedule situations.

Franks vigorously complained and stated that continued application of Archer's current policy would destroy both his division's cost and delivery performance. He stated that they were in a highly competitive market and any policy which jeopardized their cost or delivery performance was unsound. He also pointed out that of the four product divisions, his division was unquestionably the most efficient producer, due primarily to the fact that he refused to operate on any but normal lead times.

To obtain an overall viewpoint management asked the remaining division managers for their comments regarding the acceptability of the current production planning and control system. They all had numerous complaints and reservations about the current system. The managers of building products and of structures products both admitted that it might not be the best possible system, but they were unwilling to support Franks's opinion that the system was unworkable and that it required immediate revision. Their basic comment was that they felt they could live with the current system, and they were apprehensive that an immediate major change in the system might merely compound existing problems. The opinion of a majority of the managers suggested that the problem warranted looking into, but that any decision for changing the system should be delayed until a more opportune time. Fred Jenkins, manager of the military division, admitted that the current system had problems and stated that it was conceivable that a superior system could be developed. He saw no current obstacles, however, which couldn't be overcome under the current system and visualized no real need for going to a basically different system. He suggested that the problem might be solved most expeditiously by "requiring the machinery division to adapt to the situation rather than trying to tailor the entire firm to its needs."

In view of the fact that the machinery division initiated the issue and was the only division currently overly concerned with the issue, and also to prevent logrolling between the divisions, it was decided that the machinery division should independently study the problem and make specific recommendations to the central management.

Franks assigned his special staff assistant, James, to the job of investigating possible alternative solutions to this problem. He suggested that James concentrate on uncovering as many alternative solutions as possible and arrange a meeting in approximately one week to discuss the alternatives in hopes of selecting one or two for complete analysis. Franks felt it was important not to overlook any possibilities but also to realize that all possibilities could not be completely investigated in the time available. Exhibit 2 is an outline of the information, including five proposed alternatives for improving performance, that James prepared for the meeting.

James stated that none of these alternatives was necessarily mutually exclusive or all-inclusive in terms of solving the problem. He felt that a study of the organizational and procedural aspects of the problem and a study of the physical needs of the manufacturing division should be made and be included as a part of the final report that was to be submitted to top management. The current question, however, was to decide which of the alternatives considered, or possibly some other alternatives, warranted further study and what additional information should be gathered before preparing and submitting a final recommendation to the central management.

# EXHIBIT 1

## Operation start and completion dates versus acceleration ratio

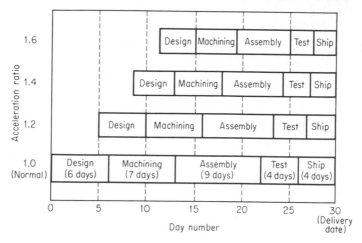

# EXHIBIT 2

## Outline of study for improving manufacturing division deliveries

I. Current condition of the manufacturing division.
   A. Increasing percentage of behind-schedule completions.
   B. Increasing overtime.
   C. Increasing parts shortage at assembly.
   D. Increasing use of special priorities.
   E. Increasing schedule revision activity.
   F. Increasing competition between product divisions for preferential treatment by manufacturing division.
   G. Increasing total production requirements.
   H. Intermittent work shortages and work overloads in specific departments.
   I. Increasing number of late tooling completions.
II. Possible causes for decline in performance.
   A. Unavailability of parts.
   B. Tight schedules.

   *C.* Variable work loads.

   *D.* Inadequate manufacturing capacity.

   *E.* Unclear overall company objectives.

   *F.* Inadequate tooling.

 III. Proposed alternatives to improve performance.

   *A.* Require each product division to adopt a common procedure for calculating due dates without the use of acceleration ratios.

    1. This would eliminate the argument for preferential treatment and make the due date a logical and automatic basis for resolving schedule conflicts.

    2. Each product division would be given fair and equal consideration. The current overload condition might be substantially reduced if most of the slack were removed from existing schedules.

    3. A justifiable basis for requesting and assigning overtime would be provided.

   *B.* Devise a priority rule which would consider both the due date and current scheduling procedure used by each division. This would accomplish the same as alternative "A" and allow each division to continue using its current scheduling procedures involving acceleration ratios or any new procedure as long as it made its procedure known to the manufacturing division.

   *C.* Assign a particular portion of the total parts manufacturing capacity to each product division and require that all unused capacity be made available to any division requiring extra capacity.

    1. This would allow each product division to make independent plans which would not be in conflict with other divisions.

    2. The manufacturing division would no longer need to resolve interdivisional conflicts.

    3. Top management could determine the relative emphasis to be given to each division's activities.

    4. Each division would be required to plan and level its load to obtain maximum utilization of assigned capacity.

   *D.* Create specific priority classes.

    1. Priority classes:

     *a.* Jobs whose assembly requirements permit normal handling procedures.

     *b.* Jobs which must be started immediately or within three days to meet assembly requirements.

     *c.* Jobs which, even if started immediately, would fail to meet assembly requirements.

2. Specify a limited number of jobs that each product division could submit per month to the manufacturing division in each of these three priority classes.
3. This would reduce the number of expedited jobs and allow departments to devote additional attention to operational efficiency.
4. Overall capacity and output of the manufacturing division would be increased.

E. Completely autonomize the manufacturing division and make it compete with outside sources for all business.
1. This would carry out the principle of divisional independence to its ultimate degree.
2. The true advisability of maintaining a manufacturing service division would be tested once and for all.
3. The manufacturing division would be forced to operate in an efficient manner.

# DISCUSSION QUESTIONS

1. Were the arguments valid for a centralized manufacturing facility and against a partitioned manufacturing facility? Why?
2. What problems resulting from the introduction of the new production planning and scheduling scheme using acceleration ratios should have been anticipated?
3. What are some of the possible reasons that Franks received little active support from the managers of the other product divisions?
4. Did Archer display sound thinking in partially ignoring scheduled completion dates?
5. Is Archer's suggestion sound to require all divisions to use a completely common production planning and scheduling procedure?
6. What are the basic elements to a satisfactory and lasting solution?
7. On the basis of your answer to question 6, discuss the merits of each of the solutions suggested by James.
8. Was assigning the responsibility of finding a satisfactory solution for PEMCOA's problem to Franks a wise procedure?

# REFERENCES

Buffa, Elwood S.: *Modern Production Management* (New York: John Wiley & Sons, Inc., 1961), chap. 16.

MacNiece, E. H.: *Production Forecasting, Planning and Control* (New York: John Wiley & Sons, Inc., 1957), chaps. 13–17, 20, 21.

Magee, John F.: *Production Planning and Inventory Control* (New York: McGraw-Hill Book Company, 1958), chaps. 6–9.

Moore, Franklin, G.: *Manufacturing Management* (Homewood, Ill.: Richard D. Irwin, Inc., 1961), chaps. 40, 41.

# THE SAMSON GORE TOOLING

"In tooling you just have to learn to live with time pressures. We are always caught in a squeeze play between the engineers and the manufacturing people." John Brady, tooling foreman of the Springfield division of the Abaco Company, was recounting his recent experience with the most unusual tooling job he had ever supervised.

Yes, the Samson gore tooling job was certainly an unusual one, but basically it had the same managerial characteristics as any tooling job that we do—insufficient lead time and lots of unexpected problems.

It seems that the engineers never want to release the drawings to us. This is true on normal projects with normal requirements, but on something with the enormous size and special requirements of the Samson, I suppose this hesitancy is easily understandable. The engineers like to keep tinkering with one scheme after another until they must make up their mind. Even after the drawings are released, they make changes; consequently the men building the tooling never know exactly where they stand. Often it becomes necessary to modify the theoretical ideas advanced by engineering after the men in the shop recognize that they are not practical.

Sure, I was late with the tooling. The manufacturing superintendent was on my neck every day. I told the top brass that I needed six months to do the job properly. They scheduled four months for the job, but the drawings were so late that I only had two months before the tooling was supposed to be ready. As it was, I took about four months, but I believe that the responsibility for the delay should be charged entirely to the engineers.

The Abaco Company was one of the major airframe manufacturers and had produced substantial numbers of large aircraft for both commercial and military applications. As national defense needs changed the requirements for aircraft decreased, and the company directed its effort toward seeking orders to produce missiles and other products for the growing aerospace industry. The company was awarded a large contract for the design and manufacture of the first stage of the Samson booster to be used in the Helios project. The Helios project was one of several major programs of the Government Space Research Agency (GSRA) designed for the exploration of the moon.

The Helios program involved three steps: the first two steps were to be earth orbital flights, and the final step was the landing of an expedition to explore the moon and return to earth. The final step would use a Samson booster to launch the Helios spacecraft for its round trip to the moon.

The Helios spacecraft was to be composed of three sections or modules. The first, or command module, contained the living quarters for four men and was the only unit to be returned to earth. The second, or service module, was to provide the power for space travel. The third, or moon exploration module (MEM), would land on the moon and would be launched back into lunar orbit to rendezvous with the other two modules that had been circling the moon awaiting the return trip to earth.

In order to get the Helios spacecraft into space flight, the three-stage Samson booster was to be used as the launching vehicle. Each Samson stage consisted of fuel tanks for kerosene or liquid hydrogen and liquid oxygen, and power engines to burn the liquid propellant. Each stage in turn would provide thrust and be jettisoned when its fuel was consumed. The first stage was to provide 8½ million pounds of thrust at lift-off, the second 1½ million pounds, and the third 250,000 pounds. The Samson booster was designed to launch a 50-ton spacecraft to the moon or place a 115-ton space station in earth orbit. When ready for launching, the three-module Helios spacecraft placed on top of the three-stage Samson launch vehicle would stand 392 feet in height (approximately the height of a 40-story building) and weigh about 7 million pounds. The general arrangement is shown in Exhibit 1.

The first or lower stage of the Samson booster consisted primarily of five thrust engines mounted at the end and two large tanks—the fuel tank for kerosene or liquid hydrogen and a tank for liquid oxygen (the LOX tank). When assembled, the first stage was to be 35 feet in diameter and 148 feet high with four fins projecting outward from the body. A thrust structure was used to connect the engines to the fuel tank. An intertank connected the fuel tank to the LOX tank. At the other end of the LOX tank a forward skirt was mounted which then attached to the interstage of the second stage of the booster. The thrust structure, intertank, and forward skirt were essentially large circular pipes which connected the engines and tanks together.

In addition to these primary structural members, the first stage also contained a large number of pipes, fittings, valves, electrical devices, mechanical devices, and other apparatus. John Brady's group was requested to make the tools to manufacture the shaped ends of the large tanks.

The exteriors of the LOX tank and the fuel tank were each 35 feet in diameter; the LOX tank was 62 feet high and the fuel tank was 48 feet high. The 35-foot circular shell of the tanks formed the exterior surface of the launch vehicle. The ends of the tanks, called bulkheads, had a semiellipsoidal (dish-shaped) configuration and were 35 feet in diameter and approximately 13 feet high. Although dish-shaped ends for tanks were not uncommon, the sheer size and close tolerances required for the Samson tank bulkheads presented an unusual manufacturing challenge, particularly for the tooling involved.

The Abaco Company had two main manufacturing divisions: one located in New England and the other at Springfield. At the time the Samson booster job was being considered, the Springfield division work load was very low and the company was anxious to obtain new business to utilize the capacity of that division. GSRA negotiated with several contractors before placing the order for a few units of the first stage of the Samson booster to be used for experimental purposes. The negotiations not only involved price considerations but also the capabilities of the potential suppliers to provide scientific and engineering personnel to complete the necessary development work and drawings that were required, the availability of manufacturing facilities, the past performance of each company on projects of comparable size and complexity, and the plans proposed by each potential contractor for handling the technical, production, and managerial aspects of the project. In addition, the GSRA took into consideration the ability of each company to expand from the few units to be produced under their current procurement program to a potential program of several hundred units if the project was successful.

Included in Abaco's proposal was the plan of the company to establish a scientific and engineering liaison group at Charlestown, which was the location of the GSRA headquarters. The enormous size of the first stage prevented it from being shipped by either rail or truck. As a result the company planned to establish a new Gulf division near the mouth of the Mississippi River, where the parts could be assembled and the finished boosters could be loaded directly onto large barges and towed through the Gulf of Mexico around the southern tip of Florida to the final launching site at Cape Kennedy. The company's proposal stipulated that the parts would be fabricated at the Springfield division and moved by land transportation to the new Gulf division. In effect, the Springfield division would become a subcontractor to the Gulf division, which would have overall responsibility for the Samson booster program and would administer the prime contract received from GSRA. The company's proposal was accepted and the Abaco Company was awarded a contract for the tooling and production of a few units of the first-stage Samson booster job by GSRA. A cost-plus-a-fixed-fee type of contract was issued for the work.

After the contract was received, the executives to be involved in the program at the Springfield division were briefed on the requirements, and managerial responsibilities were established for the various aspects of the program. Responsibility for preparing plans for fabrication was delegated to George Sloan, manager of the manufacturing development section. George Sloan had a good technical education and extensive experience as a workman, foreman, and superintendent in a variety of shops at the Springfield division. In his department he had a number of staff members whose combined backgrounds of technical education and practical shop experience covered all the types of manufacturing skills performed by the company.

The general plan of manufacturing was to be developed by Sloan for approval by the Springfield division management and then submitted to the Gulf division for their approval. Following this, the plan was to be sent to the company's engineering staff at Charlestown for technical evaluation and the preparation of detailed engineering and production drawings for the tooling as required by the manufacturing plan. The engineers at Charlestown were in constant contact with the GSRA staff for the purpose of coordinating new ideas and for obtaining official GSRA approval for each document. Since the contract was on a cost-plus-a-fixed-fee basis it was necessary for the company to obtain GSRA authorization for the expenditure of funds as each step in the program was developed.

George Sloan had participated in preparing the proposals submitted by the company to GSRA. He had been kept informed of the negotiations which had taken place between the contracting officer of GSRA and the representative of the company. As a result he was aware of three major problems: (1) severe time pressures, (2) incomplete design, and (3) conflicting tooling philosophy.

In April, 1961, the Russian cosmonaut Yuri Gagarin became the first person to orbit the earth. The Russian success in space aroused the executives of the United States government, and in May, 1961, President Kennedy in a special message to Congress proposed a national goal of landing a man on the moon and returning him safely to earth before the 1960 decade was over. A few months later Congress authorized the funds for this goal, and one of the several programs involved was given the name "Project Helios." Thus, the moon race moved forward with top priority, and the Helios program was put on a crash basis. Many activities involving research, development, and manufacturing, which normally would have been done sequentially over a longer time span, were now to be done concurrently under tremendous pressures of time. Sloan felt that this policy would ultimately have an impact on every level of the organization.

The scientific and technical problems involved in the Helios project required manufacturing skills to be used to the limit of "the state of the arts." Although the general physical design for the Samson tanks had been established, the detailed manufacturing procedures had not been outlined, and Sloan was aware that manufacturing techniques would be required which they had never used before. The specifications for the tank bulkheads were an example of the type of problems that he faced. These bulkheads were designed to use aluminum plate 1 inch in thickness to be sculptured to as thin as $\frac{1}{4}$ inch depending on the location of fittings and other mating members. The thickness of the plate at any point of the bulkhead could not vary by more than $\pm 0.008$ inch from the specified dimension, and the contour of the bulkhead had to be held within $\pm \frac{1}{8}$ inch of the designated shape.

A final difficulty that Sloan faced was in the difference in tooling philosophy between the Springfield division and the GSRA engineers. Because of the previous long production runs at the Springfield division their manufacturing people were accustomed to very high-quality tooling designed to maintain tolerances over long runs, to minimize the cost of production, and to use appropriate jigs and fixtures which permitted the employment of lower-skilled labor than might otherwise be required. In contrast to such practice, the GSRA programs generally involved the production of only one or two units as prototypes or for experimental purposes, and the tooling typically used was of simple design and relatively inexpensive. Although simple tooling would require more direct labor in manufacturing, it was believed by GSRA that the extra manufacturing cost was more than offset by the savings obtained in using low-cost tooling. This difference in philosophy was apparent during the contract negotiations when estimates for the tank bulkhead tooling were submitted for consideration by various parties as follows:

| Source of estimate | Tooling estimate for gore sections |
|---|---|
| GSRA tooling engineers | $42,000 |
| GSRA production manager | 57,000 |
| Gulf division engineers | 79,000 |
| Springfield division engineers | 87,000 |

The original tooling concept involved dividing the bulkhead into small sections which could be formed in a simple press using kirksite dies at 300 pounds pressure per square inch. The estimating was done on the basis of the estimator's experience with previous similar jobs where rates had been developed for direct labor man-hours per pound and for direct material dollars per man-hour or per pound of product.

At the time the negotiations were underway, the Springfield management was aware that the tooling allowances being discussed were far lower than the costs they normally expected to incur on such projects. They were fearful, however, of making too much of an issue over this since there were a number of competitors who were also seeking the business, and the tooling costs were only a very small part of the total estimated cost. Since the contract was to be let on a cost-plus-a-fixed-fee basis, they counted on appropriate adjustments which could be made in the contract price for changes after the award was made. Even during the contract negotiations, however, it became clear to the contracting officers of GSRA that their estimates (listed above) would be insufficient, and they finally agreed to allow $85,000 for the tank bulkhead tooling in the overall contract estimate.

As a first step in preparing the manufacturing plan for the bulkheads George Sloan carefully reviewed the ideas and estimates for the use of kirksite dies that had been presented in the negotiations for the contract. During his review, a basic policy change occurred in the Samson project, and the quantity of tanks to be produced was increased from a few units to several hundred units. The change to quantity increased the estimated cost of the production work to over $200 million. After careful study of the implications of the change in quantity he concluded that the preliminary ideas and estimates were inadequate and uneconomical and that it would be best for him to take a fresh approach to the problem. He felt certain that a greatly improved tooling program could now be justified. Even though such a tooling program might involve a substantial increase in tooling costs, these costs could be more than offset by the potential reduction in manufacturing man-hours and the resulting reduction in manufacturing costs.

The dished ends of small tanks normally could be fabricated in a single piece by means of a press using male and female dies. The ends for the Samson tanks, however, were so large that there was no press in the world big enough to do the job from a single plate. The tentative design discussed during the contract negotiations proposed to fabricate the Samson tank bulkheads in seventeen pieces which would then be welded together in the final assembly. Exhibit 2 indicates the general design. One piece was to be a 54-inch-diameter polar cap which could be shaped on a standard draw press. The remainder of the bulkhead was to consist of eight gores (curved, pieshaped pieces). Each gore was so large that it in turn had to be made into two parts—an apex section and a base section. The large base section was a dished trapezoidal shape, and the smaller apex section was dished and almost triangular in shape. George Sloan investigated several methods of manufacture which are described in the following paragraphs.

1. *Draw process.* The gore sections could be manufactured by "drawing" in a press using male and female steel dies. The dies would be very expensive to obtain and there was only one press in the United States which was large enough to handle the job. This press was owned by a competitive company. It would take approximately two years to obtain delivery of a new press large enough for the task.

2. *Bump forming.* This method frequently was used in the manufacture of large steel tanks, the forming of large plate sections for shipbuilding, and the fabrication of other irregular, large flat surfaces. Using this method, large plates were first shaped in one direction by being passed through rollers or by use of a power brake which made a series of small parallel bends or creases to form the curvature. The shaped plate was then dished on a "bump" press. Bumping consisted of supporting the plate at a few points by wooden chocks. A single vertical arm of the press then pressed on one spot of the plate to flex a small concave section. The plate progressively was moved from point to point so that the press arm could flex the concave curvature over the entire plate. This method required relatively little tooling but was very time-consuming, and it was very difficult to hold the tolerances required for the Samson gore job. It also was very difficult to obtain smooth continuous curvature and almost inevitably the plates would contain flat areas.

3. *Guerin process.* This process involved the use of a press with a single die on one side of a plate and with a constrained rubber pad on the other side. When the press applied pressure to the pad it forced the plate into the shape of the die. There was no press available that was large enough for the sections involved in the Samson gore program.

4. *Stretch press forming.* Under this method a special press was used that grasped the ends of the plate and pulled to stretch the plate. While under tension the plate was forced against a die of the proper configuration to obtain the concave shape. There was no press available large enough for this job and it would take approximately $2\frac{1}{2}$ years to get a new press of the proper size.

5. *Smaller gore sections.* It was proposed that the bulkhead be divided into sixteen gores instead of eight gores. This would permit the gore sections to be pressed out by either the draw process or the Guerin process. The design would require double the amount of welding. This proposal was turned down by the GSRA engineers because they felt that it involved an unacceptable risk of rupture of the tank under high fuel pressure.

6. *Explosive forming.* This recently developed method of forming was still in the experimental stage. It consisted of placing a plate over a cavity in a die and arranging a watertight seal between the die and the plate. The assembly was then submerged in water. An explosive charge was fired in the water, and the high pressure generated by the explosion forced the plate to assume the configuration of the die.

7. *Bulge forming.* This was not a common method of forming, but George Sloan had seen the method work some years earlier on stainless steel coffins and on sinks formed for low-cost housing and trailers. A plate was mounted over and sealed to a chamber into which oil or water could be introduced under high pressure. A single cavity die then was placed on top of the plate to be fabricated, and the die was clamped securely to the plate and hydraulic chamber. Hydraulic pressure introduced into the chamber then forced the plate up into the die cavity to assume the proper configuration. This method had possibilities for significant potential savings since no press was required and only a single female die was used.

After further consideration it appeared to George Sloan that the explosive-forming method and the bulge-forming method offered the best possibilities for this job. In each of these methods only a single die cavity was required. It was decided to test each method on a small scale. The explosive-forming method was found to be very difficult to control. The cavity under the plate had to be exhausted to a very high vacuum because the rapid shaping of the plate under the explosion caused the air in the cavity to compress and heat, resulting in an undesirable "air burn" of the die. It also was necessary to clamp the edges of the plate rigidly to prevent wrinkling. Wrinkling was particularly bad when sculptured plate was used, and it appeared necessary to use only flat plate in the explosive method. This posed a very difficult problem of sculpturing the plate after forming. The use of the explosive was somewhat dangerous and quite messy when the water in the tank was blown out in all directions. Even with the use of flat plate it was difficult to maintain the required tolerances.

The experiments with small-scale bulge forming proved to be promising, although a number of practical difficulties were encountered. In order to stretch the plate into the cavity it was necessary that very high hydraulic pressure be used. This pressure might go up to 1,500 pounds per square inch and would create a difficult problem of sealing the plate to the hydraulic chamber. The problem was finally solved by developing a rubber ring with two lips: one lip sealed against the plate and the other sealed against the hydraulic chamber. The greater the hydraulic pressure the more tightly the seal was formed. The use of the rubber ring for a seal was developed after considerable experimentation with a rubber bladder which had been used to confine the water. The bladders were very expensive and subject to frequent rupture. The rubber ring was a simple and inexpensive solution to the problem.

Another difficulty with the bulge-forming method was the necessity of tightly holding the plate in position during the drawing process. This was accomplished by means of serrated clamps located around the periphery of the plates which prevented the plates from drawing in and wrinkling while they were formed to the configuration of the cavity.

Another problem with the bulge-forming method was to find appropriate clamping methods for holding the cavity die, plate, and hydraulic chamber together. Mechanical clamps attached by hand were clumsy and time-consuming to install and remove. As a result it was decided to design the tooling with a number of hydraulic clamps which could be applied and removed quickly.

The idea of bulge forming the gore section was finally adopted by the manufacturing development section of the Springfield division. After extensive review, discussion, and debate, the radically new tooling concept was accepted by both the Gulf division and GSRA. Prior to acceptance of the new tooling plan, however, GSRA engineers and estimators gave very careful attention to the cost analysis, which indicated that although the tooling costs would be increased by over $1,800,000, the expected savings in manufacturing costs would be more than double that amount.

Development of the detailed tooling drawings was undertaken by the Gulf division engineers at Charlestown. The drawings were then to be supplied to the Springfield division for fabrication of the tooling and manufacture of the tank sections.

The final design for the tank gore tooling included many unusual features. Since the forming area of the plates was about 20,000 square inches, and the hydraulic pressure was to be about 1,500 pounds per square inch, the maximum total pressure on the plate and the cavity die was over 30 million pounds. To contain this great force the structure holding the cavity die was to be made from a special grade of high-strength T-1 alloy steel and the die surface was to be made of epoxy plastic resin. This resin was tough and had the special property of zero shrinkage when formed by a casting method.

There were to be two sets of hydraulic pumps: one operating at 1,500 pounds per square inch to fill the hydraulic chamber for the bulging operation, and another pumping system operating at 5,000 pounds per square inch for operating the hydraulic clamping devices that exerted 30 million pounds of clamping pressure. It was necessary to design the tooling to contain the following safety features:

1. Assurance that pressures greater than 1,500 pounds per square inch could not be applied to the hydraulic chamber. Higher pressures might break the tooling apart with dangerous explosive force.

2. The supply of water under pressure was to be shut off immediately in case of a leak between the hydraulic chamber and the aluminum plate being formed.

3. Assurance that pressure could not be built up inside the hydraulic chamber until the clamping devices were fully secured.

4. Arrangements making it impossible to release pressure on the clamping devices until the hydraulic chamber pressure was completely released.

When the final design plans were released to the Springfield division (see Exhibit 3), a detailed materials list was prepared and the purchasing department was authorized to proceed with the necessary procurement. The aluminum plate to be fabricated into the bulkhead sections was specified as grade 2219 in a thickness of 1 inch. The normal purchasing procedure for buying aluminum plate involved the use of the following contract statement:

> By acceptance of this order, seller certifies that materials and/or finished parts shall be controlled and tested in accordance with, and will meet specified order requirements and applicable specifications and that applicable records are on file subject to examination and will be furnished to the buyer upon request.

In order to meet GSRA requirements for reliability control it was necessary to obtain signed test reports indicating the original lot and heat number from the mill, the specific chemical analysis, yield, tensile strength, per cent elongation, and per cent reduction. These data became part of the information collected to permit the tracing of every piece in the assembled tank back through each operation to the raw material (in this case aluminum plate) and then tracing the raw material back through its steps of manufacture to the original melt. This elaborate record keeping system was required so that if a failure occurred in any piece it would be possible to locate every other similar piece which might be susceptible to failure.

The aluminum plates were to be sculptured prior to being rolled and shaped by the bulge-forming method. Sculpturing involved the tapering of the plate to reduce the thickness where the strength requirements permitted thinner material, so that every pound of unnecessary weight could be eliminated. The degree of tapering was not uniform across the plate because thicker sections were required at points of attachment for fittings and for interior baffles. This irregular sculpturing could be performed by chemical milling or by machine milling. Chemical milling involved the coating of the aluminum plate with a protective covering except in the areas in which the metal was to be reduced in thickness. The metal was then submerged in a special chemical solution which dissolved the exposed surface and, by using appropriate control procedures, complex sculpturing could be accomplished. The Springfield division did not have large enough equipment to do the necessary chemical milling but could subcontract the job to a firm on the West Coast which had the necessary capabilities. A special "make or buy" committee was designated to analyze this situation and they recommended that the sculpturing be done within the Springfield division by machine milling.

The company had been a pioneer in the development of numerically controlled machines. By adapting one of the numerically controlled mills in the plant, they were able to produce the necessary sculpturing accurately and at a relatively low cost. In effect, the decision to use numerical control transferred a significant amount of direct labor from the shop to the engineering department which prepared the necessary instructions for the computer, which in turn controlled the numerically controlled machines.

Since the manufacture of the bulge-forming tooling had to precede the production of the bulkheads, there was more than sufficient lead time to obtain the aluminum plate and do the necessary sculpturing. The major difficulty for the purchasing department involved the procurement of the materials and parts required for the tooling.

The first material needed for the tooling was a special grade of alloy steel in thicknesses of 1 to 2 inches. Over 300 tons of steel plate was needed and GSRA required the same degree of traceability for the steel plate as was required for the aluminum plate.

Normally this type of order required about six weeks of lead time to have the plates rolled at the steel mills and delivered to the plant. Because of the delay in releasing the engineering drawings the Springfield division was requested to reduce the lead time of every operation in order to get back on schedule. Consequently, the purchasing department was requested to obtain the necessary steel plate within four days. Bob Winter, the buyer, received authorization to proceed with the procurement on Thursday afternoon. How could he get some of the steel plate into the plant by Monday morning so that fabrication of the tooling could begin? He asked himself several questions:

1. Where could he locate the special steel plate since it was a special grade normally obtained directly from the mill but possibly available from a few specialty supply companies?

2. If he had to deal with a specialty supply company, could he

obtain the necessary quality certification and test certificates required by the specifications?

3. How could he stimulate some competition so that he could get the best possible price?

4. Should he try to use a steel "finder" (sometimes called a "black market" operator) who would locate the steel and arrange delivery for a premium charge?

5. How could he minimize the freight charges?

6. Should he order the material cut to the specific size required by the shop, thus eliminating the purchase of waste material and the charges for freight on such material; or should he buy large standard-sized plates to be cut at the plant?

It was apparent to Bob Winter that any attempt to obtain a special rolling from a steel mill was out of the question. Over the years as a buyer, he had developed many personal contacts in the trade and decided to call a number of companies by long-distance phone to see if he could locate the material or get some clues to where it might be found. A full afternoon of long-distance telephoning produced nothing. In desperation he decided to call a friend who was a purchasing agent in a construction company located in Ohio whom he had met as a member of the National Association of Purchasing Agents. He thought that this company had used the special grade of alloy steel which he was seeking and might have some suggestions as to where he could find such material in inventory. The friend suggested a number of supply companies which he knew had stocked the material, but warned Winter to be careful about obtaining legitimate test certificates.

Winter finally was able to locate the necessary steel in six different supply companies located in St. Louis, Chicago, Seattle, and San Francisco. He received quotations that were the standard warehouse price in each location and he also obtained the specific sizes of material which were available in each warehouse. He then checked with the manufacturing people to correlate the sizes of plate available with the sizes that were required in terms of the final cuttings to be made. Next, he checked the freight charges from the different supply companies to Springfield by rail and truck and prepared an ordering and traffic schedule that would meet the actual shop requirements, piece by piece, and still minimize the incoming freight charges. Some pieces were ordered from St. Louis by truck on a special handling basis at a premium charge in order to have them available the following Monday morning. Other materials from the distant warehouses were scheduled to be shipped by rail under the most economical rate schedule.

Although Winter was able to avoid paying premium prices for immediate delivery from the supply companies, he estimated that he could have saved about 35 per cent of the $154,000 he paid for the material and freight if he could have waited six weeks to obtain the steel from a rolling mill. As another alternative, he estimated that if he could have had enough time to send out invitations to the supply companies for competitive bidding and used the most economical transportation method, he could have saved approximately 10 per cent of the actual cost.

In commenting on this particular procurement, Bob Winter's supervisor in the purchasing department complained about the increasing pressure placed on the buyers to get material into the plant to avoid delays in production. He felt his department was being expected to make up the lead time that was lost by others and this resulted in many small emergency orders, quick reaction time that necessitated shortcuts from normal purchasing procedure, increased paper work, and difficult administrative control problems to handle the many exceptions required from normal procedure.

The large size of the bulge-forming tools and the huge pressures to be contained by the tooling required the welding of the heavy special alloy steel plates into a massive structure. It was necessary to make many welds close together, and this apparently created severe stresses that resulted in excessive cracking of the welds. This was unacceptable, and John Brady, the tooling foreman, and various consulting experts from the steel companies that manufactured the steel plate were called in to find a satisfactory solution.

After repeated failure to find a satisfactory solution to the cracking problem, John Brady finally remembered a conversation which he had with the welding foreman at a shipyard when they were both attending a technical convention. He immediately called him long-distance and the shipyard welding foreman suggested a number of steps that he had discovered were useful in dealing with the special type of plate involved. He indicated that one of the arts to avoid cracking in welding this type of plate involved the use of a low-tensile-strength welding rod rather than the high-tensile-strength welding rod that had been specified. Extra welding rod could be deposited on the welds to obtain the necessary tensile strength. Prior to welding the plates together they had to be preheated to over 200°F. The welding had to be done with special coated rod that formed a gas around the welding arc to prevent oxygen and nitrogen from being absorbed by the weldment. The welders had to be taught new techniques in connection with the length of the welding arc, the pattern of weaving the rod as it moved along the welding seam, and other procedural refinements. The practical advice from the shipyard foreman was instrumental in solving the problems which had stumped the experts.

The large and difficult welding operations required the employment of many new welders and the retraining of welders already on the payroll. In order to get the tooling ready as quickly as possible for production, it was necessary to do the welding on a three-shift seven-day-week basis. At peak operations almost 200 welders were employed. The high temperature of the steel plates, the close working quarters, and the need for eye protection from the welding arc created very difficult environmental working conditions for the welders. In addition to their head shields they were required to wear special asbestos suits and gloves. In spite of this protection, or because of it, the welders could only work a few minutes at a time in the high environmental heat. In order to keep the job moving along, it was necessary to have teams of welders who could alternate on the job. Thus one team would be welding while the other team would be resting. Approximately every half-hour they reversed positions.

As the work of building the tooling proceeded, there was a constant flow of minor design changes which complicated the coordination problem, particularly between the various shifts. The supervisors on each shift kept a log book to record comments on what had transpired during each shift and to relay information or instructions for the supervisors on the following shift. They also came in a little early and stayed a little late in order to have personal contact with the foremen on the preceding and following shifts. In many cases the welders themselves started coming in early and staying late to improve coordination between shifts, but the supervisors had to discourage this practice so that labor laws and overtime restrictions were not violated.

John Brady studied the design of the bulge-forming tooling intensively and preplanned the detailed operations into what he believed was an optimum sequence. These individual operations then were scheduled on a Gantt chart, which was displayed in the supervisor's office. Each day the actual progress was posted to this chart so that actual conditions could be checked quickly against the predetermined schedule and behind-schedule operations could be identified easily and given the necessary attention. Based on previous experience the tooling foreman estimated the man-hours required for each operation, which then were tabulated in accordance with the schedule to establish the manpower requirements for each period of time.

Brady estimated that about 20 per cent of the labor cost could have been saved if he had not been required to work under such severe time pressures that required the complex multiple-shift coordination, the training of new employees, and the difficult environmental conditions under which the work was done. About 140,000 man-hours of direct labor was needed for completing the tooling, including the welding; installing the mechanical, electrical, and hydraulic equipment; and testing the tooling ready for production. Knowing that some day he might have to justify his costs and time schedule, John Brady kept a personal daily diary that he felt would be useful to prove good performance even if the costs and elapsed time exceeded the original estimates.

After the steel structure was welded the final cavity configuration was formed from epoxy plastic resin by molding it against a master plaster pattern. Because of the large size of the aluminum plates to be formed, it was assumed that a certain amount of springback would take place and that the shape of the die had to allow for such springback. When the full-sized die was actually tested it was discovered to everyone's surprise that there was little or no springback. This necessitated a new epoxy plastic die being recast into the steel die box. This, however, was a relatively inexpensive operation compared to changing the configuration if a steel die had been used.

During the testing operation several of the hydraulic clamping devices were broken when full pressure was applied, and it was necessary to replace a number of steel pins for the rocker arms with material of higher strength. Eventually, the bulge-forming tooling was completely tested, it was approved by the local Government Resident Inspectors in behalf of GSRA, and the tooling went into production manufacturing the gore sections for the Samson tank bulkheads.

The specifications for the bulge-forming tooling not only involved the design but also indicated the processes to be followed in manufacturing the tooling. This required surveillance and approval at specified checkpoints by local inspectors representing GSRA. The Springfield division, because of its long history as a supplier to various agencies of the government, was under the surveillance of the Government Resident Inspectors; and responsibility for surveillance of the Samson program was delegated to them by GSRA. Exhibit 4 illustrates the channels of communication which existed for the organizations involved in this program.

The primary channel of communication was supposed to be between the Springfield division and the Gulf division. Information and instructions, however, frequently flowed directly between GSRA and/or the Charlestown engineers to the Springfield division. In addition, the Government Resident Inspectors often interpreted the instructions and directives at the local level in behalf of GSRA. One of the manufacturing supervisors at the Springfield division complained that, "We are like a dog that has three leashes on its collar, being pulled in three different directions by three different people." On the other hand, another supervisor felt that the multiple contacts which were practiced permitted a lot of red tape to be eliminated and permitted direct contacts to be made between the people specifically involved in a given problem, rather than requiring the problem to pass through a number of formal echelons of "paper shufflers" who were not in a position to make much of a contribution to the particular problem involved.

Exhibit 5 shows the final issue of the weekly control chart maintained by the tooling services group, a part of the industrial engineering section. This chart was an independent control device from the Gantt control chart maintained by the tooling foreman. In addition to Exhibit 5 there were other control charts for support tools, such as dollies, slings, overhead lifts, and fixtures used to handle the bulge-forming tools. The weekly cutoff of data was Thursday night, and by Monday morning the information had been summarized, posted to the charts, and the charts duplicated and distributed to the various executives involved in the manufacturing operation.

In reviewing the history of the contract for the gore tooling Henry B. Campbell, who handled the formal financial administration of the contract, pointed out that the original statement of work to be performed under the contract was very loose since the specifications and design were not completed and a very small quantity of units was required at the time the contract was placed. In effect, therefore, he felt the original contract really provided for the spending of a certain sum of money rather than providing for a specific product. When quantity requirements were increased—and as the design concepts were clarified, the drawings were produced, and the specifications were issued—the GSRA released a series of work directives which provided authorization for the Gulf division and the Springfield division to proceed under the contract for certain limited phases of work.

As these new ideas developed and the understanding of the total work package became clearer, amendments were issued to the original contract incorporating the new quantities and new provisions and providing for the additional tooling man-hours and increased tooling costs resulting from the changes. These tooling cost increases, however, permitted a greater reduction in the costs of the manufacturing work due to the improvement in the manufacturing man-hours that were made possible by the improved tooling. A total of seventeen amendments to the original contract were issued which increased the estimated cost for tooling under the cost-plus-a-fixed-fee type of contract to $1,910,000. The final actual allowed cost for the tooling ended up at $1,897,000.

Because of time pressures and informal contacts between the people in the various organizations, the actual work at the Springfield division often was undertaken before the formal work directives and amendments to the contracts could be issued. This prevented the local government finance officer from auditing many of the costs as they were incurred and prevented him from approving payment under the cost reimbursement provision of the contract. As a result the Springfield division accumulated a large backlog of work-in-process costs which were not promptly paid for by the contracting agency. This was not the basic intention of the original contract, and it was necessary for GSRA to issue a special letter to the local finance officer permitting him to make payment in advance of the official issue of amendments to the contract, subject to possible disallowance in the postaudit review.

Because of the type of contract involved, which exposed the company to a minimum of cost risks, the profit allowance was small—being slightly under 5 per cent on the final target cost. Other forms of contracts would have permitted a higher profit. Campbell felt that in the future the company should avoid cost-plus-a-fixed-fee type contracts and instead attempt to obtain fixed-price incentive type contracts, which afforded a better opportunity for a greater profit. He recognized, however, that this would require more reasonable time schedules to be established and that the design concepts and specifications of the program would have to be more clearly defined than was the case in the present program.

Campbell was also disturbed by the multiple channels of communication which existed and by the difficulty he had in formalizing many of the changes into the contract which had been informally agreed to by the engineers and the manufacturing people. At one point there had been a complete breakdown of understanding, when one group of executives negotiated the cost of a major revision in the program at a substantially lower figure than had been anticipated by another group in the organization. When the misunderstanding was uncovered, it created some conflict with the contracting officer at GSRA and it became very embarrassing to the Springfield division negotiators to arrange a correction of the original plan that they had presented. Campbell felt that there should be a "single point of entry" for information and contract authorization.

"All's well that ends well, I guess" was the overview judgment of Lou Handler, staff assistant in the production manager's office. He pointed out that the Springfield division's previous experience with the government agencies had been to receive broad overall objectives from their customer, who then left them relatively free to work out the details of the program. On the Samson program, however, the overall objectives had not been completely clarified at the beginning of the program, and both the GSRA people and the Gulf division people were constantly involved in many of the details of the program at the Springfield division. Lou Handler was given the assignment of reviewing the overall program in order to make an evaluation and recommendations for company policy and procedure in the future if a similar type of program was undertaken. In considering his assignment, he indicated the point of view he planned to use in making the evaluation: "Our big job is not to avoid problems but to learn how to respond to new problems economically, faster, and with better coordination."

# EXHIBIT 1

## Samson launch vehicle with Helios spacecraft

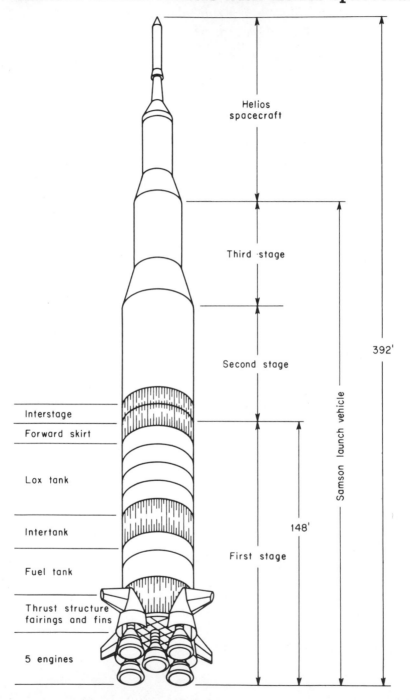

## EXHIBIT 2

# Tank showing construction of bulkheads

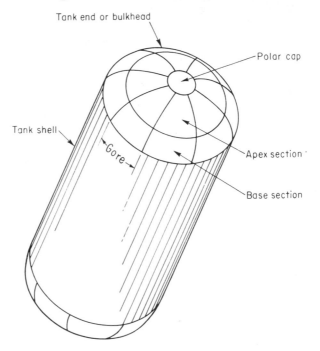

# EXHIBIT 3

## Schematic diagram of cross section of bulge-forming tool

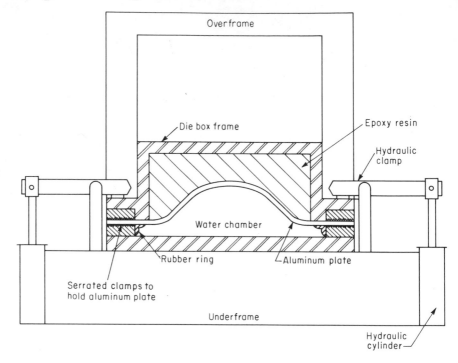

# EXHIBIT 4

## Channels of communication

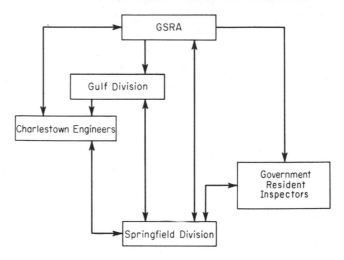

# EXHIBIT 5
# Weekly control chart

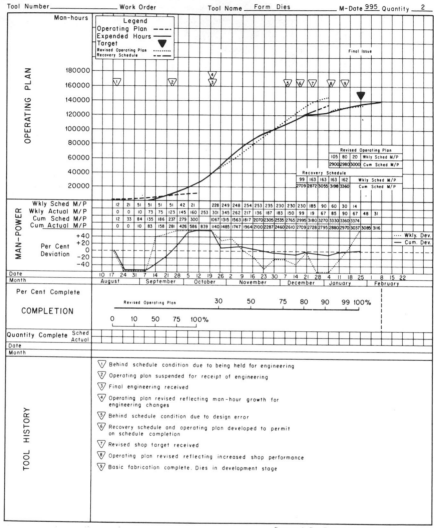

Tool Number_____ Work Order _____ Tool Name __Form Dies__ M-Date _995_ Quantity __2__

Per Cent Complete

COMPLETION

Quantity Complete Sched / Actual

Date
Month

TOOL HISTORY

1. Behind schedule condition due to being held for engineering
2. Operating plan suspended for receipt of engineering
3. Final engineering received
4. Operating plan revised reflecting man-hour growth for engineering changes
5. Behind schedule condition due to design error
6. Recovery schedule and operating plan developed to permit on schedule completion
7. Revised shop target received
8. Operating plan revised reflecting increased shop performance
9. Basic fabrication complete. Dies in development stage

Prepared By: Tooling Services Group
Operations And Control Unit
Industrial Engineering Section

# DISCUSSION QUESTIONS

1. What are the factors to be considered in determining a tooling "philosophy"?

2. What is a Gantt chart? Design a chart that would be suitable for control of the tooling operation.

3. What factors should have been considered in the "make or buy" decision regarding sculpturing of the aluminum plate?

4. Could the pressure on the purchasing department have been avoided or at least alleviated? If so, how?

5. How do you account for the fact that the solution to the welding problems was suggested by a "practical" shipyard foreman rather than by the "experts"? What kind of attitude should management take toward practical men versus theoretical experts?

6. What can be done, if anything, to improve the complex communication problems between the various agencies, divisions, departments, and sections?

7. What kind of contract would you recommend for this kind of job? Why?

8. What specific policy matters should Lou Handler consider? What are your recommendations regarding these policy issues?

# REFERENCES

Buffa, Elwood S.: *Modern Production Management* (New York: John Wiley & Sons, Inc., 1961), chap. 13.

Ireson, W. Grant, and Eugene L. Grant (eds.): *Handbook of Industrial Engineering and Management* (Englewood Cliffs, N.J.: Prentice-Hall, Inc., 1955), sec. 10.

Maynard, H. B. (ed.): *Industrial Engineering Handbook* (New York: McGraw-Hill Book Company, 1956), sec. 6, chap. 2; sec. 7, chap. 6.

Rago, Louis J.: *Production Analysis and Control* (Scranton, Pa.: International Textbook Company, 1963), chap. 6.

Schaller, Gilbert S.: *Engineering Manufacturing Methods,* 2d ed. (New York: McGraw-Hill Book Company, 1959), chap. 12.

# SIERRA INSTRUMENT COMPANY

Success was causing considerable concern to supervisor Hugh Poltier. Although his value analysis department in the purchasing division had been in existence for less than a year, the studies made by Poltier and his staff had resulted in substantial savings for the Sierra Instrument Company. This had led to an expansion of the department's activities which, it seemed to Poltier, was causing the department to lose some of its earlier effectiveness.

At first the value analysis department had conducted studies only on items suggested by buyers in the purchasing division. Under this arrangement the value analysts were able to spend as much as 90 per cent of their time on investigations that had brought about significant improvements. The balance of their time was spent in answering inquiries from buyers and advising them whether certain items would justify an analytical investigation. The majority of the items suggested by the buyers proved to be worthwhile. It was felt, however, that these suggestions represented only a small fraction of the opportunities for value analysis arising in the purchasing division. It was decided, therefore, that all items requisitioned for procurement through the purchasing division would be screened by the value analysis department before action was taken by the buyers. This procedure required the value analysts to spend more than half their time screening requisitions and greatly reduced the time available for fruitful investigations. Hugh Poltier was worried that if this trend continued his department would become a bottleneck with increasing amounts of burdensome red tape and that the savings resulting from value analysis would be more than offset by the added cost of the organization and procedure for making the value analysis.

The Sierra Instrument Company was an old and well-established firm located in Ashtabula, Ohio. It was organized in the early 1920s by several young engineers to manufacture speedometers and other dashboard instruments for the growing auto industry. The depression of the 1930s had forced the company to expand their line of mechanical-electrical equipment to supply other industries, but their major activities, by far, continued with the auto industry. This was intensified during World War II when they were heavily involved in supplying equipment for tanks as subcontractors to the major auto companies who held the prime contracts. They did, however, develop some experience as prime contractors on a few small orders for specialty products with several military agencies.

After the war the revival of auto manufacturing again commanded the exclusive attention and efforts of the company. But after only a few years of capacity production, a new trend in the auto industry brought serious jeopardy to the company. Vertical integration by the major auto companies caused one after another of Sierra's products to be produced in the shops of the auto manufacturers or their wholly owned subsidiaries. Sierra Instrument was forced to seek out new markets in which their mechanical-electrical skills in designing and manufacturing could be used, e.g., the aircraft industry. By 1950 their business with the aircraft industry, though relatively small, was diversified and growing; and they were involved with the development of many new items for a number of airframe and aircraft engine companies. The advent of the Korean War greatly increased their volume to the extent that their major efforts and volume of business were with the aircraft industry.

During the next several years the company enlarged its staff of engineers and scientists in order to engage in the extensive amount of research and development work that was essential for success in the aircraft and missile industry. This led to a wider range of products of increasing complexity in which the importance of quality, performance, and reliability was dominant. In this respect the company was successful in reorienting its original limited activities as only an auto parts and equipment supplier, i.e., mass production in huge volume of simply designed standard products at the lowest possible cost.

In 1957, limited funds required the Air Force to cut down on its procurement. This caused some aircraft programs to be canceled, others were reduced in size, many were slowed down or delayed, and all programs were subjected to close scrutiny relative to costs. Sierra Instrument Company did not escape the pressure of customers who became more demanding, competitors who offered more and/or cut price, and increasing internal overhead rates caused by a decrease in the production rate.

The management at Sierra was thus goaded into action. They began by requesting an analysis from the cost department. This analysis pointed to some possible minor improvements but concluded that in general the company's costs and prices were in line. An observation was made, however, that 30 per cent of average costs consisted of direct labor charges and 45 per cent consisted of expenditures made through the purchasing division. It became evident to the management that a small improvement in purchasing effectiveness could result in savings equivalent to a large improvement in other functions. The purchasing division agreed to make a determined effort to reduce costs by means of a cost improvement program.

In the first phase of the program the buyers were instructed to tighten up on their suppliers. Many existing subcontracts were reopened and some price reductions were obtained, but often these suppliers made up their price reductions by skimping on quality. Many vendors slowed up on their deliveries as other more profitable business was given schedule preference, or overtime work on Sierra's orders was discontinued. Strong emphasis was placed on price competition by the buyers, with the result that frequently the low bidder and contract winner was a vendor that did not know his exact costs. Vendors began to expect to bargain with the buyers, and it was discovered that some suppliers entered a high first bid so that they could satisfy the buyer by lower prices during negotiation (to the levels that they previously would have submitted on the first bid). Sierra developed a trade reputation as a chiseler, and several good vendors stopped responding to bid invitations.

The second phase of the cost reduction activity was a value analysis program that was instituted in the purchasing division by having each supervisor meet with his buyers, explain the meaning of value analysis, and emphasize the importance of each buyer using this new technique. This phase (as well as the first phase) was received by the buyers with negative enthusiasm. After several months no beneficial results were discernible from the value analysis program.

Continued pressure for cost reduction finally led the chief purchasing agent to the third phase of the cost reduction program within the purchasing division. He set up a separate value analysis department in which the technique could receive concentrated and specialized attention as a support activity for the buyers in the division. In order to bring in a fresh point of view, Hugh Poltier was hired to be the supervisor of the new department. He came from another industry where price competition was severe. Although he did not have specific experience with the aircraft industry or with value analysis as such, his previous fine record as a member of management, his technical and business training, his diplomatically effective way of dealing with difficult people and situations, and his natural curiosity and imagination seemed to qualify him for the job.

Two buyers were assigned to work in the new department, and Poltier embarked on an intensive self-education program for himself and his staff. He visited several companies which were successful in using value analysis, including the General Electric Company and the Ford Motor Company which had pioneered in establishing formal value analysis programs after World War II. From this self-study evolved a set of concepts and policies for the department.

Poltier viewed value analysis as "a science for the removal of unnecessary costs without impairing desired functions." This would be accomplished by specialized evaluation of the factors influencing the cost of an item; in many ways it was similar to the kind of specialized evaluation made by stress engineers, patent attorneys, contract coordinators, industrial engineers, or other specialists who from time to time would be called on by a buyer for assistance.

By November, 1957, the department was ready to begin operations and all buyers were requested to submit items for study. The types of items desired were not defined carefully, but it was generally understood that they might be items which the buyer was having trouble placing with a competent supplier, in which the price seemed too high for the use intended for the item, or where it appeared a change in design could result in savings. Within 6 months 57 items were analyzed. Of these, 22 items were not improved significantly, but 35 items yielded $367,000 in cost reduction.

Poltier operated largely on an informal basis with the buyers. First, he established the various functions desired from an item and the relative importance of each function. Thus, the aspects of the design or procurement which affected performance or reliability within the indicated specifications were considered. At times appearance, comfort, or convenience functions were treated as important, but generally these received minor consideration. Pride of ownership, pride of authorship, and perpetuation of habits or practices were never given serious consideration.

After the functional aspects were clearly established, consideration was given to the detailed design, the materials to be used, the processing method required, and the purchasing procedure to be followed. Where necessary, additional information was obtained from whoever might be helpful (including vendors) in providing facts or making suggestions or evaluations. Imaginative alternatives that might be considered included changes in design, materials, or processes; use of standard parts; locating more highly qualified vendors; utilizing economic order quantities; or elimination of the item altogether by changing other items.

After the alternatives were evaluated (with heavy use of common sense) and a decision was made (in which the practicability of convincing others was carefully considered), a program of persuasion was undertaken with the persons involved in any of the changes. If this resulted in agreement, the value analysis department continued to coordinate to assure that the course of action agreed upon was implemented and that the experience gained would improve the next design or the next purchase.

Poltier's group generally was well accepted, and he believed that the lack of conflict was due to his informal manner of operation and because his recommendations were only advisory to others. In addition, only a few buyers submitted suggestions, with the others indicating that they had no problems which needed attention. Poltier was convinced, however, that there were serious hurdles blocking these buyers from submitting other items that he was sure could benefit from value analysis. He was puzzled, however, as to how to motivate the buyers to screen more ideas from their individual operations and submit them to the value analysis department.

Poltier discussed the problem with his superior, the chief purchasing agent, who decided that the success to date of the department justified its operation on a more formal basis to achieve further results in the shortest possible time. This led to the departmental order that all requisitions for procurement would be screened by the value analysis department before the buyer took action.

# DISCUSSION QUESTIONS

1. What hurdles might be blocking many buyers from participating on a voluntary basis in the value analysis effort?
2. Is a specialized department for value analysis really necessary? Should it be part of the purchasing division?
3. What do you think of the present administrative arrangement?
4. What suggestions do you have for Poltier?
5. What do you think Poltier means by calling value analysis a "science"? Is it any different from getting a "best buy"?
6. What kind of a background should a value analyst have?

# REFERENCES

England, Wilbur B.: *Procurement Principles and Cases,* 4th ed. (Homewood, Ill.: Richard D. Irwin, Inc., 1962), chaps. 2, 3, 5.

Westing, J. H., and T. V. Fine: *Industrial Purchasing,* 2d ed. (New York: John Wiley & Sons. Inc., 1961), chaps. 2, 15.

# SONIC AIRCRAFT
# CORPORATION

The Sonic Aircraft Corporation had a practice of building "mock-ups" or full-sized models of the planes they produced. Although the value of mock-ups to the sales program, engineering design, and production planning was evident, the number and types of mock-ups that the company should build were not easy to determine.

The Sonic Aircraft Corporation had used four different classes of mock-ups, as follows:

Class I
A. This class of mock-up was used in the early design stages to develop preliminary engineering information for the following purposes:
   1. *Structural type of mock-up.* To review the overall perimeter configuration and space relationships of major structural elements.
   2. *Nonstructural type of mock-up.* Equipment and systems mock-ups were developed to study the space requirements for specific systems and equipment.
B. Type of construction, extent of completeness, and tolerance requirements were defined by engineering. Generally, only a limited portion of the plane was built in mock-up form to loose tolerances. There might be several separate vehicles, each built for a different section of the plane.
C. The information required to accomplish this development was transmitted in the form of limited layouts and coordination sheets.

## Class II

A. This class of mock-up was used to develop firm engineering information for the final structural design. It also was used to develop specific locations and space arrangements for systems and equipment.
B. The engineering information required to accomplish this class of development included drawings, layouts, and coordination sheets.
C. Fabrication was of wood or metal, whichever was the most economical. Standard manufacturing tolerances were maintained where production parts were available; otherwise "dummy" parts to less rigid tolerances were used.

## Class III

A. This class of mock-up was used primarily by the manufacturing departments to determine final configuration and dimensions for certain nonstructural parts.
B. The nonstructural work which required final development by the use of the mock-up prior to the issuance of production releases were:
  1. *Tubing.*
     a. To determine and establish tube routing and attachment points.
     b. To establish tube samples prior to "proof-fit" on the first production airplane. (Once the tubing was tested in the Class III mock-up, it was released for production. However, the production tube was tested in the first plane before large quantities of the tubing were produced. This test was called "proof-fit.")
  2. *Wire.* To determine and establish wire lengths and hookups.
  3. *Cables,* To establish cable lengths and turnbuckle locations prior to "proof-fit" on the first production airplane.
  4. *Insulation.* To establish templates for production use.
  5. *Production.*
  6. *Illustration.* To obtain information for production and assembly instructions.
C. The engineering data required for building both structural and nonstructural parts for the mock-up were the "firm advance production information" which authorized fabrication of production quality parts.
D. Installations of equipment and systems were made in the Class III mock-up on an "if and as required" basis. Only those detailed parts which were necessary for the needs of manufacturing were installed in the mock-up vehicle.

## Class IV

A. This class of mock-up was used primarily to sell planes. It helped the customer visualize the color combinations of the interior furnishings, the passenger loading and seating arrangement, the type and arrangement of passenger service facilities, etc.

B. The engineering information required to accomplish this class of development included drawings, layouts, and coordination sheets.

C. Fabrication of the shell was of wood or metal, whichever was the most economical. Tolerances were not critical. The interior furnishings were produced to duplicate the furnishings which would be installed in the finished product. However, the customer might suggest changes in the color, material, or arrangement after viewing the mock-up. The electrical, mechanical, hydraulic, and other similar equipment not normally visible to passenger or crew were not installed.

In summary, Class I was merely a model of a fractional part of the plane used by the engineers to establish general space relationships, such as a mock-up of the cabin to determine how high the pilot's seat should be in order to provide ample visibility. Class II was also an engineering mock-up, but more complete than Class I and including the space relationships of the systems and equipment to be installed. Class III was a complete model of the plane including hydraulic tubing, electrical wiring, cables, and insulation. Class IV emphasized the interior appearance of the plane. All four classes were to full-size scale. Class III was built to production tolerances, whereas the Class I, II, and IV mock-ups had less rigid tolerances.

For each new series of planes, separate Class IV mock-ups were built for the sales group; and several Class I vehicles, a single Class II mock-up, and a single Class III mock-up were built for engineering and manufacturing. The construction work was performed by a special mock-up manufacturing shop which was separate from the production shops. Class I mock-ups usually were built from wood, Class II and IV mock-ups were a combination of wood and metal with production parts used whenever possible, and the Class III mock-up was manufactured almost entirely with production parts.

There were three critical problems encountered with the mock-up program. First, there was a definite lack of space in which to build and store the bulky mock-ups. Second, the cost of building these models was very great—sometimes more than it cost to build the actual plane once it was in production. Third, there was a need to reduce the flow time in manufacturing the mock-ups.

The Sonic Aircraft Corporation had found it was impossible to design and manufacture their complex planes economically and expeditiously without models and mock-ups. It was very difficult to visualize every dimensional aspect of each part and its relationship to the whole. One group of engineers designed the structure, another the power plant, another the landing gear, another the ventilating system, etc. Class I mock-ups helped the engineers visualize the basic design requirements, while Class II mock-ups served as a means of coordinating the design overlap which existed among the individual engineering groups.

Exhibit 1 illustrates the general stages and order of airplane assembly. The wing and body structures were assembled separately. These assemblies were the basic structural shells, without the wiring, tubing, etc. At another assembly area the nonstructural units which could be assembled independent of body or wing were processed, e.g., engines. At each subsequent stage additional tubing, wiring, instruments, insulation, furnishings, etc., were added until the assembly was complete.

It was very difficult to determine the best installation sequence without the aid of mock-ups. For example, should the oxygen system be installed during the assembly of the body section or during final assembly? The Class III mock-up was used to help make an optimum plan concerning such decisions.

A member of the top-management group of Sonic Aircraft had suggested that the company should eliminate the Class II mock-ups and thereby eliminate one of the vehicles which was normally built. This would require that a single mock-up serve the needs of both engineering and manufacturing. John Fowler, the originator of the suggestion, summarized the advantages of combining the two classes of mock-ups as follows:

1. Material costs would be saved by eliminating the Class II vehicle.
2. Manpower costs would be reduced for mock-up construction.
3. Flow time could be reduced.
4. The critical space requirement problem would be eased.
5. Engineering commitments on design would be forced to be made earlier in the program.

Previously, the first three classes of mock-ups were constructed in the time sequence as shown in Exhibit 2. The three stages overlapped. Thus construction of Class III, for example, could begin before the engineers released firm commitments on design of all sections of the plane. Under Fowler's plan Class II and Class III would be combined as one vehicle and the flow time schedule would be as shown in Exhibit 3. The Class II work on the vehicle would phase out gradually as the phase III work was added to the mock-up. At time $X$ (Exhibit 3) the manufacturing groups could start their work on certain sections of the plane, and when time $Y$ was reached the engineering groups would have completed their design work and their need for the vehicle terminated. After time $Y$ the vehicle would be completely available to the manufacturing groups.

The company decided to adopt Fowler's suggestion and combine Class II and III mock-ups. Many months later the following results of their decision were reviewed by top management:

1. Combining the two vehicles did not reduce the flow time.

2. Engineering did not meet their commitment. Class III work was delayed and could not start until all Class II work was nearly complete.

3. Engineering never terminated their work. They maintained a sustaining engineering effort which resulted in continued improvements of design long after the plane was in production. As a result, their redesign changed production parts which in turn required the continual rebuilding of the Class II/III mock-up.

4. The mock-up shop attributed the man-hours expended over target to the use of a common vehicle for Class II and III mock-ups (see Exhibit 4).

After reviewing the results and particularly the costs, Fowler maintained that the additional cost of mock-up construction was due to the efforts of manufacturing to combine too many model variations in one mock-up. When the design of any one of these variations changed, it became necessary to reconstruct the mock-up. Further, Fowler believed that there was an advantage to this program which had not been recognized. Engineering had been required to make earlier design commitments and this, in turn, would reduce the number of out-of-sequence installations. Thus, by requiring the planning to be completed earlier than on other programs, the installation would be more efficient.

It was true that engineering releases were closer to schedule than ever before, but there were no comparative figures to determine savings, if any, on the assembly costs. Engineering was very unhappy about the pressure forced on them by this program, and some executives doubted if engineering would be willing to accept the same arrangement for the next program.

At this time the production program for a new commercial transport plane was being planned. Fowler was asked to make a presentation to top management and engineering regarding his recommendations for mock-ups in this new program.

# EXHIBIT 1

## Production scheduling

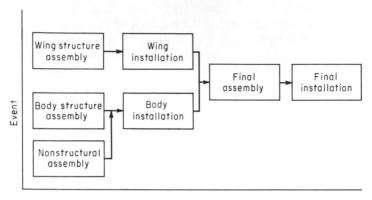

# EXHIBIT 2

## Normal construction schedule for mock-ups

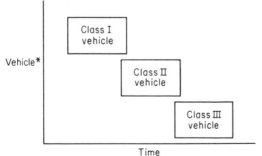

*A vehicle is used to describe a specific mock-up unit.

# EXHIBIT 3

## Proposed construction schedule for mock-ups

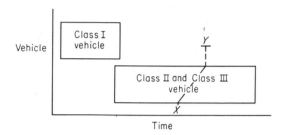

# EXHIBIT 4

## Mock-up man-hour summary

|  | Estimated target man-hours | Actual man-hours | Per cent expended |
|---|---|---|---|
| Class I: |  |  |  |
| Vehicle development | 96,621 | 97,977 | 102 |
| Miscellaneous engineering support | 53,673 | 39,331 | 73 |
| Total estimated target | 150,294 |  |  |
| *Target reduction | 15,294 |  |  |
| Total target | 135,000 | 137,308 | 102 |
| Class II: |  |  |  |
| Vehicle development | 186,011 | 380,693 | 202 |
| *Target increase | 93,000 |  |  |
| Total target | 279,011 | 380,693 | 136 |
| Class III: |  |  |  |
| Vehicle development | 200,300 | 364,644 | 182 |
| *Target increase | 120,200 |  |  |
| Total target | 320,500 | 364,644 | 113 |
| Program total target | 734,511 | 882,645 | 121 |

* The original forecast of man-hour requirements was adjusted.

# DISCUSSION QUESTIONS

1. Would mock-ups be useful to companies which were not in the aircraft industry? Why?

2. How can manufacturing cope with engineering changes which occur during production?

3. What reasons can you advance for maintaining the mock-up construction shop as a separate organization?

4. Which potential advantage did Fowler list which impressed you the most? Why?

5. Do you think the company would gain by combining the Class II and III mock-ups? Why?

6. Why might an estimated target, as illustrated in Exhibit 4, be changed during a program?

7. Do you think the forecast illustrated in Exhibit 4 is reasonable?

8. Can engineering be placed on a time schedule?

9. Should a company use a "crutch" to solve a problem, e.g., a devious method of getting early engineering commitments?

# REFERENCES

Bethel, Lawrence L., Franklin S. Atwater, George H. E. Smith, and Harvey A. Stackman, Jr.: *Industrial Organization and Management*, 4th ed. (New York: McGraw-Hill Book Company, 1962), pp. 151–170.

Buffa, Elwood S.: *Modern Production Management* (New York: John Wiley & Sons, Inc., 1961), pp. 342–370.

# SOUTHERN HYDRAULIC SUPPLIES COMPANY

The Southern Hydraulic Supplies Company was a distributor of hydraulic supplies in the Gulf states area. Southern handled standard hydraulic fittings, tubing, and similar items. Generally Southern carried an entire line for each manufacturer whose products it handled and provided local stocks for rapid delivery to customers. The items that Southern stocked were mainly used in the maintenance, modification, and manufacture of trucks, off-highway construction equipment, and machine tools. In some cases, these standard lines were also of high enough quality for use in aircraft and military production.

Southern had grown from a small two-man operation to a $15 million per year business in a span of twenty-five years. The growth of its dollar volume was based on an excellent reputation for good service coupled with the general expansion of industry in the Gulf states. From its inception Southern had been a profitable business in sound financial condition.

In spite of the continued growth of profits in absolute terms, however, Southern found that profits as a percentage of sales declined to well below the level that the company had enjoyed in the past. When management became aware of the seriousness of the problem, it was decided to undertake a thorough review of policies and procedures in the areas that could have significant influence on costs and profits—namely, product line, sales methods, stock handling and storage methods, billing and record keeping, and inventory replenishment. The last area was included as a major area for study because the company had been experiencing increasing difficulty with out-of-stock situations and unbalanced inventories.

Up until the time that the review of the inventory replenishment policies and procedures was begun, there had been no formal study of this phase of the company's operations. Since maintaining inventories was one of the company's major functions, Southern had always used experienced personnel to control the placing of orders and had relied on their judgment to make correct decisions. One thing that became immediately apparent as this phase of Southern's operations came under scrutiny was that the inventory replenishment problem had become vastly more complicated in recent years since the variety of items carried had tripled from what it was five years previously to more than 15,000 separate stock items. Since no formal study had been made previously of the inventory replenishment operations, it was decided as a first step to get some general information about order placement costs and inventory carrying costs and also to analyze in detail several typical items of inventory.

Several years earlier Southern had installed an IBM punched card system for maintaining inventory records and writing purchase orders. The data processing equipment also was used for other record keeping functions and in order to efficiently schedule this equipment the inventory records were updated only once weekly. Purchase orders were also prepared on a schedule of once each week. Purchase requisitions were turned in daily by the supervisors responsible for various types of stock, and these were accumulated until Friday when they were used to initiate purchase orders. In effect this meant that review of the inventory levels occurred once every five days, and, in fact, almost all the supervisors turned in their purchase requisitions only once each week immediately before the scheduled machine run. This caused no particular scheduling or processing problem because the purchase requisitions were themselves punched cards on which the stock man wrote the quantity desired, which was then keypunched into the card. In total, the out-of-pocket cost of preparing and processing a requisition, preparing a purchase order, and making other necessary record changes was estimated to be $2.50 per order.

Analysis of the company records indicated that the following were reasonable estimates of the variable cost per year of carrying inventories (as a percentage of dollar value of average inventory):

|                        | Per cent |
|------------------------|----------|
| Capital cost           | 6        |
| Obsolescence           | 5        |
| Insurance              | 1        |
| Taxes                  | 1        |
| Storage and handling   | 8        |
| Total                  | 21       |

One of the typical items of inventory which were analyzed in detail was a small hydraulic fitting. The fitting was purchased for $4 and sold for $5. The manufacturer from whom Southern procured the fitting did not offer any quantity discount on the fitting, but it would not fill orders for less than fifty fittings without adding a flat charge of $25 to the order. For this particular item, there were other distributors in Southern's immediate vicinity that could supply a comparable fitting made by another manufacturer. Because of this, orders which Southern could not fill immediately were lost, and Southern's sales manager felt that the company lost at least another dollar per fitting in other lost business and lost goodwill in addition to the dollar of lost margin on the fitting.

The fitting was ordered from the manufacturer located about 1,500 miles away and shipped to Southern by truck. An analysis of the time taken to receive the fittings from the day the purchase order was prepared until the fittings were received indicated that this varied between five and fourteen working days. The historical record of the time between the preparation of the purchase order and receipt of the fittings is shown in Exhibit 1. It was estimated that inspection of the shipments, preparation of receiving reports, and related activities cost Southern $2.25 per order.

The customer daily orders for one full year (260 working days) were tabulated for this fitting and are shown in Exhibit 2. Further analysis of the records pertaining to this fitting revealed the fact that the replenishment orders for the fitting were always for lots of 500 and that the amount of stock on hand averaged about 115 units on the days that purchase orders were issued for replenishment stock.

# EXHIBIT 1

## Analysis of procurement lead times

(Working days between order issue and delivery of merchandise) *

| | |
|---|---|
| 8 | 11 |
| 12 | 14 |
| 6 | 9 |
| 5 | 8 |
| 7 | 9 |
| 8 | 7 |
| 8 | 6 |
| 9 | 8 |
| 13 | 13 |
| 9 | 10 |
| 10 | 7 |
| 8 | 7 |
| 11 | 12 |
| 7 | 10 |
| 8 | 9 |
| 5 | 10 |
| 7 | 7 |
| 6 | 8 |
| 9 | 14 |
| 7 | 6 |

* Average lead time = 8.7 days.

# EXHIBIT 2

## Analysis of demand for one year

(Sales per day) *

| | | | | | |
|---|---|---|---|---|---|
| 35 | 9 | 17 | 16 | 20 | 0 |
| 0 | 8 | 4 | 0 | 0 | 19 |
| 0 | 0 | 28 | 11 | 13 | 29 |
| 17 | 17 | 25 | 16 | 7 | 18 |
| 36 | 0 | 27 | 0 | 0 | 11 |
| 6 | 28 | 20 | 13 | 14 | 29 |
| 0 | 0 | 0 | 24 | 0 | 14 |
| 5 | 29 | 7 | 11 | 10 | 0 |
| 11 | 9 | 0 | 0 | 41 | 19 |
| 18 | 0 | 8 | 27 | 8 | 31 |
| 0 | 0 | 0 | 26 | 0 | 10 |
| 4 | 0 | 18 | 0 | 9 | 16 |
| 16 | 23 | 28 | 6 | 22 | 0 |
| 25 | 0 | 20 | 0 | 0 | 27 |
| 0 | 17 | 22 | 26 | 0 | 18 |
| 19 | 8 | 0 | 13 | 44 | 14 |
| 14 | 13 | 0 | 0 | 24 | 0 |
| 32 | 31 | 16 | 21 | 0 | 0 |
| 15 | 8 | 31 | 17 | 7 | 38 |
| 0 | 0 | 24 | 22 | 40 | 3 |
| 17 | 25 | 16 | 0 | 9 | 17 |
| 18 | 11 | 0 | 10 | 0 | 0 |
| 10 | 0 | 0 | 42 | 0 | 21 |
| 30 | 43 | 14 | 0 | 0 | 15 |
| 15 | 9 | 36 | 18 | 21 | 0 |
| 0 | 0 | 11 | 0 | 16 | 9 |
| 12 | 12 | 0 | 12 | 0 | 14 |
| 21 | 22 | 3 | 27 | 23 | 0 |
| 23 | 15 | 30 | 4 | 19 | 6 |
| 15 | 0 | 12 | 19 | 25 | 23 |
| 12 | 7 | 0 | 17 | 0 | 12 |
| 0 | 15 | 10 | 0 | 2 | 22 |
| 19 | 10 | 0 | 34 | 15 | 0 |
| 37 | 33 | 20 | 17 | 12 | 34 |
| 0 | 26 | 14 | 21 | 0 | 5 |
| 13 | 0 | 21 | 0 | 32 | |
| 0 | 6 | 0 | 18 | 8 | |
| 18 | 20 | 17 | 13 | 0 | |
| 20 | 13 | 37 | 24 | 5 | |
| 14 | 7 | 19 | 33 | 15 | |
| 19 | 0 | 0 | 26 | 20 | |
| 18 | 0 | 0 | 0 | 30 | |
| 0 | 39 | 35 | 18 | 23 | |
| 10 | 19 | 16 | 0 | 0 | |
| 15 | 16 | 13 | 16 | 11 | |

* Average demand per day = 13.1.

# DISCUSSION QUESTIONS

1. In what lot sizes should the hydraulic fittings be ordered?
2. At what stock level should an order for fittings be placed?
3. Based on the information available, what possibilities appear to be present for improving inventory management procedures?

# REFERENCES

Buffa, Elwood S.: *Modern Production Management* (New York: John Wiley & Sons, Inc., 1961), chap. 7.

Fetter, Robert B., and Winston C. Dalleck: *Decision Models for Inventory Management* (Homewood, Ill.: Richard D. Irwin, Inc., 1961).

Magee, John F.: *Production Planning and Inventory Control* (New York: McGraw-Hill Book Company, 1958), chaps. 4, 5.

# SPECIFIC ELECTRIC
# COMPANY

Each Tuesday morning Joe Bennett, general foreman of the finishing department of the Specific Electric Company, came to work an hour early to analyze his weekly indirect and overhead cost allocation report. The report specified the individual overhead and indirect cost allocations charged against his department for the previous week. The charges were broken down into fifty-two classifications, of which approximately twelve were applicable to Bennett's department. The report was distributed Monday night during the latter part of the night shift and consisted of all charges up to and including the termination of operations on the previous Friday or Saturday, depending on whether a five- or six-day workweek was in force. Figures on the report were stated in terms of an absolute and percentage deviation of actual charges from budgeted amounts for the "current week," "last week," and "year to date."

Ever since the new electronic data processing system was installed, which allowed the determination of these allocations to be made on both a current and detailed basis, Joe Bennett was able to maintain his aggregate charges below the budgeted amounts on both a weekly and year-to-date basis. Individual item charges, however, occasionally exceeded their respective budgets. Whenever this happened, Joe Bennett conducted a vigorous investigation to determine the cause. Having determined the reason, he even more vigorously attempted to correct or eliminate the problem. This generally resulted in one of three courses:

1. Action within his department to reduce future charges below their respective budgeted amounts

2. Action to change the budgeted figure

3. Action to change the calculation procedure by which the specific allocations were made

The second and third courses of action had previously been effective ways for solving the problem of exceeding the budget. This was primarily due to the fact that the system was quite new and a good many bugs had to be worked out. The system had now been in use for over a year and requested changes in budget allowance or in allocation procedure were becoming very difficult to justify. This was primarily due to the fact that errors or improper procedure now rarely occurred, and also because the cost department refused to approve any changes unless accompanied by overwhelming evidence supporting the merit and value of each change requested. It was the cost department's conviction ". . . that the system had been in operation long enough to work out the major problems and it was time to stop making changes and operate the system in an efficient manner." It was also felt that the constant introduction of changes made cost comparisons among time periods of little value. The only changes which currently were processed in a routine manner were errors in data and errors in the application of the formal procedure.

Joe Bennett noticed that in the last three reports his inventory holding cost allocation and his special priority cost allocation were rising and were currently 5 and 10 per cent above their respective weekly budgeted amounts. The total year-to-date charges in each of these classifications were still below the budgeted amount but would quickly exceed their respective budgets if the current trend was not arrested. The inventory holding cost allocation was a 1 per cent per month charge on the value of each department's stores inventory at the beginning of each cost allocation period. The current estimate of the finishing department's stores inventory was $4,352,000. The special priority cost allocation consisted of a $25 charge for each purchase requisition for which a special-handling priority was requested.

To determine the validity or invalidity of the figures and to prevent the continuation of any possible undesirable·trends, Bennett called Jim Driscoll, his chief stores clerk, into his office to discuss the matter in detail. Jim Driscoll admitted that he was aware of an increase in the number of special-handling purchase requisitions initiated by his people but was completely unable to understand how the inventory holding cost allocation could be above the budgeted amount. He stated that his clerks kept a continuous record of the value of receipts and disbursements and that the total inventory value had been decreasing for several weeks. Moreover, the department had been operating at maximum capacity for over three months, thus being allowed the maximum budget amount for each cost classification. He said, however, that in checking his own inventory figures with those of the cost department, the cost department stated that his figures were way off.

Although he was unable to reconcile the two sets of figures, the possibility that his figures were way off was entirely inconceivable to him. Jim, however, admitted that the increase in special priority purchase requisitions could possibly have resulted from the failure of a new employee to properly post stores disbursements during the first three weeks of his employment. The error was such that it did not result in all postings being incorrect. Jim indicated that this problem had been corrected with respect to current and future postings but all past posting errors could not be conveniently corrected until the arrival of the next shipment of each item which was incorrectly posted. In cases where the posting error caused the stock card count to be substantially greater than the actual number of parts on hand, a stockout could result before a reorder was placed. In such cases a special-handling priority would have to be affixed to the original purchase requisition. If the difference were in the same direction but not of sufficient magnitude, the stockout might occur after the reorder was placed with a vendor but before the actual receipt of the new order. In this case also, unless the purchase order was en route, a special priority would have to be requested to expedite the purchase order so as to prevent an excessive delay in the finishing department's operations.

If the opposite error resulted, i.e., the stock and count was less than the actual count, no shortage would occur; rather, new parts would arrive ahead of their actual need and cause temporary excess inventory. The posting errors, therefore, could possibly explain the unexpected buildup of stores inventories, the discrepancy between the stores and accounting department's inventory estimates for the beginning of the last cost allocation period, and the increase in special priority cost allocations.

Joe Bennett felt that this was a logical, but certainly not an excusable, explanation of the problem and was very unhappy about the situation. He communicated these feelings to Jim Driscoll in saying ". . . I don't go for this kind of sloppiness. You had better see that it doesn't happen again. If it does, we'll find some way of making you wish it hadn't. . . ."

Joe Bennett then questioned Jim as to what remedial action he planned to take to prevent next week's special priority cost allocation from exceeding the budget. Jim stated that there was little if anything he could do but make a 100 per cent check of the inventory, which could cost over $4,000 and would be sure to cause the cumulative year-to-date budget figure to go well into the red. His estimate was based on the assumption that it would take 5 minutes each to physically inventory the 7,000 different items stocked and that a wage cost amounting to $3.86 per hour would be incurred. The high wage rate was due to the fact that this work could only be done on an overtime basis. A complete check would take about 7 weeks if each of the four stock clerks was placed on a 60-hour workweek, which was the maximum time allowed under the existing labor contract without incurring double pay.

The union contract provided that work beyond 8 hours per day or 40 hours per week was to be paid at time and a half, and it further stated that double time must be paid for all work in excess of 60 hours per week, any daily work in excess of $10\frac{1}{2}$ hours per day, any Saturday work in excess of 8 hours, and all Sunday and holiday work. Overtime penalties were cumulative in that time-and-a-half work performed after 60 total hours of work required double pay. Similarly, double pay work performed after 60 total hours of work required triple pay. Work in excess of 8 hours of work on Sunday or a holiday also required triple pay.

The $4,000 estimate included the cost of a supervisor and union steward who would also have to be paid overtime wages, as there was currently no second shift working and a union employee (stores clerk) was not allowed to work without a supervisor and union representative present. Since none of the stores clerks was a union steward, the steward required to be present could not be used to assist in the inventory check; neither would he be allowed to work at his regular job unless he was at the head of his department's overtime list. Also, since this was not regularly scheduled overtime in his department, he could refuse to work without incurring prejudice to his performance record, attendance record, or future overtime privileges. If the union representative were a machine operator, it would be difficult to assign him a machine job without also calling in a tool crib attendant, a chip puller, and an inspector. As a result it was generally considered impractical to work overtime except on a full departmental basis or in cases of extreme emergency.

Joe then questioned Jim as to how many extra priorities might have to be issued before all the errors would be worked out. Jim said that he had no idea. All he knew was that last week thirty special priorities had to be assigned because of posting errors. Joe commented, "You mean that in two months we can be charged over $6,000 for special priorities? That's more than the annual budget for special priorities. You'd better get your thinking hat on quick and find some way out of this predicament. I don't intend to have a whole year's worth of cost saving effort go down the drain over something like this. Let me know what you plan to do first thing tomorrow morning."

Jim Driscoll returned to his office and reflected on his problem. If in fact the situation was at its worst possible condition, it might well be worth sustaining the estimated $4,000 cost of the inventory review; however, if the situation was only minimal, this would be an unwise move. The only basis upon which to make a decision was to get a reliable estimate of the true error in the inventory stock records. In the time available it appeared that a small sample check would be the only practical basis upon which to make a decision.

While in college Driscoll had taken some courses in mathematics and statistics. Although Jim realized that these skills were rusty from lack of use, he felt confident that with a little help and the use of some reference material he could refresh himself enough to handle the calculations for his sampling problem.

By the time Jim was able to locate someone who could give him advice on how to take a sample, what calculations to make, and loan him a book[1] on sampling statistics, the day shift was over. He therefore asked one of his clerks to work overtime and to assist him in taking the sample. Under the union agreement Jim himself was not supposed to work on such tasks, but he was able to convince the clerk that this was a desperate situation and the clerk went along with the plan. They selected their sample by starting at random in one of the twenty file drawers which contained the inventory record cards. They selected every seventieth part card from which they recorded both the part number and the indicated amount on hand. They then made an actual count of the parts in the stock bins and noted any difference between the part card count and the actual on-hand count. In total they were able to obtain this information for 105 item numbers. Of the 105 item numbers checked, eight errors were found. Four of the errors were positive, i.e., the part card count was greater than the actual count, and four errors were negative. A positive error represented a potential stockout condition, whereas a negative error could only result in a premature reorder which, as previously stated, would cause temporary excess inventory. Negative errors would cause an underestimate of the true aggregate inventory value, and if sufficient in number, could possibly explain the difference between the accounting department's and Jim's aggregate inventory value figures.

Jim spent the rest of the night working out the result of his sample and was happily awaiting the arrival of Joe Bennett the next morning. When Joe Bennett arrived, Jim Driscoll greeted him and handed him the memo that he had prepared (see Exhibits 1–5). Joe reviewed and discussed the report with Jim. Joe admitted that although he did not fully understand the analysis it looked as though Jim had "lucked out" again. He commended Jim on his clear thinking and ingenuity in using a sampling technique in what appeared to Joe to be a very unusual manner. He said to Jim, "You sure have taken a lot off my mind. Let's get together for lunch and celebrate."

[1] Edward C. Bryant, *Statistical Analysis*, McGraw-Hill Book Company, New York, 1960.

# EXHIBIT 1

## Memo

To:       Joe Bennett, General Foreman
From:     Jim Driscoll, Chief Stores Clerk
Subject:  Inventory posting errors

With regard to our discussion of yesterday I would like to bring the following facts to your attention:

1. In a sample of 105 items having a total inventory value of $35,380 only 8 incorrect postings were located that totaled $25.73 (Exhibit 2).

2. The errors were equally divided between positive errors (items for which the part card balance exceeded the actual bin amount on hand) and negative errors (items for which the actual bin amount exceeded the part card balance on hand) (Exhibit 2).

3. No error exceeded $7\frac{1}{2}$ per cent of the actual number of parts on hand. This indicates that none of the items checked represents a serious stockout threat, as a $7\frac{1}{2}$ per cent safety stock based on the order quantity is maintained on all items (Exhibit 2).

4. Since none of the part numbers sampled represented a serious stockout threat, one can be 95 per cent certain that potential stockouts due to current stock record card errors are less than 3 per cent (Exhibits 3 and 4).

5. An aggregate inventory evaluation with an error of less than $\pm3$ per cent can be obtained by pricing out current inventory records. This amounts to a maximum error of approximately $122,000 based on a total inventory value of $4,325,000 (Exhibit 5).

Overall it can be concluded that the number of stockouts incurred last week due to posting errors is not representative of current and future expectations. The likelihood of a similar occurrence this week and in the future is extremely small.

Finally, since it will require only a moderate amount of extra clerical effort, it is suggested that the stock card records be priced out at the end of the current cost allocation period and that the figure obtained be used to either validate or invalidate the cost accounting department's next estimate of aggregate inventory value for our department.

# EXHIBIT 2

## Summary of stock card errors

| Part number | Reorder quantity | Unit value | Part card balance | Inventory count | Quantity difference | Per cent error | Dollar error |
|---|---|---|---|---|---|---|---|
| A | 35 | $35.80 | 14 | 13 | +1 | +7.1 | $ +35.80 |
| B | 250 | 4.13 | 61 | 60 | +1 | +1.7 | +4.13 |
| C | 410 | 3.75 | 128 | 136 | −8 | −6.3 | −30.00 |
| D | 85 | 8.92 | 38 | 40 | −2 | −5.3 | −17.84 |
| E | 500 | 1.38 | 143 | 140 | +3 | +2.1 | +4.14 |
| F | 350 | 3.90 | 75 | 71 | +4 | +5.6 | +15.60 |
| G | 45 | 26.40 | 21 | 22 | −1 | −4.5 | −26.40 |
| H | 140 | 11.16 | 65 | 66 | −1 | −1.5 | −11.16 |
| Total | | | 545 | 548 | −3 | | $ −25.73 |

# EXHIBIT 3

## Cell frequency distribution of stock card errors

| $X$ (cell midpoint for 2% cells) | $F$ (frequency) | $FX$ | $X^2$ | $FX^2$ |
|---|---|---|---|---|
| 8 | 1 | 8 | 64 | 64 |
| 6 | 1 | 6 | 36 | 36 |
| 4 | 0 | 0 | 16 | 0 |
| 2 | 2 | 4 | 4 | 8 |
| 0 | 97 | 0 | 0 | 0 |
| −2 | 1 | −2 | 4 | 4 |
| −4 | 1 | −4 | 16 | 16 |
| −6 | 2 | −12 | 36 | 72 |
| −8 | 0 | 0 | 64 | 0 |
| Total | 105 | 0 | | 200 |

# EXHIBIT 4

## Calculation of potential runouts

$$P(x \le a|n,p) = \sum_{x=0}^{a} {}_nC_x p^x (1 - p)^{n-x}$$

where $P(x \le a|n,p)$ = Probability of $a$ items or less (in a sample of $n$ items) having a specified characteristic if a proportion $p$ of the total population has the specified characteristic

$$ {}_nC_x = \frac{n!}{x!(n - x)!} $$

The maximum proportion $p$ of items in a population which will yield no more than a 5 per cent chance of zero occurrences in a sample of 105 items is given by the following equation:

$$.05 = \frac{105!}{105!0!} p^0 (1 - p)^{105}$$

$$(1 - p) = \sqrt[105]{.05} = .972$$

$$p = 2.8 \text{ per cent}$$

# EXHIBIT 5

## Determination of aggregate inventory evaluation error

$$\bar{x} \text{ (mean)} = \frac{\Sigma FX}{N} = \frac{0}{105} = 0$$

$$s^2 \text{ (variance estimate)} = \frac{N\Sigma FX^2 - (\Sigma FX)^2}{N(N - 1)} = \frac{105 \times 200 - 0}{105 \times 104} = 1.92$$

$s$ (standard error of estimate) $= \sqrt{1.92} = 1.39$ per cent

95% confidence limits $= \bar{X} \pm 2s = 0 \pm 2 \times 1.39 = \pm 2.78\%$

Hence aggregate dollar value of inventory error is less than $\pm 2.78$ per cent.

# DISCUSSION QUESTIONS

1. Is Jim Driscoll correct in stating that the sample indicates with 95 per cent assurance that fewer than 3 per cent of the stock card balances are in error by more than 7½ per cent?

2. On the basis of the sample taken, what limits can you place on the per cent of the total stock card records which are in error?

3. On the basis of the sample taken, what limits can you place on the per cent of the total stock card records which contain a negative error, i.e., balance less than actual inventory? A positive error, i.e., balance greater than actual inventory?

4. Was Jim Driscoll's statement about the aggregate error in the inventory records accurate?

5. Would there be any advantage in attempting to determine the aggregate inventory value directly from the sample rather than determining the amount of error in the inventory records?

6. What kind of a sampling procedure did Jim Driscoll use? Might there have been a better method?

7. Does sampling appear to be a useful way to estimate the aggregate inventory on a weekly basis?

8. If a total inventory check were required, how should it be organized?

9. What caused the difficulty reported in this case? How could it have been avoided?

10. How important were the budget system and the electronic data processing system in the situation of this case?

11. How would you proceed to reconcile the differences between the records of the accounting department and Driscoll's records?

12. Do you believe Driscoll should have worked out the sampling problem himself, or should he have turned it over to an "expert"?

13. What somewhat unique or original way of using sampling can you visualize in your own area of interest or responsibility?

# REFERENCES

Bryant, Edward C.: *Statistical Analysis* (New York: McGraw-Hill Book Company, 1960), chaps. 2–6.

Cochran, William G.: *Sampling Techniques* (New York: John Wiley & Sons, Inc., 1953), chaps. 1–6, 8.

Freund, John E., and Frank J. Williams: *Modern Business Statistics* (Englewood Cliffs, N.J.: Prentice-Hall, Inc., 1958), chaps. 9–12.

Grant, Eugene L.: *Statistical Quality Control*, 2d ed. (New York: McGraw-Hill Book Company, 1952), chaps. 13–15.

Neter, John, and William Wasserman: *Fundamental Statistics for Business and Economics* (Boston: Allyn and Bacon, Inc., 1961), chaps. 6, 10–12.

# JOHN STARK

John Stark was one of 647 employees in the purchasing department of the Celerity Company located in the Philadelphia area. Celerity was one of the major manufacturers employing over 25,000 people and producing stoves, washing machines, oil burners, vacuum cleaners, refrigerators, and other electrical-mechanical appliances. John Stark had recently received a master's degree in business administration with honors from the Wharton School of Finance and Commerce, and he had joined Celerity with great enthusiasm. This was his first major professional job, and he was anxious to succeed in his assignment as a buyer of small hardware. Three months later, however, John Stark's enthusiasm about his job had changed, and he felt frustrated and bitter. He became so disturbed about his situation that he actively began to seek other employment and only retained his job with Celerity to keep "beans in the oven" until he could locate another job. As an employee and a professional, he felt so distraught that he decided to write about his situation to his former professor at Wharton who had recommended the job to him. His letter follows:

Dear Professor Dobbins:

This letter pertains to my present position and the intense dissatisfaction that I am experiencing.

Upon your recommendation I joined the purchasing department at the Celerity Company approximately three months ago. After being keyed to peak performance during graduate school, I was anticipating being in a position where I could make a positive contribution. However, the actual situation is the exact antithesis of these anticipations. It is ex-

tremely frustrating and also depressing to be honed to a fine edge by
advanced education and then be committed to a mundane, mechanical,
and routine job.

The people in this organization think small. It is definitely the fault
of a management that has become divorced from operations. Jobs have
been so finely categorized, and responsibilities so minutely divided, that
individual initiative has evaporated. Further, impositions in the form of
extreme regimentation have reduced employees to a plodding, unthink-
ing, uninspired lot.

Through the mechanisms of five-minute coffee breaks, forty-minute
lunch periods, whistles, whistles, whistles, and the final insult of time
clocks, capable and willing people are soon transformed into mechanical,
disloyal beings. It is my firm conviction that if more activities were left to
individual initiative, a self-imposed honor system would produce a rapid
and more efficient work flow through the Celerity Company complex.

Another source of irritation is the noise level in "the office." It sometimes reaches such a level that it drowns out the all-important "quitting
time" whistle. How management expects anyone to think under these
conditions is beyond me. And of course the answer is self-evident because
management does *not* expect anyone to think!

I realize that the expense of putting each person into a partitioned
office would be prohibitive; however, the situation could be easily improved by sectionalizing buying groups through the use of movable partitions. Telephones are ringing constantly, and to assure that each is heard,
employees turn up the bell to full volume. You can imagine the overall
effect of hundreds of telephones ringing at maximum volume.

Celerity is a technically-oriented company with engineering talent
accorded preferential treatment. Engineers can be likened to commis-
sioned officers in a military organization, with nontechnical people filling
the ranks. This situation is logical in view of the company's competitive
position depending on continued technological superiority. However, this
preference is overemphasized, with resulting resentment by nontechnical
personnel.

Engineers are not required to punch a time clock, do not have
Pavlovian-type coffee breaks (where salivary gland reactions are triggered
by whistles), are not restricted severely at lunch times (may even take
enough time to go out to lunch), and in general are accorded respect
with the assumption that they possess normal discretion and human in-
telligence. The result is much more job enthusiasm and dedication, which
partially explains Celerity's continued technical excellence and marketing
success. Some engineers are even known to work overtime, during the
week and on Saturdays, without overtime pay!

Salary levels further reflect this disparity in treatment of the two
groups. The purchasing department is notorious for miserly salary levels

and extended promotion periods. I am surrounded by personnel wearing five-year buttons who are still below the supervisor level. In fact, my hiring salary rate was higher than the present income of many unfortunates who have been here six or more years. My lead buyer has been with Celerity for over eleven years and is still not making enough to enable him and his family of five to take trips on his three-week vacation. Furthermore, he has not received a raise (not even a cost-of-living raise) in the past two years. He is not alone, because many senior employees have not received raises and are openly grumbling about it. Impressive titles are handed out in lieu of monetary rewards. These titles are apparently part of the Celerity Company fringe benefits, which incidentally are inferior in comparison with those of the more progressive companies. It is a fact that the best way to get a raise or transfer at Celerity is to terminate and get rehired into a new job classification.

The personnel in purchasing are intelligent and competent people who have been sincerely dedicated in the past but who are stymied in their advancement to a supervisor's position. The tragic part of this situation is that a supervisor's position only allows one to work overtime without pay! Many buyer supervisors are making considerably less than $10,000 per year and will remain at that pay level for years. In engineering the average hiring rate is $550 per month at the present, and it keeps going up each year. The comparable rate for beginner purchasing department employees with equivalent education, skill, and responsibility is at least $100 per month less. Many people in purchasing are college graduates, but the salary levels are not commensurate with education.

Most new people hired in the department to do buying start at the lowest classification of buyer trainee and assist a buyer. Because of my education I got a break and started one rung higher on the ladder as a buyer. I am supposed to report to my lead buyer, a pleasant but unimaginative fellow who has been with Celerity for over eleven years. Actually, however, I am supervised by the buyer supervisor to whom my lead buyer reports.

My buyer supervisor is a really dedicated person and makes a sincere effort to do his job well. He had three years of college and is in his early thirties. He has been with Celerity for six years. As an administrator he gets along well with his staff, but he tends to be too easy with the vendors in an endeavor to be popular.

My buyer supervisor reports to the section supervisor, for whom I have great respect. He was trained as an engineer and is a very precise individual. His observations are keen, and his command of the situation is comprehensive. He believes in thorough consideration of a subject before commenting on it. His favorite expression to the people in our section is: 'It's better to remain silent and be thought dumb than to speak and remove all doubt." He doesn't say much unless he knows what he is talking about.

There are no personal frictions or administrative problems in our group, but this is not true of other groups. Some of the supervisors tend to be somewhat crude, and they seem to be lacking in administrative ability. It looks to me as though several have been advanced to supervisory positions only by reason of their years of service and supposed knowledge of detail. In general, however, I sense no serious frictions or resentments against the supervisors since everyone recognizes that we are all hampered by the same restrictions of the system.

It is interesting to observe the current campaign going on to upgrade the purchasing department by hiring only college graduates. Many senior employees are not college people, which creates a somewhat paradoxical situation. Presumably the college graduates will advance faster because of their educational advantage, but if they are advanced over the heads of the senior employees then Celerity will lose its best trained and most experienced employees. If the college graduates are not moved up fast, they will leave and seek better positions. Senior employees have resigned themselves to a life of mediocrity and low salaries, but it is doubtful that the aggressive, ambitious college graduates will commit themselves to this future.

Incidental irritations are traffic to and from the plant, gravel parking lots, long walking distances, and insolent, suspicious gate guards. I realize that traffic is an enigma and that Celerity has done about all it can to alleviate the situation with staggered shifts and sections. Parking lots are of course expensive due to land acquisition costs. Nevertheless, it adds insult to injury to put up with all those other things and then have to walk at least fifteen to twenty minutes to and from the car. The daily fight for a parking place, plus getting shoes and car covered with mud or dust (depending on the season), does not help matters.

Guards are instructed to be suspicious of everyone and several are naturally insolent (maybe because of their "power" position). This attitude on the part of the guards epitomizes the overall company atmosphere. Management can take an object lesson from "old biddy" schoolteachers and unsuccessful military officers who fail because of improper, suspecting attitudes. Celerity expects its personnel and suppliers to be positive-minded in relationships with the company. If management would only reciprocate, not only with its suppliers, but more importantly with its employees, then many of the problems outlined will cease to exist.

Please accept this letter as a sincere effort to relate some of the problems faced by Celerity and not just a collection of gripes. This "bottom of the barrel" approach may be somewhat emotionally charged, but it nevertheless contains some basic facts that may be useful for an objective analysis and corrective recommendations.

Thank you for your help in finding me this position. I hope you don't think of me as being ungrateful just because it hasn't worked out to my complete satisfaction as yet. I am only seeking a worthy challenge and hope to enjoy the fruits of my efforts as much in the business world as I did in your graduate seminars.

Cordially yours,

John Stark

# DISCUSSION QUESTIONS

1. How serious are the charges John Stark has made about his job situation? Can you classify the charges by ranking them from most important to unimportant?

2. Why do the difficulties exist?

3. What can be done about them?

4. Stark claims that the people in the organization "think small." Yet he says they are intelligent, competent, and sincerely dedicated. How can you reconcile the apparently contradictory statements?

5. In his letter John Stark gives his evaluation of various supervisors. How much reliability can you place on his observations?

6. He states that the company expects its personnel and suppliers to be positive-minded. What does this mean?

7. Stark complains about insufficient compensation but at the end of his letter says he is only seeking a "challenge." What do you think he really wants?

8. What does his letter say about John Stark himself?

9. Does his letter suggest that highly educated personnel need different handling than those with less education? If so, what recommendations do you have for a supervisor who has to deal with this problem?

# REFERENCES

Heckmann, I. L., Jr., and S. G. Huneryager: *Human Relations in Management* (Cincinnati: South-Western Publishing Company, 1960).

Lawrence, Paul R., et al.: *Organizational Behavior and Administration* (Homewood, Ill.: The Dorsey Press, Inc., and Richard D. Irwin, Inc., 1961).

Leavitt, Harold J.: *Managerial Psychology* (Chicago: The University of Chicago Press, 1958).

# THE STRETCH PRESS CASE, PART A

Gene Rock was an economic analyst in the equipment analysis unit of the missile and space division of the Transcontinental Aircraft Company. Transcontinental was the direct descendant, after several corporate mergers and acquisitions, of one of the oldest and most respected manufacturers of airplanes in the country. In recent years the evolution of the aircraft industry had led to the formation in most aircraft companies, Transcontinental among them, of separate divisions to handle the manufacture of missile and space vehicles apart from airframe manufacturing. At Transcontinental the missile division—later renamed the missile and space division—had been established as a division separate from the aircraft division in the early 1950s.

Gene Rock's job in the equipment analysis unit of the missile and space division was to prepare and evaluate data relating to requests for major equipment purchases by the manufacturing departments. The results of the analyses and investigations performed by Rock were included in the proposed capital budget—a total request for capital funds presented to the manufacturing department manager, the missile and space division capital expenditures committee, and the missile and space division manager. The manager of the missile and space division then recommended allocations of funds for capital expenditures on the basis of an evaluation of both the economic and intangible factors presented for each proposed purchase. His recommendations were passed on to the company's president and board of directors for approval.

For several years William Stensen, superintendent of the metal forming shop in the missile and space division, had requested a new stretch

335

press for his shop to replace two older stretch presses. A stretch press is a machine which places metal extrusions or sheets under tension. While under tension, additional pressure is applied by means of dies or forms to obtain complex configurations. Each time the request was made, management had not approved allocation of funds to the project.

Gene Rock had again received a request from Stensen to include the new stretch press in the request for capital funds being prepared for consideration by the manager of the missile and space division. Although the economic and intangible factors associated with acquiring the press had been analyzed in previous years, it was necessary for Rock to reinvestigate the proposed purchase since the condition of the existing machines and other factors changed from year to year.

Stensen's request was for a new 300-ton capacity Simpson stretch press, model LO 300, estimated to cost $500,000. It would have a scrap value estimated at $60,000 at the end of its estimated economic life of 10 years. The new press would replace two older presses, an Eimer 300-ton press and a Simpson 90-ton press. Both of the presses had been installed by the company about 20 years previously, during the Second World War. Originally they were obtained as government property, but they were purchased from the government after the war and became property of the Transcontinental Aircraft Company. The presses had been moved several times as the manufacturing facilities were reorganized and were now in the metal forming shop of the missile and space division.

As the first step in the analysis of the proposed purchase, Gene Rock requested equipment condition reports on the machines to be replaced. These were prepared by an engineer from plant services and are shown in Exhibits 1 and 2. As shown in Exhibit 1, the Eimer press was acquired from the government at a cost of $30,000. Subsequently the press was modified, and $5,000 was spent on new jaws to hold material in the machine. Although it was not shown on the equipment condition report, Rock determined from other records and discussions with the plant services engineer that the design was engineered in about 1940 and the machine was one of the first designed and built by that manufacturer. The condition code of O-3 on the equipment condition report indicated that in the opinion of the plant services engineer the machine was in poor condition and could probably be disposed of only as scrap. The Eimer press was used principally for the shaping of extrusions.

As shown in Exhibit 2, the Simpson press was built in 1941 and acquired from the government after the war at a cost of $20,000. Although rated at 90 tons, the press had been "beefed up" to the point where it was approximately the equivalent of a 135-ton machine. The machine was used principally for sheetwork but could also handle extrusions. The bed of the machine had been lengthened so that the original length limit of 22 feet for sheets had been increased to 32 feet. The Simpson press as shown on the equipment report was also in O-3 condition although the plant services engineer estimated that at a cost of about $25,000 for parts and labor this press could be rebuilt to factory-new condition. As scrap the machines had a market value of about $2,500 each or $5,000 total.

To get more information regarding the request for the new stretch press, Gene Rock arranged to meet with the shop superintendent, Stensen. At the meeting Stensen recounted some of the history of the two presses. When acquired early in World War II, the presses had operated rather poorly with considerable downtime—Stensen estimated it at about 50 per cent. By 1954 both machines had been extensively rebuilt. At that time particular attention was given to improving the hydraulic systems, which subsequently resulted in a considerable reduction in the downtime of the machines.

Stensen pointed out that even though the machines were presently operating satisfactorily, they might fail completely at any time. Because of their ages and condition their remaining life was unpredictable—they might last for five more years or they might last only a week. He was convinced that, because of the heavy work load, sudden failure of these vital machines would be disastrous. When they failed, the company would have to replace them or subcontract all stretch press sheet forming.

Stensen then recounted some of the operating difficulties with the present machines and the advantage of the new stretch press. One of the principal advantages of the new stretch press was that it would have curved jaws that conformed to the configuration of design of the part, instead of the straight jaws on the present machines. The advantage of curved jaws was that aluminum sheets being stretched into curved shapes would stretch more evenly and with less loss of material because the transition from the straight jaw to the final curved shape would be reduced or eliminated. Substantial savings would result in lower material costs due to a reduction of the amount of metal trimmed away and in fewer losses from rejections because of uneven stretching. In addition, the jaws in the new machine would be movable and would be fully powered so that the forces which stretched the metal could be applied more evenly and in the correct direction.

From the standpoint of ease of setup the new machine would result in substantial time savings. The jaws on the proposed machine were wedge action, which eliminated the necessity of inserting shims in the jaws to achieve even gripping of the material. Inserting shims on the old machines was a job which required a considerable amount of skill and, if improperly done, could result in a safety hazard. If the material was not gripped evenly, there was the possibility of the material flying out of the jaws when pressure was applied.

The new press would also be equipped with more sensitive automatic controls and tension-sensing and recording devices. These would permit a much closer regulation of the stretching process and greater evenness of stretching in the material with resultant improvement in quality. The improved controls on the new press offered the possibility of extending the range of materials which could be formed by the stretching method. The increasing use of materials such as steel and titanium which could not be handled on the old stretch presses was a major factor in reducing the usefulness of the old presses in the missile and space field.

Upon further investigation of the uses and capabilities of the present and proposed machines, Gene Rock discovered that the stretch presses were used mainly for forming aluminum parts. This method of forming had been found to be very useful in the manufacture of aircraft parts because of the stretch press's ability to obtain compound curves which could not be done by any other process. As an example, stretch forming was used to produce aircraft skins in one piece which were formerly fabricated from several pieces. This reduced assembly time and increased the structural strength of the skin.

He also discovered that over 50 per cent of the work done on the stretch presses was support work for the aircraft division. Part of the reason for the high proportion of support work was that the metal forming shop of the missile and space division had production capability which the aircraft division lacked. As a matter of fact, in addition to the work done in the missile and space division shops, the aircraft division found it necessary also to contract for some of its requirements for stretch-formed parts with other aircraft manufacturers with stretch-forming capacity. Another reason for the high proportion of support work for the aircraft division was the fact that aluminum parts of the sort which could be formed on the old stretch presses were not required in as great quantities as formerly because of changes in the design of missiles and space vehicles. The missile and space division stretch presses consequently were not used to capacity by divisional work.

The proposed machine, however, was capable of handling either aluminum or light gauges of the harder metals, such as steel or titanium. The improved automatic controls were a prime reason for the added capability since the precise control of the pressure and elongation forces between the yield point (the point at which the stress causes a permanent set to take place in the metal) and the ultimate fracture point differed by as little as 10 per cent.

At one time the possibility of obtaining an 800-ton dual control press rather than a 300-ton press was considered since this would permit the forming of a wider variety of parts made from steel and titanium. The cost of over $1 million, however, seemed to eliminate this alternative as a reasonable one because the future requirements for parts made of stronger metals were difficult to determine and because it was felt that explosion forming might one day be a more suitable process.

Having familiarized himself with the circumstances surrounding the request for the new press, Gene Rock turned his attention to collecting actual and estimated operating cost data on the present and proposed machines. This information was used in preparing the basic comparisons of operating cost on which the economic justification of the new machine would be based. The major sources of data were cost accounting records containing operating information on the present machines and Stensen, the superintendent of the metal forming shop, who provided some estimates on costs of operation of the old machines as well as of the proposed press. To corroborate some of the estimates Rock also consulted with the engineer from plant services who had prepared the condition reports shown in Exhibits 1 and 2. The engineer was sufficiently familiar with the equipment so that he could judge roughly the reasonableness of some of the estimates such as scrap loss and labor savings.

The cost accounting records indicated that about 12,000 hours of direct labor were charged to the Eimer and Simpson presses each year. The average labor rate for workers on these machines was $3 per hour. Stensen estimated that the improved automation controls and wedge action jaws on the new press would result in savings of about 4,000 hours per year in direct labor.

While it also might be possible to reduce the labor rate per hour on the new machine because of the lowered skill requirements in setting the jaws, Stensen felt that it would be difficult to prove that the workers now running the two old machines could really be replaced by lower paid workers. In explaining this point Stensen also pointed out that although the labor rate might stay about the same, it would certainly be easier to keep the new machine working at full capacity in spite of absences and turnover of employees. In the past, if the man who was skilled in setting the jaws and operating the stretch controls was absent or left the company, there was a substantial temporary decrease in production.

Because of the curved jaws and automatic controls on the proposed press, there would be a substantial reduction in material requirements. The straight jaws on the old machines made it necessary to allow a large excess of material on either side of the curved section being formed so that the metal could make the transition from a curved to a straight surface between the die and the jaws without undue stressing or wrinkling. The amount of excess metal which had to be removed and scrapped after the forming process often amounted to 50 per cent of the total amount of material used. The curved jaws of the new machine would reduce the transition and reduce the scrap loss by 75 per cent or more in many cases. Also, the lack of precise control and even application of pressure on the old presses often resulted in additional material loss when the entire part was ruined in the stretching process and had to be scrapped. Much of this would be eliminated by the new press. Based on this, Stensen and Rock arrived at a joint estimate that at present operating rates the new press would reduce material costs from $100,000 per year on the old machines to $50,000 per year on the new press, a saving of $50,000 per year.

In contrast to the complete material loss when parts had to be scrapped, some of the parts were salvaged by reworking in various ways. Cost accounting records revealed an average of about $17,000 a year of rework cost attributable to the old Eimer and Simpson presses. Stensen said that these costs would be almost entirely eliminated by the new press.

Having determined the direct savings which would result from the acquisition of the new press, Rock turned his attention to the indirect savings which might occur. Stensen indicated that supervision of the operators of the new press would be simplified but that there would be no chance of reducing costs since none of the supervisors could be eliminated. Similarly, the time of other indirect labor, such as forklift drivers, would be reduced, but no employees would be directly eliminated by the installation of the proposed press.

The accounting department, however, charged some services such as janitorial services, time keeping, shop supplies, etc., on the basis of direct labor hours. Since the new press would require fewer labor hours, there would be a saving by a reduction in this charge. The accounting department grouped all these items under the name "nonlabor maintenance" and charged these items at $2 per direct labor hour. There was another indirect charge made by the accounting department which was also based on direct labor hours: fringe benefits. The accounting department estimated that fringe benefits amounted to 20 per cent of the direct labor rate.

The prorata nonlabor maintenance charge mentioned above did not include the cost of maintenance above the normal amounts. The accounting department classified these additional maintenance costs as indirect costs but maintained separate records of the amounts expended for various machines. In the case of the Eimer and Simpson presses which would be replaced, the additional maintenance was averaging about $4,000 per year. Stensen guessed that there would be no such charges against the new press, and his judgment was confirmed by the plant services engineer. This information completed all of the data that Gene Rock required for his economic analysis.

Gene Rock began his analysis by filling out the "Capital Equipment Investment Analysis Data Sheet" (Exhibit 3), on which was summarized all of the pertinent cost information. The data sheet was divided into three parts. The first part was a comparison of the investments in the existing equipment and in the proposed equipment. In the second part the yearly utilization of the present and proposed equipment was recorded. Annual operating cost estimates were computed and compared in part three. Gene Rock filled in Exhibit 3 and determined that the total prospective saving in direct costs attributable to the proposed investment in the modern press was $79,000. Total indirect cost savings of $14,000 added to this gave a total annual operating cost savings of $93,000 if the modern stretch press were purchased.

The final step in the economic analysis was the calculation of the rate of return and payoff period after income taxes. In order to do this it was necessary to fill out the "Investment Analysis" (Exhibit 4) and to determine the net cash flow after income taxes. On this form were recorded the cash flows, depreciation, and income taxes resulting from the proposed investment for each of the ten years of the life of the equipment.

The totals from the analysis shown in Exhibit 3 were recorded on lines 1 to 4 of Exhibit 4 and summarized on line 5. The payment (negative cash flow) for the initial investment in the proposed machine was assumed to occur at the beginning of year 1 (considered as time 0) and was entered on line 1 in column 0 as a negative figure. Cash savings for each of the ten years were recorded on lines 2 and 3. The cash inflow from the sale of the old equipment was assumed to occur at the end of the first year and was recorded on line 4. On line 1, the second column for the tenth year shows the positive cash flow which would result from the sale of the asset at the end of its economic life. It was recorded separately to distinguish it from the taxable cash flow resulting from the operating savings realized in the tenth year. Total cash flow before income tax was found by adding lines 1 to 4 and was shown on line 5.

The depreciation charges for each year were computed on a "Depreciation Schedule" (Exhibit 5) and recorded on line 6 of Exhibit 4. The company used the sum-of-years digits method for computing depreciation. The depreciation charges were then subtracted from the cash flow in line 5 to give taxable income on line 7. The Federal corporate income tax was computed on the basis of the current normal tax rate plus the surtax rate, and the amount of the tax was indicated on line 8. The income tax was then subtracted from the cash flow in line 5 to give the cash flow after income taxes shown in line 9. Line 10 was the cumulative cash flow after income taxes and indicated the "crude" payoff period after taxes when the figures therein changed from minus to plus.

The cash flow after income tax was entered on the form "Calculations to Determine Prospective Rate of Return" (Exhibit 6). The form was used to find the rate of interest at which the present value of the net cash flow over the expected life of the asset equals zero. The rate of return found in Exhibit 6 was then recorded together with the crude payoff period from line 10 of Exhibit 4 on the "Investment Analysis Summary" (Exhibit 7). This last form also indicated the cost of the asset, the total savings (before allowing for investment costs), and the net income (after allowing for investment costs).

# EXHIBIT 1

Equipment Condition Report

| | | | |
|---|---|---|---|
| Property No. | 4-FH-3547 | Serial No. | 235689 |
| Location: Plant | Missile | Shop | Metal forming |
| Date built | 1941 | Date acquired | 1946 |
| Acquisition cost | $30,000 | Modifications | $5,000 |
| Manufacturer | Engineering Research Corporation | | |
| Description and capacity | Hydraulic stretch press, Eimer—300-ton | | |
| Condition code | O-3 | Est. rebuild cost | |

Remarks    Machine is too slow. Maintenance has been extremely high. Overage. Machine has been modified with some parts deleted. Five-year labor maintenance. 2,000 hours @ $2.75 = $5,500.

Recommended disposition    Scrap.

Survey made by    N. S. Neer    Date    9/26/61

Plant Services

# EXHIBIT 2

Equipment Condition Report

Property No.     4-FH-6733          Serial No.     345902

Location: Plant     Missile          Shop     Metal forming

Date built     1941          Date acquired     1946

Acquisition cost     $20,000          Modifications

Manufacturer     Simpson Corporation

Description and capacity     Hydraulic stretch press, Simpson—90-ton

Condition code     O-3          Est. rebuild cost     $25,000

Remarks     Maintenance has been high. Machine is too slow for present needs.
Overage. Five-year labor maintenance. 2,600 hours @ $2.75 = $7,150.

Recommended disposition     Scrap or rebuild completely.

Survey made by     *N. S. Neer*          Date     9/27/61

Plant Services

# EXHIBIT 3

## Capital equipment investment analysis data sheet

(All figures rounded to nearest thousand dollars)

Date: _____

Equipment _____
Using organization _____    Analyst _____

### Equipment Investment Comparison

*Present equipment*    *Proposed equipment*
1. Description _____    Description _____

2. Date acquired_____    Installation date_____
3. Original cost_____    Installed cost_____
4. Equipment life_____    Equipment life_____
5. Est. market value_____    Est. scrap value_____
6. Condition code_____
7. Est. rebuild cost_____

### Utilization comparison

8. Total direct labor hours per year____    Total direct labor hours per year_____

9. Labor rate/hour_____    Labor rate/hour_____

### Annual Operations Comparison

| *Direct costs:* | *Estimated for present equipment* | *Estimated for proposed equipment* | *Savings* |
|---|---|---|---|
| 10. Labor | | | |
| 11. Materials | | | |
| 12. Scrap rework | | | |
| 13. Tooling | | | |
| 14. Inspection | | | |
| 15. Other | | | |
| 16. Total direct costs | | | |
| *Indirect costs:* | | | |
| 17. Labor | | | |
| 18. Nonlabor maintenance | | | |
| 19. Material handling | | | |
| 20. Fringe costs | | | |
| 21. Power | | | |
| 22. Maintenance | | | |
| 23. Other | | | |
| 24. Total indirect costs | | | |
| 25. Other first-year costs | | | |
| 26. Total cost | | | |

# EXHIBIT 4

## Investment analysis

### (In thousands of dollars)

Equipment _____    Date _____

|  | End of year | | | | | | | | | | | |
| Savings analysis | 0 | 1 | 2 | 3 | 4 | 5 | 6 | 7 | 8 | 9 | 10 | 10* |
|---|---|---|---|---|---|---|---|---|---|---|---|---|
| 1. Asset cost | | | | | | | | | | | | |
| 2. Direct savings | | | | | | | | | | | | |
| 3. Indirect savings | | | | | | | | | | | | |
| 4. Gain on sale of asset | | | | | | | | | | | | |
| 5. Total cash flow before income tax | | | | | | | | | | | | |
| 6. Less depreciation | | | | | | | | | | | | |
| 7. Taxable income (5 minus 6) | | | | | | | | | | | | |
| 8. Federal income tax† | | | | | | | | | | | | |
| 9. Cash flow after income tax (5 minus 8) | | | | | | | | | | | | |
| 10. Cumulative cash flow after income tax | | | | | | | | | | | | |

\* Salvage value.

† Based on current normal tax rate plus surtax rate.

# EXHIBIT 5

## Depreciation schedule, sum-of-years digits method

(In thousands of dollars)

Equipment _____
Original cost _____
Est. salvage value _____
Amount depreciated _____
Asset economic life _____

| Year | Depreciation fraction | Depreciation decimal | Annual depreciation |
|------|-----------------------|----------------------|---------------------|
| 1 | | | |
| 2 | | | |
| 3 | | | |
| 4 | | | |
| 5 | | | |
| 6 | | | |
| 7 | | | |
| 8 | | | |
| 9 | | | |
| 10 | | | |
| 11 | | | |
| 12 | | | |
| 13 | | | |
| 14 | | | |
| 15 | | | |
| 16 | | | |
| 17 | | | |
| 18 | | | |
| 19 | | | |
| 20 | | | |

# EXHIBIT 6

## Calculation to determine
## prospective rate of return

(In thousands of dollars)

Equipment _____

| Year | Cash flow after income taxes | Present value | | | | | |
|------|------|------|------|------|------|------|------|
| | | $PV_{SP}$ %* | PV | $PV_{SP}$ %* | PV | $PV_{SP}$ %* | PV |
| 0 | | | | | | | |
| 1 | | | | | | | |
| 2 | | | | | | | |
| 3 | | | | | | | |
| 4 | | | | | | | |
| 5 | | | | | | | |
| 6 | | | | | | | |
| 7 | | | | | | | |
| 8 | | | | | | | |
| 9 | | | | | | | |
| 10 | | | | | | | |
| 10† | | | | | | | |
| Sum | | | | | | | |

* Present value single payment factor at trial interest rate (from Appendix C)
† Salvage value.

# EXHIBIT 7
## Investment analysis summary

Equipment _____

| | |
|---|---|
| Asset cost | |
| Total income (savings) after income tax | |
| Net income after income tax | |
| Crude payoff period after income tax | |
| Rate of return after income tax | |

# ASSIGNMENT

Make the necessary calculations to evaluate the proposed purchase of the new stretch press.

# REFERENCES

Bierman, Harold, Jr., and Seymour Smidt: *The Capital Budgeting Decision* (New York: The Macmillan Company, 1960), chap. 2.

Grant, Eugene L., and W. Grant Ireson: *Principles of Engineering Economy*, 4th ed. (New York: The Ronald Press Company, 1960), chap. 8.

Ireson, W. Grant, and Eugene L. Grant: *Handbook of Industrial Engineering and Management* (Englewood Cliffs, N.J.: Prentice-Hall, Inc., 1955), sec. 3.

Morris, William T.: *The Analysis of Management Decisions*, rev. ed. (Homewood, Ill.: Richard D. Irwin, Inc., 1964), chap. 3.

# THE STRETCH PRESS CASE, PART B

Gene Rock, economic analyst in the equipment analysis unit of the missile and space division of Transcontinental Aircraft Company, had collected the data necessary for an analysis of a proposal to replace two existing stretch presses in the division's metal forming shop with a modern stretch press (see Part A). The investigation brought out the facts that the existing presses were nearly twenty years old and were in danger of failing at any time and that the work capability of the existing presses was limited in regard to much of the present work being performed by the shop. Material scrap losses were high because of the straight jaw configurations and manual controls of the present machines. These losses could be greatly reduced by the curved jaw configuration and automatic controls of the proposed press. Labor, maintenance, and other costs could also be substantially reduced if the proposed machine were purchased.

The economic comparison of the present and proposed presses and the investment analysis of the proposed press were contained in Gene Rock's report to his supervisor, Boyd Cutter, equipment analysis unit manager. It was Cutter's job to supervise the assembly of all departmental requests for authorization for capital expenditures into a single capital budget request which was presented to the manager of the missile and space division. In addition to assembling the budget requests, the equipment analysis unit served as a first screening step in the submission of capital requests.

The system worked in general as follows. Individual departments initiated all requests for capital expenditures. The originating department identified the equipment or other capital improvement desired and made an estimate of the item or items which was submitted to the equipment analysis unit. Along with this information the originating department was expected to provide a justification for the request in the form of supporting data or arguments.

Besides processing the requests into a single document for presentation to the division manager, the equipment analysis unit had the authority to delete items from the budget request if there was insufficient justification or if the items were obviously of low priority as compared to other requests. When the system was first initiated, many items were deleted; but with experience the requesting departments were able to anticipate which marginal items were likely to be deleted, and they refrained from submitting them. In cases where requests were deleted, the equipment analysis unit generally discussed the item with the requesting department and explained the reasons why the item was deleted. In most instances, the person initiating the request agreed to the deletion of the item as a result of this discussion.

The kind of analysis done by Gene Rock on the stretch press was one method which the equipment analysis unit used to determine whether to include an item in the budget request. On smaller items, typically those items under $20,000, detailed analyses of the type developed for the stretch press were not made. Instead, the items were included in the budget request if, on the basis of a more general statement of need, they seemed to warrant inclusion in the budget. The type of analysis performed on the stretch press was not always applicable on all items over $20,000 which were requested to provide new capabilities. The type of analysis used for the stretch press was used only for equipment which was intended to replace existing equipment or methods and where comparisons could be made of the relative costs of operation of present and proposed equipment. On new program equipment, such comparisons were usually not possible and, instead, the items were assigned priorities based on subjective estimates of the importance of the items. These estimates were made by the equipment analysis unit.

Another important function of the equipment analysis unit was to obtain an accurate cost estimate for any item requested. Usually this was obtained by actually contacting vendors and obtaining price quotations. Taxes, transportation charges, installation costs, peripheral equipment costs, and other extra costs were also added to the base equipment price —items which the requesting department often neglected to do. As an example, in the case of the stretch press the original departmental cost estimate was $400,000, in contrast to the final estimate of $500,000 for the press which included allowances for installation charges and additional equipment. The equipment analysis unit was extremely careful in obtaining good cost estimates since management was very reluctant to make special authorizations for extra funds when cost estimates were too low.

After the cost estimates were obtained and the analyses of the requests were completed, the equipment analysis unit assembled the requests into a tentative manufacturing department capital assets budget for the next six months. Items lacking sufficient justification by the requesting department, items which were clearly not economically sound, and items which were not compatible with the long-range business plan for the missile and space division were not included in the tentative budget. The budget was divided into sections for the three major current activities in the manufacturing department: the general shops, the Pluto program, and the Paul Revere system. A sample page (the page on which the stretch press appeared) of the form used is shown in Exhibit 1. For each item listed, a cost estimate, rate of return, date required, lead time, program classification (shown in column PRG), and cash outlay commitment by quarter were included. Only those items costing over $20,000 were listed out on this form in detail. Those items costing less than $20,000 were included in a lump sum amount at the end of each budget section, and the only detailed information supplied was a simple listing of the names of the larger items making up about 65 per cent of the lump sum. The items costing over $20,000 which were not analyzed for rate of return because they did not replace present equipment were given priorities of A, B, C, or D in the rate-of-return column. The exact meaning of the priorities was never spelled out in detail; however, everyone agreed that "A" items were absolutely necessary and "D" items were not very critical. There was no formula or scale for converting a letter priority to a percentage rate of return for comparison purposes.

Each line item on the form in Exhibit 1 was also supplemented by a summary sheet with written discussion to justify the item. A sample page of the form, containing summary information regarding the stretch press, is shown in Exhibit 2. The purpose of the supplementary sheets was to provide an opportunity to present a discussion of the intangible factors bearing on the purchase of the equipment.

After the tentative budget was prepared by the equipment analysis unit, there was a series of reviews, at any one of which an item might be deleted. The first review was by the manufacturing department manager and a committee of executives from the department. The second review was by the missile and space division capital expenditures committee. This committee analyzed the requests of the various departments in detail, made constructive criticisms on the presentations, and, in some cases, either deleted an item or sent the request back to the originating department for further justification. The third step was review and approval by the missile and space division manager and his executive committee. Final review and approval of the company-wide capital budget was by the president and board of directors of Transcontinental.

In the case of the stretch press, after Gene Rock had completed his analysis and turned it in to Boyd Cutter, the head of the equipment analysis unit, it was decided that the metal forming shop should provide further justification for the press by additional analysis of the intangible benefits associated with purchasing the press. Accordingly, Stensen, the shop superintendent, was asked to supply a new and expanded discussion of the intangible benefits. Boyd Cutter also felt that the stretch press was not completely compatible with the long-range business plan but should probably be included in the tentative budget because it was a critical piece of equipment in the stretch-forming operations which should be reviewed at a higher level.

The stretch press request was included in the tentative budget as shown in Exhibits 1 and 2. The manufacturing department manager and the committee of executives from the department reviewed the budget and approved the stretch press as one item to be included in the budget request sent on to division level for review. At the division level, the capital expenditures committee reviewed the stretch press proposal along with other items in the budget and submitted the budget to the division manager.

During the deliberations of the division capital expenditures committee, the stretch press proposal was discussed at some length, partly because of the substantial investment involved and partly because two committee members were convinced that this was a questionable investment for the division.

One man pointed out that the projected return on the investment was lower than the rate for other proposals and that the press capability did not seem compatible with the long-range business plan for the division. He said, "Since the division will be primarily concerned with making missiles out of steel, titanium, and the harder metals, a press to form aluminum and light-gauge metals may well be useless to us in the near future. There is a very likely possibility that we will not be making anything out of aluminum before long. Here we have an analysis based upon an economic life of ten years. Why, we can't even be sure what we'll be doing in five years, let alone ten years."

The other objector said, "Even if the present presses do fail, we can farm out the skin forming work to other aircraft manufacturers."

Another committee member pointed out, "Yes, but if we do we will have to pay for his overhead and profit as well as for transporting the formed sheets 1,000 or 2,000 miles. On this basis the investment in the proposed press is even more attractive."

Another member said, "That's very true. In addition, we would have no control over the production scheduling for our work. This could be disastrous to production schedules for the commercial and military aircraft division. After all, we do a considerable amount of support work for them in our shops."

To this the first objector replied, "Well, if the aircraft division needs the press so bad, why don't they buy one themselves, instead of tying up half a million of our money?"

Another member recountered, "But the fact remains that half the work done on the press is for the missile and space division. It seems to me that we are taking entirely too narrow a view of this matter. We should consider this kind of proposal not only from the division's standpoint, but also from the standpoint of doing what is best for the entire company."

Because opinion in the committee was rather sharply divided, it was decided that the proposal should be submitted to the division manager with the arguments on both sides of the question.

# EXHIBIT 1 Departmental capital budget request summary

Division: *Missile and Space*

Department: *Manufacturing*     Budget Period: *First half, 1962*

| Item number | Item | Capital amount | Expense amount | Total amount | Rate of return | PRG | Date required | Lead time | Commitments by quarter in thousands | | | |
|---|---|---|---|---|---|---|---|---|---|---|---|---|
| | | | | | | | | | 1st | 2d | 3d | 4th |
| 18. | Hydraulic brake press | $ 25,000 | $ 5,000 | $ 30,000 | A | Pl. | | | | | | |
| 19. | Induction furnace | 26,000 | 2,000 | 28,000 | 4.6 | S.S. | | | | | | |
| 20. | Stretch press | 500,000 | | 500,000 | * | S.S. | | | | | | |
| 21. | Profile mill | 100,000 | 2,000 | 102,000 | 16.1 | P.R. | | | | | | |
| 22. | 20-foot press brake | 73,000 | | 73,000 | D | Pl. | | | | | | |
| 23. | Inert gas welding chamber | 160,000 | | 160,000 | A | P.R. | | | | | | |
| 24. | Precision grinders (2) | 66,000 | | 66,000 | 13.1 | S.S. | | | | | | |
| 25. | Electric discharge machine | 50,000 | 4,000 | 54,000 | C | Pl. | | | | | | |
| 26. | Vertical boring mill | 200,000 | 80,000 | 280,000 | B | P.R. | | | | | | |
| 27. | 12-foot squaring shear | 30,000 | 5,000 | 35,000 | D | P.R. | | | | | | |
| 28. | Vertical profile mills (3) | 150,000 | 10,000 | 160,000 | 23.4 | S.S. | | | | | | |
| | Total | | | | | | | | | | | Total |

* Rate was shown on original summary.

# EXHIBIT 2  Capital budget item request

First half, 1962

Division: _____ Missile and Space
Department: _____ Manufacturing

Quantity: _____1_____  Description: _____ Modern stretch press, 300-ton capacity

Manufacturer: _____ Simpson _____  Model or Type: _____ LO 300 _____  S.C.C. No.: _____

Alternative Mfg.: _____  Model or Type: _____  S.C.C. No.: _____

Justification (Airplane model(s) process spec. no., etc.):

The extrusion and skin stretch-forming facilities available within the missile and space division are technologically and functionally obsolete. The existing machines considered for modernization and replacement were built in the 1940s and have deteriorated to the point where replacement is mandatory if in-plant capacity and capability are to be maintained.

It is proposed that a Simpson model LO 300 with 32-foot length capacity, elongation and yield-sensing devices, and 80-inch-wide curved sheet holding jaws be procured to replace and modernize the existing stretch press facility. The proposed machine will have two tension cylinders capable of exerting 150 tons at any angle of pull. It will be capable of forming high-tensile steels and exotic materials at slow speeds and will be equipped for elevated temperature part forming.

Out-plant stretch-forming capacity will continue to be utilized. The upgrading of existing in-plant facilities is not intended to change existing "make or buy" policies but will permit a more efficient operation and an extension of stretch-form capabilities to include the high-strength materials which will be used on advanced programs.

Acquisition of a modern stretch press will result in operating economies. Less excess material is required using curved jaws, scrap will be reduced by proper elongation control, maintenance and repairs to the old machinery will be eliminated, and labor requirements reduced. The new machine will cost approximately $500,000. Savings will provide a * rate of return and a * year payoff period. The resale of the two existing machines will realize approximately $5,000. The existing machines have been recommended for retirement by the facility department. These machines will be scrapped upon activation of the requested machine.

It is recognized that some programs included in the division business plan could require stretch-forming equipment in the 1,600-ton range (800 tons per tension cylinder). The replacement of the existing obsolete equipment with a machine of this size has been considered. However, configuration, size, and process definition for the advanced projects (spinning, stretching, explosive forming) are not considered firm enough for the investment required (approximately $1 million). It has been concluded that the requested 300-ton press would be adequate for the majority of future vehicle forming requirements and could most efficiently produce current and anticipated transport work loads.

# EXHIBIT 2 (Continued)

The design of future aircraft and space vehicles utilizing such materials as René 41; B120VCA titanium; 2020T6, 2024T81, and T86 aluminum; stainless steel; magnesium; and beryllium places a greater demand on close control of forming parameters than do present-day aircraft materials. It is recognized that the technological as well as economic penalties for not having the proper capability will impose engineering design limitations and force utilization of inadequate machine tools. Reliance on outside capabilities usually presents intolerable time delays. The decision to maintain a modernized stretch-form and wrap capability favors the proposed request.

Requested by: _____
Approved by: _____

Approved by: _____

Program Manager

| Item number | Capital amount | Expense amount | Total amount | Rate of return | PRG | Date required | Lead time | Commitments by quarter in thousands | | | |
|---|---|---|---|---|---|---|---|---|---|---|---|
| | | | | | | | | 1st | 2d | 3d | 4th |
| | $500,000 | | $500,000 | * | All | 3/63 | 12 mo. | 500 | | | |

* Data were shown on original request.

# DISCUSSION QUESTIONS

1. What additional factors should be taken into account beyond those discussed in the case?

2. How do you evaluate the procedures established in this company for making capital equipment decisions?

3. Assume you are the division manager. What would your decision be?

4. How important are the Federal tax laws in influencing capital equipment decisions?

# SWEPTWING AIRCRAFT COMPANY

The manufacturing research and development group of the Sweptwing Aircraft Company was responsible for developing manufacturing methods for new processes and changes in existing processes. A change of material was regarded as a change of process. In addition, this group developed the tools and facilities necessary for each new process and was responsible for helping to get such changes adopted in manufacturing. A new process was not released until it had been tested by using production equipment and trained production people. When the research and development group was convinced that the proposed process was workable, a production test was scheduled. This test was operated under the supervision of the research group, but employed production workers. If the test was satisfactory, the research group prepared instructions and procedures for the process and issued instructions to the manufacturing supervisors and workers who were to be employed in using the process.

The manufacturing research and development group had been requested to develop a process to manufacture titanium ducts for a new supersonic airplane. The purpose of the ducts was to supply air for cabin air conditioning and wing anti-icing. The peculiar stresses of jet flight required the use of metals with high strength characteristics; therefore, most of the ducts were made of stainless steel in the first subsonic jet airplanes. The cost of the duct system on the supersonic airplane was estimated at $36,000 if titanium was used as the basic material, compared with $28,800 a plane if stainless steel was used. A reduction of 150 pounds of weight per plane, however, justified the additional cost, and the decision was made to use titanium.

The process for the production of titanium ducts was tested and released to manufacturing. Tubes ranging from $1\frac{1}{4}$ to 6 inches in diameter, with wall thicknesses from 0.015 to 0.042 inch, were specified for the pneumatic systems. The minimum centerline bend radius of elbows $4\frac{1}{2}$ inches in diameter and smaller was $1\frac{1}{2}$ times the tube diameter. The preferred bend radii for all tubes were specified at twice the tube diameter.

There were four major methods in general use for bending elbows in tubes: (1) ram or press forming, (2) roll bending, (3) compression bending, and (4) draw bending. The first three methods were relatively simple and normally were used to bend heavy wall tubing.

Ram forming was accomplished by placing a tube between two supports and passing the ram and tube between the supports. Roll bending consisted of passing the tube through a series of power-driven rolls. Compression bending utilized a special tube-bending machine and was accomplished by wiping the tube around a stationary bend die. These three methods, however, were not satisfactory for thin wall tubes. The bending of thin wall tubing used in airplane pneumatic ducts required the use of draw bending in order to form the parts without wrinkling, fracturing, or collapsing the tubes.

The draw-bending process was done on a conventional aircraft type tube bender (Exhibit 1). The tube was confined between two pairs of semicircular dies: the bend die and the clamp die, and the wiper die and the pressure die (illustrated in Exhibit 2). A mandrel was inserted inside the tube to provide internal support. The end of the mandrel consisted of a series of ball sections connected together by flexible joints that permitted the balls to assume various bend positions. The ball sections were sized to the inside diameter of the tube, and by being positioned in the bend area they prevented the collapse of the tube. After the tube was bent the mandrel was readily withdrawn.

To make the bend, the bend die and clamp die rotated in unison while tightly embracing the tube. As the tube was bent it was drawn through the stationary wiper die, which tended to pull on the metal located in the inside curvature of the tube. The pressure die traveled with the tube and applied a reaction force in the direction of the bend, which tended to push on the metal located in the outside curvature of the tube. To aid the flow of metal in the bend area, the tube and dies were heated to temperatures ranging up to 500°F, depending on the size and other factors.

Because the use of titanium thin wall tubing was relatively new, several problems were encountered:

1. *Problems of straightening tubes.* A substantial amount of the ductility of the titanium material was removed in fabricating or welding

the material into tubing. The tube specification incorporated a straightness requirement which could be satisfied only by straightening the tube after welding. The straightening operation reduced the ductility in the material as much as 20 per cent and was partly the cause of high rejection rates on severely bent elbows. Annealing the tube after welding or straightening did not provide a solution to the problem because warpage occurred in the tube and additional straightening or a sizing operation was required. This problem was partially solved by relaxing the straightness tolerance from 0.015 to 0.030 inch per foot to reduce the amount of straightening necessary after welding.

2. *Tube bending speeds.* Titanium tubing had a tendency to neck down severely in local areas. It was concluded that the reason for this was the close proximity of the yield strength to the ultimate strength. Rapid bending did not provide the time necessary for the work hardening stresses to equalize over a large area. Thus, severe neck down and usually fractures occurred when the local forming stresses were not applied at a slow rate in the material being bent.

An optimum tube bending speed was not established because the properties of titanium material varied substantially. Other factors such as the lubricant and the tube diameter tolerances also affected tube bending speeds. Bending speed, therefore, was left to the tube bender's discretion.

3. *Tool wear rates.* Mandrel and wiper die wear rates had to be controlled closely to provide reliable tube bending (see Exhibit 3). If the mandrel and wiper dies were permitted to wear more than 0.005 to 0.008 inch, insufficient tool confinement resulted. Large pressure die forces were used to compensate for the lack of tool confinement which prevented the proper flow of metal into the bend area and caused excessive stretching which often resulted in a fracture. Severely worn tools were believed to create a high elbow failure rate.

The following tube bending techniques were developed for the new program:

1. *Selection of tube bending temperature and heat source.* Mechanical property tests, at elevated temperatures coupled with actual bending tests, revealed that a temperature range from 400 to 500°F appeared to provide the best ductility for commercially pure Grade A-40 titanium. Conventional aircraft tube benders were to be used for the elevated temperature forming; however, it was felt that temperatures higher than these would be detrimental to the equipment. Electric cartridge type heaters were selected as the best source of heat for the elevated temperature tools. This method provided the reliability, low cost, and easy mainte-

nance and temperature control characteristics desired. Bending tests proved that not all of the tools had to be heated. Satisfactory results were obtained by using only a heated pressure die and mandrel body. Tube bender maintenance was reduced by not heating the bend die and wiper die in order that the massive bearings in the bend die spindle not be subjected to the high temperatures of the pressure die and mandrel body.

2. *Selection of lubricant and tooling materials.* Friction, lubricant, and actual bending tests indicated that the selection of lubricant and tooling material was critical. Most of the tooling materials tested showed an affinity for cohesion to titanium, and conventional lubricants did not provide the film strength desired to separate the tools from the work piece.

Experiments proved that SAE 4340 steel, heat-treated to a hardness of Rockwell C 45-48, was adequate for the pressure die because it did not slide against the tube. The wiper die and mandrel, however, had to contend with sliding friction, and none of the ferrous alloys tested was satisfactory for this application. Ampco Grade 21 aluminum bronze was found to be a satisfactory material for this application. The friction and galling tests indicated that high graphite content grease should provide acceptable lubrication properties for elevated temperature titanium tube bending. This lubricant, however, was not completely satisfactory in production runs. Frequently minor galls occurred for no explainable reason, and it was necessary to supplement the lubricants with a phosphate conversion coating. Phosphate conversion coating was first applied to the tubes by dipping them in a mixture of sodium phosphate, potassium fluoride, and hydrofluoric acid. This mixture combined with the titanium to produce a thin titanium phosphate fluoride coating on the tube surface. The coatings prevented the tooling material from coming in direct contact with the titanium base metal and provided a low coefficient of friction.

Satisfactory lubrication was finally achieved in production runs by using phosphate conversion coated tubes lubricated with graphite greases.

3. *Tube bender modification and heat source equipment.* On conventional tube benders the pressure die mounting carriage normally was permitted to travel freely with the tube as it was being drawn into the bend area. During early titanium tube bending tests it was determined that a pressure die booster was required. The pressure die booster system consisted of a hydraulic cylinder mounted on the aft end of the pressure die mounting carriage. The cylinder was mounted in such a manner that it could apply a forward thrust load on the pressure die, thus pushing or boosting the tube through the bend cycle. This push accomplished two things: (1) it helped feed material into the bend area, and (2) it reduced the tension strain on the outside of the bend, thus permitting the neutral axis to be moved as far out into the elbow

as possible, which in turn reduced the amount of elongation required in bending the tube.

The pressure die booster cylinder had to be capable of maintaining a constant load on the pressure die that could be controlled up to the maximum static friction force between the die and tube. A speed control was provided so that the pressure die would not slide against the tube. If sliding occurred, galling resulted.

The tube benders were adapted to handle heated tools. Insulation, to prevent excessive bearing temperatures, and electrical leads, to supply power to the electric cartridge heaters, were required. The heated pressure die was mounted on a transit insulated adapter plate to prevent heat absorption into the pressure die carriage bearings. Electrical leads ran directly from bus bars on power panels to supply power for the cartridge heaters in the pressure die. The mandrel body was also heated by a cartridge heater connected to a power panel.

The power panels consisted of two controllers and two automatic rheostats, one each for the mandrel and pressure die. Temperature of the tools was monitored by thermocouples. The electrical current supply to the power panels was 30 amperes at 440 volts.

The cost of $36,000 per plane for a duct system was based on a 5 per cent scrap factor. Titanium prices ranged from $12 to $15 per pound, while scrap material was valued at approximately $1 per pound. Sometime after the tube bending process had been released to manufacturing it was determined that the spoilage rate was approximately 20 per cent, rather than the forecasted rate of 5 per cent.

The manufacturing R and D group had spent 3,600 engineering man-hours, 4,300 shop man-hours, and $33,000 worth of material developing this process. Bob Lancaster, the manager of the R and D group, requested a member of his staff to make an investigation to determine the cause of the difficulty and to decide whether additional research was warranted to improve the process. Sometime later the following audit report was submitted to Lancaster.

## Titanium Tubing Audit Report

It did not appear that straightness was checked in terms of stated requirements. Further, a survey of several drawings revealed that no ovality tolerance was given on these drawings. Purchase orders and affidavits did not specify any ovality tolerance either. This point merits further investigation, but it does not seem that this would create any problem in the fabricating of pneumatic ducts.

# WELD QUALITY

There does not seem to be any problem of weld quality. A number of cracks in seam welds were experienced during the bending operation. They do not seem to be excessive in number when related to cracks initiating in other areas. It must be expected that the weld always will be an area weaker than the rest of the tubing.

# SURFACE DEFECTS

Dents, gouges, and scratches were at an acceptable level indicating that the finish, the handling, and the packaging of the material are of good quality.

Pits in the material, outside the weld, create some concern. They can be repaired by welding, but their frequency seems to be increasing. We recommend that a metallurgical investigation be made to determine their origin.

# CHEMISTRY

Information from vendors' affidavits and chemical laboratory log books has been collected to compare the product with specification requirements. Being commercially pure titanium, gases and impurities alone were recorded. These results were very satisfactory. Gases and impurities were well below the specified limits, even suggesting that changes to lower these limits might be in order.

# MECHANICAL PROPERTIES

It should be remembered that the mechanical properties are those of the sheet used to make the tube. No data on the tube itself were available. Some significant conclusions can be derived from this information, especially in the light of the forming problems explained later.

1. The ultimate tensile strength is well above the minimum specified limits.

2. From past tests it appears the upper yield point, where the metal begins to have permanent deformation, barely fits within the specification

limit, indicating that the specification may not be in complete agreement with the actual capabilities of the producers. Consequently, it is an illusion to consider the suggestion previously made to lower the upper specification limit to alleviate forming problems. Moreover, an unknown amount of cold work is introduced during the fabricating of the tube and the data available are not the best for a study of ductility properties.

3. The per cent elongation from tests of incoming materials has averaged 26.3 per cent with a standard deviation of 2.24 per cent. The control limits agree fairly well with the lower specification limit of 20 per cent and the upper specification limit of 33 per cent. This is highly significant, for the material must elongate properly if the bend is to be formed without defects. These figures, however, should be compared to the narrow range of 30.5 per cent and 31 per cent respectively of the elongation values recorded for the test materials reported by the manufacturing research and development group in making their evaluation. A simple computation shows that there are less than five chances in one hundred of the shop getting material from stores with an elongation as good as or better than the material used by manufacturing research and development during their evaluation.

## RECEIVING REJECTIONS

Records of incoming material rejections for the previous twelve months were reviewed and the results summarized (Exhibit 4). The overall rejection percentage was very low. There was practically no material scrapped. The main cause of rejection was poor X-ray film. This did not mean that the material was poor but merely that the X-ray method of taking pictures and the interpretation (of one vendor at least) were poor. Liaison between the receiving inspection laboratory and the vendor seems to have solved this problem.

## DIMENSIONAL INSPECTION

The tubing was inspected for dimensions and there were practically no rejections for such discrepancies. The outside diameter was measured to the nearest 0.001 inch. This is in accordance with the procurement specification. There was a difference of opinion between the shop and the receiving inspection unit about outside diameter tolerance. The shop inspection took a series of measurements on 4.5- by 0.020-inch tubing and reported the results to receiving inspection. (The statistical distribution of these measurements is shown on Exhibit 5.) It is apparent that a large percentage of this tubing is oversize. There seems to have been a misunderstanding in receiving inspection about specification change on outside diameter tolerance. In fact the tolerance 0.0025 to 0.007 inch for tubing under 6 inches outside diameter has never been changed; this same tolerance is called for on the original specification.

## FABRICATING

This audit disclosed that tube bending was by far the most critical problem. This was realized by the organizations involved before this audit was initiated. However, reliable figures on the magnitude of the problem were not readily available.

During the period January 1 to August 6, 176 rejection tags were written on titanium tubing. A breakdown of the causes for rejection is presented (see Exhibit 6). These rejections involved 2,180 feet of tubing, of which 1,094 feet (50.2 per cent) was scrapped. Important as it may seem, the figures give a very incomplete picture of the actual scrap because most of the material which fractured during bending did not pass through inspection and is accounted for under different headings, such as "machine setup" or "tool tryout." The actual consumption of material related to the needs should provide more accurate information.

Up to August 8, 84,000 feet of tubing was issued. The total quantity per airplane was 864.2 feet. According to the production program approximately 67 airplanes sets or 57,900 feet should have been required to this date. The difference between these two figures is very large and cannot be accounted for only by engineering changes. Undoubtedly, the material scrapped is a large percentage of the material procured. The estimated 20 per cent rejection rate seems very conservative.

Using a median price for computation and taking into account the relative quantities of different sizes used, the average cost of ducting material is $7.75 per foot. The cost of rejections in material alone would then be 78 planes × $7.75 × 864/100 = $5,223 annually for every 1 per cent of rejection rate, with the present program. This is over $100,000 a year for a 20 per cent rejection rate.

Exhibit 6, based on the analysis of rejection tags, indicates that cracking during bending is the most frequent cause of rejection, accounting for the largest percentage of all rejections written during the first months of this year and probably for most of the unwritten rejections as well. Next frequent causes were excessive wrinkles, dents, gouges, collapsed areas, etc., all traceable to bending problems. Rejections not related to bending amounted to less than 10 per cent of the total rejections.

It is evident that real forming difficulties are experienced by the shop with titanium. Compared to stainless steel, the vastly increased difficulty of bending titanium tubing is explainable by the differences in the structure and mechanical properties between the two materials.

Manufacturing research and development made an excellent evaluation, but as already indicated, did not take into account material variability permitted by the specification. A detailed analysis of the causes of rejection is not within the scope of this audit, but if it is made it should involve correlation studies of such factors as material properties, surface condition, lubrication, tubing-to-tooling clearance, temperature (for hot bending), clamping pressure, and other machine settings. This definitely requires a systematic approach in which statistical techniques, such as used in experimental design and analysis of variance, should prove a valuable tool.

It is in the tradition of the shop not to use a manufacturing plan for tube fabrication. This undoubtedly cuts down on the paper work but does not provide the operator with a guide as to how to do the job most effectively. Manufacturing started to record dimension and temperature settings on cards a few weeks ago to avoid unnecessary tryouts. The cards will be used every time a job is repeated.

## MATERIAL CONTROL

Operating procedure "Tubing—Pneumatic Ducts—Material Control" has been revised and was reissued on August 6. The purpose of the revision was to explain the current method of accounting for raw materials. This operating procedure does not place any limit on the amount of material which can be procured for machine setup, tool tryout, material losses, etc. This allows wide latitude in the issuing of material in any quantity and explains why the analysis of rejection tags alone does not provide conclusive evidence why material is scrapped.

## WELDING AND INSTALLATION

Because of the amount of time spent on material and forming problems, it has not been possible to audit welding and installation specifications in detail. There does not seem to be any unusual problem in these areas. Analysis of rejection tags for the period January 1 to August 6 shows that only 3 from a total of 176 tags were charged to weld defects. This seems to be a very good quality level.

Final assembly shops reported some problems in duct assembly which do not seem to be unique to titanium tubing. These problems are related to duct and flange alignment and to the installation of clamps and seals.


## CONCLUSION

The fabrication of titanium pneumatic ducting is the cause of a serious rejection problem. Important savings are possible through improvement of material forming properties and institution of adequate process control on the forming operations. These improvements require coordinated action from engineering, manufacturing, and quality control.


## RECOMMENDATIONS

1. An improved method must be used to provide an accurate evaluation of the rejection rate. This is important for cost control as well as for providing a yardstick to measure improvements. An analysis of the rejection rate based on rejections tags is essential.

2. Much of the out-of-tolerance tubing has passed through the stores department with inspection conducted on a sampling basis. It does not seem feasible to reinspect 100 per cent for dimensions on all the tubing in stores. A new sampling standard should be preceded by tests conducted by manufacturing research and development to determine the effect of out-of-tolerance dimensions on bending properties.

3. A realistic attempt should be made to encourage the manufacturer to produce material with better forming properties. This is contingent upon producers' capabilities, however. Changes to the specification should be made to make tolerance requirements more specific and to improve the control over the mechanical properties of the tubing.

4. Process control of tube forming operations is nonexistent. There is an urgent need for coordinated action. It may be some time before specifications enforceable by quality control are available, but work toward this goal should be started at once. Interim steps can be taken, such as reevaluating and developing tube bending information, and having manufacturing and quality control determine the list of critical processing steps and establish satisfactory control limits.

5. In the engineering manual information on titanium tube bending and forming should be more specific. Bend radius and angle limitations should be reviewed for compatibility with the least acceptable material.

6. Drawings and purchase orders should be reviewed and, if necessary, completed to specify the tolerance on ovality.

After receiving the audit report, Lancaster met with representatives from engineering, manufacturing, purchasing, and quality control. The following proposal was suggested for distribution to all parties concerned.

## Review Committee Report

1. Purchasing and processes unit:
   Update the present procurement specification to:
   a. Relax the straightness requirement from 0.015 to 0.030 inch per foot.
   b. Include a minimum limit on ductility to control the amount of work hardening originating at the vendor plant.
   c. Include a metallurgical check to identify nonuniform material.
2. Engineering unit:
   Change the wall thickness or basic design, as required to improve bending capability of those elbows causing the most problems.
3. Purchasing unit responsibility:
   a. Provide for an inspection at the vendor plants to assure that procurement specification provisions are maintained before the material is shipped.
   b. Purchasing should compare the current inventory status of material on hand against actual production requirements to assure material availability.
4. Parts control area:
   a. Group similar material types and sizes for joint release to reduce setup time and waste of setup material.
   b. Shortages of ducts to be picked up on the next lot of work orders released.
5. Shop responsibilities:
   Assign to a responsible party, preferably an experienced bend operator, the duties of:
   a. First part check.
   b. Measuring tool wear.
   c. Control of tool wear.
   d. Report of equipment malfunctions causing rejections.
6. Quality control unit responsibilities:
   a. Review receiving inspection methods and procedures to minimize flow time of incoming materials.
   b. Incorporate a foolproof method of segregating incoming material to assure the separation of low-quality but acceptable material and high-quality material which fully meets all requirements of the specifications. The high-quality material to be designated and reserved for bending. A color code system was suggested as a means of identification for segregation.

7. Tooling unit responsibilities:
   a. Measure and record wear on tooling, during and after use, to determine wear rate.
   b. Provide duplicate tooling if warranted to minimize downtime due to lack, or repair, of tooling.
   c. Simplify designed tools.
   d. Improve the control of heat required for bending within the required range.
   e. Provide oversized tooling for oversized tube material, if necessary.
8. Facilities unit responsibilities:
   a. Overhaul and redesign the actuating mechanisms to provide positive action cylinders.
   b. Eliminate any undesirable machine features formerly required for aluminum tube bending.
   c. Keep the equipment in a state of good repair.
   d. Improve the reliability of maintaining the proper temperature for the tools and dies.
   e. Refine the controlling systems on all benders to allow a more positive relationship between the bend die and the pressure booster cylinder.

Lancaster decided that the problem of rejection could be solved by instituting this program and without additional research in refining the process. Three months later, however, no significant changes in the rejection rate were noted. During this period it was discovered that the purchasing group was ordering linear quantities of titanium tubes based on the exact dimensions of the elbow, when in reality there was an average of 8 inches of waste at each end of the duct where the tube bender gripped the material. Increased quantities of titanium were scheduled to start arriving within thirty days.

# EXHIBIT 1

## A tube bending machine

# EXHIBIT 2

## Typical tube bending tools

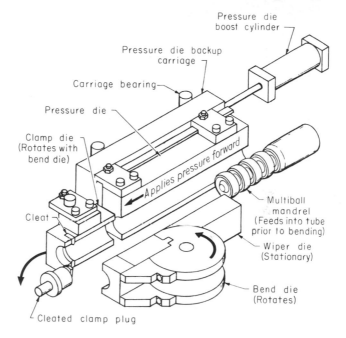

# EXHIBIT 3

## Typical tool wear

| Accumulated mandrel wear, inches | Accumulated wiper die wear, inches | Number of elbows bent |
|---|---|---|
| 0.0013 | Less than 0.001 | 50 |
| 0.0021 | 0.0015 | 100 |
| 0.0052 | 0.0037 | 200 |
| 0.015 | 0.009 | 500 |

# EXHIBIT 4

## Titanium pneumatic tubing rejections on receiving inspection

| Specification | Date | Reason | Disposition |
|---|---|---|---|
| AMS 4941 | July 18 | 2 | 4 |
| AMS 4941 | Aug. 16 | 3 | 1 |
| AMS 4941 | Nov. 21 | 2 | 2 |
| AMS 4941 | Feb. 1 | 2 | 2 |
| AMS 4941 | Feb. 1 | 2 | 2 |
| AMS 4941 | Feb. 1 | 2 | 2 |
| AMS 4941 | Mar. 8 | 4 | 1 |
| AMS 4941 | Mar. 27 | 4 | 1 |
| AMS 4941 | Apr. 10 | 4 | 2 |
| AMS 4941 | Apr. 10 | 4 | 2 |
| AMS 4941 | May 3 | 4 | 1 |
| AMS 4941 | May 3 | 4 | 2 |
| AMS 4941 | June 12 | 4 | 2 |
| AMS 4941 | July 11 | 4 | 1 |

CODE:

*Reason*
1 = Code marking incorrect
2 = Failed tensile test
3 = Wrong material
4 = Poor exposure or incomplete X-ray film
*Disposition*
1 = Rejected (returned to supplier)
2 = Accepted on retest
3 = Rework or scrap
4 = Use as is

# EXHIBIT 5

## A-40 titanium pneumatic tubing

(Statistical distribution of outside diameter measurements taken on 4.5- by 0.020-inch stock material in shop, June 19)

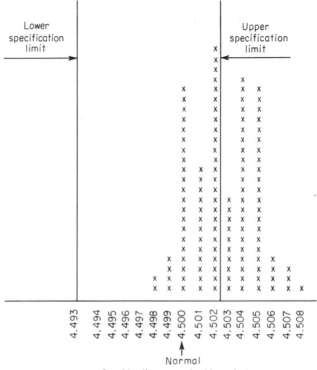

Outside diameter of tubing, inches

# EXHIBIT 6

## Titanium pneumatic tubing: causes of rejections in shop

(Based on 176 rejection tags issued between January 1 and August 6)

| | |
|---|---|
| 42 Cracks and rupture (Outside weld area) | |
| 11 Cracked seam welds | |
| 25 Wrinkles or dents | |
| 16 Gouges on holes | |
| 15 Pits or scratches | |
| 6 Collapsed areas | |
| 7 Wrong bend or material | |
| 5 Undetermined bending damage | |
| 1 Thin out | |
| 3 Assembly welding defects | |
| 176 Total | |

# DISCUSSION QUESTIONS

1. After reviewing appropriate sections of the suggested reading, make a list of the technical terms and significant details of the case you do not understand. How much should a nontechnical administrator understand regarding such technical matters?

2. What is causing the large number of rejections of ducts?

3. Should manufacturing research and development refine the process for manufacturing titanium ducts?

4. What suggestions, other than those mentioned, can you think of which will improve manufacturing's effectiveness in producing titanium ducts?

5. Are any of the procedures of the manufacturing research and development group in conflict with the manufacturing department?

6. What effect will increased quantities of titanium have on rejections, if any?

7. How could you calculate the value of saving a pound of weight on a supersonic plane?

# REFERENCES

Heyel, Carl: *Handbook of Industrial Research Management* (New York: Reinhold Publishing Corporation, 1959).

Marks, Lionel S. (ed.): *Mechanical Engineers' Handbook*, 6th ed. (New York: McGraw-Hill Book Company, 1958).

Quisin, James B.: *Yardsticks for Industrial Research* (New York: The Ronald Press Company, 1959).

Schaller, Gilbert S.: *Engineering Manufacturing Methods*, 2d ed. (New York: McGraw-Hill Book Company, 1959).

# TEEM AEROSPACE CORPORATION

Phil Wagenar was beginning to "cool off" as he sipped his coffee in the executive dining room of the Teem Aerospace Corporation. He and Dale Johnson were relaxing for a moment after their presentation to the selection board regarding their recommended placement of a major subcontract for the reaction controls system for the X284 airplane. Phil Wagenar, senior design engineer, was still insisting that his point of view was right: "I tell you, Dale, your procurement evaluation system is no damn good—you can switch it around to get any answer you want. It's just a numbers game." With some resignation Dale Johnson, section manager in the purchasing department, repeated his attitude: "What have you got that's better? When you have a large number of variables that must be evaluated and summed up, our system gives us the best compromise decision which can be adequately justified."

The selection board had just adjourned to give its members time to study the facts presented by the analysis committee regarding the reaction controls system. A meeting had been scheduled for the following day at which time a final decision regarding this major procurement was to be made.

The Teem Aerospace Corporation was one of the largest producers of commercial and military aircraft. Its Tucson division was located in Tucson, Arizona, and was engaged in a major effort to design and manufacture the X284 airplane. The X284 airplane was to be a very advanced concept. Although it was a manned aircraft, its extremely high altitude capabilities and its long range gave this fighter-bomber some of the characteristics of a missile. When the prime contract for the X284 had been placed with Teem by the Air Force it had been agreed that the reaction controls system would be subcontracted. The purpose of the reaction controls system was to assist the aerodynamic surfaces in providing vehicle attitude control in that area of the flight in the upper atmosphere where the aerodynamic surfaces were not effective. The subcontractor was to design the reaction controls system to performance specifications provided by Teem, with some of the general characteristics of the hardware indicated but with the detail design left to the supplier. The specifications provided such information as the envelope space limitations, weight limitations, fuel to be used, number and type of major parts, thrust levels of the nozzles, response times, and other technical information which established the necessary constraints.

The reaction controls system was to consist of a hot gas generator, propellant control system, hot gas transmission lines, thrust control valves, and nozzles. The system was to provide control torques to the vehicle pitch, roll, and yaw axes by valving off hot gas as required through the thrust control valves and nozzles. The gas generator and propellant control system were to maintain pressure in the system by burning fuel as required to supply the nozzles. The fuel supply chosen for the system was to be cryogenic hydrogen drawn from the main storage tank of the airplane. The hydrogen was to be burned with liquid oxygen to raise its temperature and thus provide an efficient energy source. An important design requirement of the system was that the hot gas generator was to be "fail-safe." In the event of failure (either electrical or mechanical) of the controls system or the fuel metering valves, the hot gas generator was to be designed so that a "burn through" would not occur which could result in flame or gases being emitted from the system. The thrust control valves were to be operated either by the pilot or by the automatic flight control system. The valves were to be of an "on-off" type to provide high reliability and low leakage.

For major procurements, such as the reaction controls system for the X284, a well-developed system of vendor selection had been established at Teem. The buyer assigned to the reaction controls system was Tom Osborne. He was to collect all of the appropriate information regarding each of the vendors to be considered for the award. This information was to be submitted to an analysis committee which was responsible for making a selection recommendation to the selection board for final approval.

Tom Osborne set out to prepare a list of potential vendors to whom invitations for bids (IFB) would be submitted. He carefully reviewed the requisition and related specifications, and discussed the project with his supervisor, Dale Johnson, section manager in the purchasing department, and with the designers in the engineering department. In order to secure the best hardware for the program, the following items regarding potential subcontractors were considered:

1. Companies with known capabilities, including original research skills.
2. Companies which previously had made presentations to Teem indicating their capabilities in the field of this procurement.
3. Contacts and discussions that Tom Osborne and other buyers had with people in the industry.
4. Recommendations that had been presented by other Teem divisions and other companies.
5. A thorough review of data—information and brochures—that were on file in the Teem procurement office.
6. Companies which had sent letters indicating interest, experience, and capability.
7. Review of trade magazines to identify the names of corporations with indicated interest in secondary power applications. A study was also made of *Thomas' Register of American Manufacturers* for companies that were listed in this field.
8. Suggestions and recommendations made by Air Force personnel.

Based on the above factors Tom Osborne was able to obtain names of twenty-three companies which could be considered as potential vendors. He reviewed this list with Dale Johnson, and they decided to compare the known characteristics of each company with the proposed work statement. This comparison was intended to reduce the list to companies which had experience in the following areas:

1. Experience in the particular or related systems on missiles or airplanes
2. Experience with hydrogen/oxygen fuel systems
3. Known management, engineering, and manufacturing capabilities in the general product line of the procurement

This comparison reduced the list of potential bidders to fourteen. The remaining names were then reviewed with personnel in the engineering department, finance department, and other departments that were able to provide information of a preliminary nature regarding each vendor's past performance for on-time delivery, quality, financial responsibility, and security clearance status.

This resulted in a refined list of eight potential sources. The list of eight names was submitted to the chief purchasing agent for his approval and he in turn submitted the list to the Air Force plant representative for final approval. Upon receipt of the Air Force approval of the bid list, Tom Osborne was ready to forward the invitations for bids requesting proposals and quotations to the eight vendors as soon as the IFB was released by the analysis committee. The preparation of this list had taken approximately two weeks from the time Tom Osborne had first received the official requisition from the engineering department.

During the time that the bid list was being prepared, an analysis committee had been organized consisting of Dale Johnson from the purchasing department as chairman of the committee; Phil Wagenar, the design supervisor in charge of preparing the specifications for the reaction controls system; a supervisor from the quality control department who was familiar with developmental and experimental work and had extensive experience with subcontractors; and a foreman from the manufacturing department who had general information regarding the primary types of manufacturing involved in the reaction controls system and also had experience in evaluating subcontractors. The four members of the analysis committee were mature executives with broad backgrounds in the aircraft industry, and each had a reputation for exercising objective judgment.

The first task of the analysis committee was to set up a system of assigning points to each vendor which would form the basis of making the award to the winning company. They selected the major factors to be considered as follows:

1. Technical
2. Management
3. Financial
4. Manufacturing
5. Quality control

Each of the factors was then broken down into criteria which were of significance with reference to the specific program involved. The criteria for each factor were then weighted as shown in Exhibit 1.

The criteria for each factor were broken down further into subcriteria; the management factor is shown in Exhibit 2. There were two basic principles involved in the establishment of the detailed subcriteria. First, there was a recognition that vendor selection required judgment in making the final decision. It was difficult, if not impossible, to arrive at a single overall judgment decision directly. It was believed, therefore, that the overall large and difficult problem could be broken down into a series of smaller problems. Each of the smaller problems more readily lent itself to a solution which could be related to other solutions to obtain an overall judgment which could be substantiated and justified.

The second principle in setting up detailed criteria was to provide a basis for evaluating each vendor independently on an absolute basis, rather than relating each vendor to the other vendors and rating them on a relative judgment basis. It was expected that an absolute rating basis would involve less bias than a relative rating basis.

In evaluating each criterion, all vendors first were given the full value of the points assigned on the preliminary assumption that each vendor met the requirements of the criterion. Points were then deducted from the maximum points allowed as deficiencies were observed.

The thought process in evaluating each subcriterion is illustrated in the following examples for Exhibit 2. Subcriterion I-C involved the "make or buy" plan. For this item the vendor was requested to identify how much he planned to make and how much he planned to buy. Particular attention was given to critical items of the design which the vendor was expected to make rather than buy in order assure that the vendor had control of the manufacturing process for the critical items. A check also was made as to whether the vendor intended to make items that could be purchased at a lower cost or with better quality.

Subcriterion II-A of Exhibit 2 pertinent to corporate structure was investigated regarding centralization versus decentralization of control. Did the local functional executive report to the local plant manager or to the functional manager at the headquarters office? Was this a good or bad arrangement? What degree of control, effectiveness of communication, and lines of responsibility and authority existed between the functional executive at the local level and the functional executive at the headquarters level? To whom did the quality control executive report? Was the support to be received from the corporate headquarters real or imaginary? What was the role of the board of directors and the president as compared to the role of the manager at the divisional levels?

Subcriteria listed under IV of Exhibit 2 for management controls concerned the effectiveness of the specific controls used by the vendor for the program being procured. Elaborate controls were not necessarily required. The simplest controls that would adequately do the job were considered superior to elaborate controls that might involve greater costs without improving the effectiveness. Where coordination was necessary between the prime contractor and the subcontractor with reference to reports, the control systems were checked for compatibility. A check was made to determine if reports were prepared on a timely basis so that action could be taken promptly to correct an undesirable situation.

After preparation of the criteria list the anlysis committee reviewed the invitations for bids to be certain that the vendors were requested to submit sufficient information to evaluate technical and cost criteria. The invitations for bids were also checked to minimize unnecessary information that might be requested regarding the other criteria. This policy had resulted from past situations when too much detail had been requested from vendors. The excessive detail had caused high bidding cost for the vendors, and some members of management had charged that the analysis committees were "grading papers for the best science fiction writers" rather than evaluating companies. It was planned that the technical cost data submitted would permit the vendors to be reduced to three or four. A field survey of each of these companies then would be made to provide the remaining detailed information required by the analysis committee to reach a final recommendation.

Upon release of the invitations for bids by the analysis committee, Tom Osborne sent out the invitations to the eight vendors remaining on the proposed bidders' list. Five weeks later six companies had responded. Two companies declined to submit proposals. The six proposals were given a preliminary evaluation by the analyis committee and two companies were eliminated as unacceptable because their proposals failed to meet the technical requirements of the specifications. The four companies remaining in the competition were as follows:

Bullard Scientific Company
Military Division of the Eastern Corporation
R. J. Matterson Company
Amalgamated Manufacturers, Inc.

Amalgamated was a large company prominent in its field, but there was a question as to whether their proposal complied with the basic design requirements. The analysis committee decided to field survey all four companies and to verify whether there was compliance by Amalgamated with the technical requirements of the procurement.

Tom Osborne headed up a team of functional specialists who then visited each vendor for about two days and prepared documentation covering each of the criteria established by the analysis committee. These written statements by the functional specialists were submitted to the analysis committee along with other information collected by the buyer.

Each member of the analysis committee first evaluated his own area of specialization. Dale Johnson from the purchasing department handled the management and financial factors with the assistance and advice of the other members of the committee. The evaluation of each factor then was reviewed by the entire committee and resulted in the scores assigned to each vendor as shown in Exhibit 3. Having reached this step in the procedure all that remained was to relate the values of each factor to one another and to compare the resulting points with the prices which were submitted.

The responsibility for weighting the factors relative to one another was assigned to the selection board. This information was withheld from the analysis committee until the members of the analysis committee had evaluated the criteria for each factor. This was to prevent possible bias on the part of the members of the analysis committee who might give too much attention to the heavily weighted factors and give inadequate attention to the factors receiving little weight. For the reaction controls system the selection board assigned the following weights:

|  | Per cent |
|---|---|
| Technical | 50 |
| Management | 15 |
| Financial | 15 |
| Manufacturing | 10 |
| Quality control | 10 |
| Total | 100 |

The weights then were applied to the score given each vendor for each factor and resulted in the assignment of points shown in Exhibit 4.

The prices proposed by the four bidders were as follows:

| Bullard | $5,784,562 |
|---|---|
| Eastern | 3,334,652 |
| Matterson | 4,763,970 |
| Amalgamated | 2,858,079 |

Since Amalgamated was the low bidder their proposal was again carefully reviewed, particularly because of the technical question involved in their design. This concerned the fail-safe feature of the generator. Their design involved a mechanical device to adjust for failure, but the mechanical device itself was subject to failure. Even though the scoring procedure for technical criteria only provided a penalty of two points for this design difficulty, it was finally decided by the analysis committee to eliminate Amalgamated because of noncompliance with the design specifications.

The analysis committee now faced the necessity of a final recommendation. Tom Osborne pointed out that Bullard had received 5.8 points more than Eastern but their bid was higher by almost $2.5 million than the bid submitted by Eastern. He suggested, therefore, that the award be made to Eastern since the designs submitted by both companies were acceptable. Phil Wagenar, the engineer on the committee, violently objected to such a suggestion. He insisted that Bullard's design was significantly superior to that submitted by Eastern and he felt the superiority of the design justified the increase in cost.

Normally the analysis committee was expected to submit a unanimous recommendation to the selection board. After a great deal of discussion, however, Phil Wagenar held out for Bullard while the other three members of the analysis committee insisted on Eastern. When it became apparent that complete agreement could not achieved, it was decided to submit Eastern as the recommendation of the analysis committee, with the dissent of Phil Wagenar noted, to the selection board.

As a result of the nonunanimous recommendation, the selection board requested each point of view to be elaborated. Tom Osborne pointed out that a change in the weighting of the various factors could change the total point relationship. He indicated that the range of weights assigned in previous competitions had varied as shown in Exhibit 5. By assigning the weights shown in Exhibit 6, Osborne was able to illustrate equal total points for Bullard and Eastern. Since this equalized the relative point advantage previously held by Bullard over Eastern, he felt that there should be no question about the award being made to the lower bidder.

Phil Wagenar presented a different point of view. He insisted that the original weighting of the selection board established the relative importance of each factor for this specific procurement and should not be changed. Further, he pointed out that the criteria used for evaluating the financial factor also included an allowance for price, as shown in Exhibit 1. He believed that price should not be considered twice. If price was included in the point system, then the actual prices should not be considered. On the other hand, if the actual prices were to be considered separately, the price criterion should be removed from the point system. He had made such a recalculation and presented an adjusted point table as shown in Exhibit 7. Here the difference between the two vendors had increased from 5.8 to 8.7 points which he suggested substantiated his recommendation of making the award to Bullard.

Tom Osborne countered this argument by pointing out that although the point system included consideration of price, the dollar difference between the acceptable bidders was of such magnitude that it did not receive adequate consideration in the point system evaluation. Of the 15 points total weight allocated to the financial factor, only 4.5 were allocated to price consideration. The lowest bidder received 4.5 points. Deductions for prices higher than the lowest bid from the 4.5 points were based on the following formula:

$$\text{Deduction for price for a given vendor} = \text{weight} \times \left( 1 - \frac{\text{lowest bid}}{\text{vendor bid}} \right)$$

By this method of allocating points for price there was only 1.6 points difference in the total evaluation for the price criterion between Bullard and Eastern.

In the discussion which followed it was claimed that the point system could not compensate for severe conditions. As an example, it was indicated that if the point system were employed literally a proposal would be penalized only 2.00 points for lack of a fail-safe combustor, 0.75 point if the company had no management experience on a similar job, 0.50 point if there was inadequate space in the plant to accomplish the manufacturing task, 1.00 point if the supplier did not possess proper inspection equipment, and 0.75 point if their financial stability was questionable. Under these circumstances a supplier could score 95 points but still, obviously, be incapable of meeting the requirements of the procurement.

Phil Wagenar retaliated by suggesting a further flaw in interpreting the points. He claimed that the weighting of each factor should not be applied to the total score within each factor but to the range between the lowest and the highest score awarded for each factor. To illustrate this he presented Exhibit 8 showing that the score range of 63.7 for the financial factor caused this item to receive undo importance as compared to the technical factor which had a score range of only 14.4. He contended this occurred even though the selection board had provided factor weights in which the technical factors were to be given primary consideration. Based on this argument he recalculated the raw scores as shown in Exhibit 9, and reassigned the points as shown in Exhibit 10. On the basis of this calculation he claimed that Bullard had an overwhelming advantage in the competition and should receive the award. After Phil Wagenar's presentation several members of the selection board indicated that they would like to study the new data in the exhibits before making a final decision. As a result, an adjournment was called after scheduling a meeting for the following day when the final decision was to be made.

# EXHIBIT 1 Criteria and weights for major factors

| Technical | Management | Financial | Manufacturing | Quality control |
|---|---|---|---|---|
| 40 Design approach | 20 Plan | 30 Cost proposal (price) | 20 Departmental experience | 20 Policy |
| 25 Technical capability | 26 Organization | 15 Strength | 15 Plan | 25 Operational system |
| 15 Development plan | 14 Manpower | 15 Accounting system | 13 Facilities | 15 Technical capability |
| 8 Reliability | 20 Controls | 10 Financial capability | 6 Skills | 10 Facilities |
| 7 Specification conformity | 5 Experience | 20 Cost control | 10 Tooling | 15 Reliability |
| 5 Release of proprietary rights | 10 Reliability | 10 Estimating technique | 16 Controls | 15 Record system |
| | 5 Labor relations | | 8 Quality assurance | |
| | | | 7 Improvement plan | |
| | | | 5 Training | |
| 100 Total | 100 Total | 100 Total | 100 Total | 100 Total |

# EXHIBIT 2

## Management subcriteria

| | | Points |
|---|---|---|
| I. Management plan | | 20 |
|   A. Adequacy of plan—consistent with program requirements; depicts understanding of problems with logical solutions and actions | | 10 |
|   B. Compliance with proposal instructions | | 3 |
|   C. "Make or buy" plan (including procurement) | | 7 |
| II. Management organization | | 26 |
|   A. Corporate structure | | 5 |
|   B. Specific management organization, depth, lines of authority, experience | | 12 |
|   C. Organizational stability | | 4 |
|   D. Support organization | | 5 |
| III. Manpower (total) | | 14 |
|   A. Requirements and availability | | 7 |
|   B. Manpower acquisition plan | | 5 |
|   C. Effect of current and future business on manpower program | | 2 |
| IV. Management controls | | 20 |
|   A. Adequacy of management controls (time and dollars): type, frequency, effectiveness | | 12 |
|   B. Top-management participation | | 5 |
|   C. Corrective action by management: what, how, effectiveness | | 3 |
| V. Management experience | | 5 |
|   Similar projects or jobs successfully managed of a similar complexity and magnitude | | 5 |
| VI. Reliability | | 10 |
|   Management participation: | | |
|   A. Policy | | 3 |
|   B. Procedures | | 3 |
|   C. Organization | | 4 |
| VII. Labor relations | | 5 |
| | Total = | 100 |

## EXHIBIT 3
### Factor scores

|            | Tech. | Mgt. | Financial | Mfg. | Q.C. |
|------------|-------|------|-----------|------|------|
| Bullard    | 64.4  | 92.1 | 82.1      | 66.0 | 63.0 |
| Eastern    | 50.0  | 86.8 | 82.1      | 71.0 | 80.0 |
| Matterson  | 63.4  | 79.5 | 43.4      | 55.0 | 52.0 |
| Amalgamated| 51.6  | 83.5 | 100.0     | 69.0 | 66.0 |

## EXHIBIT 4
### Factor points

|            | Tech.  | Mgt.   | Financial | Mfg.   | Q.C.   | Total   |
|------------|--------|--------|-----------|--------|--------|---------|
| (Weights)  | (50%)  | (15%)  | (15%)     | (10%)  | (10%)  | (100%)  |
| Bullard    | 32.2   | 13.8   | 12.3      | 6.6    | 6.3    | 71.2    |
| Eastern    | 25.0   | 13.0   | 12.3      | 7.1    | 8.0    | 65.4    |
| Matterson  | 31.7   | 11.9   | 6.5       | 5.5    | 5.2    | 60.8    |
| Amalgamated| 25.8   | 12.5   | 15.0      | 6.9    | 6.6    | 66.8    |

## EXHIBIT 5
### Range of weights
(Per cent)

|      | Tech. | Mgt. | Financial | Mfg. | Q.C. |
|------|-------|------|-----------|------|------|
| High | 55    | 15   | 20        | 20   | 25   |
| Low  | 35    | 5    | 10        | 10   | 10   |

# EXHIBIT 6

## Factor points based on revised weights

|            | Tech. | Mgt. | Financial | Mfg. | Q.C. | Total |
|------------|-------|------|-----------|------|------|-------|
| (Weights)  | (35%) | (5%) | (15%)     | (20%)| (25%)| (100%)|
| Bullard    | 22.5  | 4.6  | 12.3      | 13.2 | 15.7 | 68.3  |
| Eastern    | 17.5  | 4.3  | 12.3      | 14.2 | 20.0 | 68.3  |

# EXHIBIT 7

## Adjusted factor points
( Price criterion not included in financial factor )

|            | Tech. | Mgt.  | Financial | Mfg. | Q.C. | Total |
|------------|-------|-------|-----------|------|------|-------|
| (Weights)  | (50%) | (15%) | (15%)     | (10%)| (10%)| (100%)|
| Bullard    | 32.2  | 13.8  | 14.6      | 6.6  | 6.3  | 73.5  |
| Eastern    | 25.0  | 13.0  | 11.7      | 7.1  | 8.0  | 64.8  |
| Matterson  | 31.7  | 11.9  | 5.4       | 5.5  | 5.2  | 59.7  |
| Amalgamated| 25.8  | 12.5  | 15.0      | 6.9  | 6.6  | 66.8  |

# EXHIBIT 8

## Range of scores, adjusted basis

|                  | Tech.  | Mgt.  | Financial | Mfg.   | Q.C.   | Total   |
|------------------|--------|-------|-----------|--------|--------|---------|
| High             | 64.4   | 92.1  | 100.0     | 71.0   | 80.0   |         |
| Low              | 50.0   | 79.5  | 36.3      | 55.0   | 52.0   |         |
| Range            | 14.4   | 12.6  | 63.7      | 16.0   | 28.0   | 134.7   |
| (Adjusted weights)| (10.7%)| (9.3%)| (47.4%)   | (11.9%)| (20.8%)| (100.0%)|

## EXHIBIT 9

### Scores above minimum score, adjusted basis

(Price criterion not included in financial factor)

|            | Tech. | Mgt. | Financial | Mfg. | Q.C. |
|------------|-------|------|-----------|------|------|
| Bullard    | 14.4  | 12.6 | 60.8      | 11.0 | 11.0 |
| Eastern    | 0     | 7.3  | 41.3      | 16.0 | 28.0 |
| Matterson  | 13.4  | 0    | 0         | 0    | 0    |
| Amalgamated| 1.6   | 4.0  | 63.7      | 14.0 | 14.0 |

## EXHIBIT 10

### Factor points based on Exhibit 9*

|            | Tech. | Mgt. | Financial | Mfg. | Q.C. | Total |
|------------|-------|------|-----------|------|------|-------|
| (Weights)  | (50%) | (15%)| (15%)     | (10%)| (10%)| (100%)|
| Bullard    | 50.0  | 15.0 | 14.3      | 6.9  | 3.9  | 90.1  |
| Eastern    | 0     | 8.7  | 9.7       | 10.0 | 10.0 | 38.4  |
| Matterson  | 46.5  | 0    | 0         | 0    | 0    | 46.5  |
| Amalgamated| 5.6   | 4.8  | 15.0      | 8.7  | 5.0  | 39.1  |

$$* \text{Points} = \text{weight} \times \frac{\text{score above minimum}}{\text{range of scores}}$$

# DISCUSSION QUESTIONS

1. What are the limitations and strengths of a point system evaluation?
2. Was the double consideration of cost justified?
3. Using a point system evaluation, how do you compensate for extremely good or extremely bad features which have been designated a small number of points?
4. Do you accept the proposed use of the range of scores rather than the total scores in calculating the factor points?
5. If you were a member of the selection board, how would you vote?

# REFERENCES

Buffa, Elwood S.: *Modern Production Management* (New York: John Wiley & Sons, Inc., 1961), chaps. 2, 20.

England, Wilbur B.: *Procurement: Principles and Cases,* 4th ed. (Homewood, Ill.: Richard D. Irwin, Inc., 1962), chaps. 8, 9.

Koontz, Harold D., and Cyril J. O'Donnell: *Principles of Management,* 2d ed. (New York: McGraw-Hill Book Company, 1959), chap. 23.

# TORSION TRACTOR COMPANY

In March, 1961, the Torsion Tractor Company received an order from the Air Force for 400 tractor-van units to be used in moving missiles and electronics gear for a new weapons system then under development. Two hundred of the vans were to be used in moving missiles between production and maintenance facilities and the missile sites; the other two hundred vans were to be equipped with electronics gear used in maintaining and checking out the missiles. Although the missile vans were somewhat larger than the electronics gear vans, the gross weight when loaded was approximately the same. Because of the greater than normal load requirements and the necessity for reliable operation at high road speeds over both flat and mountainous country, Torsion Tractor redesigned one of its commercial tractor models to meet Air Force specifications and performance requirements. The major changes were a more powerful engine and an improved transmission and rear axle. The transmission was a heavier-duty design built to closer tolerances than the commercial model. In place of the standard two-speed rear axle on the commercial model, the military model had a two-speed rear axle with different gear ratios designed for heavier loads and built to closer tolerances than the commercial two-speed axle.

After the military tractor was designed, Torsion Tractor found that several commercial customers were also interested in the heavier-duty tractor design. The company obtained orders from them for 100 tractor units to be used in both on- and off-highway hauling in the western part of the country.

The delivery schedule for the military tractor-van units was twenty per month to begin in January, 1962. The first order for forty tractors from a commercial customer was scheduled to be delivered at a rate of ten per month beginning in April, 1962. The second order for sixty tractors from a second commercial customer was scheduled to be delivered at a rate of ten per month beginning in August, 1962. As soon as the contracts were received, the Torsion Tractor Company developed a master production schedule for the fabrication and assembly of both the van and tractor units. In the case of the military contract, it was imperative that the delivery schedule be met since missiles and electronics gear being manufactured by other weapons systems contractors could not be made operational without tractor-van units. The delivery schedules for the commercial units were also important since the market for commercial tractors was a highly competitive one, and customers viewed the ability of manufacturers to meet delivery dates as an important factor in placing orders. The heavy-duty tractor units designed by Torsion had also aroused considerable interest in the industry with the result that several competitive manufacturers were bringing out tractor models with similar capabilities which would be available for commercial delivery in late fall of 1962.

The Torsion Tractor Company was located in Pittsburgh where it owned one large plant at which all the vans and tractors were manufactured. The plant was equipped with a foundry, machine shops, and supporting facilities for the fabrications of parts. There was one area devoted exclusively to the assembly of vans in which each van was kept in one position while all assembly work was done. Tractors, however, were assembled by moving them through successive positions in a line. Different tractor models were all assembled on this one line with each position on the line performing the same type of work on each tractor as it moved down the line. A diagram of the tractor assembly line is shown in Exhibit 1.

The Torsion Tractor Company produced many of the van and tractor parts in its own plant, but purchased other parts as complete assemblies. Tractor and van frames, side panels, door panels, and floor panels were typical of the items fabricated in the Torsion shops. Wheels, axle assemblies, engines, transmissions, and radiators were typical of the items purchased as completed units from other manufacturers.

In the new heavy-duty tractor model the redesigned transmission and the two-speed axle assemblies were critical purchased parts. The new heavy-duty design of both required machining and finishing tolerances closer than those that had been used in previous commercial models. For transmissions, the Milwaukee Machine Tool Company had been a reliable supplier in the past, and Torsion selected them as the supplier for the new transmissions for the heavy-duty tractor. Rear axle assemblies had previously been procured from three sources:

Michael & Sons in Cleveland, West Coast Products in Oakland, California, and Milwaukee Machine Tool. Michael & Sons was a smaller company with limited production facilities; however, they had been a competent supplier of single-speed axles in the past. On occasion, the limited capacity of their production facilities had led to some slight delays in delivery, although this was never a serious problem. West Coast Products owned a large, modern facility in Oakland equipped with a wide variety of up-to-date machine tools. They had been a very capable supplier of two-speed rear axles and were generally better regarded than Michael & Sons. In general, the two-speed axles were more complicated than the single-speed axles produced by Michael & Sons and required tolerances which would be difficult for Michael & Sons to attain with the equipment in their plant. Milwaukee Machine Tool had served as a subsidiary source of two-speed axles, supplying about one-third of Torsion's requirements. There were two other companies in the country who supplied two-speed rear axles to competitors of Torsion, but these had never been used as suppliers by Torsion because of the satisfactory relationship with West Coast Products and Milwaukee Machine Tool. Also the quantity of two-speed rear axles purchased by Torsion was such that more than two sources of supply would lead to substantially higher costs because of short runs and the necessity for multiple sets of tools.

When the matter of procuring the new military two-speed axle came under consideration by Torsion, Michael & Sons was quickly ruled out as a possible source both because of the lack of capacity and the fact that the new two-speed axle would require even closer tolerances than the commercial two-speed axle and much closer tolerances than the single-speed axles with which Michael & Sons was experienced. Milwaukee Machine Tool had the plant capacity for both the transmission and rear axle contracts, but it was felt that it would not be a good policy to procure both the new transmission and rear axle from one manufacturer. This left West Coast Products, the other supplier of two-speed axles, as the logical choice, and a contract was negotiated with them for the production of the axles with delivery scheduled to support the master schedule for the fabrication and assembly of the tractor-van units. The contract called for production of the axles according to designs supplied by Torsion Tractor. In total the contract with West Coast Products was for 400 axles plus an initial order of 15 spares which the Air Force intended to locate at various depots around the country. The total contract amount was $606,500, of which $456,500, was for the axles themselves and $150,000 for the design and procurement of tooling and special equipment necessary for the production of the new two-speed axles. Although the production quantity was only 400, the quality of the tooling was such that is could be expected to be satisfactory for the manufacture of several thousand units. Under the contract, the tooling and special equipment was to be the property of the Air Force, but was to be located in the plant of West Coast Products. The quantity of tooling and special equipment was sufficient to support a production schedule of 25 axles per month on a two-shift five-day-week basis, which was West Coast's normal operating schedule.

After the contract for axles for the military order was negotiated, Torsion Tractor received the two commercial orders and negotiated a second contract with West Coast for axles for the 100 units for commercial use. No spares were ordered initially for the commercial units. The contract for axles for the commercial units was for $110,000. Of the $1,100 per unit contract amount, West Coast Products paid $50 per unit to the Air Force for the use of the Air Force-owned tooling and special equipment. Because of the overlap in the contracts requiring a 30-unit-per-month production rate, West Coast anticipated operating on a partial third-shift basis and with some overtime to meet the schedule for both contracts.

West Coast Products did not intend to produce all the parts for the new two-speed axles in its own plant. Standard nuts, bolts, and washers, some of the small fittings, a portion of the axle housing, and such things as gaskets and oil seals were procured from outside sources. About 40 per cent of the total parts in the axle assembly was contracted for by West Coast from other suppliers. The delivery schedules for these purchased items, in turn, were developed to support the axle fabrication schedule in West Coast's plant, although some small items were ordered in a single quantity sufficient to cover the entire requirements for both contracts.

The axles were shipped via rail from West Coast's plant in Oakland to Pittsburgh. Although transit time varied, it was assumed that the axles would arrive in Pittsburgh two weeks after shipment from Oakland since that was the longest time ordinarily experienced in transit. On one or two occasions, shipments had taken longer because of misrouting of cars, but these cases were very exceptional. Torsion Tractor's purchasing department scheduled the rear axles to arrive six weeks or thirty working days prior to the scheduled shipment dates of finished tractor units. Normally ten working days were required to receive the axles, uncrate and inspect them, and place them in the parts inventory. The axles remained in inventory another fifteen working days before being moved to position C on the assembly line (see Exhibit 1) where they were assembled into the tractor unit. The tractor units were ready for shipment five working days after moving into position C. The cumulative schedule for delivery of axles to Torsion, movement of axles to position C, and shipment of completed tractor units is shown in Exhibit 2.

Through the early fall of 1961 all schedules for the design and production of parts for the new tractor unit were met by both Torsion Tractor and its suppliers. There were some difficulties with last-minute design and tooling changes; however, such things were anticipated and problems were corrected as they arose. Torsion Tractor had an excellent reputation for on-time deliveries and was willing to expend the necessary effort to expedite anything which might delay the schedule. By late fall, parts from various suppliers were arriving on regular schedules, and the Torsion Tractor plant was building up to the scheduled production rate on parts produced in the plant. Deliveries of the axle units from West Coast Products began in the middle of November, 1961, at a rate of twenty per month. Starting in the middle of February, 1962, this rate was increased to thirty per month. The first tractor unit was completed on December 29 and shipped to the Air Force as scheduled on January 2, 1962. Although minor production problems caused a good deal of overtime work in December and January, deliveries proceeded on schedule at the twenty-per-month rate programmed for the first quarter of 1962.

By the end of March most of the early production problems had been solved so that overtime work was no longer necessary to meet delivery schedules. In fact, Torsion's manufacturing manager, Pete Burger, was pleased to find that a drop in man-hours expended per unit was sufficiently large so that no overtime would be necessary to meet the accelerated delivery rate of thirty units per month scheduled to begin in April, 1962.

On April 1 Pete Burger was in his office reading several monthly reports when the purchasing agent, Chet Beyer, rushed in with a telegram he had just received from West Coast Products. The telegram notified Torsion Tractor that the shop employees of West Coast had gone on strike as of midnight, March 31, and that deliveries of axles would cease immediately. The telegram had come as quite a surprise to Beyer since West Coast Products was well known for its good relations with its employees, and a sudden strike was completely unexpected. One reason why West Coast Products was considered to be such a reliable vendor was that its shop employees averaged fifteen years' service with the company and there had never previously been a strike of any consequence.

In addition, the employees had for years participated in a retirement program which involved the placement of nonvoting stock of the company into a fund from which retirement benefits were paid. Since the level of benefits was determined by the value of the stock in the fund, the employees had an immediate interest in the profitable operation of the company. In effect, the strike by employees against the company was, in part, a strike against themselves, particularly in view of the fact that the retirement fund held about 50 per cent of the total outstanding stock of the company. Perplexing as the situation was, however, the matter of immediate concern was the effect of the strike on operations at Torsion Tractor.

Chet Beyer felt that there was no immediate cause for concern with regard to the supply of the standard two-speed axles for Torsion's regular line of commercial tractors. Although West Coast was filling about two-thirds of Torsion's two-speed axle requirements, Chet Beyer was sufficiently familiar with the operations of Milwaukee Machine Tool, the supplier of the other third, that he was confident Milwaukee Machine Tool could temporarily fill all of Torsion's requirements for standard commercial two-speed axles by working overtime and adding some second-shift work. However, West Coast Products had been selected as the sole source of supply for the heavy-duty axles for the new tractor, because of the relatively small number of axles required, and no alternative source was immediately avaliable. This presented Torsion Tractor with a possible serious situation in meeting schedules on the new tractor if the strike were not settled quickly.

Pete Burger's first action was to call in Sid Euler, head of production planning for the Torsion plant, to notify him of the situation with regard to the axles for the new tractor model. In the ensuing discussion, Chet Beyer pointed out that, although shipments had ceased on March 31, axles should continue to arrive until about the middle of April since two weeks' supply was always in transit. Referring to his shipment schedules, as shown in Exhibit 2, Sid Euler estimated that there were enough axles on hand or in transit to support delivery schedules until June 1. The discussion ended with Chet Beyer volunteering to get more information about the strike and to check into other possible sources of supply. Although Sid Euler could think of nothing that could be done by the people in Torsion's plant to remedy the situation, he volunteered to talk to the assembly superintendent about the problem. For the moment, the situation was not critical, but it would become critical in the near future if something were not done.

Chet Beyer called Oakland and was able to reach the assistant manufacturing manager at West Coast Products. The assistant manufacturing manager said that the strike had occurred as a result of a series of incidents involving the disciplining of several shop employees for minor infractions of rules. While the strike did not involve any major issues, both management and the shop employees were adamant that the other side back down from its position, and it was difficult to say how long the strike would last. While discussing the situation with the assistant manufacturing manager, Chet Beyer discovered that West Coast had an inventory of completed parts on hand which had not yet been assembled into completed axles, although the exact number of each part was not immediately available. Chet Beyer inquired about the possibility for delivery of these parts to Torsion Tractor, but he could not get any commitment since the employees were picketing the plant and no one was available to prepare the parts for shipment.

Following his conversation with West Coast, Chet Beyer spent the rest of the afternoon contacting Michael & Sons, Torsion's supplier for single-speed axles, and the two firms that supplied two-speed axles to Torsion's competitors to see whether they could supply the axles which West Coast could not supply. In these conversations, Beyer explained the situation briefly, emphasizing the importance of the delivery of the tractors to the defense effort. He also emphasized the exploratory nature of his inquiry and that he would like an estimate of the company's ability to supply the required axles. Michael & Sons was more than anxious to obtain the extra business, although it would strain their facilities to the utmost. Michael & Sons estimated that they could begin deliveries three months after an order was received if the tooling in West Coast's plant were moved to their plant. If new tooling had to be obtained, deliveries could commence in five months. One of the firms which supplied axles to Torsion's competitors did not feel that it had sufficient plant capacity to be able to supply the axles; the other firm was interested in the business and had adequate facilities to handle the order. This firm's estimate of delivery dates was about the same as Michael & Sons had given.

Dan Dailey, the tractor and van assembly superintendent, was quite concerned when Sid Euler informed him of the strike at West Coast Products. Dan Dailey had worked hard to smooth out various difficulties that had arisen in the production of the first tractor and van units, and it was disappointing to him to see the delivery schedule upset at this point by something beyond the control of the plant. He also pointed out several effects that an interruption in the assembly of the tractor units would have on his department. While the new tractor units constituted only one-third of the total current work on the tractor assembly line, additional workers had just been hired and trained to increase the capacity of the line. These workers would have to be released or underutilized if production of the new tractors were halted. Either of these alternatives would be quite expensive. Also, the assembly superintendent pointed out that Torsion's machine shop and foundry and the plants of Torsion's vendors were delivering other parts which would accumulate rapidly if production ceased. Slowing down or halting deliveries of these other parts would be expensive and might lead to further delays once production was resumed since many of the parts were not standard and required special setups and tooling.

Early the next morning, April 2, Pete Burger called a meeting in his office of Chet Beyer, Sid Euler, Torsion's sales manager, and a representative of the Air Force who had been stationed at Torsion's plant because of the importance of the tractor-van order. Both the Air Force representative and the sales manager emphatically stated that something had to be done to maintain the delivery schedules. In the case of the Air Force, the schedule for an entire weapons system depended on the delivery of the tractor-van units. As far as the commercial units were concerned, the sales manager felt that for competitive reasons deliveries had to be made on schedule at all costs, even if it meant losing money on the tractors. When Chet Beyer mentioned that some finished parts were awaiting assembly at West Coast's plant both the sales manager and the Air Force representative suggested that every effort be made to move the parts out of the plant and ship them to Pittsburgh for assembly in Torsion Tractor's plant.

Chet Beyer called West Coast Products immediately and persuaded West Coast to assign several administrative employees who were not on strike to the preparation for shipment of as many complete sets of parts as were on hand. Meanwhile the Air Force representative, working through military channels, made arrangements to provide a mixed military and civilian police guard to assure unmolested movement of the parts from the plant. Within two days, as many complete sets of parts as were available were moved out of the plant and shipped from Oakland via airfreight to Torsion Tractor's plant at Pittsburgh. There Torsion undertook assembly of the parts at its own expense. When the axles were assembled, this would add another fifteen axles to the number already on hand, providing sufficient stock to meet deliveries as scheduled through June 15.

On Monday, April 8, one week after the crisis began, Pete Burger invited Chet Beyer, Sid Euler, Dan Dailey, the sales manager, the Air Force representative, and the foundry and machine shop superintendent to his office to again discuss the situation. A call to West Coast Products immediately before the meeting had revealed that there was no change in the strike situation, although the management at West Coast Products doubted that the strike could conceivably last very long. Sid Euler opened the meeting with a report of the exact status of the axle supply and its relation to tractor shipment schedules. With the axles on hand, those in transit, and the ones being assembled from parts, enough of the new two-speed axles were on hand to maintain shipments as scheduled through June 15. If assembly of commercial units were stopped immediately and military units only were assembled and shipped, delivery of military tractors could be maintained as scheduled through July 15.

Chet Beyer then reported on his conversations with Michael & Sons and the other firm which had indicated willingness to take over completion of the axle contract. Discussion of the possibility of changing suppliers resulted in the group arriving at the conclusion that this was not an attractive alternative. If the tooling at West Coast's plant were moved out, deliveries could not commence before the early part of July. Also, if the strike ended while the tooling was being moved, West Coast could not get back into production. Procuring another set of tooling would not only be expensive but would also delay delivery for another two months, until the early part of September. And, if the strike ended while the second set of tooling was being procured, the cost of the second set of tooling would be a total loss. It also seemed unlikely that the strike would last long enough to require changing to another supplier. Of course, there was no guarantee that the strike would be short lived.

As the discussion progressed, Dan Dailey, the assembly superintendent, suddenly announced that he had just thought of a partial solution to the problem. He suggested that Torsion Tractor build a dolly in its shops to take the place of the rear axle assembly. The dolly could be placed under the rear of the tractor at position C on the assembly line, which would permit movement of the tractor through positions D and E with the dolly in place rather than the rear axle. The tractors could then be stored outside the plant on the dollies until such time as the rear axles were available. Although this would not solve the delivery problem, production could proceed at a close to normal pace with the tractors being completed to a point such that the only remaining work would be to install the axle assembly. Utilizing dollies in this fashion would prevent a shutdown of the assembly line and the preceding operations. The sales manager and Air Force representative did not feel that this was in any sense a solution to their problems of getting the tractors completed; however, they did agree that the dollies merited further investigation as a means of preventing a total shutdown of work on the tractors after the supply of axles was exhausted. Dan Dailey agreed to take up the matter of the design and fabrication of the dollies with the engineering and manufacturing departments and report back to another meeting of the group on Wednesday, April 10.

On Wednesday morning, the same group that had attended the Monday meeting assembled once again in Pete Burger's office. Dan Dailey reported that the engineering department felt that it could easily draw up plans for a dolly which could be used in place of the rear axle assembly while the tractors were being worked on in the assembly department. The engineering department estimated that labor and materials for the dollies would cost $200 to $225 plus the cost of engineering drawings. One possibility was to build a dolly for each tractor unit, leaving the dolly with the tractor while it was stored outside the plant awaiting the axle assemblies. A more economical system seemed to be to build five to ten dollies and use them only while the tractors were being worked on. The tractors could then be put on blocks while awaiting the rear axles, and the dollies would be available for reuse.

However, an engineer in the engineering department had come up with still another idea which might be feasible, although considerably more expensive. The engineer suggested that, instead of building dollies which wouldn't help much to get the tractors actually delivered, it might be possible to redesign one part of the standard two-speed rear axle housing and several fittings so that standard commercial two-speed rear axles might temporarily be used instead of the new heavy-duty axles. The engineer had pointed out that installation of the standard two-speed axles would affect performance somewhat, because of the difference in gear ratios and the necessity for limiting the permissible speed, but they would be serviceable until they could be replaced with the new heavy-duty axles when the supply of these units again became available. This would permit Torsion to deliver the tractor-van units to the Air Force so that outfitting and testing could be begun, and, if necessary, they could be put into modified service.

The engineer had estimated very roughly that the cost of modifying standard two-speed rear axles, installing them in the tractors, later removing them, and converting them back to the standard two-speed axle configuration would total about $500 to $600 per unit plus the cost of engineering work to determine what modifications would be necessary and to prepare drawings. At the production rate of thirty units per month, this solution would cost Torsion Tractor between $15,000 and $18,000 per month plus the initial engineering costs.

After Dan Dailey had completed his presentation of these two alternatives, Chet Beyer pointed out that the second alternative, that of using the standard two-speed axles temporarily, would raise still another problem. Milwaukee Machine Tool, the firm which produced the standard two-speed axles, had already received a large increase in work load because of the shifting of part of the standard two-speed axle work from West Coast Products. Using standard two-speed axles instead of the new heavy-duty axles would place an even heavier burden on Milwaukee. Any additional two-speed axles would certainly have to be manufactured on second and third shifts for which Milwaukee would have to be paid a premium. As a first estimate, Chet Beyer guessed that Milwaukee would be forced to charge an extra 15 per cent because of the extra costs involved. At a thirty-per-month delivery rate, this would add almost $5,000 more per month to the costs estimated for conversion of the axles alone.

# EXHIBIT 1

## Schematic diagram of tractor assembly line
### (Not to scale)

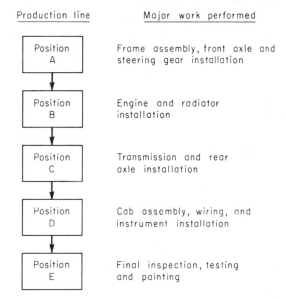

Production line

Position A — Frame assembly, front axle and steering gear installation

Position B — Engine and radiator installation

Position C — Transmission and rear axle installation

Position D — Cab assembly, wiring, and instrument installation

Position E — Final inspection, testing and painting

# EXHIBIT 2

## Cumulative master schedule
## for production of tractor units

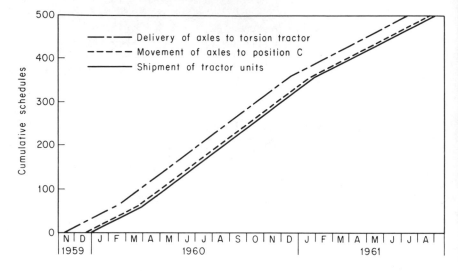

# DISCUSSION QUESTIONS

1. What is the relationship between the contract price for the axles to be used in the Air Force tractors and the price for the axles to be used in the commercial tractors? What justification might there be for this relationship?

2. Could Torsion Tractor have shut down the production of the new tractors to avoid any extra expenses because of the lack of axles?

3. At the time that the last meeting was held, what alternatives were available to Torsion Tractor? What risks and costs are associated with these alternatives? What course of action would you follow?

4. Did Torsion Tractor follow good procurement practice in obtaining its source of supply for the new axles?

# REFERENCES

Buffa, Elwood S.: *Modern Production Management* (New York: John Wiley & Sons, Inc., 1961), chap. 2.

England, Wilbur B.: *Procurement: Principles and Cases,* 4th ed. (Homewood, Ill.: Richard D. Irwin, Inc., 1962), chaps. 8, 9.

Ommer, Dean S.: *Materials Management* (Homewood, Ill.: Richard D. Irwin, Inc., 1962), chaps. 12, 14.

# TRAVELHOMES, INCORPORATED

Travelhomes, Incorporated, a major producer of a varied line of standard and special aluminum vacation and house trailers, was entering the final phase of a major expansion program. In order to complete the outfitting of the new facility, considerable amounts of equipment and supplies were still required. Due to an underestimate of the cost of the new facilities, the amount budgeted for the expansion was already overspent and the company's cash position had become very low. One increase in the original loan obtained to finance the expansion had already been granted and a recent informal inquiry for a further increase had received a very negative response from the lending agency.

One of the remaining potential sources of funds was the internal generation of cash through a reduction of in-process inventories. Each departmental supervisor was, therefore, asked to review his operating policies with the objective of reducing the amount of in-process inventory within his area of operation.

Travelhomes, Incorporated, was organized into three sections: (1) the parts manufacturing section, (2) the subassembly section, and (3) the final assembly section. The parts manufacturing section consisted of five manufacturing departments which produced all in-plant parts used by the other two sections. The subassembly section consisted of two departments: (1) chassis subassembly and (2) interior subassembly. These departments supplied the chassis and all the in-plant–produced interior furnishings used in the final assembly of the firm's line of trailers.

The final assembly section assembled the trailer bodies, attached them to the chassis, and outfitted the interior of the trailer. All items not produced within the other two sections were purchased from outside sources. The completion of the current expansion program would substantially reduce the number of fabricated and subassembled items purchased, and increase the purchase of raw materials to fabricate and subassemble these items in-plant.

Jim Hawkins, supervisor of the interior subassembly department (ISA department), was aware that his operation utilized large stores of fabricated and purchased parts and thought that there might be some opportunity for a reduction of in-process and purchased goods inventories within his area of operations. ISA operations consisted primarily of assembling parts drawn from ISA stores and directly forwarding the completed subassemblies to the final assembly section. A major portion of the items assembled in the ISA department were produced in batches of one to ten items. Most work was done on a modified assembly line basis with each line and crew capable of producing a wide variety of similar items. For example, there was a ceiling-height cabinet line, a counter and sink line, a corner cabinet line, a "converta-lounge" line, an interior paneling line, etc. Most items were of unitized design, and 90 per cent of the structural components were common to a large number of subassemblies. Surface components were largely standardized in size and shape but were available in numerous colors and finishes. On the basis of the current two-shift operation most subassemblies required a maximum of two working days to complete once actual work on the item had commenced.

In rechecking scheduling procedures Hawkins noticed that all operations of the parts manufacturing and subassembly sections were based on the final assembly section's advance and current assembly schedules. The advance schedule indicated planned production levels of each basic type of trailer by month for six months in advance and indicated to what extent these plans were backed by firm sales orders. This schedule was updated monthly to reflect the latest market forecasts and weekly to reflect new orders and cancellations of existing orders.

The current schedule indicated planned production by specific trailers for four weeks in advance. Expected starting and completion times for all trailers scheduled within the initial two weeks of the four-week period covered by the current schedule were shown. For the last two weeks only the specific trailers to be produced and the week in which they were to be completed were shown. The current week of the current schedule was considered to be fixed except in the case of an extreme emergency or the cancellation of a special trailer. In the latter case a standard trailer as nearly similar as possible was generally substituted. Very little flexibility existed as there was only a three-day planned lead time between the completion of subassembly work and the start of final assembly work on any given trailer. Lengthening of this lead time had often been discussed, but the bulky and fragile nature of the subassemblies hindered such a change. The fragility of the subassemblies resulted primarily from the use of the trailer wall to provide the basic rigidity of the structures. To store the subassemblies in larger than current quantities would require considerable additional floor space, special storage racks, or temporary bracing within the subassemblies. All these alternatives represented a substantial increase in cost over the current method of manufacturing and handling. Scratching and marring, already troublesome, would become an increasing problem as the number of items, length of time, and amount of handling and storage increased.

The second week of the current schedule was also considered firm except for extremely close substitutions and changes in sequences that met with the approval of the supervisor of the subassembly sections. Changes in the third and fourth weeks were allowed provided all necessary subassemblies could be completed in time. This seldom offered any real problem in view of the fact that all fabricated parts were supposed to be available to the subassembly department thirty working days prior to their officially scheduled need date.

About 5 per cent of ISA subassemblies were completed two to three days behind schedule. Under the three-day planned lead time, this often allowed only a matter of hours to inspect the completed subassemblies and move them approximately $\frac{1}{4}$ mile to the final assembly section. Reducing the scheduled lead time between subassembly and final assembly had been considered, but was rejected as being impractical. Any failure to provide the final assembly section with completed subassemblies on schedule evoked drastic reactions from top management and was to be avoided at almost any cost. Increased manufacturing cost appeared to be the major cause of management's irritation. Any work not capable of being performed on the assembly line frequently left the assembly crew with idle time, as the shortage of a single subassembly often prevented the installation of several major items. Installing items after a trailer left the assembly line required the use of higher paid labor and often took up to three times as many man-hours as was required when the work was done in its normal sequence on the assembly line. In extreme cases a temporary item would have to be installed to allow the continuation of assembly procedures. This required the subsequent off-line removal and replacement of the item. On the basis of these facts action to either reduce or lengthen the current three-day safety lead time between subassembly and final assembly appeared inadvisable.

The situation was somewhat different in the case of completion dates for fabricated parts required for subassembly. As already stated these parts were scheduled to arrive at ISA stores approximately thirty working days prior to the expected runout date for existing parts in stock. Fabricated parts stocks were reviewed weekly and a reorder was placed whenever the supply on hand was less than that required to meet the current and master production schedules for a period equal to the standard lead time for the part plus thirty days. The thirty-day cushion was instituted to assure that no stockouts occurred at subassembly time.

With the six-week (thirty working days) safety lead time between the scheduled completion time of fabricated parts and their ultimate need at subassembly, few parts shortages were experienced in the ISA department. A detailed survey indicated that over a period of one month only 1 per cent of the parts used reached a zero or actual stockout level. There were, however, a substantially greater number of parts which reached a low but not a stockout level prior to the arrival of the succeeding batch of parts. These stockouts and other relatively infrequent minor difficulties were the main causes for the late completions in the subassembly department.

In view of management's desire to reduce in-process inventories and the negligible number of late parts arrivals and completions within the ISA department, it was believed that the thirty-day safety lead time between the scheduled completion date for fabricated parts and their scheduled subassembly requirement date could be reduced. In attempting to arrive at a reasonable figure, Hawkins received suggestions for reducing the safety lead time by five to twenty-five days. There was common agreement that a slight increase in parts shortages at subassembly could be tolerated but that 2 to $2\frac{1}{2}$ per cent per month was the absolute limit. It could not be agreed upon, however, to what extent the thirty-day cushion could be reduced without exceeding the 2 to $2\frac{1}{2}$ per cent lateness restriction. Furthermore, it was not known how much each day's reduction in the cushion would affect the total value of in-process inventories.

The point had arrived when a decision was required and the problem was assigned to Henry Barnes, general stores superintendent. It was felt that his experience and relative independence from the ISA department would yield both a practical and an unbiased decision. Barnes had been in on several of the meetings devoted to discussing this problem and realized that any decision unsupported by cold hard facts would place him in a difficult position. If he recommended a large reduction in the current safety lead time, members of the ISA department would be extremely unhappy. If he recommended a very small cut, general management might override his recommendation.

In studying the problem, Barnes arrived at the following conclusions:

1. There was no apparent disagreement, but also no sound reason for agreement, on the 2 to $2\frac{1}{2}$ per cent per month maximum limit for parts shortages tolerable in the ISA department.

2. It was almost certain that management would make an arbitrary decision to reduce substantially the thirty-day safety lead time if a strong argument was not made for a more moderate reduction.

3. The only available sources of quantitative information relating to the problem were the master subassembly schedules, ISA stores records, and the advance and current master assembly schedules.

4. A complete analysis of the available records was impossible in the time available and at best only a small sample could be analyzed.

Barnes decided to take a sample of 100 of the approximately 1,000 fabricated parts used in the ISA department and simulate what would happen if the thirty-day cushion were reduced by various amounts of time. He felt that the ISA stores records would offer all of the information necessary for a valid decision.

When a new batch of parts arrived in the subassembly stores area the batch number and quantity were immediately noted on the proper stock record card and the card placed in a special incoming file. As soon as a stock attendant had time, he would count any identical parts remaining from previous batches and note this figure in his notebook. He would then consolidate the old and new parts, making some attempt to arrange the old parts so that they would be disbursed ahead of the new parts. When he had finished physically placing the new parts into stock, he would update the stock record card for the item involved. Updating consisted of selecting the proper stock record card from the incoming file, correcting the previous "balance on hand" for overages or shortages determined from the count, and adding the amount received in the new batch. The stock card was then placed in the regular file. Any discrepancy between the stock card balance and the physical count exceeding 4 per cent of the reorder point quantity was noted on a stock deviation report which was sent to Barnes. As parts were dispatched from the stores area, each disbursement was recorded on the appropriate stock record card and a new "balance on hand" figure was entered on the card. Barnes felt that these data contained more than adequate information to determine a valid answer to the in-process inventory problem.

In selecting his sample for study Barnes chose a part card at random from the stock record card file and then selected every tenth successive part card for which a new batch had been completed at least one month, but not more than four months, before the sampling date. By selecting parts in this manner he felt he had both a random and a current sample. For each of these parts he designated the receipt date of the most recent batch of parts as day zero and noted the balance of old parts on hand on that day. He also noted the actual usage of the part by week for four weeks beyond the receipt date. From this information he intended to calculate how much later the new batch could have arrived before an actual stockout would have occurred. Exhibit 1 shows the information that Barnes obtained from the inventory records.

In addition to obtaining this information Barnes talked with several individuals in the purchasing and accounting departments. From these individuals he acquired the following information:

1. The average fixed cost of writing and handling a purchase order was $25.

2. The average fixed cost of writing and handling an in-plant manufacturing order was $35.

3. Thirty-five per cent of the firm's total direct labor costs was charged to setup and miscellaneous downtime. (The largest and smallest amounts charged against any single order were $3,500 and $20, respectively, during the past six months.)

4. The current cost of capital for all essential investments was specified to be 25 per cent before taxes.

5. Total variable inventory costs including depreciation, taxes, deterioration, maintenance, records, etc., were $0.05 per dollar of inventory per year (inventory valued at labor and material, plus overhead).

6. The current company average direct labor and overhead rates were $3 per hour and 200 per cent, respectively.

7. Material costs for parts varied from 5 to 55 per cent, but averaged about 15 per cent of the total parts value.

# EXHIBIT 1　　Summary of data for 100 selected stock cards

| Line no. (1) | Part no. (2) | Unit cost (3) | Actual usage following day 0, quantity in units | | | | Avg. weekly | | Balance on hand, day 0 | | | Reorder quantity | | |
|---|---|---|---|---|---|---|---|---|---|---|---|---|---|---|
| | | | Week 1 qty. (4) | Week 2 qty. (5) | Week 3 qty. (6) | Week 4 qty. (7) | Qty. (8) | Amount (9) | Unit qty. (10) | Amount (11) | Time coverage† (12) | Unit qty. (13) | Amount (14) | Time coverage† (15) |
| 1 | 31-276 | $ .38 | 270 | 285 | 193 | 310(*) | 264.5 | $ 101 | 1,048 | $ 398 | 4.0 | 4,000 | $ 1,520 | 15.1 |
| 2 | 31-743 | 4.18 | 57 | 46 | 81 | 46(*) | 57.5 | 242 | 223 | 932 | 3.9 | 1,000 | 4,180 | 17.3 |
| 3 | 31-927 | .91 | 60 | 63 | 61 | 87(*) | 67.8 | 62 | 241 | 219 | 3.6 | 1,200 | 1,092 | 17.7 |
| 4 | 33-001-3 | 4.80 | 16 | 8 | 17○ | 21* | 15.5 | 77 | 42 | 202 | 2.7 | 200 | 960 | 12.9 |
| 5 | 33-427 | .38 | 115 | 98 | 130 | 86(*) | 107.3 | 41 | 375 | 143 | 3.5 | 2,000 | 760 | 18.6 |
| 6 | 34-010-F | 5.18 | 15 | 19 | 21 | 24(*) | 19.8 | 104 | 77 | 399 | 3.9 | 250 | 1,295 | 12.6 |
| 7 | 35-113 | .75 | 201 | 305 | 175 | 269(*) | 237.5 | 179 | 995 | 746 | 4.2 | 3,500 | 2,625 | 14.7 |
| 8 | 35-114-7 | 1.38 | 15 | 21 | 42 | 37(*) | 28.8 | 40 | 89 | 123 | 3.1 | 450 | 621 | 15.6 |
| 9 | 35-791 | 15.00 | 28(*) | 41 | 17 | 25 | 27.8 | 420 | 2 | 30 | .1 | 400 | 6,000 | 14.4 |
| 10 | 38-642 | 5.17 | 19 | 11 | 27 | 41(*) | 24.5 | 129 | 63 | 326 | 2.6 | 350 | 1,809 | 14.3 |
| 11 | 38-695 | 10.40 | 7 | | | 5(*) | 3.0 | 31 | 9 | 94 | 3.0 | 50 | 520 | 16.7 |
| 12 | 41-320-K | 3.87 | 17 | 26 | 42 | 28(*) | 28.3 | 108 | 103 | 399 | 3.6 | 400 | 1,548 | 14.1 |
| 13 | 41-342 | 1.98 | 50 | 10 | 5 | 17(*) | 20.5 | 40 | 71 | 141 | 3.5 | 350 | 693 | 17.1 |
| 14 | 42-650 | 4.08 | 250 | 210 | 15 | 68(*) | 135.8 | 555 | 510 | 2,081 | 3.8 | 2,500 | 10,200 | 18.4 |
| 15 | 42-780 | 32.60 | 15 | 21 | 13○ | 21* | 17.5 | 587 | 52 | 1,695 | 3.0 | 300 | 9,780 | 17.1 |

| | | | | | | | | | | | | | | |
|---|---|---|---|---|---|---|---|---|---|---|---|---|---|---|
| 16 | 42-960 | 7.41 | 4 | 9⊛ | 7 | 6 | 6.5 | 52 | 7 | 52 | 1.1 | 100 | 741 | 15.9 |
| 17 | 45-320-B | 3.94 | 157 | 142 | | 227⊛ | 131.5 | 520 | 486 | 1,915 | 3.7 | 2,000 | 7,880 | 15.2 |
| 18 | 45-780 | 32.60 | 17 | 76 | 49 | 21⊛ | 9.5 | 326 | 32 | 1,043 | 3.4 | 150 | 4,890 | 15.8 |
| 19 | 47-150 | 100.41 | 81 | 1 | 3○ | 107⊛ | 78.3 | 7,832 | 293 | 29,420 | 3.7 | 1,400 | 140,574 | 17.9 |
| 20 | 47-980 | .76 | 10 | | | 16* | 7.5 | 6 | 20 | 15 | 2.7 | 120 | 91 | 16.0 |
| 21 | 48-327-4 | 1.85 | 17 | 38 | 27* | 8 | 22.5 | 43 | 81 | 150 | 3.6 | 400 | 740 | 17.8 |
| 22 | 48-472 | 2.15 | 8 | 6 | 13 | 9⊛ | 9.0 | 19 | 29 | 62 | 3.2 | 150 | 323 | 16.7 |
| 23 | 49-133-F | .08 | 7 | 5* | | ○ | 3.0 | 1 | 10 | 1 | 3.3 | 50 | 4 | 16.7 |
| 24 | 49-375 | .73 | 17 | 17 | 11 | 15⊛ | 15.0 | 11 | 53 | 39 | 3.5 | 250 | 182 | 16.7 |
| 25 | 49-643 | 1.40 | 71 | 38 | 47* | 83○ | 59.8 | 84 | 192 | 269 | 3.2 | 1,000 | 1,400 | 16.7 |
| 26 | 50-000 | 1.98 | 38 | 21 | 19 | 65⊛ | 35.8 | 71 | 150 | 297 | 4.2 | 750 | 1,485 | 20.9 |
| 27 | 50-721-A | 2.37 | 27 | | | 27⊛ | 13.5 | 33 | 46 | 109 | 3.4 | 200 | 474 | 14.8 |
| 28 | 62-375 | 3.61 | | | 42 | 10⊛ | 13.0 | 47 | 48 | 173 | 3.7 | 200 | 722 | 15.4 |
| 29 | 63-473 | 1.40 | 21 | 27 | 32 | 17⊛ | 24.3 | 34 | 93 | 130 | 3.8 | 400 | 560 | 16.5 |
| 30 | 63-581-7 | 11.20 | 127 | 89 | 120 | 103⊛ | 109.8 | 1,232 | 399 | 4,469 | 3.6 | 2,000 | 22,400 | 18.2 |
| 31 | 65-800 | 17.10 | 17 | 27 | 29⊛ | 19 | 23.0 | 393 | 69 | 1,180 | 3.0 | 400 | 6,840 | 17.4 |
| 32 | 65-871-C | .87 | 5 | | ○ | 5* | 2.5 | 3 | 7 | 6 | 2.8 | 50 | 43 | 20.0 |
| 33 | 67-243-9 | .96 | 27 | 17 | 37 | 17⊛ | 24.5 | 24 | 91 | 87 | 3.7 | 400 | 384 | 16.3 |
| 34 | 68-279 | 2.73 | 39 | 31 | 47 | 29⊛ | 36.5 | 101 | 143 | 390 | 3.9 | 600 | 1,638 | 16.4 |
| 35 | 69-435 | 7.23 | 117 | 89 | 113 | 107⊛ | 106.5 | 774 | 368 | 2,661 | 3.5 | 1,800 | 13,014 | 16.9 |
| 36 | 69-575-B | 1.19 | 21 | 17 | 16 | 20⊛ | 18.5 | 23 | 69 | 82 | 3.7 | 300 | 357 | 16.2 |
| 37 | 70-107 | 4.11 | 201 | 187 | 765 | 183⊛ | 209.0 | 859 | 731 | 3,004 | 3.5 | 3,500 | 14,385 | 16.7 |
| 38 | 70-842 | 9.20 | 181 | 162 | 75 | 207⊛ | 156.3 | 1,435 | 574 | 5,281 | 3.7 | 3,000 | 27,600 | 19.2 |
| 39 | 73-521-L | 1.37 | 115 | 87 | 45 | 117⊛ | 91.0 | 125 | 304 | 416 | 3.3 | 1,500 | 2,055 | 16.5 |
| 40 | 74-375 | 13.50 | 5 | 5 | 5 | 5⊛ | 5.0 | 68 | 20 | 270 | 4.0 | 100 | 1,350 | 20.0 |

# EXHIBIT 1  (Continued)

| Line no. (1) | Part no. (2) | Unit cost (3) | Week 1 qty. (4) | Week 2 qty. (5) | Week 3 qty. (6) | Week 4 qty. (7) | Avg. weekly Qty. (8) | Avg. weekly Amount (9) | Unit qty. (10) | Amount (11) | Time coverage† (12) | Unit qty. (13) | Amount (14) | Time coverage† (15) |
|---|---|---|---|---|---|---|---|---|---|---|---|---|---|---|
| | | | Actual usage following day 0, quantity in units | | | | | | Balance on hand, day 0 | | | Reorder quantity | | |
| 81 | 128-363 | $ 3.11 | 207 | 151 | 172 | 88‡ | 154.5 | $ 482 | 725 | $ 2,255 | 4.7 | 2,500 | $ 7,775 | 16.2 |
| 82 | 128-421-A | 4.19 | 19 | 27 | 15 | 17(*) | 19.5 | 84 | 69 | 289 | 3.5 | 250 | 1,047 | 12.8 |
| 83 | 128-421-B | 2.16 | 25 | 25 | 31 | 25(*) | 26.5 | 58 | 97 | 210 | 3.7 | 450 | 972 | 17.0 |
| 84 | 128-911 | 7.20 | 25 | 24 | 23 | 25(*) | 24.3 | 173 | 91 | 655 | 3.7 | 400 | 2,880 | 16.5 |
| 85 | 128-987 | 1.40 | 51 | 62 | 60 | 35(*) | 52.0 | 73 | 179 | 251 | 3.4 | 800 | 1,120 | 15.4 |
| 86 | 130-401-N | 3.50 | 13 | 13 | 13 | 13(*) | 13.0 | 46 | 46 | 161 | 3.5 | 200 | 700 | 15.4 |
| 87 | 130-728 | 28.74 | 241 | 361 | 99 | 511(*) | 303.0 | 8,708 | 921 | 26,470 | 3.0 | 5,000 | 143,700 | 16.5 |
| 88 | 140-316-4 | 51.30 | 47 | 45 | 62* | 37○ | 47.8 | 2,452 | 145 | 7,439 | 3.0 | 800 | 41,040 | 16.7 |
| 89 | 141-263 | 11.07 | 27 | 35 | 31 | 17(*) | 27.5 | 310 | 98 | 1,085 | 3.6 | 450 | 4,981 | 16.4 |
| 90 | 141-317 | 16.10 | 69 | 117 | 27 | 49‡ | 65.5 | 1,063 | 349 | 5,619 | 5.3 | 1,100 | 17,710 | 16.8 |
| 91 | 141-511-C | .92 | 81(*) | 148 | 96 | 153 | 19.5 | 18 | 1 | 1 | .1 | 2,000 | 1,840 | 102.6 |
| 92 | 143-521 | .48 | 14 | 18 | 18* | 30○ | 17.5 | 9 | 53 | 25 | 3.0 | 300 | 144 | 17.1 |
| 93 | 143-611 | 1.40 | 19 | 9 | 26 | 38(*) | 23.0 | 32 | 76 | 106 | 3.3 | 400 | 560 | 17.4 |
| 94 | 145-201-F | 1.93 | 40 | 10 | 13 | 27(*) | 22.5 | 44 | 90 | 174 | 4.0 | 350 | 675 | 15.6 |
| 95 | 145-621 | 2.60 | 15 | 19 | 19 | 13(*) | 16.5 | 44 | 64 | 166 | 3.9 | 300 | 780 | 18.2 |

| (1) | (2) | (3) | (4) | (5) | (6) | (7) | (8) | (9) | (10) | (11) | (12) | (13) | (14) | (15) |
|---|---|---|---|---|---|---|---|---|---|---|---|---|---|---|
| 96 | 145-792-D | 27.10 | 50 | 21 | 9 | 38⊛ | 29.5 | 813 | 89 | 2,412 | 3.0 | 500 | 13,550 | 16.9 |
| 97 | 145-920 | 14.87 | 47 | 17 | 26○ | 38* | 32.0 | 476 | 95 | 1,413 | 3.0 | 550 | 8,178 | 17.2 |
| 98 | 148-760 | 31.07 | 14○ | 17* | 28 | 7 | 16.5 | 528 | 15 | 466 | .9 | 250 | 7,767 | 15.2 |
| 99 | 148-790 | 7.07 | 53 | 51 | 39 | 47⊛ | 47.5 | 339 | 164 | 1,160 | 3.5 | 800 | 5,656 | 16.8 |
| 100 | 148-321-K | 2.16 | 487 | 362 | 712 | 653⊛ | 553.5 | 1,197 | 1,862 | 4,022 | 3.4 | 10,000 | 21,600 | 18.0 |
| | | | | | | | | $50,975 (total) | | $147,904 (total) | 3.2 (avg.) | | $846,514 (total) | 17.6 (avg.) |

Columns (2) to (7), (10), and (13) taken from data on stock record cards.

$$\text{Column (8)} = \frac{\text{columns (4) + (5) + (6) + (7)}}{4}$$

Column (9) = column (3) × (8)
Column (11) = column (3) × (10)
Column (12) = column (10) ÷ (8)
Column (14) = column (3) × (13)
Column (15) = column (13) ÷ (8)

* Indicated in columns (4) to (7) to identify the week in which a stockout would have occurred due to actual usage if reorder quantity had not been received. ○ Indicates similar information based on average usage rather than actual usage. ⊛ indicates * and ○ stockout conditions would have occurred during the same week.

† Time coverage = number of weeks supply on hand based on average weekly usage.
‡ Indicates that a stockout would not have occurred during the four weeks after day 0 even if the reorder quantity had not been received.

# DISCUSSION QUESTIONS

1. Draw suitable charts for summarizing the data collected by Barnes with respect to:
a. The distribution of actual safety lead times
b. The acceptable reduction in safety lead times
c. The per cent of items which constitute the bulk of ISA stores inventory value
2. What justification, if any, might there be for the thirty-day lead time for fabricated parts and only a three-day lead time for subassemblies?
3. What would be the effect of each day's reduction in the thirty-day lead time between receipt of parts and subassembly?
4. From the data provided, how much can the lead time be reduced?
5. What other ways, if any, are there for reducing in-process inventories?
6. What effect would using economic order quantities (EOQ) have on average in-plant inventories?
7. What problems not stated in this case might arise from a reduction of in-process inventories?
8. What action would you take?

# REFERENCES

Buffa, Elwood S.: *Modern Production Management* (New York: John Wiley & Sons, Inc., 1961), chap. 16.
Hunt, Pearson, Charles M. Williams, and Gordon Donaldson: *Basic Business Finance* (Homewood, Ill.: Richard D. Irwin, Inc., 1961), chaps. 3, 10–13.
Magee, John F.: *Production Planning and Inventory Control* (New York: McGraw-Hill Book Company, 1958), chaps. 2–4.
Moore, Franklin G.: *Manufacturing Management* (Homewood, Ill.: Richard D. Irwin, Inc., 1961), chap. 38.

# THE UNITED
# ELECTRONICS COMPANY

Tom Hinshaw worked in the manufacturing department of the United Electronics Company. When the company was awarded a missile contract by the Air Force, he was assigned to determine the type of manufacturing system which should be used in the assembly of circuit cards. The decision was to be based on the product and environmental requirements, manufacturing assembly techniques, capabilities of the workers, training facilities, time available for training, and costs.

United Electronics was a well-established firm. This was, however, the first contract the company had secured in the manufacture of the more exotic types of electronic products. Consequently, the company wanted to do an outstanding job so as to establish an excellent reputation in this type of business.

The firm manufactured commercial broadcasting equipment and analog computers in one division of the company, outboard motors in a second division, and military products in a third division. The outboard motor division was no longer profitable and the board of directors had decided to close this division within the next year. The president had stated in announcing this decision to the press: "The company will absorb the 2,000 displaced workers in our expanding military division."

## PRODUCT AND
## ENVIRONMENTAL REQUIREMENTS

The Air Force specified modular construction in the manufacture of missiles and supporting ground equipment. This involved the use of circuit cards which could be plugged into larger assemblies to facilitate manufacturing, testing, and replacement. Even though the circuit cards were all of the same dimension, the circuits and the combination of components placed on the card varied a great deal. It was common to have production runs where no more than 5 or 10 identical cards were assembled and seldom where there were more than 100 identical cards in a single production run.

The dimensions of all of the circuit cards were the same (8 by 5⅜ by ⅛ inches thick). The cards were made of a phenolic or epoxy resin laminate reinforced with glass, cloth, or paper fibers. On one side of the card the electronic circuit was etched or printed in copper or silver. On the other side of the card the location numbers of the various components were printed to assist the operator in making the assembly. Holes were drilled in the card so that the wires from the components (e.g., diodes, capacitors, resistors, condensers, transistors) could be placed through the holes and connected to the circuitry on the other side of the card. When all the components were in place, the etched side of the card was placed in a solder bath to connect the components to the circuitry. The solder remained wherever the card was etched and where the wires from the components came through the card. Each card included a multi-post connecting plug which provided a means of connecting the card to a larger electronic circuit. Hundreds of different circuit cards were connected to create the electronic equipment for the missile.

The Air Force required that United Electronics comply with the same environmental standards which were used by other manufacturers of advanced missiles. This included rigid control of humidity, temperature, and dust.

Maintaining the correct humidity and temperature was not difficult; however, controlling the dirt, dust, grease, and other contaminates presented problems which had never been faced before. Controlled areas were to be isolated from uncontrolled areas and from each other by double-door air locks which served as entries, exits, and dressing rooms. Workbench tops had to be covered with a hard, smooth finish. Walls and ceilings were to be painted with a nonflaking epoxy paint for easy and frequent washing. Floors needed to be surfaced with glasslike vinyl or otherwise sealed against dust. No sweeping or dusting was permitted. Cleaning had to be done on frequent schedules with damp cloths, damp mops, or vacuum cleaners. In addition, mops and cloths had to be lint free.

Air from the outside had to pass through filters which removed 80 to 85 per cent of all atmospheric dust, with a complete air change every six minutes. Persons entering the clean area had to walk over a mechanical vacuum and brushing system installed in the floor which scrubbed the soles of their shoes and removed all dirt.

Most companies engaged in this type of work had their employees clothed in white laboratory coats, head coverings, white gloves, and in certain cases lintless white socks over their shoes. Furthermore, necessary paper work had to be enclosed in polyethylene film because exposed paper and paper products tended to carry lint.

Most of these requirements established to control environmental conditions had proved to be meaningful; that is, the control measures had been justified on the basis of scientific research. Hinshaw, however, could find no evidence to support the requirement that employees wear laboratory coats or white uniforms of one kind or another. In fact, the manager of one company which Hinshaw visited stated, "We spend $35,000 a year in laundering laboratory coats, and we have no information to show that wearing or not wearing these coats makes any difference in controlling the dust."

## MANUFACTURING ASSEMBLY TECHNIQUES

The component parts used in the manufacture of circuit cards required special handling. For example, it had been determined that clipping the soldered ends of a resistor with hand clippers exposed the resistor to extreme shock; bending the leads resulted in upsetting the uniform flow of soldering; and dropping the parts could change their operating characteristics. The production assembly line had to be designed in consideration of the critical requirements for handling the parts, the environmental conditions surrounding the manufacturing process, and the unskilled workers assigned to assemble the components to the circuit cards. Instructions had to be conveyed to the workers in such a manner as to facilitate assembly without error.

Tom Hinshaw discovered that one approach which had been used successfully was a system of audio-visual aids. This system captured, stimulated, and retained the know-how of processes and experiences by combining the forces of sight and sound with good planning. It was a sensory presentation utilizing sequentially planned instructions verbally recorded on magnetic tape and supporting visual aids reproduced on 35-millimeter color slides, strip film, or cards that were synchronized with the sound instructions to assist in the transfer of information to individuals. Its basic objective was to improve communication from the planner to the worker on the assembly line.

The worker received verbal assembly instructions through an earplug (note the worker to the left in Exhibit 3) and a visual interpretation of the proper assembly procedure by the synchronized showing of slides. The slides were flashed on the screen to the left of the control panel in front of the operator. A package of slides is visible directly below the control knobs in Exhibit 3, and tapes for the instructions are stored on the shelf above the control knobs.

Tom Hinshaw talked to the representatives of the firm which manufactured the audio-visual equipment. He was told that an audio-visual system was applicable when a majority of the following questions could be answered in the affirmative:

1. Is the operation repetitive?
2. Is the operation fairly complex?
3. Is sufficient volume involved?
4. Can quality be improved?
5. Can experience requirements be reduced?
6. Will better communications result?

Hinshaw was told that an audio-visual system proved to be an invaluable aid in training because it stimulated both the auditory and visual senses. Psychological research had proved that an individual could learn better when he could both see and hear than when he could only see *or* hear. The benefits which were realized in the use of over 200 audio-visual stations in production assembly at another major electronics manufacturer were pointed out as follows:

1. Defects per hour were reduced 40 to 55 per cent.
2. Instruction time was reduced 50 to 75 per cent.
3. Learning cycle was reduced noticeably.
4. Operation tension and fatigue were relieved.

It was suggested that the above findings provided striking evidence that audio-visual system application in the assembly area resulted in important gains. The significant increase noted in quality alone stood as a positive and revolutionary gain that would more than justify the audio-visual installation.

Tom Hinshaw talked to repesentatives of the Acme Electronics Corporation. This company had installed audio-visual (A-V) aids to provide detailed instructions for their workers on the assembly line. Bob Johnson, coordinator for the A-V program at the Acme Electronics Corporation, summarized the results of their program as follows:

1. A-V effected a 26 per cent cost saving for the program. Projection of the data to include completion of the balance of the current program yielded an anticipated gross savings of 34.8 per cent. Implementation at the start of the production program would have yielded a higher percentage saving by obtaining full advantage of the difference in learning curves between A-V and written detailed planning. A-V had proved to

be a useful tool for controlling direct labor man-hour expenditures. The cost reduction benefits obtained were not all from just the equipment, however. Much of the time and cost savings were derived from the operational techniques used to achieve successful A-V planning. These techniques were careful operation sequencing, good time standard application, planning responsibilities centered in one person, complete knowledge of shop capabilities and method of operation, and monitoring of engineering projects for advanced data about forthcoming changes.

2. A-V did not affect quality significantly, as measured by defects discovered during inspection and test. This indicated the efficiency of the previous reliability program which had reduced defects to a low of 0.4 per cent prior to the A-V program. A brief test, however, indicated that use of the special A-V program had reduced inspection time about 21 per cent while improving the uniformity of inspection.

3. Training the assemblers was very easy. A program of five minutes' duration was prepared to orient the assemblers to the use of A-V. Factory supervision furnished additional training thereafter on the job. It was necessary, however, to provide special training for the planners so that they would prepare appropriate information which could be utilized directly in the A-V program.

Johnson concluded his statement by saying that he was writing a report to the management of the Acme Electronics Corporation recommending the A-V planning techniques be used for all future programs of the type in which his company was now engaged. He gave Tom Hinshaw copies of a cost comparison chart (Exhibit 1), comparing the labor man-hour expenditures of the old method and the A-V method; a summary of a questionnaire given to the A-V operators (Exhibit 2); and a picture of the A-V work station as it was set up by the Acme Electronics Corporation (Exhibit 3).

The information summarized in Exhibit 1 had resulted from a special situation. Acme Electronics had planned to process 55 assemblies using a conventional planning and assembly process. After the original planning had been completed, the total assembly requirements had been increased to 80 units. It was decided to plan and assemble the additional 25 units by A-V. These units were assembled concurrently with units 25 to 38 and 45 to 55 which were made by conventional methods. Exhibit 1 shows the direct labor man-hours per unit for the original 55 assemblies made by conventional methods in comparison to the projected man-hour requirements. The A-V group of 25 assemblies was plotted on the same chart as the conventional group so that units made at the same time were plotted congruently. A comparison was then made of actual man-hours for the assemblies of each group against the projected man-hour requirements. Although the cumulative total requirement for the 55 conventional assemblies was 18.2 direct man-hours more than forecast, it required 178.5 fewer direct man-hours for the 25 assemblies where A-V was used.

The two assembly stations illustrated in Exhibit 3 were typical of the A-V section at Acme Electronics. The circuit card was placed in a holder directly in front of the worker. The bins to the upper right and left contained the components required in the assembly. The deck of 35-millimeter slides is shown directly above the rack with the various jars. Above the slides and to the left is the screen for viewing the slides. Above the slides and to the right are the controls for operating the unit. The front panel of the A-V unit was pulled out when the operator wanted to install a new sound tape. (Note boxes of extra tapes directly above the control panel.) Once the unit was started, the synchronized word instructions (note operator's earphones) and colored pictures proceeded through the entire assembly sequence at a predetermined rate. The operator could, however, increase the speed, stop, or reverse the process.

Tom Hinshaw was impressed by this audio-visual technique. He summarized the benefits that might be derived from the use of this technique by United Electronics as follows:

1. Reduce operator instruction time
2. Reduce distractions
3. Reduce skill requirements of the employee
4. Reduce the volume of paper work needed
5. Reduce the shop loading problem
6. Insure the optimum work rate
7. Provide maximum operator flexibility
8. Assure maximum uniformity of output

Tom was convinced that his company should install A-V equipment. Fifty A-V units would be needed to perform the work. He decided, however, to visit Neutronics Propulsion Laboratories, Inc., inasmuch as that company was a leader in the production of advanced electronic gear. He was surprised to find that this company used another assembly technique. Fred Waters, production manager of Neutronics Propulsion Laboratories, Inc., described their system to Tom Hinshaw as follows:

We assume that our employees have little skill and little ability to follow instructions. Further, we want to spend very little time training them. Our approach, therefore, is to break the job down into its smallest function and have each person do a single, or at least a very limited number of operations. We can quickly instruct an employee how to recognize and place a single component in the right location in a circuit card. It would be more difficult to train an employee to follow the instructions necessary to put all the components on the card (there may be as many as 160 components).

THE UNITED ELECTRONICS COMPANY 423

We have found that this system has given us better quality of production and lower production costs. However, there are certain disadvantages which we have also discovered. First of all, this type of production is repetitious and could be boring to the worker; second, we have found that it is more difficult to load the shop and balance the work stations when we have individuals doing a specialized task; and third, we find it more difficult to utilize our inventory of parts effectively.

Waters gave Tom Hinshaw a copy of an instruction sheet which was used to show the worker how to locate the correct placement of the part he was to install (Exhibit 4), and a picture of the arrangement of an assembly station (Exhibit 5). The assembly workers at Neutronics Propulsion Laboratories, Inc., were given an instruction chart (see Exhibit 4) which showed the location of all the components on the circuit card by component and number. For example, if there were two resistors on the card these parts would be R-1 and R-2. Below the schematic drawing the components were listed by part number, standard time, quantity, component designation, and special assembly instructions. The specific assemblies to be made at each work station were circled, e.g., the worker receiving the instruction card shown in Exhibit 4 would install R-24, R-33, and R-11.

The standard time included an allowance for self-instruction, i.e., the time required by the operators to determine the placement of the parts to be assembled (those circled) by identifying their location on the chart. Each assembly for a series of cards would be the same, and the worker would quickly develop skill in assembling the parts. When a run of cards was finished, it was necessary to give each assembly worker a new instruction card, and in many instances an inventory of different components, for the next assembly run.

## TRAINING FACILITIES AND TIME

United Electronics maintained an in-plant school for new employee orientation and for teaching employees new skills. The school facility and staff could provide instruction on procedures for a maximum of 250 employees a day using a lecture and visual aids approach. If employees were to be trained in the use of tools or techniques, e.g., soldering, riveting, wiring, etc., the school could handle 150 employees a day.

## WORKER CAPABILITIES

About 1,500 of the 2,000 workers of the outboard motor division were men. Of these men, about 50 planned to retire. It was forecast that many others would find jobs outside the company. Perhaps 1,000 men and 400 women wanted jobs in the military division of the company. The 400 women had been engaged in assembly and packaging activities in the outboard motor division. Most of the 1,000 men had been involved in manufacturing and assembly operations. A few were skilled workers, but a majority of these men were without any special skill.

Tom Hinshaw decided to estimate the cost of the three different kinds of assembly he was considering for United Electronics. These estimates were based on definite equipment prices and forecasts of the number of assembly workers and planners required. Tom realized that these forecasts would be subject to question. He would have to support them on the basis of his own experience and the insights he had gained from his visits to Acme Electronics and Neutronics Propulsion Laboratories.

*Cost Estimates*

A-V system:

| | |
|---|---:|
| Audio-visual units | $   600   each |
| Work stations with accessories | 450   each |
| Sound mastering equipment | 1,450 |
| Photo module | 925 |
| Other | 1,000 |

All other systems:

| | |
|---|---:|
| Work stations with accessories | $250   each |

Assembly workers required:

| | |
|---|---:|
| Assembly of total card (usual technique) | 65   workers |
| Assembly of total card (A-V technique) | 50   workers |
| Specialized assembly | 48   workers |

Planners required:

| | |
|---|---:|
| Assembly of total card (usual technique) | 30   planners |
| Assembly of total card (A-V technique) | 36   planners |
| Specialized assembly | 40   planners |

Labor costs:

| | |
|---|---:|
| Assembly labor (including overhead) | $5.20   per hour |
| Planning labor (including overhead) | 6.40   per hour |

Space requirements would be the same for all three systems.

The initial missile contract would be completed in two years.

Two hundred twenty days were scheduled for assembly and one hundred fifteen days were scheduled for planning. No overtime work should be required.

It was estimated that the materials cost for preparing slides would be offset by a reduction in paper forms.

There would be 73 different cards in the program; and although as many as 4,000 cards of one kind would be required, no more than 50 would be assembled in a single continuous run.

# EXHIBIT 1

## Direct labor man-hour expenditures: conventional, A-V, and projected

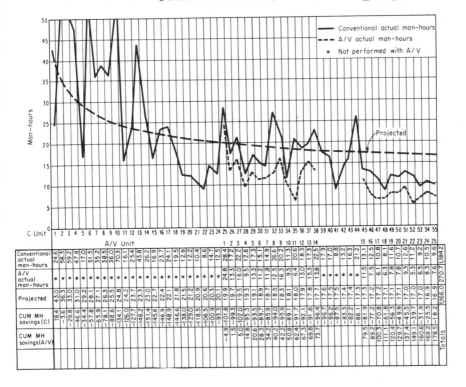

# EXHIBIT 2

## A-V operator questionnaire

A. General background of the operators

   1. How long have you been doing this type of assembly work?     Average operator 2 years 9 months

   2. Did you have previous experience with using the audio-visual aids?

| | Yes | No |
|---|---|---|
| | 1 | 12 |

   3. How long have you been using the audio-visual aids?     Average operator 2 months 3 weeks

   4. Approximately how many assemblies have you built with the audio-visual aids?     Average of 35

   5. Have you used the audio-visual aids to build assemblies which you have never built before?

| | Yes | No |
|---|---|---|
| | 9 | 4 |

   6. Were you given enough instructions and training to operate properly the audio-visual unit at the beginning?

| | Yes | No |
|---|---|---|
| | 11 | 2 |

B. Operator attitude toward the A-V aids

   1. Do you like working at the audio-visual work station?

| | Yes | No |
|---|---|---|
| | 10 | 3 |

   2. Do you like to use both audio and visual aids?

| | Yes | No | No Ans. |
|---|---|---|---|
| | 7 | 5 | 1 |

   3. Would you prefer working with the audio-visual aids or conventional process planning?

| | A-V | Pro. |
|---|---|---|
| | 10 | 3 |

C. The audio-visual work station environment

   1. Does the light in the area make it difficult for you to see the detail on the slide?

| | Yes | No |
|---|---|---|
| | 5 | 8 |

   2. Does the noise in the area make it difficult to hear the instructions?

| | Yes | No |
|---|---|---|
| | 1 | 12 |

   3. Are the part bins arranged so that you can readily locate and obtain the required parts?

| | Yes | No |
|---|---|---|
| | 13 | 0 |

   4. Do you feel more fatigued using A-V aids than following the conventional process planning?

| | Yes | No |
|---|---|---|
| | 5 | 8 |

   5. Do you find when using the A-V aids you are able to concentrate more fully on your work and are less subject to distractions?

| | Yes | No |
|---|---|---|
| | 9 | 4 |

   6. Does music in your earphone between instructions make your job more pleasant?

| | Yes | No | No Ans. |
|---|---|---|---|
| | 11 | 0 | 2 |

   7. Is it easier for you to assemble electronic packages using the assembly jig on the A-V work station than the cardholder used at regular workbenches?

| | Yes | No |
|---|---|---|
| | 6 | 7 |

## EXHIBIT 2     (*Continued*)

D. Operations

| | | Yes | No | |
|---|---|---|---|---|
| 1. | Would you prefer a woman's voice giving the instructions? | Yes<br>1 | No<br>12 | |
| 2. | Do you feel that the instructions are given with sufficient detail to allow you to do the job properly? | Yes<br>8 | No<br>4 | No Ans.<br>1 |
| 3. | Do you follow the general sequence of operations given to you by the A-V unit? | Yes<br>10 | No<br>3 | |
| 4. | Do you always check part bins and workbench to assure the availability of necessary parts, tools, and materials? | Yes<br>8 | No<br>5 | |

## EXHIBIT 3

### Assembly station using audio-visual epuipment at the Acme Electronics Corporation

# EXHIBIT 4

UNITED ELEC 17

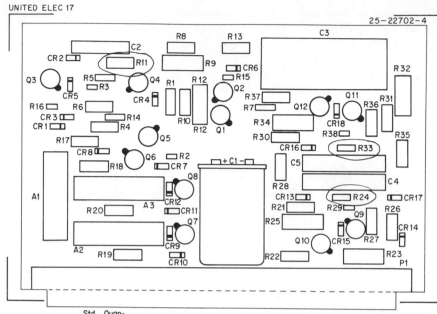

25-22702-4

| Part number | Std. time | Quan- tity | Description | Reference | | Miscellaneous | |
|---|---|---|---|---|---|---|---|
| 25-22702-7 | | 01 | ETCHED BOARD | 25-22702-6 | C 1201 | | 0 |
| C 45 BM 1 | .64 | 01 | P1 KEY 9, 29 | | 2 | | 0 |
| NAS 601-6 | | 03 | SCREW | | 2 | | 0　2 |
| 441-0326-001 | | 01 | C1 | 450 | 1 | 5010, TYPE 52, BMS5-60 | 101 |
| | 2.71 | | | 29-18092-1 | 1 | SOLDER 5052, USE HT SINK | 1011 |
| 25-22702-5 | | 01 | WIRE | | F | 20 MIL-W-3861, TYPES, TIN-CT | 2 |
| C 15 AF 13-26 | | 1 | CLIP | 29-18207-3 | 1 | | 2041 |
| MS 20470 A 4 | 1.79 | 3 | RIVET | | 2 | HD F/S, DRIVE .035-.050 | 2042 |
| | | | | | 6 | | |
| 443-0151-016 | | 03 | R15, 29, 38 | 43 | 1 | | 321 |
| 443-0151-069 | | 01 | R16 | 6.8 K | 1 | | 321 |
| 443-0151-079 | | 01 | R2 | 18 K | 1 | | 321 |
| 443-0151-087 | | 01 | R3 | 39 K | 1 | | 321 |
| 443-0152-042 | | 01 | R14 | 2.40 K | 1 | | 322 |
| 443-0152-046 | | 01 | R7 | 3.60 K | 1 | | 322 |
| 443-0152-051 | | 01 | R5 | 5.60 K | 1 | | 322 |
| 443-0152-060 | 3.08 | 02 | R24, 33 | 13.0 K | 1 | | 322 |
| 443-0153-034 | | 01 | R6 | 240 | 1 | | 420 |
| 443-0153-035 | | 04 | R17-20 | 270 | 1 | | 420 |
| 443-0153-046 | | 01 | R1 | 750 | 1 | | 420 |
| 443-0153-048 | | 01 | R4 | 910 | 1 | | 420 |
| 443-0153-049 | | 02 | R26, 35 | 1.0 K | 1 | | 420 |
| 443　0153　050 | | 02 | R21, 30 | 1.1 K | 1 | | 420 |
| 443　0153　051 | 3.36 | 01 | R11 | 1.2 K | 1 | | 420 |

# EXHIBIT 5

## Assembly work station Neutronics Propulsion Laboratories, Inc.

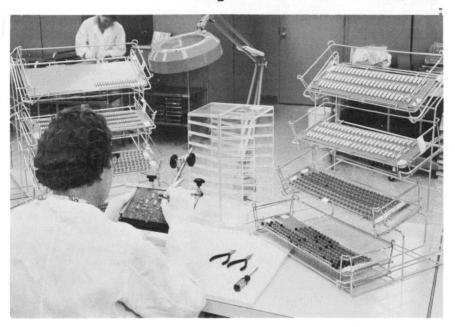

# DISCUSSION QUESTIONS

1. What additional alternative systems might be designed to assemble the cards?
2. What are the advantages and disadvantages of each system?
3. Do you think workers would prefer to assemble an entire circuit card or to specialize by assembling a particular component to the card?
4. Would more planning be required if the A-V technique is used? Why?
5. Which system should Tom Hinshaw recommend for United Electronics?
6. Do you believe Tom's forecast of manpower requirements is realistic?
7. Analyze and evaluate the information in Exhibit 1.

# REFERENCES

Buffa, Elwood S.: *Modern Production Management* (New York: John Wiley & Sons, Inc., 1961), pp. 286–340.

Johnson, Richard A., Fremont E. Kast, and James E. Rosenzweig: *The Theory and Management of Systems* (New York: McGraw-Hill Book Company, 1963), pp. 257–278.

# THE U.S. CAR COMPANY

The military division of The U.S. Car Company, a large manufacturer in the fabricated metal products industry, had received a military production contract to manufacture a small number of Army tanks. This order was to be produced according to the prototype which had been originally designed and built by The U.S. Car Company under an earlier developmental contract. The production contract (cost-plus-a-fixed-fee type) specified payment on the basis of actual costs plus a fixed fee that amounted to 10 per cent of the estimated cost. It contained no mention of which portion of the project should or should not be subcontracted.

The following year, shortly after the tank was in production, the Army decided to purchase several hundred more tanks and entered into negotiations with The U.S. Car Company for a follow-on order. The proposal for this contract, however, specified that a substantial portion of the dollar value of the contract should be subcontracted with small business firms.

One of the items under consideration in the "make or buy" analysis was a cabinet which housed an atomic shell. The design of the cabinet was rather complex. Each panel was detachable, and yet it had to fit securely with the other sections. The cabinet was designed to protect the occupants of the tank against chance radiation and to protect the shell against physical damage and excessive moisture. Further, it was necessary to ventilate the cabinet. There were from four to eight of these units in every tank, depending on the kind of installation. U.S. Car believed that this was an item which they wished to make, but the Army representatives felt differently and maintained that these cabinets were a logical item to subcontract. They insisted that U.S. Car follow this suggestion.

The contracting officer supported his position for subcontracting the shell cases under the provision stated in the following section of the Armed Services Procurement Regulations:[1]

> Proposed "make" items shall not be agreed to when the products or services under consideration:
> (i)  are not regularly manufactured or provided by the contractor, and are available—quality, quantity, delivery, and other essential factors considered—from other firms at prices no higher than if the contractor should make or provide the product or service; or
> (ii) are regularly manufactured or provided by the contractor, and are available—quality, quantity, delivery, and other essential factors considered— from other firms at lower prices.
> However, such items may be agreed to if the contracting officer determines that the over-all cost of the contract or of the program to the Government would be increased if the item were bought.

As a result of the reluctance of U.S. Car to agree to treat the cabinet as a buy item, the contracting officer arranged for a revision in the prime contract for the tanks so that the shell containers would be procured separately as an independent prime contract under advertised bidding procedures on a fixed-price-redeterminable type of contract with a downward only price revision clause. The shell containers would then be provided to the tank manufacturer for installation as government-furnished equipment.

The managers of The U.S. Car Company were very upset by this turn of events. They felt that there was a fundamental issue involved. First, they believed that it was their right to select that portion of the prime contract which they wanted to build and that portion which they desired to subcontract. Second, they felt the production of cabinets was of particular importance to them inasmuch as the Army was likely to place this material in every tank that was in operation.

John Calvin, the director of the military division of The U.S. Car Company, pointed out in the negotiations that very few small business firms, if any, could build the cabinet. The tolerances were small, the openings and fittings were irregular, and the radiation shielding requirements were critical. At first the Army representatives paid little heed to these arguments; however, when the invitation to bid on the cabinet was released it did not contain a provision to restrict the contract to small business firms. Thus, The U.S. Car Company had an equal right

---

[1] See Appendix A. Section referred to is in ASPR 3-902.3.

to bid on the cabinet contract along with other large and small companies. Calvin suspected that his admonitions had disturbed the contracting officer sufficiently so that he wanted to protect the project in case there were no small businesses qualified to bid or that excessively high bids might be received if only small businesses were permitted to participate.

On June 29, the cost estimating staff of The U.S. Car Company received a program study authorization from John Calvin to prepare a technical and cost proposal for the manufacture of cabinets for atomic weapons. The proposal was due no later than July 21.

At the time the proposal study was undertaken, The U.S. Car Company was manufacturing 40 cabinets on the production contract and had completed approximately 20 of these units. The balance of the units was in process. The request for quotations for the new production program involved 2,834 additional cabinets. Calvin indicated to the cost estimators that proposals were being solicited by the Army from many competitive companies and that it was imperative that the technical and cost proposal prepared by The U.S. Car Company be extremely competitive. There were certain factors to be considered in connection with this request for bids:

1. The contract would be awarded in September with production to start at once.

2. No request for new facilities would be allowed.

3. Tooling and/or testing equipment, if required, could be charged against the contract.

All the other procurement rules were the same as those found in the typical Army Ordnance request for quotation except that the contract type to be used would be a fixed-price-redeterminable type, downward only.

The management of The U.S. Car Company considered that it was rather strange for this type of contract to be specified. Representatives of the Army explained, however, that they wanted every company to submit a careful bid. There would be no chance to redetermine the price upward if a mistake was made in the estimate of costs.

S. E. Paulsen, director of the planning department of The U.S. Car Company, was responsible for preparation of the cost estimate, and he decided to prepare the bid for this proposal himself. In planning his strategy he made these assumptions:

1. The top management of U.S. Car was very anxious to get this business.

2. For U.S. Car to secure this contract they must be extremely competitive to overcome Army Ordnance's impression that this contract should be provided by another contractor.

Therefore, Paulsen decided on the following strategy:

1. He would make an all-out effort to prepare an extensive proposal document.
2. He would attempt to reduce costs to a point where Army Ordnance could not refuse to give the business to U.S. Car.
3. The bid would be made on the basis of strict compliance with the specifications originally established in the U.S. Car prototype contract without exceptions, proposed changes, or restrictions.

In making the proposal, Paulsen decided to call in people from the finance, cost accounting, production, and purchasing departments. This was to be an all-out effort to make a bid which would not only be the very best bid U.S. Car could make but also would be a realistic bid which could be justified to Army Ordnance. It was decided that the standard bidding and cost procedures which had been used in the past would not be sufficient in this instance. For example, the practice of estimating the cost of purchased parts and material on the basis of past experience would not suffice. Paulsen intended to contact the various vendors and get actual commitments from them in terms of the very lowest prices they would quote. The quantities ordered, upon which the quoted prices would be based, would be for the entire contract. Further, if any of the parts were standard and were used on other jobs, the prices quoted were to reflect lower prices made possible by the larger quantities resulting from company-wide purchases.

The costs covering the manufacture of these cabinets were forecast in great detail. First, production performance on the forty-cabinet order was carefully analyzed. Exhibit 1 shows the indicated costs (8.6 per cent higher than the contract estimate) on the first production contract for forty cabinets. These costs were based on actual costs for the twenty cabinets completed, plus an estimate of the cost likely to be incurred to complete the remaining work. Production labor costs had been collected for each cabinet. Based on the results of the completed twenty units it appeared that the forty-cabinet contract would follow a 90 per cent improvement curve. Previous work of the same general type, however, had ranged from a low of 77 per cent to a high of 95 per cent improvement curve. Paulsen decided to depend largely upon advice from the manufacturing supervisors regarding the improvement factor to be used in estimating the new contract.

Paulsen held a meeting with the manufacturing group to develop ways to reduce cost on the follow-on contract. He prepared the following questions as a means of stimulating the people in manufacturing to think of other ideas for reducing costs:

1. Could raw material costs be reduced by purchasing metal to actual cutting size?

2. Could quality rejections of the final product be eliminated by adding inspection at critical points in the manufacturing process?

3. Should a straight-line technique be used to assemble the cabinets? Could conveyors be used to facilitate the assembly?

4. Should the tools used to manufacture the forty cabinets be used for this contract, or should new tools be manufactured? (New production tooling would cost $40,000 and could reduce production labor costs by 6 per cent.)

5. Could inventories be reduced by careful scheduling?

Paulsen felt quite confident about winning the contract. He knew that The U.S. Car Company was the only company which had any experience in building cabinets of this type and that the specifications and standards in the proposal were those established by The U.S. Car Company in its original developmental contract. Furthermore, top management had indicated its willingness to reduce profits to 5 per cent, if necessary, in order to get the contract.

If The U.S. Car Company won this contract, it would be operating at 105 per cent capacity. (Two shifts, five days a week was regarded as 100 per cent capacity.) At the time this cost proposal was to be prepared, the company was operating at 80 per cent capacity.

Calvin had suggested to Paulsen that at least three different price estimates be prepared for study and analysis:

1. Based on the unit costs as incurred in the first contract (see Exhibit 1)

2. Using a 90 per cent improvement curve, using material costs from the first contract, and allowing an 8 per cent profit

3. Using an 85 per cent improvement curve, an 8 per cent reduction in material cost, and a 5 per cent profit margin

Paulsen knew that even if he prepared several estimates for study, he would eventually have to make a specific recommendation. There was some justification for using a better than 90 per cent improvement curve, inasmuch as this program had been planned more carefully than previous programs. On the other hand there was a great deal of risk involved in the estimates; e.g., the prices quoted by vendors were not necessarily firm contracts. Furthermore, unforeseen production problems could occur. Finally, there was a danger of bidding much lower than the competitive situation required in order to get the contract.

By July 18 Paulsen and the planning department had finished the proposal, it was reviewed and approved by Calvin, and then it was forwarded to J. D. Walters, vice-president of The U.S. Car Company, for final authorization. The following day Calvin received the letter from Walters shown in Exhibit 2. Calvin had also received a summary of the expenses in making the proposal from Paulsen as shown in Exhibit 3.

# EXHIBIT 1

## Total indicated costs for the forty cabinets on the first production contract

| Costs | Cabinet structure | Internal brackets | Miscellaneous | Total |
|---|---|---|---|---|
| Tool labor | | | $1,940 | $ 1,940 |
| Tool material | | | 176 | 176 |
| Inspection labor | $    186 | | 25 | 211 |
| Production labor | 5,725 | $    316 | | 6,041 |
| Manufacturing overhead | 9,972 | 534 | 338 | 10,844 |
| Production material | 10,230 | 977 | 280 | 11,487 |
| Total | $26,113 | $1,827 | $2,759 | $30,699 |

| Labor rates | |
|---|---|
| Tooling | $3.42 per hour |
| Inspection | 3.22 per hour |
| Production | 3.10 per hour |

| Overhead rates | |
|---|---|
| Manufacturing | $5.24 per hour of direct labor |
| Administrative | 17.5% of manufacturing costs |

# EXHIBIT 2

July 19

Mr. Calvin:

You asked for comments on the proposal for atomic cabinets. In reviewing the technical proposal just in the light of its coverage of the subject matter, I have two comments:

1. In the section titled "Program Schedules" we might have pointed out our plan for minimum work in process and minimum raw material inventory.

2. We seem to be somewhat repetitive in the two sections "Manufacturing Experience and Capability" and "Manufacturing Plan." This might be necessary, but in future proposals we should make sure that any repetition adds strength and not just words.

My real negative criticism of the proposal is not with the material, but with the atmosphere, attitude, whatever appears to make such overdocumentation necessary. I get quite confused listening to and reading about the need to cut overhead—then finding that we must spend so much effort on a relatively simple, straightforward proposal. All that should have been required is a one-page letter saying that U.S. Car is building these to specifications, we will deliver to the schedule, and the cost will be XX dollars.

All we can do is raise the question, "Is this necessary—and why?" This I intend to do.

/s/  J. D. Walters

# EXHIBIT 3

## Cost of preparing proposal

| | |
|---|---:|
| 200 hours of planning overhead @ $5 | $1,000 |
| 62 hours of flip chart work @ $4 | 248 |
| 254 hours of artwork @ $3.50 | 889 |
| 33 hours of varityping @ $4 | 132 |
| Material cost | 270 |
| Total | $2,539 |

# DISCUSSION QUESTIONS

1. Prepare the three estimates Calvin suggested. Are there any other estimates you believe should be made based on other assumptions?
2. What bid would you recommend?
3. To what degree should the bid be based on the company's expected costs or on the probable action of competitors?
4. What price do you believe competitors might bid on this contract?
5. What factors were involved in considering lower costs on the follow-on contract rather than in using the actual cost of manufacturing the first forty units?
6. What advantages and/or disadvantages would a smaller company have over The U.S. Car Company in bidding on this contract?
7. What do you think of Walter's letter to Calvin?
8. Is $40,000 in new production tooling justified?

# REFERENCES

Buffa, Elwood S.: *Modern Production Management* (New York: John Wiley & Sons, Inc., 1961), pp. 41–54, 583–596.

Niebel, Benjamin W., and Edward N. Baldwin: *Designing for Production* (Homewood, Ill.: Richard D. Irwin, Inc., 1963), pp. 40–46.

Rago, Louis J.: *Production Analysis and Control* (Scranton, Pa.: International Textbook Company, 1963), pp. 462–466.

Timms, Howard L.: *The Production Function in Business* (Homewood, Ill.: Richard D. Irwin, Inc., 1962), pp. 196–206.

# VESUVIUS, INC.

Vesuvius, Inc., was engaged in the production of military reconnaissance and fighter aircraft and guided missiles. The company was located in a large city in the Middle West and maintained two plant sites in that city. In addition the company leased space for storage in government-owned warehouses located adjacent to a former airfield on the outskirts of the city. Aircraft production was concentrated at plant number 1, which had been developed during the Second World War as a fighter production facility. Adjacent to plant number 1 were a flight strip and three smaller buildings built to house administrative offices and supporting facilities. (See Exhibit 2, attachment A, for a layout of the plant site.) The three smaller buildings had been added one at a time as increased work at the plant made expansion necessary. The most recent addition was building C, which had not yet been utilized fully since it was built to provide more additional space than was actually required at the time of completion. Plant number 2 was devoted exclusively to missile work and was located at some distance across town from plant number 1.

In the years since plant number 1 and the adjacent buildings had been constructed, numerous changes had taken place in the location of production shops, storage areas, and administrative departments. The changes were necessary to accommodate altered space and facilities requirements caused by the expansion and contraction of departments due to fluctuations in the amount and character of contracts for aircraft production obtained by Vesuvius. Because of the frequency of changes, a separate space requirements unit had been established in the industrial engineering department to analyze current and future space requirements in the plant and surrounding buildings and make adjustments in space allocations when needed.

The most recent problem to come to the attention of the space requirements unit was a request by the supervisor of the finishing and corrosion proofing shop in plant number 1 to double the size of the shop. The function of the finishing and corrosion proofing shop was to put the final surface finish on certain sheets and other structural shapes and then seal the surface against corrosion. These sheets and shapes were exposed to environmental conditions which required special protection to their surfaces. The shop also performed a close inspection to detect any imperfections in either the surface finish or corrosion proofing. After the parts were finished, various smaller parts were attached to them in the buildup shop; these subassemblies were sent to the body and wing assembly shops to be incorporated into completed assemblies, which were then sent to the final assembly line. It had been the experience of the buildup shop that the fabrication of the subassemblies often resulted in damage to both the surface finish and the corrosion proofing of the parts which had just come from the finishing and corrosion proofing shop. As a result, the finishing and corrosion proofing shop had a crew assigned to the buildup shop who routinely inspected the subassemblies and corrected the damage done to the surface finishes during the subassembly buildup. Because of the nature of the process it was much easier to finish the surface of unassembled sheets and shapes, and later repair minor surface damages after subassembly, than to do all the subassembly work with unfinished materials and then finish the entire subassembly.

The request by the supervisor of the finishing and corrosion proofing shop was for an additional 20,000 square feet of floor space, an amount which would double the existing floor space of the shop. The request was accompanied by a brief description of the use which would be made of the additional space. It was the intention of the supervisor of the finishing and corrosion proofing shop to bring all of the inspection and refinishing work now being done in the buildup shop back into the finishing and corrosion proofing shop. This was to be accomplished by transferring some of the subassembly operations being done in the buildup shop to the finishing and corrosion proofing shop. Instead of finishing and inspecting sheets and structural shapes in one shop, later reinspecting them in another shop after other parts were attached, and then correcting any damage occurring during subassembly, it would thus be possible to eliminate one inspection and correct any damage in the original shop which was best equipped for the work. Such an arrangement would also have the advantage of making one shop alone responsible for the delivery of completed corrosion-proofed subassemblies to the body and wing assembly shops. Tentative approval had been given to the plan by the head of the manufacturing department if it was economically feasible and appropriate space could be arranged.

It was customary in the space requirements unit to assign one man to investigate each request for an additional space allocation and prepare a factual report of the circumstances surrounding the request. After this report was prepared, the space requirements unit would then consider the question of allocating additional space in the light of total space requirements throughout the plant. In the case of the request for additional space for the finishing and corrosion proofing shop, Sid Norton was assigned the job of gathering the facts of the case; his report to Ted Broom, the head of the space requirements unit, is shown in Exhibit 1.

Broom studied Sid Norton's report and returned it to Norton with the comment that the proposed expansion of the finishing and corrosion proofing shop appeared to be a reasonable request and that Norton should proceed with a detailed analysis of how such an additional allocation of space to this shop could be made. Essentially the problem which Sid Norton faced was to determine what alternatives were available in terms of moving departments and reallocating space or constructing new space, and also to determine the cost of each of these alternatives. Sid Norton spent several weeks analyzing the various alternatives available and discussing them with plant personnel who would be affected by any space reallocations. After his analysis was completed, Sid Norton submitted the report shown in Exhibit 2 to his supervisor, Broom.

Broom studied the report and then arranged for a meeting to include all the department heads and supervisors whose space allocations might be affected by any of the possible moves. In preparation for the meeting, he also obtained an estimate of possible increases in contract quantities which were being considered by the Air Force. Although it was highly speculative to consider these additional units, Broom wanted to have some idea of the effect that the increased business could have on the analysis. Based on the figures obtained by Broom, Sid Norton made the rough estimate that the savings of $215,000 quoted by him in his first memo to Broom would be raised to $315,000 if the additional business were obtained. This additional saving was due largely to the fact that the new business would overload the buildup shop and the finishing and corrosion proofing shop if the latter were not expanded, resulting in about nine months of third-shift operation at an additional cost of $100,000. The proposed expansion of the shop would provide sufficient space so that this third-shift operation would be unnecessary.

Prior to the meeting with the department heads from affected units, Broom was faced with the problem of evaluating each of the alternatives and being prepared to present his recommendation for discussion by these men. After the meeting, Broom planned to submit his recommendation to the head of the manufacturing department.

# EXHIBIT 1

## Memorandum

December 15

To:      Ted Broom, Head, Space Requirements Unit, Industrial Engineering
         Department
From:    Sid Norton
Subject: Additional space allocation for finishing and corrosion proofing shop

A study has been made to determine the estimated cost savings to be realized by incorporating subassembly work involving parts processed in the finishing and corrosion proofing shop into the work package in the finishing and corrosion proofing shop.

The plan would be implemented for production scheduled during the next 3½ years. During this production period a total of 1,100 aircraft are scheduled for completion.

The present work package in the finishing and corrosion proofing shop is limited to the following operations:

1. Clean
2. Finish surfaces
3. Apply corrosion proofing
4. Inspect

The proposed work package in the finishing and corrosion proofing shop would consist of the following operations:

1. Clean
2. Finish surfaces
3. Apply corrosion proofing
4. Assemble parts into subassemblies
5. Repair damaged surfaces
6. Inspect

The results of the study indicate that 20,000 square feet of additional floor space will be required to add these operations to the work package. Total savings in labor and related charges are estimated to be $200,000 for the next 3½-year period based on work already scheduled. The savings will be approximately equally divided over the 3½ years.

There are three potential advantages in expanding the work package in the finishing and corrosion proofing shop:

1. Consolidation of all surface finish work in one shop will permit greater flexibility of crew assignments. The savings realized should approximate $25,000.

2. Improved operating conditions in both the finishing and corrosion proofing shop and the buildup shop will produce savings of another $75,000.

3. The third advantage would be increased quality since only one shop will be responsible for the entire work package. This should result in a reduction in rework and in the cost of rework when it is necessary. Inspection man-hours also will be reduced. Savings of approximately $100,000 will be possible by reducing the cost of rework and reducing the number of quality control personnel required.

In addition, according to the present planned production schedule, a third shift for the finishing and corrosion proofing shop will be required two years from now for a period of three months. The overtime will be required because of the lack of space for planned production levels. The loss of production hours, due to the shorter 6½-hour shift, will cost approximately $15,000.

To recapitulate, the expansion of the finishing and corrosion proofing shop as outlined above will result in savings of $200,000 from increased efficiency plus savings of $15,000 with the elimination of third-shift operations, or a total saving of $215,000 on currently planned production.

Revision of the present production sequence to incorporate the proposed changes would require advance planning. A schedule buildup is necessary to develop flow time for the additional operations in the finishing and corrosion proofing shop. Also, implementation of this plan will require earlier delivery of purchased items to support the program.

number 2, although some construction work would be necessary to make the area suitable for the mills. Since about half of the spar mill work is for missile production in plant number 2, there would be no difference in transportation costs if the mills were moved. Savings due to the relief of some congestion if the mills were moved to this larger area are estimated at about $10,000 per year. The cost of moving the mill and preparing the area in plant number 2 is estimated at $200,000.

2.42. *Relocate parts storage.* Parts storage is used to supply parts to the wing and body section buildup area and the final assembly area. The present location is not the most efficient since it is physically removed from the using areas. The parts storage could be relocated in two-story racks between the buildup and final assembly areas. The cost of constructing the storage racks and moving the parts is estimated to be $550,000, including relocation of some equipment in the buildup and final assembly areas. Yearly savings in improved efficiency due to relocating the storage area are estimated at $40,000.

2.43. *Relocate wire shop.* The best location for the wire shop would be in building C, close to the mock-up area and engineering department. If the wire shop were moved to building C, it is estimated that there would be savings of $20,000 per year due to the ease with which the wire shop could fit wiring on the mock-ups in the same building. There are two alternatives possible if the wire shop is moved to building C:

2.431. *Relocate engineering.* The engineering activities now located in building C can be moved away from that area with practically no loss of efficiency. Space which can be leased for $4 per square foot per year is available one block from the plant site. The total cost per year of this space would be $80,000. A new building to house these engineering activities could be built in several locations on the plant site for an estimated $200,000.

2.432. *Utilize part of mock-up area.* The mock-up area in building C is currently underutilized. The wire shop could occupy part of the mock-up area for two years until the expected expansion of the mock-up area requirements forced the wire shop out of the mock-up area. The present cost of moving some of the mock-ups and preparing the area for the wire shop would be $50,000. At the end of the two years, the wire shop would have to be moved into the engineering area of building C with the costs as shown in 2.431 above.

# EXHIBIT 2, ATTACHMENT A
## Main plant and building layout

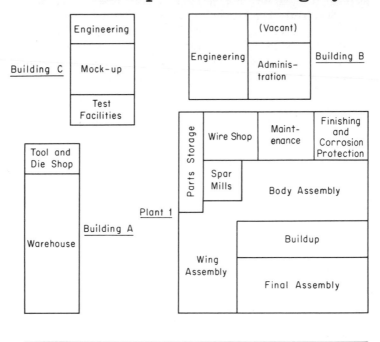

Flight Strip

# DISCUSSION QUESTIONS

1. What recommendation should Broom make? Support your answer with a cost comparison (before taxes) of each alternative. In your cost evaluation, compare the alternatives on the basis of: (a) ignoring the time value of money, (b) 12 per cent minimum return (before taxes), and (c) 6 per cent minimum return (before taxes). Also, consider two extreme economic life assumptions: (a) savings stop at the end of this program, and (b) savings continue indefinitely. What would be an appropriate life assumption for this proposal?

2. What would be the intangible benefits and disadvantages for each of the departments involved resulting from the various alternatives suggested? What weight should they be given in the recommendations?

3. What reactions to his proposal would Broom be likely to encounter?

4. What effect would the inclusion of income taxes have on your cost comparisons in question 1?

# REFERENCES

Bierman, Harold, Jr., and Seymour Smidt: *The Capital Budgeting Decision* (New York: The Macmillan Company, 1960), chap. 2.

Grant, Eugene L., and W. Grant Ireson: *Principles of Engineering Economy,* 4th ed. (New York: The Ronald Press Company, 1960), chap. 8.

Ireson, W. Grant, and Eugene L. Grant: *Handbook of Industrial Engineering and Management* (Englewood Cliffs, N.J.: Prentice-Hall, Inc., 1955), sec. 3.

Morris, William T.: *The Analysis of Management Decisions,* 2d ed. (Home-Wood, Ill.: Richard D. Irwin, Inc., 1964), chap. 3.

# YORK CONTAINER
# COMPANY

The York Container Company was established in 1920, and by 1960 it had become one of the "big five" manufacturers in the container producing industry. The industry included large, medium, and small companies. The large companies had decentralized their production facilities throughout the country. They engaged in active competition with each other by emphasizing customer service. The smaller manufacturers competed by offering price reductions ranging from 2 to 6 per cent, coupled with less service.

John Flint, the production planning manager of the Midwest plant of the York Container Company, faced a problem involving employment policy, inventory control, and production planning. Early in December the home office in New York City had dictated a new policy directing all branch plants to stabilize employment of production line workers to the maximum extent that such a policy was possible. During the past year employment of production line workers had fluctuated with seasonal requirements from a high of 150 to a low of 30. Flint believed, however, that it would be possible to stabilize employment at around 88 production line workers ±25 per cent.

The Midwest factory was one of the company's oldest plants and, although unionized, it enjoyed favorable relations with its employees. For years this branch had followed a policy of hiring and laying off employees as required by market demands. It drew largely upon transient workers and college students to fill manpower needs during the busy summer and fall months. When college students left at the end of summer to go back to school, the factory had to hire and train a new group of employees for one or two months' work. Joe Asplund, the personnel director, estimated that it cost $75 to hire and train a new employee, and $25 to terminate one. During the previous year this cost had totaled $16,500. In contrast to the changes in employment levels of production line workers, the supervisory, maintenance, lithographing and enameling, and tinplate department employees were hired on a permanent basis and, therefore, the number of people in these categories did not fluctuate with changes in seasonal demand.

The Midwest plant had twelve standard can lines and two frozen food container lines. The cans manufactured were of several types and sizes. Most cans were classified as open top cans, i.e., the top was not sealed on the can until after the can had been filled. Some cans (e.g., beer cans) were manufactured differently from the typical fruit or vegetable can. These cans were sprayed with a protective coating on the inside of the can. The frozen food containers came in a variety of materials and shapes. For example, the carton for frozen strawberries was made of paper with metal ends. The can lines produced cans at rates varying from 100 to 450 cans per minute, depending upon the size and complexity of the can. As a general rule, the larger the can, the slower the rate of production. The two frozen food container lines produced at an average rate of 180 per minute. Standard can lines could only be used to produce beer cans and open top cans, and frozen food container lines could only be used to produce frozen food containers. A list of the can sizes most frequently produced at this plant, together with production rates, appears in Exhibit 1.

A line changeover typically withdrew the line from production for two days and resulted in a cost of $600. This cost included the wages of two maintenance men who made the mechanical changeover, material scrap, and a $400 charge for lost production capacity. The latter figure was based on approximately sixteen hours of lost line time at a cost of $25 per hour. Line operators and supervisors could be reassigned to other jobs during such changeovers. A line that had been idle, however, could be restarted again without any additional setup costs, provided it was used to produce the same-sized can. During the previous year setup costs for line changeovers amounted to $14,400. Machine lines scheduled to be in operating condition on January 1 included two beer lines, two frozen food lines, and three open top can lines producing for can numbers 4, 5, and 9, respectively.

In past years the factory had operated two shifts during the peak season, running about ten can lines on the first shift and six on the second shift. In addition, two frozen food container lines were operated on each shift. The shift hours were:

First shift        7:00 A.M. to   3:30 P.M.
Second shift       3:30 P.M. to 12:00 P.M.

Each shift included a one-half-hour lunch period. The average first-shift hourly pay rate for line operators and supervisors was $2.50 and $5, respectively. A 15 per cent premium was paid to both line operators and supervisors for second-shift operations. A 50 per cent overtime premium was paid for all overtime work not exceeding 20 hours per week per crew (maximum of 4 hours per day), and a 100 per cent premium for any overtime work exceeding 20 hours per week per crew (or 4 hours per day). The maximum practical overtime per crew was 32 hours per week.

The bulkiness of the cans, the highly seasonal demand for the product, and the low unit sales value of an individual item appeared to make it expensive to stabilize production. A typical can measuring $3\frac{1}{4}$ inches in diameter and $4\frac{1}{4}$ inches in height sold for $0.045 each in freight car lots (125,000 cans of this size). This meant that a cubic foot of the product had a sales value of approximately $1.75. A freight car contained approximately 3,200 cubic feet of shipping space. Storage space in the factory for the finished cans amounted to 50,000 square feet, and when stacked to a height of 10 feet (the maximum), 500,000 cubic feet. The empty cans were stored in cardboard cartons which could be used to package the filled cans.

There was no immediate alternative use for inside storage space; hence depreciation, building taxes, etc., were considered a fixed cost and no specific charge was levied for the use of this space. A monthly charge, however, equal to 1 per cent of the average monthly inventory value was applied to cover variable costs for capital investment in the inventory, deterioration of inventory, other handling and maintenance costs, etc., associated with the use of both inside and outside storage space.

Adequate warehouse space was available nearby at a monthly rate of 4 cents per square foot (10 feet high). The rent was determined by the maximum number of square feet used in any single month. To load, transport, and unload a freight car lot of cans from the factory to an outside warehouse cost an additional $100 per car. Rental charges for outside warehouse space and transportation charges thereto were incurred only when the inventory exceeded the in-plant storage capacity of 500,000 cubic feet. Shipments were made directly to the customers from the outside warehouses.

Deliveries fluctuated between 30 freight carloads per month to more than 300 cars per month. Exhibit 2 illustrates the percentage of carloads of each can type sold, and Exhibit 3 shows the sales forecast which Flint intended to use in planning production for the next year. Flint expected to have 73 line operators and 7 supervisors on the payroll as of December 31, 1960. Finished goods inventories as of the same date were estimated to consist of 72 carloads of can number 1, 20 carloads of can number 4, and 12 carloads of can number 5.

Sales forecasts were typically optimistic, but not sufficiently so to justify either specific or general reductions by the production planning group. Production plans were made so that the amount forecast for any given month was planned for production in the same month. Sufficient flexibility existed in delivery dates and production capacity that more specific planning could be delayed until the month prior to actual production. Hence, if the sales forecast called for fifteen carloads of can number 4, it was sufficient to plan for the production of fifteen carloads of can number 4 anytime during the month of January.

Each type of can line required a specific number of workers. The beer cans, the open top cans, and the frozen food containers required thirteen, eleven, and twelve operators, respectively, plus a supervisor for each line. The detailed manpower requirements for each of these lines are shown in Exhibit 4.

Each operator held a specific job classification which required him to perform a given task on each of the lines. In addition to being able to perform these specific tasks all operators except those holding the lowest classification were required to be able to perform all jobs of classifications lower than that which they currently held. Each operator, however, was required to be paid on the basis of the job classification held rather than the job performed. Since the range between the lowest and highest hourly wage rate was only $0.35 per hour, it was not excessively costly to have employees work outside of their basic job classification. Moreover, if the assignment appeared to be extensive the operator's classification could be changed. Hence, under existing operating policies the labor force was almost infinitely flexible.

All workers, unless otherwise indicated, were male employees. The listed requirements for production line workers do not include any of the employees who worked in the preparatory departments: e.g., the men unwrapping the loads of tinplate, the men who lithographed and enameled the sheets, and maintenance men (machinists and millwrights). The average pay rate for these workers was also $2.50 per hour.

# EXHIBIT 1

## Properties of cans manufactured at Midwest plant of York Container Company

| Can number* | Approx. size (diam. × height), inches | Production rate | | Manufacturing cost, $/carload |
| | | cans/ line-shift† | carloads/ line-month‡ | |
|---|---|---|---|---|
| 1 | 2¾ × 4¾ (beer) | 216,000 | 30 | $3,200 |
| 2 | 3¼ × 4¼ | 168,000 | 30 | 2,800 |
| 3 | 4 × 4¾ | 156,000 | 45 | 2,300 |
| 4 | 3 × 4¾ | 168,000 | 25 | 2,500 |
| 5 | 3½ × 2 | 168,000 | 15 | 4,000 |
| 6 | 3 × 4½ | 168,000 | 25 | 2,800 |
| 7 | 6¼ × 7 | 48,000 | 50 | 1,500 |
| 8 | 4 × 5½ | 139,000 | 50 | 2,100 |
| 9 | Miscellaneous | 144,000§ | 25 | 2,600 |
| 10 | Frozen food container | 86,000 | 10 | 3,500 |

\* Can number was a local plant code used for convenient identification. It was not related to the standard can size number used in the industry. Can numbers 9 and 10 were used to designate groups of special dimension cans or containers, most of which were infrequently produced and each of which required its own dimension identification.

† Line-shift is based on average output per line during eight hours of normal operation.

‡ Line-month is based on a single shift operating twenty-one days per month.

§ Average production rate.

# EXHIBIT 2

**Approximate sales breakdown by can number according to the percentage of carloads shipped by Midwest plant during the past year**

| Can number | Approximate percentage |
|---|---|
| 1 | 30 |
| 2 | 16 |
| 3 | 14 |
| 4 | 12 |
| 5 | 5 |
| 6 | 5 |
| 7 | 3 |
| 8 | 2 |
| 9 | 8 |
| 10 | 5 |
| | 100 |

# EXHIBIT 3

## Anticipated inventory and equipment status, December 31, 1960, and sales forecast for 1961

(Carloads)

| | Can number | | | | | | | | | | Total |
|---|---|---|---|---|---|---|---|---|---|---|---|
| | 1 | 2 | 3 | 4 | 5 | 6 | 7 | 8 | 9 | 10 | |
| Lines in operation (Dec. 31, 1960) | 2 | | | 1 | 1 | | | | 1 | 2 | 7 |
| Inventory on hand (Dec. 31, 1960) | 72 | | | 20 | 12 | | | | | | 104 |
| Sales Jan., 1961 | 6 | | | 15 | 9 | | | | | | 30 |
| Sales Feb., 1961 | 12 | | | 25 | 12 | | | | 5 | | 54 |
| Sales Mar., 1961 | 21 | | | 55 | 39 | | | | 30 | | 145 |
| Sales Apr., 1961 | 39 | | | 55 | 57 | | | | 30 | 5 | 186 |
| Sales May, 1961 | 36 | 24 | | 50 | 42 | 40 | | | 25 | | 217 |
| Sales June, 1961 | 102 | 90 | | | | 40 | | 5 | 20 | 5 | 262 |
| Sales July, 1961 | 150 | 81 | 18 | | | 20 | | 20 | | 28 | 317 |
| Sales Aug., 1961 | 111 | 81 | 81 | | | 20 | 10 | | | 43 | 346 |
| Sales Sept., 1961 | 90 | 42 | 81 | | | | 40 | 25 | | 21 | 299 |
| Sales Oct., 1961 | 81 | 21 | 81 | | | | 10 | 25 | | 33 | 251 |
| Sales Nov., 1961 | 15 | | 54 | 15 | | | | | | 17 | 101 |
| Sales Dec., 1961 | 27 | | 36 | 15 | | | | | | 41 | 119 |
| Total | 690 | 339 | 351 | 230 | 159 | 120 | 60 | 75 | 110 | 193 | 2,327 |

# EXHIBIT 4

## Workers required to operate lines

(Number of workers excluding supervisors)

| Job title | Beer can | Open top can | Frozen food container |
|---|---|---|---|
| Slitter operator | 1 | 1 | 1 |
| Tin and body blank feeder | 1 | 1 | 1 |
| Spray operator and line tender | 1 | 1 | 2 |
| Bottom end feeder (female) | 1 | 1 | 1 |
| Inspector | 3 | 1 | 2 |
| Packer and sealer (female) | 1 | 4 | 2 |
| Folder and stitcher | 2 | 0 | 1 |
| Checker | 1 | 1 | 1 |
| Car loaders | 2 | 1 | 1 |
| Total | 13 | 11 | 12 |

# DISCUSSION QUESTIONS

1. What kinds of gains may accrue from stabilizing employment?
2. What alternative methods exist for stabilizing employment?
3. What are the relative costs of stabilizing employment by the methods you suggested in your answer to question 2 above?
4. What limits would the stabilization of employment within the desired limits of 88 line operators ±25 per cent place upon the output capacity of the York Container Company?
5. Outline the approach that you would take in solving York's labor stabilization problem.
6. Develop a production plan that you suggest will minimize the total cost for the operation during 1961. (Assume inventory levels predicted by Flint for December 31 were normal for the end of the year and that there are twenty-one working days per month.)
7. What is the cost of stabilizing the labor force within the prescribed limits?
8. What are some of the advantages and disadvantages of your solution?

# REFERENCES

Bowman, Edward H., and Robert B. Fetter: *Analysis for Production Management,* rev. ed. (Homewood, Ill.: Richard D. Irwin, Inc., 1961), pp. 79–143.

Buffa, Elwood S.: *Modern Production Management* (New York: John Wiley & Sons, Inc., 1961), pp. 144–199.

Holt, Charles C., Franco Modigliani, John F. Muth, and Herbert A. Simon: *Planning Production Inventories, and Work Force* (Englewood Cliffs, N.J.: Prentice-Hall, Inc., 1960), pp. 47–64, 389–405.

# APPENDIX A

## Supplemental notes regarding the Armed Services Procurement Regulations

The Department of Defense, in its procurement of military products, is one of the largest individual customers of manufactured goods in the United States. The interface relationship between private industry, represented by individual companies, and the Federal government, represented by the Department of Defense, is controlled by the Armed Services Procurement Regulations (ASPR).

ASPR is issued by the Department of Defense under authority of the Congress and establishes uniform policies and procedures relating to the procurement of supplies and services. These supplemental notes describe some of the aspects of ASPR that may have influence on the situations described in some of the cases.

## TYPES OF BIDDING

The two general methods of selecting vendors are procurement by formal advertising and procurement by negotiation. Formal advertising means procurement by competitive bids involving the following basic steps:

1. Preparation of the invitations for bids describing the requirements clearly, accurately, and completely, but avoiding unnecessarily restrictive specifications or requirements which might unduly limit the number of bidders.
2. Publicizing the invitations for bids in sufficient time to enable prospective bidders to prepare and submit bids before the time set for a public opening of the bids.
3. Submission of bids by prospective contractors. Generally any organization is privileged to submit bids if they are capable of meeting the requirements of the procurement.
4. Awarding the contract after the bids are publicly opened to that responsible bidder whose bid will be most advantageous to the government based on price and other factors. Almost always, however, the contract is awarded to the bidder offering the lowest price.

Procurement by formal advertising is specified as the preferred method for placement of contracts by government agencies. When, however, there are special circumstances, procurement by negotiation is permitted. Such circumstances include conditions of national emergency; purchases involving small amounts of money; limited number of suppliers; situations where competition is precluded because of the existence of patent rights, copyrights, secret processes, control of basic raw materials, or other circumstances; procurement involving experimental, developmental, or research work; classified purchases (products or services which cannot be publicly disclosed because of national security); and other reasons.

There are two main variations of negotiated procurement:

1. Sole source negotiated bidding where the buyer deals with only one company as the supplier of a particular product or service. This is generally avoided by the buyer whenever possible.

2. Competitive negotiated bidding where the buyer deals with two or more companies each of which submits proposals. The buyer makes the award to one or more companies which he decides offer the best combination of quality, reliability, delivery, price, and other factors of significance. Generally only those suppliers who can demonstrate that they are qualified as suppliers of the particular material or services desired are invited to participate in negotiated bidding. Prior to the awards there may be extensive discussion and negotiations between the buyer and the suppliers involved on all phases of the contract, including price. There are many types of contract which may be used.

## TYPES OF CONTRACTS

Prime contracts involve contracts between the government and a commercial supplier, otherwise known as the first-tier supplier. Subcontracts refer to purchases made by the prime contractor from suppliers on the second tier who may in turn place further subcontracts to the third tier, etc.

There are many types of contracts used by the government to meet a wide variety and volume of supplies and services. Among the many factors to be considered in determining the type of contract are the following two dominant factors:

1. The degree of risk or responsibility assumed by the supplier
2. The amount and type of profit incentive offered to the suppliers to achieve or exceed specified standards or goals of cost or performance

At one end of the contract spectrum is the firm fixed-price type of contract in which the buyer pays a predetermined price and the supplier assumes full responsibility in the form of profits or losses for all costs that are under or over the firm fixed price. At the other end of the spectrum is the cost-plus-a-fixed-fee type of contract, where the supplier's profit is fixed as to a dollar amount and the buyer assumes all responsibility for all costs over or under the original estimated target. Under such a contract, the supplier's cost responsibility is minimal. In between these two types of contracts are various other forms of contracts which may be used to compensate for the degree of uncertainty involved in a specific procurement. Cost-plus-a-percentage-of-cost contracts are prohibited by law.

A modification of the firm fixed-price contract is the fixed-price contract with redetermination which is used where it is possible to negotiate fair and reasonable firm fixed prices for an initial period but not for subsequent periods of contract performance. At some point in the contract, then, the final total price of the contract is redetermined—based on the accumulation of cost information up to that point. Such contracts can provide for either upward or downward revision of the original price. They may also provide for price ceilings.

Incentive type contracts may be used where there are sufficient uncertainties in the procurement to prevent the use of a fixed-price type contract, yet the procurement is delineated sufficiently so that a cost type contract is not required. Incentive type contracts involve the setting of a target for costs, and if the actual costs are higher or lower than the target costs the overages and underages are shared between the government and the contractor by an agreed formula. Compared to a fixed-price type of contract, an incentive type contract transfers some of the risk to the buyer; compared to a cost type contract, an incentive type contract retains a significant incentive to the supplier to strive for the lowest possible costs.

Incentive type contracts can also be made to cover performance of the product (targets based on weight, speed, etc.) and delivery time, with bonuses in proportion to the degree that target values are improved and with penalties for the reverse condition.

## SMALL BUSINESS POLICY

It is the policy of the Department of Defense to place a "fair proportion" of its total purchases with small business concerns. One of the techniques used to accomplish this objective is to set aside certain procurements which are restricted to small business firms. Generally, a small business concern is one that is independently owned and operated, is not dominant in the field of operation in which it is bidding, and does not employ more than 500 persons.

Government contracts also have provisions that require prime contractors and subcontractors to practice procedures that give fair consideration to small business concerns in the placement of their purchases.

## "MAKE OR BUY" POLICY

"Make or buy" policy refers to the determination of which items and parts are to be manufactured by a supplier in his own facilities and which items and parts will be obtained elsewhere by subcontract. Because of the many objectives of the government in its procurement policy, including the placement of a fair proportion of business with small business concerns, the contracting officer for the government is required in large procurements to be informed of and approve the supplier's "make or buy" program.

# APPENDIX B

## Supplemental notes regarding improvement curves

It is well known from experience that improvement in the amount of time required to do a job will occur when the job is repeated by a single individual, a group of workmen, or an entire work force assigned to a specific production program if the timing is not rigidly controlled by machine operations. This improvement from repetition generally results in a reduction of man-hour requirements and, hence, an improvement in costs. From empirical evidence of many production jobs, it appears that the following statement effectively describes the improvement phenomenon: *Each time the production quantity doubles, the unit man-hours are reduced at a constant rate.*[1] This relationship can be illustrated with an example in which 1,000 man-hours were required to manufacture the first unit of a product. If the constant rate of improvement is assumed to be 80 per cent then the second unit can be forecast to require 1,000 × 80 per cent, or 800 man-hours, etc., as follows:

| Unit | | Man-hours |
| --- | --- | --- |
| 1st | | 1,000 |
| 2d | 1,000 × 80% | 800 |
| 4th | 800 × 80% | 640 |
| 8th | 640 × 80% | 512 |
| 16th | 512 × 80% | 410 |

The formula can be expressed mathematically as follows:

$$Y_x = K(X)^n \tag{1}$$

and

$$T_x = \sum_{i=1}^{x} (Y_i) \tag{2}$$

or

$$T_x = K\left[\frac{(X + \tfrac{1}{2})^{n+1} - (\tfrac{1}{2})^{n+1}}{n+1}\right] \tag{3}$$

where $Y_x$ = the man-hours required for the single unit $X$
   $T_x$ = the cumulative total man-hours required from the first unit through unit $X$
   $X$ = the number of the unit for which the man-hours are being determined
   $K$ = the man-hours for the first unit
   $n = \log r/\log 2$
   $r$ = improvement ratio (80%, etc.) expressed as a decimal (.80, etc.)

Formula (1) can be readily calculated for a specific value of $X$, but formula (2) is tedious by manual calculations since it involves calculating every unit value from 1 to $X$. It can, of course, be calculated with a computer. Formula (3) is a close approximation of (2) that is satisfactory for most practical uses.

[1] This is a statement used by many companies. Other statements have been proposed and are also in use by some companies.

To eliminate the need for cumbersome calculations required by the formula, tables have been developed which give the factor for each unit and for various improvement ratios. Table I, page 464, shows such factors for unit man-hours, and Table II shows the factors for cumulative man-hours. On log-log paper, the unit man-hours plot as a straight line, as shown in the chart on page 463.

Using Tables I and II we can determine the man-hours for each unit, the cumulative total man-hours, and the cumulative average unit man-hours, for the previous example, as follows:

| Unit (1) | Unit man-hours (2) | Cumulative total man-hours (3) | Cumulative average unit man-hours (col. 3 ÷ col. 1) (4) |
|---|---|---|---|
| 1 | 1,000 | 1,000 | 1,000 |
| 2 | 800 | 1,800 | 900 |
| 3 | 702 | 2,502 | 834 |
| 4 | 640 | 3,142 | 785 |
| 5 | 596 | 3,738 | 748 |
| 8 | 512 | 5,346 | 668 |
| 10 | 477 | 6,315 | 632 |
| 100 | 227 | 32,650 | 327 |
| 1,000 | 108 | 158,700 | 159 |

The improvement ratio may vary from about 60 per cent, representing very great improvement, to 100 per cent representing no improvement at all. A very commonly experienced improvement ratio is about 80 per cent. Generally, the simpler the work the less improvement that is likely and the higher the improvement ratio that is used. On the other hand, the more complicated and difficult the work is, the greater is the opportunity for improvement and, therefore, the improvement ratio used will be a lower percentage.

On a new job it is necessary to estimate the man-hours required for the first unit. This information generally is derived from experience on work that is similar to the new situation. A second estimate is required to establish the improvement ratio. With these two factors it is then possible to predict the man-hours required for any individual unit or for any cumulative group of units by the use of Tables I and II, respectively. For example, if it is assumed that the first unit will require 850 man-hours and the improvement ratio is eighty-five per cent, then in a production lot of 20 units, the twentieth unit will require 421 man-hours (850 × .4954 from Table I) and the cumulative man-hours required for the entire lot of 20 units will be 10,540 man-hours (850 × 12.40 from Table II).

A very common problem in the use of improvement curves is to estimate the cost of a follow-on lot of production when the costs of the previous lots are known. The generalized method of solving this problem is as follows: The cost of a follow-on lot is determined by subtracting the cumulative costs of all previous lots from the cumulative cost of the previous and proposed lots combined. It should be emphasized that the method of determining the cost of follow-on lots is based on considering the total actual (or theoretical) *cumulative* costs involved; that is, the cost from the very first unit produced through the units under consideration. The application of the generalized rule for determining follow-on lot cost is illustrated by the following examples.

Assume that the 20 units previously described actually required 940 man-hours for the first unit and the entire lot of 20 required 9,875 man-hours. The ratio of the total man-hours to the first unit man-hours is 9,875 ÷ 940 and equals 10.5. Referring to Table II, we note that for 20 units we shall find a cumulative improvement factor of 10.48 for an 80 per cent improvement ratio. Based on this experience, we now have the problem of calculating a second follow-on production lot of 150 units. The cumulative number of units will be 170 (20 on the first and 150 on the follow-on lot). If we assume that the follow-on lot also will follow an 80 per cent improvement curve, then the cumulative total required for both lots will be 44,288 man-hours [equal to 940 × (45.20 + 49.03)/2 from Table II]. The follow-on lot will then require 34,413 man-hours (44,288 − 9,875).

The average man-hours on the first lot was 494 (9,875 ÷ 20) and the average man-hours on the second lot was 229 (33,413 ÷ 150).

The first unit of the follow-on lot can be expected to require 353 man-hours [equal to 940 × (.3812 + .3697)/2 from Table I for unit number 21] and 180 man-hours for the last unit [equal to 940 × (.1952 + 1879)/2 from Table I for unit number 170]. It should be noted that the factors in Tables I and II are always applied to the actual or theoretical value of the first unit.

As experience is accumulated on repetitive production operations, it is desirable to use the latest information in the calculations. Assume, for example, that the previous illustration had actual costs collected on a unit basis for selected items which were plotted on a piece of log-log paper as shown in the chart, resulting in 205 man-hours for the last unit. A straight line fitted through the latest experience (say, from unit 70 through 170) indicates an improvement curve of about 90 per cent with a *theoretical* first unit of 450 man-hours. The factors of 90 per cent and 450 man-hours would then be used in the calculation for a third lot to follow on after the second lot, assuming the latest trend is expected to continue.

# Improvement curves of unit man-hours

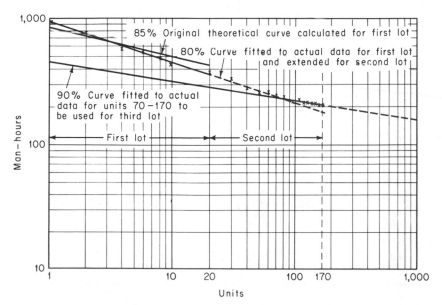

# APPENDIX B

## Table I   Improvement curves: table of unit values

| Unit | \multicolumn{8}{Improvement ratios} |
|------|--------|--------|--------|--------|--------|--------|--------|--------|
|      | 60% | 65% | 70% | 75% | 80% | 85% | 90% | 95% |
| 1 | 1.0000 | 1.0000 | 1.0000 | 1.0000 | 1.0000 | 1.0000 | 1.0000 | 1.0000 |
| 2 | .6000 | .6500 | .7000 | .7500 | .8000 | .8500 | .9000 | .9500 |
| 3 | .4450 | .5052 | .5682 | .6338 | .7021 | .7729 | .8462 | .9219 |
| 4 | .3600 | .4225 | .4900 | .5625 | .6400 | .7225 | .8100 | .9025 |
| 5 | .3054 | .3678 | .4368 | .5127 | .5956 | .6857 | .7830 | .8877 |
| 6 | .2670 | .3284 | .3977 | .4754 | .5617 | .6570 | .7616 | .8758 |
| 7 | .2383 | .2984 | .3674 | .4459 | .5345 | .6337 | .7439 | .8659 |
| 8 | .2160 | .2746 | .3430 | .4219 | .5120 | .6141 | .7290 | .8574 |
| 9 | .1980 | .2552 | .3228 | .4017 | .4930 | .5974 | .7161 | .8499 |
| 10 | .1832 | .2391 | .3058 | .3846 | .4765 | .5828 | .7047 | .8433 |
| 12 | .1602 | .2135 | .2784 | .3565 | .4493 | .5584 | .6854 | .8320 |
| 14 | .1430 | .1940 | .2572 | .3344 | .4276 | .5386 | .6696 | .8226 |
| 16 | .1296 | .1785 | .2401 | .3164 | .4096 | .5220 | .6561 | .8145 |
| 18 | .1188 | .1659 | .2260 | .3013 | .3944 | .5078 | .6445 | .8074 |
| 20 | .1099 | .1554 | .2141 | .2884 | .3812 | .4954 | .6342 | .8012 |
| 22 | .1025 | .1465 | .2038 | .2772 | .3697 | .4844 | .6251 | .7955 |
| 24 | .0961 | .1387 | .1949 | .2674 | .3595 | .4747 | .6169 | .7904 |
| 25 | .0933 | .1353 | .1908 | .2629 | .3548 | .4701 | .6131 | .7880 |
| 30 | .0815 | .1208 | .1737 | .2437 | .3346 | .4505 | .5963 | .7775 |
| 35 | .0728 | .1097 | .1605 | .2286 | .3184 | .4345 | .5825 | .7687 |
| 40 | .0660 | .1010 | .1498 | .2163 | .3050 | .4211 | .5708 | .7611 |
| 45 | .0605 | .0939 | .1410 | .2060 | .2936 | .4096 | .5607 | .7545 |
| 50 | .0560 | .0879 | .1336 | .1972 | .2838 | .3996 | .5518 | .7486 |
| 60 | .0489 | .0785 | .1216 | .1828 | .2676 | .3829 | .5367 | .7386 |
| 70 | .0437 | .0713 | .1123 | .1715 | .2547 | .3693 | .5243 | .7302 |
| 80 | .0396 | .0657 | .1049 | .1622 | .2440 | .3579 | .5137 | .7231 |
| 90 | .0363 | .0610 | .0987 | .1545 | .2349 | .3482 | .5046 | .7168 |
| 100 | .0336 | .0572 | .0935 | .1479 | .2271 | .3397 | .4966 | .7112 |
| 120 | .0294 | .0510 | .0851 | .1371 | .2141 | .3255 | .4830 | .7017 |
| 140 | .0262 | .0464 | .0786 | .1287 | .2038 | .3139 | .4718 | .6937 |
| 160 | .0237 | .0427 | .0734 | .1217 | .1952 | .3042 | .4623 | .6869 |
| 180 | .0218 | .0397 | .0691 | .1159 | .1879 | .2959 | .4541 | .6809 |
| 200 | .0201 | .0371 | .0655 | .1109 | .1816 | .2887 | .4469 | .6757 |
| 250 | .0171 | .0323 | .0584 | .1011 | .1691 | .2740 | .4320 | .6646 |
| 300 | .0149 | .0289 | .0531 | .0937 | .1594 | .2625 | .4202 | .6557 |
| 350 | .0133 | .0262 | .0491 | .0879 | .1517 | .2532 | .4105 | .6482 |
| 400 | .0121 | .0241 | .0458 | .0832 | .1453 | .2454 | .4022 | .6419 |
| 450 | .0111 | .0224 | .0431 | .0792 | .1399 | .2387 | .3951 | .6363 |
| 500 | .0103 | .0210 | .0408 | .0758 | .1352 | .2329 | .3888 | .6314 |
| 600 | .0090 | .0188 | .0372 | .0703 | .1275 | .2232 | .3782 | .6229 |
| 700 | .0080 | .0171 | .0344 | .0659 | .1214 | .2152 | .3694 | .6158 |
| 800 | .0073 | .0157 | .0321 | .0624 | .1163 | .2086 | .3620 | .6098 |
| 900 | .0067 | .0146 | .0302 | .0594 | .1119 | .2029 | .3556 | .6045 |
| 1,000 | .0062 | .0137 | .0286 | .0569 | .1082 | .1980 | .3499 | .5998 |
| 1,200 | .0054 | .0122 | .0260 | .0527 | .1020 | .1897 | .3404 | .5918 |
| 1,400 | .0048 | .0111 | .0240 | .0495 | .0971 | .1830 | .3325 | .5850 |
| 1,600 | .0044 | .0102 | .0225 | .0468 | .0930 | .1773 | .3258 | .5793 |
| 1,800 | .0040 | .0095 | .0211 | .0446 | .0895 | .1725 | .3200 | .5743 |
| 2,000 | .0037 | .0089 | .0200 | .0427 | .0866 | .1683 | .3149 | .5698 |
| 2,500 | .0031 | .0077 | .0178 | .0389 | .0806 | .1597 | .3044 | .5605 |
| 3,000 | .0027 | .0069 | .0162 | .0360 | .0760 | .1530 | .2961 | .5530 |

# APPENDIX B

## Table II   Improvement curves: table of cumulative values

| Units | Improvement ratios | | | | | | | |
|---|---|---|---|---|---|---|---|---|
| | 60% | 65% | 70% | 75% | 80% | 85% | 90% | 95% |
| 1 | 1.000 | 1.000 | 1.000 | 1.000 | 1.000 | 1.000 | 1.000 | 1.000 |
| 2 | 1.600 | 1.650 | 1.700 | 1.750 | 1.800 | 1.850 | 1.900 | 1.950 |
| 3 | 2.045 | 2.155 | 2.268 | 2.384 | 2.502 | 2.623 | 2.746 | 2.872 |
| 4 | 2.405 | 2.578 | 2.758 | 2.946 | 3.142 | 3.345 | 3.556 | 3.774 |
| 5 | 2.710 | 2.946 | 3.195 | 3.459 | 3.738 | 4.031 | 4.339 | 4.662 |
| 6 | 2.977 | 3.274 | 3.593 | 3.934 | 4.299 | 4.688 | 5.101 | 5.538 |
| 7 | 3.216 | 3.572 | 3.960 | 4.380 | 4.834 | 5.322 | 5.845 | 6.404 |
| 8 | 3.432 | 3.847 | 4.303 | 4.802 | 5.346 | 5.936 | 6.574 | 7.261 |
| 9 | 3.630 | 4.102 | 4.626 | 5.204 | 5.839 | 6.533 | 7.290 | 8.111 |
| 10 | 3.813 | 4.341 | 4.931 | 5.589 | 6.315 | 7.116 | 7.994 | 8.955 |
| 12 | 4.144 | 4.780 | 5.501 | 6.315 | 7.227 | 8.244 | 9.374 | 10.62 |
| 14 | 4.438 | 5.177 | 6.026 | 6.994 | 8.092 | 9.331 | 10.72 | 12.27 |
| 16 | 4.704 | 5.541 | 6.514 | 7.635 | 8.920 | 10.38 | 12.04 | 13.91 |
| 18 | 4.946 | 5.879 | 6.972 | 8.245 | 9.716 | 11.41 | 13.33 | 15.52 |
| 20 | 5.171 | 6.195 | 7.407 | 8.828 | 10.48 | 12.40 | 14.61 | 17.13 |
| 22 | 5.379 | 6.492 | 7.819 | 9.388 | 11.23 | 13.38 | 15.86 | 18.72 |
| 24 | 5.574 | 6.773 | 8.213 | 9.928 | 11.95 | 14.33 | 17.10 | 20.31 |
| 25 | 5.668 | 6.909 | 8.404 | 10.19 | 12.31 | 14.80 | 17.71 | 21.10 |
| 30 | 6.097 | 7.540 | 9.305 | 11.45 | 14.02 | 17.09 | 20.73 | 25.00 |
| 35 | 6.478 | 8.109 | 10.13 | 12.72 | 15.64 | 19.29 | 23.67 | 28.86 |
| 40 | 6.821 | 8.631 | 10.90 | 13.72 | 17.19 | 21.43 | 26.54 | 32.68 |
| 45 | 7.134 | 9.114 | 11.62 | 14.77 | 18.68 | 23.50 | 29.37 | 36.47 |
| 50 | 7.422 | 9.565 | 12.31 | 15.78 | 20.12 | 25.51 | 32.14 | 40.22 |
| 60 | 7.941 | 10.39 | 13.57 | 17.67 | 22.87 | 29.41 | 37.57 | 47.65 |
| 70 | 8.401 | 11.13 | 14.74 | 19.43 | 25.47 | 33.17 | 42.87 | 54.99 |
| 80 | 8.814 | 11.82 | 15.82 | 21.09 | 27.96 | 36.80 | 48.05 | 62.25 |
| 90 | 9.191 | 12.45 | 16.83 | 22.67 | 30.35 | 40.32 | 53.14 | 69.45 |
| 100 | 9.539 | 13.03 | 17.79 | 24.18 | 32.65 | 43.75 | 58.14 | 76.59 |
| 120 | 10.16 | 14.11 | 19.57 | 27.02 | 37.05 | 50.39 | 67.93 | 90.71 |
| 140 | 10.72 | 15.08 | 21.20 | 29.67 | 41.22 | 56.78 | 77.46 | 104.7 |
| 160 | 11.21 | 15.97 | 22.72 | 32.17 | 45.20 | 62.95 | 86.80 | 118.5 |
| 180 | 11.67 | 16.79 | 24.14 | 34.54 | 49.03 | 68.95 | 95.96 | 132.1 |
| 200 | 12.09 | 17.55 | 25.48 | 36.80 | 52.72 | 74.79 | 105.0 | 145.7 |
| 250 | 13.01 | 19.28 | 28.56 | 42.08 | 61.47 | 88.83 | 126.9 | 179.2 |
| 300 | 13.81 | 20.81 | 31.34 | 46.94 | 69.66 | 102.2 | 148.2 | 212.2 |
| 350 | 14.51 | 22.18 | 33.89 | 51.48 | 77.43 | 115.1 | 169.0 | 244.8 |
| 400 | 15.14 | 23.44 | 36.26 | 55.75 | 84.85 | 127.6 | 189.3 | 277.0 |
| 450 | 15.72 | 24.60 | 38.48 | 59.80 | 91.97 | 139.7 | 209.2 | 309.0 |
| 500 | 16.26 | 25.68 | 40.58 | 63.68 | 98.85 | 151.5 | 228.8 | 340.6 |
| 600 | 17.21 | 27.67 | 44.47 | 70.97 | 112.0 | 174.2 | 267.1 | 403.3 |
| 700 | 18.06 | 29.45 | 48.04 | 77.77 | 124.4 | 196.1 | 304.5 | 465.3 |
| 800 | 18.82 | 31.09 | 51.36 | 84.18 | 136.3 | 217.3 | 341.0 | 526.5 |
| 900 | 19.51 | 32.60 | 54.46 | 90.26 | 147.7 | 237.9 | 376.9 | 587.2 |
| 1,000 | 20.15 | 34.01 | 57.40 | 96.07 | 158.7 | 257.9 | 412.2 | 647.4 |
| 1,200 | 21.30 | 36.59 | 62.85 | 107.0 | 179.7 | 296.6 | 481.2 | 766.6 |
| 1,400 | 22.32 | 38.92 | 67.85 | 117.2 | 199.6 | 333.9 | 548.4 | 884.2 |
| 1,600 | 23.23 | 41.04 | 72.49 | 126.8 | 218.6 | 369.9 | 614.2 | 1001. |
| 1,800 | 24.06 | 43.00 | 76.85 | 135.9 | 236.8 | 404.9 | 678.8 | 1116. |
| 2,000 | 24.83 | 44.84 | 80.96 | 144.7 | 254.4 | 438.9 | 742.3 | 1230. |
| 2,500 | 26.53 | 48.97 | 90.39 | 165.0 | 296.1 | 520.8 | 897.0 | 1513. |
| 3,000 | 27.99 | 52.62 | 98.90 | 183.7 | 335.2 | 598.9 | 1047. | 1791. |

# APPENDIX C
## Interest tables

| Period | Interest rate | | | | | | | | |
|---|---|---|---|---|---|---|---|---|---|
| | 1% | 2% | 3% | 4% | 5% | 6% | 7% | 8% | 9% |
| 1 | 0.990 | 0.980 | 0.971 | 0.962 | 0.952 | 0.943 | 0.935 | 0.926 | 0.917 |
| 2 | 0.980 | 0.961 | 0.943 | 0.925 | 0.907 | 0.890 | 0.873 | 0.857 | 0.842 |
| 3 | 0.971 | 0.942 | 0.915 | 0.889 | 0.864 | 0.840 | 0.816 | 0.794 | 0.772 |
| 4 | 0.961 | 0.924 | 0.888 | 0.855 | 0.823 | 0.792 | 0.763 | 0.735 | 0.708 |
| 5 | 0.951 | 0.906 | 0.863 | 0.822 | 0.784 | 0.747 | 0.713 | 0.681 | 0.650 |
| 6 | 0.942 | 0.888 | 0.837 | 0.790 | 0.746 | 0.705 | 0.666 | 0.630 | 0.596 |
| 7 | 0.933 | 0.871 | 0.813 | 0.760 | 0.711 | 0.665 | 0.623 | 0.583 | 0.547 |
| 8 | 0.923 | 0.853 | 0.789 | 0.731 | 0.677 | 0.627 | 0.582 | 0.540 | 0.502 |
| 9 | 0.914 | 0.837 | 0.766 | 0.703 | 0.645 | 0.592 | 0.544 | 0.500 | 0.460 |
| 10 | 0.905 | 0.820 | 0.744 | 0.676 | 0.614 | 0.558 | 0.508 | 0.463 | 0.422 |
| 11 | 0.896 | 0.804 | 0.722 | 0.650 | 0.585 | 0.527 | 0.475 | 0.429 | 0.388 |
| 12 | 0.887 | 0.788 | 0.701 | 0.625 | 0.557 | 0.497 | 0.444 | 0.397 | 0.356 |
| 13 | 0.879 | 0.773 | 0.681 | 0.601 | 0.530 | 0.469 | 0.415 | 0.368 | 0.326 |
| 14 | 0.870 | 0.758 | 0.661 | 0.577 | 0.505 | 0.442 | 0.388 | 0.340 | 0.299 |
| 15 | 0.861 | 0.743 | 0.642 | 0.555 | 0.481 | 0.417 | 0.362 | 0.315 | 0.275 |
| 16 | 0.853 | 0.728 | 0.623 | 0.534 | 0.458 | 0.394 | 0.339 | 0.292 | 0.252 |
| 17 | 0.844 | 0.714 | 0.605 | 0.513 | 0.436 | 0.371 | 0.317 | 0.270 | 0.231 |
| 18 | 0.836 | 0.700 | 0.587 | 0.494 | 0.416 | 0.350 | 0.296 | 0.250 | 0.212 |
| 19 | 0.828 | 0.686 | 0.570 | 0.475 | 0.396 | 0.331 | 0.277 | 0.232 | 0.194 |
| 20 | 0.820 | 0.673 | 0.554 | 0.456 | 0.377 | 0.312 | 0.258 | 0.215 | 0.178 |
| 21 | 0.811 | 0.660 | 0.538 | 0.439 | 0.359 | 0.294 | 0.242 | 0.199 | 0.164 |
| 22 | 0.803 | 0.647 | 0.522 | 0.422 | 0.342 | 0.278 | 0.226 | 0.184 | 0.150 |
| 23 | 0.795 | 0.634 | 0.507 | 0.406 | 0.326 | 0.262 | 0.211 | 0.170 | 0.138 |
| 24 | 0.788 | 0.622 | 0.492 | 0.390 | 0.310 | 0.247 | 0.197 | 0.158 | 0.126 |
| 25 | 0.780 | 0.610 | 0.478 | 0.375 | 0.295 | 0.233 | 0.184 | 0.146 | 0.116 |
| 30 | 0.742 | 0.552 | 0.412 | 0.308 | 0.231 | 0.174 | 0.131 | 0.099 | 0.075 |
| 35 | 0.706 | 0.500 | 0.355 | 0.253 | 0.181 | 0.130 | 0.094 | 0.068 | 0.049 |
| 40 | 0.672 | 0.453 | 0.307 | 0.208 | 0.142 | 0.097 | 0.067 | 0.046 | 0.032 |
| 45 | 0.639 | 0.410 | 0.264 | 0.171 | 0.111 | 0.073 | 0.048 | 0.031 | 0.021 |
| 50 | 0.608 | 0.372 | 0.228 | 0.141 | 0.087 | 0.054 | 0.034 | 0.021 | 0.013 |

# APPENDIX C

## Table I  Present value of a single payment

| | | | | Interest rate | | | | |
|---|---|---|---|---|---|---|---|---|
| 10% | 12% | 15% | 20% | 25% | 30% | 35% | 40% | 50% |
| 0.909 | 0.893 | 0.870 | 0.833 | 0.800 | 0.769 | 0.741 | 0.714 | 0.667 |
| 0.826 | 0.797 | 0.756 | 0.694 | 0.640 | 0.592 | 0.549 | 0.510 | 0.444 |
| 0.751 | 0.712 | 0.658 | 0.579 | 0.512 | 0.455 | 0.406 | 0.364 | 0.296 |
| 0.683 | 0.636 | 0.572 | 0.482 | 0.410 | 0.350 | 0.301 | 0.260 | 0.198 |
| 0.621 | 0.567 | 0.497 | 0.402 | 0.328 | 0.269 | 0.223 | 0.186 | 0.132 |
| 0.564 | 0.507 | 0.432 | 0.335 | 0.262 | 0.207 | 0.165 | 0.133 | 0.088 |
| 0.513 | 0.452 | 0.376 | 0.279 | 0.210 | 0.159 | 0.122 | 0.095 | 0.059 |
| 0.467 | 0.404 | 0.327 | 0.233 | 0.168 | 0.123 | 0.091 | 0.068 | 0.039 |
| 0.424 | 0.361 | 0.284 | 0.194 | 0.134 | 0.094 | 0.067 | 0.048 | 0.026 |
| 0.386 | 0.322 | 0.247 | 0.162 | 0.107 | 0.073 | 0.050 | 0.035 | 0.017 |
| 0.350 | 0.287 | 0.215 | 0.135 | 0.086 | 0.056 | 0.037 | 0.025 | 0.012 |
| 0.319 | 0.257 | 0.187 | 0.112 | 0.069 | 0.043 | 0.027 | 0.018 | 0.008 |
| 0.290 | 0.229 | 0.163 | 0.093 | 0.055 | 0.033 | 0.020 | 0.013 | 0.005 |
| 0.263 | 0.205 | 0.141 | 0.078 | 0.044 | 0.025 | 0.015 | 0.009 | 0.003 |
| 0.239 | 0.183 | 0.123 | 0.065 | 0.035 | 0.020 | 0.011 | 0.006 | 0.002 |
| 0.218 | 0.163 | 0.107 | 0.054 | 0.028 | 0.015 | 0.008 | 0.005 | 0.002 |
| 0.198 | 0.146 | 0.093 | 0.045 | 0.023 | 0.012 | 0.006 | 0.003 | 0.001 |
| 0.180 | 0.130 | 0.081 | 0.038 | 0.018 | 0.009 | 0.005 | 0.002 | 0.001 |
| 0.164 | 0.116 | 0.070 | 0.031 | 0.014 | 0.007 | 0.003 | 0.002 | 0.000 |
| 0.149 | 0.104 | 0.061 | 0.026 | 0.012 | 0.005 | 0.002 | 0.001 | 0.000 |
| 0.135 | 0.093 | 0.053 | 0.022 | 0.009 | 0.004 | 0.002 | 0.001 | 0.000 |
| 0.123 | 0.083 | 0.046 | 0.018 | 0.007 | 0.003 | 0.001 | 0.001 | 0.000 |
| 0.112 | 0.074 | 0.040 | 0.015 | 0.006 | 0.002 | 0.001 | 0.000 | 0.000 |
| 0.102 | 0.066 | 0.035 | 0.013 | 0.005 | 0.002 | 0.001 | 0.000 | 0.000 |
| 0.092 | 0.059 | 0.030 | 0.010 | 0.004 | 0.001 | 0.001 | 0.000 | 0.000 |
| 0.057 | 0.033 | 0.015 | 0.004 | 0.001 | 0.000 | 0.000 | 0.000 | 0.000 |
| 0.036 | 0.019 | 0.008 | 0.002 | 0.000 | 0.000 | 0.000 | 0.000 | 0.000 |
| 0.022 | 0.011 | 0.004 | 0.001 | 0.000 | 0.000 | 0.000 | 0.000 | 0.000 |
| 0.014 | 0.006 | 0.002 | 0.000 | 0.000 | 0.000 | 0.000 | 0.000 | 0.000 |
| 0.009 | 0.003 | 0.001 | 0.000 | 0.000 | 0.000 | 0.000 | 0.000 | 0.000 |

| Period | Interest rate | | | | | | | | |
|---|---|---|---|---|---|---|---|---|---|
| | 1% | 2% | 3% | 4% | 5% | 6% | 7% | 8% | 9% |
| 1 | 0.990 | 0.980 | 0.971 | 0.962 | 0.952 | 0.943 | 0.935 | 0.926 | 0.917 |
| 2 | 1.970 | 1.942 | 1.913 | 1.886 | 1.859 | 1.833 | 1.808 | 1.783 | 1.759 |
| 3 | 2.941 | 2.884 | 2.829 | 2.775 | 2.723 | 2.673 | 2.624 | 2.577 | 2.531 |
| 4 | 3.902 | 3.808 | 3.717 | 3.630 | 3.546 | 3.465 | 3.387 | 3.312 | 3.240 |
| 5 | 4.853 | 4.713 | 4.580 | 4.452 | 4.329 | 4.212 | 4.100 | 3.993 | 3.890 |
| 6 | 5.795 | 5.601 | 5.417 | 5.242 | 5.076 | 4.917 | 4.767 | 4.623 | 4.486 |
| 7 | 6.728 | 6.472 | 6.230 | 6.002 | 5.786 | 5.582 | 5.389 | 5.206 | 5.033 |
| 8 | 7.652 | 7.325 | 7.020 | 6.733 | 6.463 | 6.210 | 5.971 | 5.747 | 5.535 |
| 9 | 8.566 | 8.162 | 7.786 | 7.435 | 7.108 | 6.802 | 6.515 | 6.247 | 5.995 |
| 10 | 9.471 | 8.983 | 8.530 | 8.111 | 7.722 | 7.360 | 7.024 | 6.710 | 6.418 |
| 11 | 10.368 | 9.787 | 9.253 | 8.760 | 8.306 | 7.887 | 7.499 | 7.139 | 6.805 |
| 12 | 11.255 | 10.575 | 9.954 | 9.385 | 8.863 | 8.384 | 7.943 | 7.536 | 7.161 |
| 13 | 12.134 | 11.348 | 10.635 | 9.986 | 9.394 | 8.853 | 8.358 | 7.904 | 7.487 |
| 14 | 13.004 | 12.106 | 11.296 | 10.563 | 9.899 | 9.295 | 8.745 | 8.244 | 7.786 |
| 15 | 13.865 | 12.849 | 11.938 | 11.118 | 10.380 | 9.712 | 9.108 | 8.559 | 8.061 |
| 16 | 14.718 | 13.578 | 12.561 | 11.652 | 10.838 | 10.106 | 9.447 | 8.851 | 8.313 |
| 17 | 15.562 | 14.292 | 13.166 | 12.166 | 11.274 | 10.477 | 9.763 | 9.122 | 8.544 |
| 18 | 16.398 | 14.992 | 13.754 | 12.659 | 11.690 | 10.828 | 10.059 | 9.372 | 8.756 |
| 19 | 17.226 | 15.678 | 14.324 | 13.134 | 12.085 | 11.158 | 10.336 | 9.604 | 8.950 |
| 20 | 18.046 | 16.351 | 14.877 | 13.590 | 12.462 | 11.470 | 10.594 | 9.818 | 9.129 |
| 21 | 18.857 | 17.011 | 15.415 | 14.029 | 12.821 | 11.764 | 10.836 | 10.017 | 9.292 |
| 22 | 19.660 | 17.658 | 15.937 | 14.451 | 13.163 | 12.042 | 11.061 | 10.201 | 9.442 |
| 23 | 20.456 | 18.292 | 16.444 | 14.857 | 13.489 | 12.303 | 11.272 | 10.371 | 9.580 |
| 24 | 21.243 | 18.914 | 16.936 | 15.247 | 13.799 | 12.550 | 11.469 | 10.529 | 9.707 |
| 25 | 22.023 | 19.523 | 17.413 | 15.622 | 14.094 | 12.783 | 11.654 | 10.675 | 9.823 |
| 30 | 25.808 | 22.396 | 19.600 | 17.292 | 15.372 | 13.765 | 12.409 | 11.258 | 10.274 |
| 35 | 29.409 | 24.999 | 21.487 | 18.665 | 16.374 | 14.498 | 12.948 | 11.655 | 10.567 |
| 40 | 32.835 | 27.355 | 23.115 | 19.793 | 17.159 | 15.046 | 13.332 | 11.925 | 10.757 |
| 45 | 36.094 | 29.490 | 24.519 | 20.720 | 17.774 | 15.456 | 13.606 | 12.108 | 10.881 |
| 50 | 39.196 | 31.424 | 25.730 | 21.482 | 18.256 | 15.762 | 13.801 | 12.233 | 10.962 |

# APPENDIX C

## Table II  Present value of an annuity

| | | | Interest rate | | | | | |
|---|---|---|---|---|---|---|---|---|
| 10% | 12% | 15% | 20% | 25% | 30% | 35% | 40% | 50% |
| 0.909 | 0.893 | 0.870 | 0.833 | 0.800 | 0.769 | 0.741 | 0.714 | 0.667 |
| 1.736 | 1.690 | 1.626 | 1.528 | 1.440 | 1.361 | 1.289 | 1.224 | 1.111 |
| 2.487 | 2.402 | 2.283 | 2.106 | 1.952 | 1.816 | 1.696 | 1.589 | 1.407 |
| 3.170 | 3.037 | 2.855 | 2.589 | 2.362 | 2.166 | 1.997 | 1.849 | 1.605 |
| 3.791 | 3.605 | 3.352 | 2.991 | 2.689 | 2.436 | 2.220 | 2.035 | 1.737 |
| 4.355 | 4.111 | 3.784 | 3.326 | 2.951 | 2.643 | 2.385 | 2.168 | 1.824 |
| 4.868 | 4.564 | 4.160 | 3.605 | 3.161 | 2.802 | 2.508 | 2.263 | 1.883 |
| 5.335 | 4.968 | 4.487 | 3.837 | 3.329 | 2.925 | 2.598 | 2.331 | 1.922 |
| 5.759 | 5.328 | 4.772 | 4.031 | 3.463 | 3.019 | 2.665 | 2.379 | 1.948 |
| 6.145 | 5.650 | 5.019 | 4.192 | 3.571 | 3.092 | 2.715 | 2.414 | 1.965 |
| 6.495 | 5.938 | 5.234 | 4.327 | 3.656 | 3.147 | 2.752 | 2.438 | 1.977 |
| 6.814 | 6.194 | 5.421 | 4.439 | 3.725 | 3.190 | 2.779 | 2.456 | 1.985 |
| 7.103 | 6.424 | 5.583 | 4.533 | 3.780 | 3.223 | 2.799 | 2.469 | 1.990 |
| 7.367 | 6.628 | 5.724 | 4.611 | 3.824 | 3.249 | 2.814 | 2.478 | 1.993 |
| 7.606 | 6.811 | 5.847 | 4.675 | 3.859 | 3.268 | 2.825 | 2.484 | 1.995 |
| 7.824 | 6.974 | 5.954 | 4.730 | 3.887 | 3.283 | 2.834 | 2.489 | 1.997 |
| 8.022 | 7.120 | 6.047 | 4.775 | 3.910 | 3.295 | 2.840 | 2.492 | 1.998 |
| 8.201 | 7.250 | 6.128 | 4.812 | 3.928 | 3.304 | 2.844 | 2.494 | 1.999 |
| 8.365 | 7.366 | 6.198 | 4.843 | 3.942 | 3.311 | 2.848 | 2.496 | 1.999 |
| 8.514 | 7.469 | 6.259 | 4.870 | 3.954 | 3.316 | 2.850 | 2.497 | 1.999 |
| 8.649 | 7.562 | 6.312 | 4.891 | 3.963 | 3.320 | 2.852 | 2.498 | 2.000 |
| 8.772 | 7.645 | 6.359 | 4.909 | 3.970 | 3.323 | 2.853 | 2.498 | 2.000 |
| 8.883 | 7.718 | 6.399 | 4.925 | 3.976 | 3.325 | 2.854 | 2.499 | 2.000 |
| 8.985 | 7.784 | 6.434 | 4.937 | 3.981 | 3.327 | 2.855 | 2.499 | 2.000 |
| 9.077 | 7.843 | 6.464 | 4.948 | 3.985 | 3.329 | 2.856 | 2.499 | 2.000 |
| 9.427 | 8.055 | 6.566 | 4.979 | 3.995 | 3.332 | 2.857 | 2.500 | 2.000 |
| 9.644 | 8.176 | 6.617 | 4.992 | 3.998 | 3.333 | 2.857 | 2.500 | 2.000 |
| 9.779 | 8.244 | 6.642 | 4.997 | 3.999 | 3.333 | 2.857 | 2.500 | 2.000 |
| 9.863 | 8.283 | 6.654 | 4.999 | 4.000 | 3.333 | 2.857 | 2.500 | 2.000 |
| 9.915 | 8.304 | 6.661 | 4.999 | 4.000 | 3.333 | 2.857 | 2.500 | 2.000 |